CHAMPIONS!

CHAMPIONS!

Hawthorn – Hill – Clark – Surtees
Stewart – Hunt – Mansell

Portraits and memories of the seven
British drivers who have won the
Formula One World Championship

CHRISTOPHER HILTON
and JOHN BLUNSDEN

Motor Racing Publications

MOTOR RACING PUBLICATIONS LTD
Unit 6, The Pilton Estate, 46 Pitlake, Croydon CR0 3RY, England

First Published 1993

British Library Cataloguing in Publication Data

Hilton, Christopher
  Champions!: Hawthorn, Hill, Clark,
  Surtees, Stewart, Hunt, Mansell
  I. Title II. Blunsden, John
  796.7092

  ISBN 0-947981-76-4

Typeset in Great Britain by
Ryburn Publishing Services, Keele University, Staffs

Printed in Great Britain by
Hartnolls Limited, Bodmin, Cornwall

CONTENTS

PART ONE

by Christopher Hilton

THE BRIDGE OF TIME

The ancient structure, laid with railway sleepers which trembled as vehicles ebbed slowly across them, had gone, gone into memory. The new structure, broad and level, was better, but that wasn't the same thing. Below it, the track no longer curved in an imperious sweep towards the bank of grandstands; the staccato chicane at the end of the curve no longer sucked racing cars into an embrace, slowing them, holding them, releasing them.

The pits opposite the grandstands, cemented breeze blocks and homely as cattle stalls, had gone into memory, too. More spacious pits spread under a communications centre, itself an edifice looming like a guardian of modernity, tall windows and television monitors and fax machines and wire rooms to send photographs full round the world.

But...

Crossing the new bridge – a conduit to the infield, the paddock and the pits just as the old one had been – you couldn't help waiting for the sleepers to tremble as generations had known them do; couldn't help surveying the track now diverted much as a river is: a right-left-left-right contortion of tight corners had replaced the sweep. It was June 1992.

By a nice historical conjunction, a second bridge had been built arching into the infield and yes, the old sleepers had been used to make its span, and yes, they still trembled. The changes were not superficial but somehow on the surface, and the soul of Silverstone lay undisturbed.

You could hear that in the sound of elderly engines rising, yearning and dying as deft hands tinkered with them, tuned them, turned them over. You could see that in the eyes of the people who wandered by them, stopping and stooping to inspect them, murmuring knowing words. "That's a 1952 Cooper-Bristol, isn't it?" Yes, and a 1952 Connaught and a 1952 HWM and a 1953 Riley and a 1946 Talbot Lago; and more, by the dozen and by the acre, sit-up-and-beg shapes, solid square shapes, pug-like shapes, but no less graceful for that; cars from memory magically still alive and breathing hard. Curious. No pathos lingered, no graveyard-scrapyard feel, and the people who stopped and stooped were young as well as old.

Near the paddock, temporary stalls sold bric-a-brac, programmes of races long ago, boxes of spare parts, badges and ensigns, almost archeological artefacts. At the front of one stall a selection of secondhand books stood wedged on a wooden rack. By coincidence or design one of them was *Champion Year* by Mike Hawthorn, describing how he became the first Briton to win the World

Formula One Championship in 1958. They wanted £25 for it, cheap or expensive depending on the depth of your nostalgia or curiosity. A goodly portion of the 10,000 spectators probably had it anyway, and could recite tracts of it. They looked that kind.

Over by the cafeteria butting onto the rear of the pit area a couple of lads sat wedged on a wooden bench nursing pints of lager. "Wonder if *he'll* get pole today?" one mused.

"Put your shirt on it," the other said evenly, "and your mortgage."

The words built another kind of bridge, linking Silverstone and the cars from memory to the *Ile Notre Dame*, a graceful, verdant island within sight of Montreal's skyscrapers – also guardians of modernity – where soon enough this June weekend Nigel Mansell would press his Canon Williams Renault out of the pits and go for his seventh consecutive pole position of the season: another decisive step towards joining Hawthorn as a British Champion, continuing the dynasty Hawthorn began and Graham Hill, Jim Clark, John Surtees, Jackie Stewart and James Hunt continued.

Many of the 10,000 at Silverstone nursed the official programme they'd bought for £1.50. You didn't need nostalgia or curiosity to be able to afford that. A black and white photograph dominated the front cover, a man seated in an open-top car wearing a flat cap, his mouth held in an open, boyish grin. It was, and is, a grin everyone remembers. The caption said *Hawthorn Memorial Race Meeting* and the text inside emphasized this was a day of celebration of the man.

Event five, a 12-lap scratch race, had five Cooper-Bristols in it of the kind Hawthorn drove in his first Grand Prix, Belgium 1952. Jean Howarth, his fiancee, would present the prizes. Ted Papsch and Brit Seddon, who'd worked for Hawthorn, were there to watch and chat and reminisce. As event five began the years fled. Hands sawed at vast steering wheels, the cars fishtailed and wobbled and drifted. In the right-left-left-right contortion each driver felt for his own racing line, some varying it from lap to lap as if they were exploring the freedom of movement rather than being constricted by it.

Round the *Ile Notre Dame* Nigel Mansell would have no such opportunities. Formula One cars hadn't drifted for a generation and if they wobbled it meant trouble. Mansell would take the same racing line almost to the inch every lap and all the other qualifiers for the Canadian Grand Prix would, too. A gain and a loss, no doubt, whatever your point of view, however deep your nostalgia.

Almost two hours after the last race at Silverstone, a five-lap handicap involving cars from as far back as 1925, Mansell did press his Canon Williams Renault out onto the *Ile Notre Dame*, but he didn't get pole. "I was not going quick enough at the right time," he would say. Conditions change and if you're co-existing on tiny fractions that's important: air temperature, track adhesion, cross wind, tail wind, following wind, no wind, the dampness of every dew drop, the extent of cloud cover; a minute molecular mini-world within the big world; a herbarium making heat.

By then the 10,000 at Silverstone had dispersed quietly. They'd supped of a long afternoon of decorum and dignity, of gutsy racing and laughter and tales of wonderful, improbable heroics. The whole atmosphere was precisely that and you could sup very safely from it; and that itself reared from memory, a crowd which disciplined itself and took its pleasure innocently in the presence of potentially lethal combat. Even a single policeman would have been an unnecessary intrusion, a discordant note. No doubt the police were present but I didn't see them.

Four weeks later Nigel Mansell won the British Grand Prix at this same Silverstone before 100,000, many of whom stormed the track while the cars were still going round, all intoxication and tee-shirts and jingoistic flags and beer bellies hanging like balconies. Sections of that crowd became a mob.

Hawthorn would not have understood. Once upon a time he stopped on his slowing down lap at this same Silverstone and accepted a pint of shandy from a marshal. No doubt everyone laughed. It was the way it was, and the way it was no longer. This book covers a lot of ground, the ground between Hawthorn with a shandy and too many of the 100,000 with a lot of beer, but it is more, we hope, than the story of the seven Britons who won the World Championship, who they were and what they did; its span reaches across five decades and mirrors social changes, not just changes inherent in Formula One. Each person, after all, is shaped by when he lives. Hawthorn, winning at Casablanca in 1958 to found the dynasty, was as much a product of that as Mansell at the Hungaroring, August 1992; the one driving in a bow tie and uniquely for the love of it, the other wrapped into a billion dollar industry which had forced itself to the outer reaches of what anybody could call sport.

A random example. In 1958 Hawthorn broke down on lap 46 of the Monaco Grand Prix when the fuel pump no longer pumped. As he walked back towards the pits he espied a pretty girl at a window, she opened her door and he went in for a glass of water. Even exercising your imagination to the full you can't see that happening to Mansell or anyone else these 30-odd years later. The jauntiness, the live for the moment to see what the moment brings has gone, gone into memory.

The dynasty interlocks. At Monaco in 1958, while Hawthorn put his Ferrari onto the third row of the grid, a Londoner just squeezed a Lotus-Climax into the race. This was the debut of Graham Hill and the first of his 176 races across 18 seasons and two Championships. Those 18 seasons spanned the entire careers of Clark, twice Champion, Surtees, the only man in the time-honoured phrase to win on two wheels and four, and Stewart, thrice Champion. Stewart retired at the end of 1973, but at Monaco that year, while he was putting his Tyrrell on pole, a young man from Surrey squeezed a March onto the ninth row. This was the debut of James Hunt and the first of 92 races and one Championship.

Hunt retired after Monte Carlo in 1979 where – not that it mattered now – the driveshaft broke on lap five. That weekend a man from Upton-on-Severn driving a March struggled to 11th in the supporting Formula Three race which traditionally featured during the Monaco Grand Prix meeting. Everybody talked about the winner of that Formula Three race, a very fast Frenchman called Alain Prost, and how good he was, how soon he would be into Formula One, what impact he'd make when he got there. Few noticed the flat-voiced Midlander who finished more than 40 seconds behind, but that was Nigel Mansell and the dynasty passed to him.

A word about the structure of this book. It was conceived by John Blunsden who felt that to have the lives of the seven World Champions within one cover would be apt as well as informative; would satisfy the curiosity of younger readers, take older readers into their memories and hopefully give both groups a great deal they didn't know. It seemed simple enough, Hilton researching the lives, Blunsden, who reported on all of them and was at Casablanca in 1958, adding personal appreciations.

A difficulty immediately became apparent: the interlocking. You cannot take the seven lives in isolation. You cannot, for example, write about Clark as if Hill hadn't co-existed (they were team-mates) and then write about Hill as if Clark hadn't co-existed. Moreover, Surtees and Stewart interlocked with Clark and Hill, each of the four careers having a direct bearing on the others. How else could it be when they were in the same races, contesting the same Championships?

To circumvent this and keep the narrative in approximate chronological order, Hilton constructs a portrait of each driver up to and including the first time they won the Championship and draws the remainder of their careers into chapters headed Echoes – which prevents the narrative from endlessly doubling back. Otherwise you'd read about Hill all the way to his death in 1975, then return to Clark in the Fifties and follow him to his death in 1968, then return to Surtees in the Fifties...

The Echoes are valuable in another way. The story of the seven is in a very real sense the story of Formula One from 1952 to 1992, season by season in an uninterrupted sequence, and they allow the seven to be doing different or similar things simultaneously. The Echoes of Winter, for example, embraces Hawthorn, Surtees, Hill and Clark over a couple of months in 1958, but never all together at the same place.

In Part Two Blunsden paints his personal portraits. For your interest, Hilton didn't see what Blunsden wrote and Blunsden didn't see what Hilton wrote, so you have, we trust, independent avenues towards the same subjects.

Many, many people have helped by giving the background and foreground, but particular thanks go to Nigel Roebuck, Grand Prix Editor of *Autosport* for his council, advice and insights. Simon Taylor, the Deputy Chairman of the magazine's publishers, Haymarket, unhesitatingly said "Yes" to a request to quote from *Autosport*.

Mattie Calder, Jim Clark's eldest surviving sister, not only gave an interview but made sure his other sisters, Isabel and Betty, were there, too. They have a merry twinkle in their eyes and surely mirror their brother; calm people, down to earth but not earthy, genuine but nobody's fool. A mixture of gentility and firmness of purpose tumbles from them. It was what he had.

Bette Hill, maternally and sharply and understandably protective of Graham's memory, was touchingly candid and kindly gave permission to quote from her book *The Other Side of the Hill* (co-authored by Neil Ewart and published by Hutchinson/Stanley Paul). Her son Damon was equally candid and handled what might have been an uncomfortable interview as if to the manner born, which is what he is.

Graham Gauld readily agreed to the use of much material he'd taped with and about Clark, and his thoroughly researched *Ecurie Ecosse* (published by himself) was invaluable in shedding light on many aspects, particularly the Stewart family.

Charlie Rous, a pillar of support in an earlier MRP book, *A Man Called Mike* (by Hilton), moved effortlessly into memory to capture Surtees' early days and was good enough to hunt out articles he'd written long ago, especially on the rider John Hartle, who was a team-mate of Surtees.

Other permissions to quote, all gratefully received, were from: Peter Garnier, *Sixteen on the Grid* (Cassell); Heinz Pruller, *Jochen Rindt* (William Kimber); Walter Hayes and Reed International Books, *Jim Clark, Portrait of a Great Driver* (Hamlyn); Brands Hatch Circuits Limited via Caroline O'Connor for Clark's 1964 lap of the circuit from the official programme; David Chappell, Sports Editor of *The Times*, for an extract from James Hunt's feature on Nigel Mansell in 1986; Peter Dick for his feature on John Frankenheimer and the making of the film *Grand Prix*; Richard Williams from his tribute to James Hunt in *The Independent on Sunday* plus tracts of an interview with 'Bubbles' Horsley which space did not permit him to use; Maurice Hamilton for a particularly perceptive paragraph or two on Hunt from his tribute in *The Observer*.

The people who shared memories or just plain helped are, in no particular order, June Brunet of the BRDC, Corinna Phillips of Silverstone, David Mills, Derek Bell, Richard Attwood, Iain Mackay, Keith Greene, Mark Wilkin of the BBC, Kevin Flynn of BBC Television Publicity, Tony Mason, Nick Brittan, Howden Ganley, David Fern of Donington, Pat Mennem, formerly of the *Daily Mirror*, David Phipps, Roger Clark, Andrew Cowan, Tony Jardine, Brian Melia, Lord Alexander Hesketh, David Benson, Tony Brooks, Jim Dunn of *The Scotsman*, Colin Wilson of the RAC, Jim Porter, Peter Warr, Alan Brinton, Peter Stayner of Marlboro McLaren International, John Watson, Peter Dick, Ann Bradshaw, Frank Williams, Ian Scott Watson, Catherine Prentice, Ian Norris, Jim Bloss, Oswald Brewis, Eoin Young for a deliciously mischievous interview, Maurice Hamilton, Martyn Pass, Marcus Pye, Vic Elford, Mark Burgess of *Karting* magazine, John Webb, Ken Tyrrell, Jeff Taylor (museums officer of the Berwickshire District Council), Jimmy Stewart, John Surtees, David Tremayne, David Sims, Bob Dance, Jim Endruweit, Ted Papsch, Innes Ireland, Jean Howarth (now happily Mrs Jean Ireland) and Roy Salvadori.

The books consulted would constitute a library of motorsport so we list only those which were primary sources of information. For basic research: *Autocourse, Marlboro's Grand Prix Guide, Rothmans' Grand Prix Motorcycle Yearbook*, the four-volume set *Grand Prix!* by Mike Lang (Haynes) and the Olivetti-Longines annual statistical compendiums, a treasure trove of the hardest of hard facts to three decimal points.

For personal versions of what happened: *Life at the Limit* by Graham Hill, *For the Record* by Niki Lauda, *When the Flag Drops* by Sir Jack Brabham, *A Turn at the Wheel* by Stirling Moss, *Faster!* by Jackie Stewart and Peter Manso, *Champion Year* by Mike Hawthorn (all William Kimber); *Graham* by Hill and Ewart, *Driven to Win* by Nigel Mansell and Derick Allsop (both Hutchinson/Stanley Paul); *Jim Clark at the Wheel* by Clark and Gauld (Arthur Barker); *Against All Odds* by James Hunt (Hamlyn); *Jackie Stewart World Champion* by Stewart and Eric Dymock (Pelham); *My Twenty Years of Racing* by Juan-Manuel Fangio (Temple); *Les Jeux du Risque* by Jacques Laffite and Johnny Rives (Michel Lafon); *The Day I Died* by Mark Kahn (Gentry); *World Champion* by John Surtees and Alan Henry (Hazleton).

For invaluable background: *Colin Chapman, The Man and His Cars* by Jabby Crombac, *Jim Clark, The Legend Lives on* by Gauld, *Fangio* by Fangio and Roberto Carozzo, Williams, *The Business of Grand Prix Racing* by Henry, *Mr Monaco* by Tony Rudd, *Grand Prix Greats* by Nigel Roebuck (all PSL); *Mon Ami Mate* by Chris Nixon (Transport Bookman Publications); *The Motor Racing Register* 1965 by Geoffrey Dempsey (MRR); *Lotus, All the Cars* by Anthony Pritchard (Aston); *The World Champions* by Pritchard (Leslie Frewin); *Grand Prix British Winners* by Hamilton (Guinness); *Autocourse History of the Grand Prix Car* by Doug Nye and the *Driver Profile* series (all Hazleton).

There is now, happily, an increasing collection of videos with archive film enabling the viewer to relive it all. The following gave that: The *Champions* series by Duke Marketing, Jim Clark, *The Legend* by Sports Seen, the season-by-season Marlboro collection covering the Seventies and *British Invasion* by Front Runner.

PORTRAIT:
MIKE HAWTHORN

"The star of the Cooper drivers is expected to be the 23-year-old Mick [sic] Hawthorn of Farnham, Surrey who at the first Goodwood international meeting proved himself a 'natural' – in other words, a driver seemingly born to fast car driving. In his first Grand Prix type of race he defeated many far more experienced drivers in more powerful cars.

"Actually, Mick who has been trained by his father, himself an old TT motorcycle and Brooklands car racer, became prominent last year in sports car racing. It took only his first appearance in a much faster car to reveal his cool and accurate judgement.

"The duels between the HWM's and the Coopers should produce the highlights of the season, and a great deal will be heard of the 'blonde [sic] giant with a nice taste in bow ties,' as one writer described him after Goodwood."

These words appeared in the June 1952 issue of the *Boy's Own* paper in an article headlined BRITISH HOPES IN GRAND PRIX RACING. I know that the very name of the magazine has become the conduit to a dreaded cliche (*Boy's Own* paper stuff, straight from *Boy's Own*, and so forth), but it *did* appear and anyway the words are particularly prophetic. A lot would be heard of Mike Hawthorn.

That June 1952 issue is interesting in many other ways. Accompanying the article, for instance, is a caption showing the "cockpit of the impeccable HWM, which will compete in Formula Two classics. Twenty-two-year-old Stirling Moss will bring youth to the helm."

The magazine reflects, quite unconsciously, perceptions of how the world was. Here is Denis Compton's famous Brylcreem advertisement (the notion of a cricketer being paid to endorse a product provoked controversy) and such articles as Good Camping Means Clean Camping, and Do You Collect Bus And Tram Tickets? An episode of Biggles preceded a profile of "sixteen-year-old Lester Piggott, boy wonder of the turf".

A certain wholesome innocence pervades every page, and maybe the misconceptions about Hawthorn began there and then. In time he'd appear in much less innocent publications and the press would fashion him into an image of what they wanted him to be, a flamboyant and devil-may-care hard-drinking Public Schoolboy. It was obvious imagery and the fact that he was a handsome man in a very dangerous activity fed it hugely. Those who knew him well don't really recognize him within it because at best he was only partially like that. They find other descriptions, a gentle, caring, concerned man, polite, guarding the common touch; a man who bore illness and pain in silence and who often kept his own counsel. Jean Howarth will be giving a great deal of evidence to support that, but suffice it so say here that she never once saw him tipsy, never mind drunk.

Former Grand Prix driver Innes Ireland (who married Jean in June 1993) is more adamant. In his deep, powerful voice he described how somewhere he'd read that Hawthorn used to drink 20 pints of beer a night. "I ask you: have you ever met *anyone* who could do that? Rubbish, absolute rubbish. Mike liked a pint in the pub. That's normal, isn't it? But 20 pints...rubbish..."

John Michael Hawthorn, born Mexborough, Yorkshire on April 10, 1929, remained a Yorkshireman all his life although the family moved to Farnham when he was three. At the risk of introducing another cliche, the customized Tyke, Hawthorn carried with him certain northern traits. He knew the value of hard work and the value of the money it brought, he was nobody's fool and, as Jean says, "if he made up his mind not to do something, particularly if he thought it not right, nothing on earth would make him."

If all this disturbs the legends of endless boozy binges, lots of loose ladies and devil-take-the-hindmost, so be it. Drinking there was, ladies there were, and the devil lurked never very far away, but we are speaking here of scale. Of course he played hard (and if you haven't you've not been truly alive) but often enough he liked silence, liked to sit in and just watch the television, he and Jean eating supper off trays.

Farnham, hard by Aldershot, is a pleasant, very southern place with agreeable detached houses peeking across leafy lanes and a whiff of prosperity. Hawthorn's father Leslie seems to have been a difficult, determined man who opened a garage – called the Tourist Trophy Garage – in Farnham in 1931 selling and tuning cars and motorbikes. Hawthorn's mother, Winifred Mary, was certainly a curious and difficult woman.

Ted Papsch, who worked in the garage, says that "Mrs H, as we called her, was a businesswoman. She'd go through the books and if there was a penny missing she would find it even if it took three weeks because she'd say 'the pennies look after the pounds'. She was very, very fond of Mike. She didn't speak about his racing but we knew in her mind she was always worried.

"She was superstitious. Once she found a robin in the showroom and that was something terrible. Apparently she had a superstition about birds and if you sent her a Christmas card with a robin on it she wouldn't have anything more to do with you. None of the number-plates on her cars had to add up to 13: she wouldn't have a one or a three and she wouldn't have numbers that added up to 13, either – like, say, six and seven, or nine two two. She either liked you or she didn't. If your face fitted you were all right. She liked me and therefore it was all right."

We shall never know what Hawthorn felt about his mother although, as it seems, he coped with her eccentricities and foibles well enough. Jean remembers vividly when Hawthorn took her home to be introduced and his mother referred to her throughout as *that woman* as in "pass that woman the salt". Such encounters can be uncomfortable and potentially explosive, but Hawthorn solved it by taking a suite in a nearby hotel so he and Jean could stay there rather than at the family home. This, Jean insists, was entirely typical of the man, protecting harmony in the most sensible, pragmatic way.

Of course, if your father has been in racing and now has a garage which tunes and works on the cars and bikes, the chances the son will follow increase.

Hawthorn recorded how even as a "tiny tot" he clung to the steering wheel of the family's Morris Cowley and "cried like mad when I had to get out." Evidently at eight he drove in the field behind the garage and would remember the "thrill I felt at first having a moving car under my control."

This is something many racers remember, the initial and subsequently powerful impetus, and it reaches like a theme all the way to a young Nigel Mansell driving a friend's ancient Austin round fields. Neither he nor Hawthorn were big enough to see over the steering wheels properly but that didn't matter. Motion, not direction, was the important thing.

As a lad Hawthorn watched racing at Brooklands, the bowl-shaped track not so far from Farnham, and the sight of cars "thundering round those towering cliffs of concrete" was "heaven." During the war, and at the age of only 14, he bought – for 30 shillings, mark you (£1.50!) – an old motorbike and renovated it himself. That proved to be another beginning.

Many – though not all – great drivers have a sympathy with mechanical matters, have more than a basic understanding of why the four wheels go round, and Hawthorn knew intimately, as Papsch, an engineer-mechanic-tuner, attests. "My first impression when I started to work for him? A fantastic man, you'd never meet a better. He was kind. He'd be in the workshop and he knew the job as well as any of us, perhaps even more. I remember an Alfa Romeo which had won Le Mans in 1933. Mike and I stripped it down and what a car that Alfa was, every split-pin chromium plated. I took the exhaust manifold to a place at Haslemere, had it stove-enammeled and so on, and I tell you Mike knew more about it than I did..."

After four years at Public School – Ardingly from 1942 to 1946 – the hands-on experience inevitably became broad because of the number and variety of cars and bikes Hawthorn would come to know. Moreover, after his schooldays he served an apprenticeship with a firm of engineers in Guildford – Dennis Bros, who made trucks, fire engines and so forth. He rode bikes, albeit old ones, which broadened the understanding further. He tried scrambles and liked the wild rush of sensations. At 18 he started to drive a 1930 Riley, tatty inside but which stood up to a hammering. It all pointed to racing, and he yearned to do that. Leslie Hawthorn yearned for him to do that, too.

Normally, fathers approach the matter of their sons exploring mortality with trepidation, if not outright hostility – and mothers are worse – but Leslie had raced himself, of course, and to offer his son less than full encouragement would almost have been unnatural.

They bought a Riley Imp and in 1949 Hawthorn did a couple of speed trials, winning the first and coming second in the second; they raced it and a Riley Imp in 1951 at such places as Goodwood, Castle Combe and others which have gone into memory like Boreham, Gamston. He won regularly.

Britain, moving in to the Fifties, was not the place you recognize today. Rationing of confectionery and coal remained in force as a reminder of the toll the war had taken, cities still bore bomb damage, but far away an Imperial presence played itself out in many a distant land. Britain counted for something and saw herself – after the United States and the Soviet Union – as the third superpower. The national decline had begun, indeed was further advanced than seemed evident, but to be British *still* represented, in the words of a poet, having won the first prize in life by birthright alone. *Circa* 1950–51–52, the notion that we were better than the rest of the world at everything persisted. Anything made abroad was crudely stamped *Foreign* and treated with suspicion as a cheap and unreliable trinket. You bought only goods stamped *Made in Britain*.

To recapture these certainties is elusive because the trough of time is too deep, too much has swilled through it, but Germany remained essentially a shattered land, a third of it administered by the British as a fiefdom, and Japan remained essentially another shattered land and an American province. The Third World remained the province of the white man, to be done with as he decreed. No person in Britain could escape these influences, any more than a child of the Nineties can escape the drastically revised position of Britain. You are shaped by when your formative years happen to be. The everyday forces are too strong to do anything else, and they are all you know.

There can be no reasonable doubt that John Michael Hawthorn succumbed to these forces and acted of his time. At every pressure point in his life – and they were many and profound – he stayed true to this: for better or worse, a British gentleman as he conceived what a British gentleman would be. That might disturb the legends again, but so be it again. He was neither saint nor sinner in the extreme sense of either term, and he nurtured private as well as public strengths. His bravery was never questioned, nor his skill. Each day of his 30 years he remained an essentially British person, perhaps quintissentially, and he'd have said: *Well, what's wrong with it?* The national doubts, the self-questioning, the decline were truly not in evidence. You cannot understand his career unless you understand this.

The Hawthorns decided that the next step must be Formula Two (easy to think of that, then, *let's have a go and why the hell not, eh?*) and by chance a family friend saw a photograph in a newspaper of the new Cooper-Bristol. The friend, a racing enthusiast, offered to buy one if Leslie would maintain it and Mike drive it. Cooper, then famous racing car manufacturers, had already sold two and were building a third.

Hawthorn was anxious to have it for Goodwood on April 14, 1952, a meeting which by tradition launched the season proper in Britain and this year would be spiced by the presence of Juan-Manuel Fangio and Jose Froilan Gonzalez, both famous drivers on a global scale and visiting from Argentina: Fangio the World Champion of the year before, Gonzalez a Ferrari driver who'd finished third in the Championship.

Fangio has described the visit. "Gonzalez and I were invited by Raymond Mays to try out his BRM. We had already heard about it in racing circles. It was spoken of as an engine which would eat up capital but never win a race. The invitation was so pleasantly offered that we could not refuse to go to England for a quick look at the new model being given its final touches. When we were with Raymond Mays he talked about the car very persuasively. At the end of our conversation he took us to the old Folkingham airfield near Bourne where a circuit had been laid out.

"Gonzalez took the wheel of the BRM first, making several laps at ever-increasing speeds. I watched his progress with interest. Then it was my turn. The car went into a skid after the first lap. I vainly tried to keep it in hand but ended up off the road, though the only damage was a broken exhaust pipe, quickly replaced. I took to the road again. One could not find fault with the car which held the road well and had remarkable acceleration."

This test completed, Fangio and Gonzalez went off to the cinema to pass the time, watching a western because "we did not understand a word of English." Gunfire on horseback is gunfire on horseback, no interpreters necessary.

"I don't know why, but I was not at ease in that place. Suddenly there were shouts, the film went off and the lights went on. Almost exactly over our heads, hunks of plaster began dropping from the ceiling. I grabbed Gonzalez's arm and yanked him out of his seat – a tough job, considering his weight – and we made for the exit, followed by other people, fleeing in panic. A second later the huge chandelier lighting the place went out, there was a frightening crash and people screamed in the darkness. Later, by the aid of a flashlight, we found that the hanging light had crashed down exactly on the two seats Gonzalez and I had just left. Five other spectators in the same row who had not got away had been seriously hurt."

If Fangio had remained in his seat the history of motor racing would have been completely altered and a direct bearing on the career of Hawthorn gone.

The Cooper-Bristol was ready for Goodwood – touch and go, much last-minute improvization. Fangio had been invited to drive one at the meeting, Gonzalez had the Thinwall Special. Hawthorn faced them with meagre experience. He'd not raced a single-seater before and, though he qualified second for the Lavant Cup, realized "I had never practised a racing start with the car." This alarming thought crossed his mind *on the starting line*. Hawthorn remembered an article in *Motor Sport* about how, at a Brighton Speed Trial, the writer had been gratified to see one of the contestants holding his revs constant rather than blipping the throttle. Hawthorn decided to do that. He dipped the accelerator and held the revs, but at that instant the flag fell so he had no notion of how many revs he'd reached.

He set off in a great surge, got round Madgwick Corner and "pressed on as hard as I could." When he'd settled he looked back and realized that not only was he leading by some distance but pulling away. He won easily and won the next race on the card, the Chichester Cup – Fangio fifth. Hawthorn finished second in the main event, the Richmond Trophy, Gonzalez winning.

Cumulatively this proved a genuine sensation and made front page news in the national press, *Unknown Briton beats Fangio*. Ted Papsch's wife "knew Mike before because I worked in Farnham as a dentist, but I always remember the day he won at Goodwood. Everyone was so thrilled and we went absolutely mad. He was a boy who enjoyed life but was nice to everyone and of course good-looking, oh yes."

Hawthorn enjoyed the immediate aftermath, enjoyed a measure of fame although in time he'd find another side to this, a pervasive, vicious one.

The world then was less rigid, less mapped and planned, less governed by rules. Contrast that with the *Federation Internationale de l'Automobile* rulebook, 1993, which is nearly an inch and a half thick and the sporting code section alone runs to 575 pages. Hawthorn entered for the Belgian Grand Prix at Spa on June 22 and simply took the Cooper-Bristol there, he and Leslie and their mechanic Hugh Sewell driving a Bedford van over with the car in the back.

Spa offered itself as a deeply intimidating place for your debut (and co-incidentally your first race of any kind on the Continent): 8.479 fast miles uphill and down dale, all of it virtually unprotected from houses, woods, ditches and farm buildings. The year before, Fangio set fastest lap averaging 120.5mph. Then (as now) it generally rained for the race, the Ardennes seeming to have a micro-climate and Spa a micro-climate within the micro-climate. Clouds close in, hovering and smothering, and unload. In the wet Spa ceased to be intimidating and presented itself as stark and nakedly terrifying, a potential graveyard.

By an irony, Hawthorn would find himself competing against some of the best of the day although not Fangio, who was nursing a broken neck after a crash, or Gonzalez who drove but a single Grand Prix during the season. That diluted the entry but still left Piero Taruffi, Giuseppe Farina and Alberto Ascari, who some equate to Fangio. They filled the front row in their Ferraris, Jean Behra in a Gordini on the second, Stirling Moss in an ERA on the fourth, a chap from Kidderminster called Peter Collins on the fifth in an HWM. Another Briton, Lance Macklin, put an HWM on the sixth. Hawthorn qualified on the third row after what he judged some quite good laps.

It rained on race day...

Hawthorn and Ken Wharton (Frazer Nash) duelled, trading places down the field while Ascari demonstrated his mastery of this circuit as he demonstrated it at so many others, leading Farina by a distance. On lap 11 Hawthorn moved in front of Wharton and so he did not see the Frazer Nash spin off at Stavelot, the fast right loop at the far side of the circuit. The car travelled backwards through a barbed wire fence. Next lap Hawthorn noticed a knot of spectators and, glancing, glimpsed the tail-end of Wharton's car protruding from woods. Later Hawthorn found out that Wharton had ducked just in time, although the barbed wire clawed its way along the car and tore Wharton's shirt. If he hadn't ducked...

Hawthorn finished fourth, a lap behind Ascari. Without diminishing this performance in any way, it was easier to finish in the points on your debut then: 10 drivers had in 1950, seven would in 1952. Only thereafter did it become progressively rarer and it is extremely rare now, only 15 in the last 30 years.

The real context of Hawthorn's achievement is that he got to the end at all – despite needing two unplanned pit stops for petrol and struggling with a clutch problem *and* despite waving to Taruffi, who was walking back after he'd spun off. A nice gesture to make, yes, but a mistake because, as Hawthorn turned, looking at Taruffi, he went off himself and narrowly avoided a telegraph pole. It frightened Hawthorn a good deal.

Collins dropped out on lap three, driveshaft. In time he and Hawthorn would become very close friends, so close that for a time their names welded, became synonymous in much the same way as those of Larwood and Voce, Nottinghamshire's opening bowlers, in the Thirties or Matthews and Finney on the football field, or Lock and Laker, the Surrey spin bowlers, in the mid-Fifties. The unusual aspect is that it almost never happens in motor racing. The great partnerships have been those of mutual benefit, Colin Chapman making Lotus cars and Jim Clark winning in them. Ordinarily drivers are too competitive, too self-ambitious to co-exist comfortably with *any* other driver. We could have likened Lock and Laker to Prost and Senna, but...

Hawthorn contested the French Grand Prix at Rouen two weeks after Spa, but the ignition failed on lap 51; two weeks after that he went to Silverstone for the British Grand Prix, where a driver called Roy Salvadori was making his debut in a Ferrari. Salvadori is a most illuminating man because the romance of racing in the Fifties touched him not at all. Quite the opposite. I quote him at length because he discourses so lucidly on the world Hawthorn had just penetrated.

What were the cars of the Fifties like? "Horrible, terrible cars. They vibrated and they were hot because you had all the pipes going through the cockpit so if you touched any part of the pipes you burned your leg. You kept away from them. You were enclosed in petrol because you needed 40 gallons to get through a race. The handling was difficult because you'd steer on the throttle, correct your angle of drift on the throttle. We could go through two or three races with one set of tyres. We'd try and get our rubber down to about 3½ mill. You wouldn't start on new tyres because they weren't at their best, you'd get them well ground in.

"The whole point was that you had very narrow tyres, and 100 horsepower with that can be just like 600 with a wide tyre. It's very difficult to give an impression of that. We went quick on the straights because we didn't have the wings to slow us down, but which also give you roadholding, so at Le Mans the Aston Martin saloon was doing 300km/h, and that's quick even by later standards – but they weren't quick through the corners: sliding all over the place. You didn't have the downforce because nobody knew about it. In Formula One you had no downforce, either.

"I've got no feel for the old-time racing. It was damned dangerous, disorganized. You've got no idea. They'd cancel practice, you wouldn't get your starting money, you wouldn't know whether your entry had been accepted until two or three weeks before the event. Scutineering was a masterpiece. The mechanics would be standing in heavy rain for about three hours trying to push their cars up to be scrutineered by an idiot who wouldn't know right from left. That's the way it went on. You'd be on circuits where you had no caravans, nowhere to get out of the wet. From memory, it always seemed to be raining. You'd be soaked to the skin, you'd come back from the track and get in your road car to have a change of clothes. You had no facilities."

These hard words are of necessity very personal to Salvadori, and however other drivers treasure the era – as they do – they contain great truths, not least that the world was less mapped, less rigid and planned. Go and have a go, why not, eh?

"Take a Grand Prix meeting at Silverstone. Let me give you an idea of what a driver did. I'd arrive at 10 in the morning and do a race for cars of up to 2 litres then another in the unlimited classification – already 200 racing miles. The Grand Prix could be up to and over 300 miles (although Silverstone in 1952 was 'only' 248) and then you'd finish off with a saloon car or GT race, four in the day. A Grand Prix driver would go right through the card."

Actually, drivers wanted to drive, and they accepted as not only natural but also desirable that they'd race all manner of cars. In later years, for example, during the International Trophy meeting at Silverstone, Hawthorn entertained – and genuinely thrilled – the crowd by flinging his Jaguar round in a Touring Car race, churning smoke from the tyres, the Jaguar leaning and craning and angling and rocketing.

In the 1952 Grand Prix Hawthorn finished third, two laps behind the winner, Ascari, Salvadori eighth and three laps down, Collins out on lap 73, ignition.

Hawthorn finished fourth in the Dutch Grand Prix at Zandvoort after qualifying on the front row, but something of historical significance moved in the background. Hawthorn, his father and Sewell stayed in the same hotel as the Ferrari team and after qualifying they all fell to talking in the only common language they had, a species of French. Aurelio Lampredi, the chief designer, and Nello Ugolini, the team manager, represented Ferrari in what, after Hawthorn had gone to bed, became a convivial drinking session – Leslie Hawthorn listening but taking no great part because evidently he lacked even a species of French. Sewell did the talking for the Brits. Clearly the Ferrari people were impressed by Hawthorn, said they'd try and give him a test drive sometime and would certainly mention his name to Enzo Ferrari himself.

Hawthorn believed that his partnership with Ferrari began then, however tenuously. As is often the way of motor racing the beginning was enacted swiftly.

After the final Grand Prix of the season – the Italian at Monza, where Hawthorn spent *an hour* in the pits with ignition trouble – Ferrari asked if he'd like to drive for them in the non-Championship Modena Grand Prix. He would, and he'd need to have a run in the car first. That would be done at Modena immediately following Monza.

While he waited for his turn at Modena – Ascari and Villoresi were also present – he went round in the Cooper, braked too late and crashed at between 70 and 80 miles an hour. He was thrown out and thought he'd killed himself.

His father didn't see the accident, but Salvadori – also present, and who should have been driving the Cooper – had a Morris Minor and ran Leslie round to the scene. Hawthorn said he was shaken but, he thought, otherwise in one piece. No medical facilities of any kind were available at this test and, worse, as they helped Hawthorn into the Morris, he went blind. Two police motorbike riders escorted the Morris to hospital where Hawthorn nervously opened his eyes and found he could see again. The skin on his back and shoulder was raw – a jumper he'd been wearing had been torn off. At the hospital they treated the raw flesh with neat alcohol. The shock of that alone can kill.

He was detained in hospital and Ugolini came to visit, said Ferrari wanted him for the following year. Hawthorn asked for a couple of weeks to weigh it up, privately hoping to get a place with a British team, then returned to England, did weigh it up, flew back to Italy and signed. He had only driven in five Grands Prix, taking 10 points from them: fourth equal in the Championship. It had happened fast, as befits a man in a hurry. All racing drivers are.

Ferrari? Salvadori is illuminating about that, too – his debut at the British Grand Prix had been in one. "A Ferrari driver was very limited in his earning capacity because he was only allowed to drive a Ferrari (in all racing). Hawthorn and later Peter Collins drove nothing else but Ferraris, so a lot of their earning power was eliminated. It was, however, prestige to drive for Ferrari.

"Start money was quite considerable in the context of the time although peanuts now and I suppose Ferrari got £1,000 and the driver half of that. The main inflow came from your contracts and the big penny arrived on January 1 when you got all your monies. I'd be with Esso, say, and Esso would find me the drives or I'd have to drive for Esso-contracted entries – that applied to the tyre companies, too – so really the money was paid before you started racing, the rest being additional.

"The Ferrari drivers were notoriously badly paid. You sacrificed quite a lot to drive for them, but Ferrari had the best cars and their argument ran, 'OK, you might not initially get the money from us but you'll have the opportunity of earning it through prize money during the season because our cars are the best.' This mirrors the passage of time, but it also mirrors the commercial aspect."

The danger cannot be avoided as a legitimate subject of discussion. Wharton might have been decapitated at Spa, Hawthorn might easily have struck the telegraph pole at Spa or the Cooper might have landed on top of him at Modena, might have burst into flames, and all this at the threshold of a career. What lay ahead? More of it. We're talking about a different mentality.

"You look at the grids through those years," Salvadori says, "you see the change of names and it was happening an awful lot, and when it did it seemed only natural. It didn't hit as hard as it possibly should. Most of those accidents were due to breakages on cars. So much happened but why it happened you could never find out afterwards, nothing left of the car, difficult to say where it all started.

"Unless you were an idiot you had to accept that percentage-wise the chances of getting written-off were high, and in some years as high as 25 per cent. Your feeling was always that it wasn't going to be you – otherwise you wouldn't have continued. *You're the clever one or the lucky one and no, it's not going to happen to you.* Did Mike rationalize it that way? Look, Mike was a go-er. I'd meet Mike on the roads and as soon as he saw you it was foot down on the accelerator, up would go two fingers. Didn't matter what car he was in, he'd be at it. He couldn't resist that any more than maybe I could. I dreaded seeing him as he went to Farnham. We occasionally met on the Kingston by-pass and then we were off trying to outfumble (outwit and outdrive) each other. He was a very competitive guy and that's the way he wanted it, you can be sure."

There would be two years at Ferrari and in only his fourth Grand Prix for them, the French at Reims, he won. That race endures for many reasons, not least that Hawthorn became the first Briton to win a Grand Prix in the modern era. Some races draw together many different strands and they interweave gloriously for a moment or two and then are gone – a car breaks down, say – but a tiny residue of races remain where the interweaving tightens and builds towards something completely momentous. Reims, July 5, 1953 was that. The grid, fastest on the right:

Villoresi	Bonetto	Ascari
(Ferrari)	(Maserati)	(Ferrari)

Gonzalez	Fangio
(Maserati)	(Maserati)

Marimon	Hawthorn	Farina
(Maserati)	(Ferrari)	(Ferrari)

Fangio remembers that "Gonzalez took off like an arrow. Knowledgeably, the experts in the stands remarked that he had assured this initial advantage by a Machiavellian plot, starting with a half-empty tank which, weighing less, would make his rivals overstress their engines. Gonzalez held the lead for a long time, followed by me, Ascari and Hawthorn, totally unimpressed to find himself alongside far more experienced drivers. When Gonzalez stopped to refuel I decided that the moment I was waiting for had arrived. I put my foot down and lost Ascari and Hawthorn.

"Suddenly my position in the lead was less secure than I thought as Hawthorn turned up in my mirror. Little by little he crept up alongside me. What a battle! Against me a very young man whose blond hair made him look adolescent; yet he had the tenacity of a true champion. Lap after lap I could not shake him off in spite of every trick of the trade. We were still side-by-side scarcely more than a yard apart. From time to time one of us nosed ahead of the other by an inch or two.

"Only towards the end of the race did Hawthorn realize he had an ace in his hand and decided to play it. It was a question of brakes, those of his Ferrari apparently in better condition than mine on the Maserati. On the last corner he waited until the very last second before braking. For an instant I thought he would go off the road but his brakes held. His audacity gave him a tiny advantage as he swung in to the finishing straight because I had to brake earlier and for a longer time."

Hawthorn knew that the race turned on the exactness of his gearchange at this final corner, a V-shaped right called *Virage de Thillois*, before the long straight, the line being nearly a mile from Thillois. Hawthorn described the two cars as inches apart going into Thillois. He "slipped" into first and hugged the apex of the corner as tightly as he could, "straightened up the wheels and simultaneously slammed the throttle wide open. The engine screamed up to peak revs but the tyres gripped." The tiny difference: enough.

Fangio remembers that "the young English driver crossed the line a hairsbreadth ahead of me. England had a new and worthy champion. I had already realized it and said so frankly when I talked with the reporters. We had seen the birth of a new ace. I warmly congratulated Hawthorn, who reddened visibly. Embarrassed, he ran his fingers through his blond locks."

Hawthorn	2h 44m 18.6s
Fangio	at 1.0s
Gonzalez	at 1.4
Ascari	at 4.6

Hawthorn wrote in *Challenge Me The Race* that he feared the spectators might have been bored watching two cars "just" passing and re-passing. It endures as an astonishing statement while hysteria gripped everyone else at Reims in the late afternoon of July 5, 1953. This hysteria rose and rose until the climax when some drivers slowed to witness it for themselves, abandoning the race altogether, and the crowd invaded the track. Quite possibly, and more than probably, a natural reticence (the fabled British reticence) inhibited Hawthorn from expressing himself fully because chaps didn't, *one* didn't, *one* took it on the chin for better or worse and never ventured the opinion that you'd thrashed the others by nerve, willpower, skill, endurance. You had the luck, that was all.

What did he really think? Only public posturing, surely, can make a man worry about whether such a race bored those present. He did not lack perception. He knew the scope and depth of the moves on lap 60 of 60, must have learned of their impact later if he didn't sense them as they happened. He could not avoid that. After all, spectators now choked the circuit, Fangio now prepared to embarrass him by telling him how good he was.

What did he really think? It is lost, and will remain lost. Even today, if he were here, the ethics would no doubt hold him and he'd choose not to say. I had the luck, that was all.

Autosport headlined their report THE RACE OF THE CENTURY and it culminated like this: "For the tenth time the leaders dead-heated over the line on the last lap, and Gonzalez led Ascari by about a centimetre. Farina panted along behind, whilst Villoresi was practically exhausted. At Thillois Hawthorn edged ahead of his rival and the Ferrari held its slender lead all down the straight with Fangio crouching down in his Maserati to try to get every ounce of speed. Down went the flag with the Ferrari about forty yards in front of the Maserati."

It was a precious moment because the rest of 1953 drifted to only fourth in the Championship with 27 points (19 counting), and 1954 would be dominated not by racing but by a much more emotive subject, the Call-Up to the armed forces. National Service, which then applied to virtually every male between 18 and 26, lasted for two years and frankly wasn't something most eagerly anticipated. (As a Sgt Major once said: "You might break your mother's heart but you won't break mine" – ominous sentiments). However, in 1954, a strong sense of duty still existed in the country at large and the Second World War lay only nine years distant, still very fresh in the memory. In that war everyone had done their bit.

A feeling existed that a subsequent generation should serve and gain some military proficiency in case of a major emergency. The Soviet Union and its satellites loomed as a direct threat, the Iron Curtain drawn down the middle of Germany with six million Communist soldiers ranged behind it, perhaps more, and in any case Britain remained a world power with responsibilities to be discharged in many, many places.

The Call-Up stretched across such a broad age span because that allowed latitude for deferment. If you were apprenticed to a trade you had deferment until you'd completed the apprenticeship. When Hawthorn joined Dennis Brothers in Guildford – he ought to have spent four years there – deferment came automatically. However, three years later he left to go to Chelsea College and the deferment lapsed. He volunteered for the RAF as air crew. Although accepted, the RAF didn't need air crew at this time so he was not yet called-up. That came in August 1952, but because he was doing so well in the Cooper-Bristol, a whole career unfolding before him and quickly, he applied for a deferment until the end of the season. And he crashed at Modena in September. He was informed that "I would not be called-up until I had passed another medical examination."

Hawthorn heard no more, although at Silverstone in 1953 a Ministry of Labour official approached him – he now drove for Ferrari – to ascertain where he lived. Hawthorn replied Italy – which put him beyond the reach of the Call-Up – but he returned to Britain subsequently that season to drive and nothing happened.

The storm broke after the non-Championship Buenos Aires Grand Prix on January 31, 1954. Hawthorn led brilliantly until the engine let go on the final lap, so brilliantly he attracted big publicity in Britain. The following day questions were raised in the House of Commons. Why hadn't this young man been called up?

He represented a tempting target, handsome, fit, famous, seemingly well-paid and living in a land of milk and honey, Italy, while poor British lads slogged out the square-bashing and discovered that patrolling the Suez Canal could be nasty (ask Blunsden). If you fell in they gave you 17 different injections immediately…

We know from Salvadori that Hawthorn wasn't particularly well-paid at Ferrari and, far from savouring the milk and honey, he was homesick, would have traded the lot for a pint. Nor in fact was he now fit in the military sense. He had a kidney complaint which he thought might have begun when his career began, getting thrown around in the Riley Imp and Sprite.

The storm rose around two sharp questions. Why, when each of his visits to England involved publicity – as a racer – had the papers not been served, and how was it possible that a young man might be fit enough for Grand Prix racing but not fit enough for National Service? As someone asked cryptically (and rhetorically), do you need to be fitter to get into the army than battle the fastest cars on earth?

That missed an immediate point. With the sheer scale of the Call-Up there had to be tight rules about fitness. Certain ailments or disabilities led to immediate exclusion. Accepting everyone would have been folly, embracing thousands and thousands of special cases needing personalized arrangements, an administrative nightmare. Moss, for example, volunteered at 17 but was turned down because of a kidney condition: much easier for the armed forces than risk the complication and responsibility of having him, although the kidney trouble in no way impaired him from racing cars.

Hawthorn drove in the Syracuse non-Championship Grand Prix on April 11 and during it, as he swerved to avoid Marimon, he hit a low wall so hard the fuel filler cap burst open, the fuel cascaded onto the exhaust pipe and the Ferrari became an inferno. At hospital an examination revealed second-degree burns to his legs and left arm. The recovery took several weeks, although Hawthorn persuaded Enzo Ferrari to let him have a test drive to see if he'd be fit for Le Mans on June 11. The test went well and Hawthorn drove from Italy to Paris with the driver who would partner him in the race, Umberto Maglioli. They spent a couple of days in Paris, but when Hawthorn popped into the *Bar de l'Action Automobile* near the *Place d'Etoile* the barmaid said Reuters, the internal news agency, had been trying to contact him. Reuters then rang and asked if he was going to England to see his father. When Hawthorn asked "Why?", Reuters told him Leslie had had an accident. Hawthorn rang the Tourist Trophy Garage in Farnham. They informed him his father had had a severe road crash the night before and "there was not much hope for him".

Hawthorn flew to England immediately, but Leslie did not regain consciousness. On the morning of the funeral the police arrived at the Hawthorn home and served him with three summonses for a trifling accident some time before when he'd brushed against a Post Office van. Sections of the press, who had been baying in a great chorus for 'the dodger' to be caught, now bayed at the insensitivity of serving the summonses at such a moment. That altered the tone of the coverage, sympathy beginning to replace outrage.

Whatever, a week after the funeral he had to report for a medical, but this only led to a further examination by an ear specialist (evidently an ear had been giving Hawthorn trouble since the crash at Syracuse and his burnt legs had by no means healed fully). In sum, he'd have to have yet another medical in the autumn. When he arrived for that he took X-rays of his kidneys – he'd suffered back pain since the age of 17 and after Syracuse had discussed this with his doctor, who had forwarded him to a specialist. The specialist ordered an operation at the end of the racing season.

The military medical people now gazed at the X-rays and said they'd have to be referred to "higher authority", something which enraged Hawthorn. He underwent the kidney operation in late October, just after he'd won the Spanish Grand Prix – the last race of the season, which made him third in the Championship – and this operation alone would debar him from National Service. And he'd be 26 on April 10, 1955 anyway, too old for it.

In his book *Mon Ami Mate* Chris Nixon has gathered some evidence, though none conclusive, that Hawthorn did spend a lot of time in Italy *circa* 1953–54 beyond the reach of National Service, although to me this seems negated by the fact that he drove in Britain eight times during those two seasons. If truly he intended to remain out of reach would he have risked coming back at all? He could have simply sat it out until April 10, 1955; nor would he have been tempted – as he was tempted – to return permanently to run the garage after the death of his father. In fact his mother agreed to do that so he could continue racing, and she ran (as Ted Papsch has already explained) a tight ship.

Hawthorn decided to leave Ferrari for the British Vanwall team for 1955, and because Stirling Moss had now joined Mercedes (from Maserati) he – Moss – wouldn't be driving Jaguars in sportscar events, so Hawthorn took that over; quite literally an ominous choice.

The Vanwall wasn't competitive. Hawthorn didn't go to the first race, Argentina, qualified only on the fifth row at Monaco, and in the race the throttle control went. Ascari was killed testing at Monza on May 26, between Monaco and the next race, the Belgian at Spa. Lancia, for whom he drove in Formula One, announced they were finishing although, as Hawthorn and everyone else noted, Ascari's partner Eugenio Castellotti competed at Spa in ostensibly a private Lancia. It had, however, full works support. Castellotti "begged" Gianni Lancia to let him have the car so he could win in Ascari's memory. This created extreme tension in the Lancia pit during qualifying. Would Castellotti's emotions overwhelm him, would he force the car towards the impossible?

He put it on pole, but the gearbox went on lap 17 of the race. Hawthorn qualified only 10th and his gearbox went even earlier than Castellotti's, on lap nine. Hawthorn held discreet talks with the Lancia personnel, who said they might not be finishing after all and wondered if he'd join as team leader. Tony Vandervell, the man behind Vanwall, was not at all pleased but had to accept it. Lancia promised Hawthorn a "definite proposition" at Le Mans, a week after Spa.

When Hawthorn got there – to partner Ivor Bueb in a D-type Jaguar – Lancia told him they'd changed their minds and were withdrawing from Grand Prix racing. Enzo Ferrari, who must have heard all this, contacted him just before the race and offered him his place back. He would resume his Grand Prix career with Ferrari at Holland on June 19, a week after Le Mans.

There's a temptation to employ the word fate about each human activity, and the word recurs in motor racing because the consequences of motor racing can be so savage. There's a temptation to retrace events and murmur *if only* this hadn't happened, or he hadn't done that, the sequence leading to the savagery would have been broken. Who knows how many major accidents never happened because, all unknowing, someone broke the sequence? Is that fate? Or is it the interplay of many random actions which are sometimes completely innocent and sometimes draw unto themselves a truly terrible sequence? However you ruminate on it, the sequence leading to the warm and cloudless afternoon of June 11, 1955 is uncanny and – if you're not a fatalist – eerily full of *if onlys*...

Hawthorn ought to have been partnered by a Scot, Jimmy Stewart, who'd competed there the year before in an Aston Martin, but lost control at the White House, hit a bank and was flung out, the car cartwheeling away from him. In *Ecurie Ecosse* Graham Gauld writes that "the accident put Jimmy out of commission for the rest of the 1954 season. In April of 1955, just prior to his first race of the season at Oulton Park with Ecurie Ecosse, he signed a contract with Jaguar to race a D-type at Le Mans with Mike Hawthorn.

"To put this into perspective, Jimmy Stewart, despite his accident at Le Mans, had been voted one of Britain's most promising young racing drivers by *Motor*

Racing magazine and so his choice by Jaguar was well merited. In his letter to Stewart, selecting him to race at Le Mans, Lofty England (the team manager) wrote, and here I paraphrase '…I am pairing you with Mike Hawthorn because I think you can match the speed of Fangio and Moss in the Mercedes.'

"Jimmy launched into 1955 with his usual enthusiasm but at the Nurburgring in May he went off the road in the Ecosse D-type and ended trapped upside down in a ditch. As he had gone through one of those Nurburgring hedges he could not be seen from the road and it was some time before he was found. Indeed it was Stirling Moss who noticed a pair of skid marks and some damage to a hedge. When Stirling stopped and looked over he found Jimmy underneath the D-type. This accident injured the same arm and on his return to Glasgow a specialist advised Jimmy that if he were to continue racing and damage it again he may lose the use of the arm altogether. Jimmy retired from motor racing without having his drive with Hawthorn."

At Silverstone, Jaguar and Lofty England tested two drivers, Don Beauman and Bueb, for a place in the team, and although both showed well Hawthorn pushed hard for Beauman, a schoolfriend whose racing cars were prepared at Hawthorn's garage. However, for Le Mans, Jaguar had paired Beauman with an Ulsterman, Desmond Titterington, but as Titterington was recovering from an accident, Norman Dewis, Jaguar's works test driver, was brought in as substitute. Bueb replaced Stewart as Hawthorn's partner.

Hawthorn described Bueb as "furious" when Beauman initially secured a drive and he, Bueb, didn't. Now, at Le Mans, Hawthorn faced a "prickly situation" partnering him, but would write that they put their relationship on a businesslike footing and got on with it. Bueb, however, had not driven in a long-distance sportscar race before and he and Hawthorn faced the formidable pairing of Fangio and Moss in the mighty Mercedes.

Britain had a large, prosperous and important motor industry. How fitting that Jaguar won Le Mans at 1951 and 1953. The power of German manufacturing was sensed, but not accurately perceived, and a great deal of anti-German feeling remained. Hawthorn, to take the most pertinent example, did not like German cars and occasionally used expletives when speaking of them.

Clearly Hawthorn could run with Fangio and Moss, but equally clearly Bueb couldn't; nor might any reasonable person demand it of him against two of the greatest drivers of this or any other era. Assuming the Jaguar and the Mercedes lasted 24 hours, Hawthorn had to construct a cushion on each of his stints to protect Bueb.

Worse, the Mercedes had innovative air brakes – flaps which, at the touch of a lever, rose above the rear of the car. Moss has described them as "fantastic" and said they improved braking enormously because you didn't risk locking wheels and they gave extra downforce. Moss judged the Mercedes could outbrake the Jaguar which, cumulatively, assumed primary importance over the 4,000 kilometres of the race. Across such an immense span – roughly the equivalent of London to the Ural mountains 1,000 kilometres beyond Moscow – small advantages magnify themselves.

Hawthorn and Fangio took the first stints, and although Fangio got the gear stick up his trouser leg whilst clambering into the Mercedes – a Le Mans start with drivers sprinting across the track to their cars, and Fangio tried Moss' trick of vaulting straight in, not opening the door – he set off in pursuit of Hawthorn, himself pursing Castellotti's Ferrari.

The race acquired a momentum which rose and rose, lifting it far beyond any normal endurance event where cars travel at a steady, predetermined pace to last the distance. The momentum broke that apart, Castellotti, Hawthorn and Fangio trading lap records; and that fed the momentum. Hawthorn and Fangio shed Castellotti and still traded fastest laps. Contemporary and subsequent accounts capture the pure intoxication of this and it's easy to see it in your mind's eye: the smooth yet chunky Mercedes, the sleek prehensile Jaguar both locked into each other and averaging 120 miles an hour in front of a vast, noisy crowd and Le Mans itself a panorama of a place, a majesterial setting for just this.

By the end of the second hour Hawthorn led and the Jaguar pits started their pre-arranged signals to bring him in to hand over to Bueb. The signals began three laps before the stop, continuing as he passed on the next. He'd come in on the one after that.

Hawthorn lapped the Mercedes of Karl Kling just before the Indianapolis turn – a corner which fed onto the long run towards the pits – and lapped the Mercedes of Pierre Levegh just after White House, within sight of the grandstand opposite the pits.

The final sequence had begun, the biggest accident in the history of motor racing had begun.

The road described a long, lazy curve to the pits, a *right* curve. Hawthorn drew up alongside the Austin-Healey of Lance Macklin. Macklin had already seen the cavalcade of much faster cars coming towards him (he'd been lapped four times) and hugged the inside, the right, keeping as far out of the way as he could. Levegh came hard, Fangio immediately behind Levegh and both of them on the other side of the road. From here the positioning of each car is crucial.

In *Challenge Me The Race* Hawthorn wrote that "as I came up alongside [Macklin] I worked out whether there was room to pass him and then pull in to the pits. In my view there was, so I kept on and then as the pits drew nearer I put my hand up, put the brakes on and pulled in. I was nearly there when out of the corner of my eye I saw something flying through the air."

There is no dispute about *what* happened. Macklin, braking as hard as he could, realized that, because the Jaguar's brakes were so superior to those of his Healey, Hawthorn was slowing faster than he could. Macklin wrenched the Healey to the left and just missed the back of the Jaguar.

Fangio says that "Hawthorn's Jaguar was about a hundred yards ahead of me. Behind him, a little to the right, was Macklin's Austin-Healey. Behind him again, but to the left this time, was Levegh's Mercedes going at full speed. Very suddenly, Hawthorn's Jaguar headed towards the pits. His unexpected braking surprised [the drivers of the] two cars following him. Macklin braked hard but in doing so inevitably found himself in line with Levegh's Mercedes as he began to skid."

With Macklin travelling across the track into Levegh's path Levegh had nowhere to go even if he had had time to consider such options. Did he have the time? Fangio says that Hawthorn's braking and Macklin's pulling out "was as quick as lightening, and that I am still alive today I certainly owe to Levegh. My stablemate raised his hand, indicating he wanted to go to the left. At that moment my foot was already on the brake. Kept on an even keel by the air brake, my Mercedes evidently lost speed, though still carrying a lot of momentum. Levegh desperately tried to pass on the left of Macklin's Austin-Healey but found that he could not make it. The right front end of the German car smacked into the left rear end of the British machine. Petrified with horror I saw the Mercedes take off."

It struck a bank and went into the crowd, landing with such ferocity that the engine wrenched free. The car bounced out of the crowd but the engine continued like a sythe. The death toll: 82. Fangio says that he watched Levegh take off "as though the Austin-Healey's tail had been a springboard. An instant later Levegh's car crashed down on the protection wall to the left and burst into flames. Even above the roar of my engine I heard the explosion, felt the repercussion in my stomach. Simultaneously a wall of fire flared up before me as though a napalm bomb had burst, sending up spirals of smoke and unidentifiable debris.

"I was less than 50 yards away and doing 120mph. No-one could have stopped in fifty yards at that speed, reduced though it was by my instinctive braking as I saw Levegh raise his hand. I saw with horror there was nothing I could do before reaching that wall of smoke and fire...I had to go on. In front of me Macklin's Austin-Healey skidded. Instinctively I passed to his right. I found myself confronted by Hawthorn's Jaguar, the first to brake and still slowing down. The English driver had evidently not calculated his pit's position correctly and finally stopped some 80 yards beyond it. How I ever managed to pass him is a mystery I have still not solved. I can only say that it was such a close shave that traces of the Jaguar's green paint were found later on the right front wing of my silver Mercedes.

"In front of me, miraculously, an opening gave me a chance to survive. I went through, weaving, my stomach weaving in sympathy and I shouted with relief as I picked up speed on the unobstructed circuit. The worst moment of my career, that very short but horribly violent nightmare, was ended. Then, instinctively, I glanced in my rear mirror. One look and I knew that an appalling tragedy had taken place."

Levegh lay among the 82 dead.

Hawthorn wrote that he saw Levegh take off and at the same instant Macklin's car came past "spinning round backwards, then slewed across in front of me towards the pits." Hawthorn remembered three people standing in front of the pit in Macklin's path "frozen with horror and the car mowed them down." The Austin-Healey then careered away to the other side of the track.

The immediate aftermath was a ghastly thing, a carnage.

The race was not stopped. Charles Faroux, the Clerk of the Course, took the brave and prudent decision to let it continue because, if he had not, spectators would have blocked every approach road and the ambulances needed as clear a run as they could get, would do for several hours. Faroux's decision inevitably drew criticisms of insensitivity. There can be no doubt he was right. Many other disputes, however, linger, like some sort of unproven spectre, many are the exhaustive investigations and reconstructions, the studying of eye-witness accounts, the wringing of conclusions from a cine-film of the accident.

The central dispute is locked, and will always be locked, onto the moment Hawthorn decided to pull over in front of Macklin. Did Hawthorn brake so hard because he himself had become intoxicated by the duel with Fangio, and the momentum of that carried him past Macklin rather than wait even a few seconds following Macklin before peeling into the pits? Did Hawthorn brake so hard because he realized he'd left it very late? Some people hold that the fact Hawthorn overshot the Jaguar pit is evidence of that.

Innes Ireland speaks with the authority of a former racing driver and is therefore in a position to understand. It's entirely natural, Ireland says, that if you have just witnessed what Hawthorn had the last thing on your mind is where your pit happens to be. You stop the car when you stop it, your thoughts back there with the catastrophe. Nor is Fangio correct in saying Hawthorn overshot his pit by 80 yards. In fact he missed it by three pits.

Jaguar and Hawthorn maintained that he had followed 'normal racing practice' in his approach to the pit stop. Many witnesses did not agree; equally many who knew Hawthorn as a superb driver *still* do not accept that he could make such an elementary error: fail to realize the limitations of Macklin's brakes in direct relation to his own. Macklin has given his own account in great detail. It is convincing. Mike Hawthorn, of course, is not here to query it, to say whatever he might wish to say or indeed say anything. Amid the lingering central dispute there is a big silence – his. He would be pilloried in the moments, days and years which followed, pilloried even after his own death.

Pierre Levegh (an assumed name) would be pilloried, also: at 50 they said he was too old, was "frightened" of the power of the Mercedes, couldn't react fast enough. Levegh's lap times over the first two hours of the race do not support the theory that he was "frightened", and if Fangio – further back than Levegh – felt powerless in the face of so much going on so quickly, what chance had Levegh?

The real cause of the accident lay in the nature of Le Mans, whatever the rights and wrongs of that June afternoon. If you ask drivers long experienced in it they say that what does frighten them is not the age of the drivers but how good they are, what frightens them is the disparity in the performance of the different cars – which in 1955 manifested itself between a Jaguar and an Austin-Healey. Macklin had already been lapped four times, remember, which translates to Hawthorn leading him by some 34 miles. We could equally apply the disparity to 1993. In qualifying a Peugeot took pole with 3 minutes 24.94 seconds, a MiG M100 (yes, truly) slowest with 5 minutes 59.15. Now imagine the approach speed of the Peugeot to the MiG...

If all the cars seriously tried to race each other, weaved and stonewalled as you see in Formula One, wouldn't accept being lapped except with reluctance and after resistance, Le Mans would never happen and never be allowed to happen. In 1955, under the impetus, Hawthorn and Fangio went racing and a disparity did manifest itself. In the end it was probably as simple as that.

Mercedes withdrew from the race, Lofty England ordered Hawthorn to continue and he won. In *Challenge Me The Race* Hawthorn does not describe his feelings about this. One didn't.

Ted Papsch – who wasn't at Le Mans but is one of those convinced Hawthorn couldn't have made such an elementary error – says: "Mike never really talked about it, not really. I think his view was 'accidents do happen and what's the good of discussing them?'" Although the fall-out proved inevitable and enormous, and the future of motor sport in several countries cast into doubt, Papsch's words are an echo of the era, the suggestion of a different way of rationalizing.

The Western Europe of today, safety-conscious about every aspect of life (sometimes to amazing extents), did not exist. Papsch's own story is instructive because it illuminates the circumstances which produced the different way of rationalizing.

"I was born in the Sudetenland of German parents and when in 1938 the German army marched in we automatically became German citizens. I had to join the army when I was seventeen and a half, was sent out to Russia and at Stalingrad I was connected to the Sixth Army. [Hitler invaded the Soviet Union in 1941; the Sixth Army, surrounded and battered to exhaustion, surrendered at Stalingrad in 1943.] We were lucky to get out. I was captured in Belgium and they shipped us to London, to Kempton Park. I couldn't speak one word of English. I didn't even know what yes and no meant."

He went to various camps, including one at Sheffield. "That was bad. When you are a prisoner of war it depends on the commandant. They took us out to work in Bedford trucks and you weren't allowed to walk, you always had to run. British soldiers carried a stick, a little bit bowed, and you had a blow across your back when you went out and one across the back when you returned."

Papsch couldn't return home because the Soviet army was now in occupation and anyway he had no idea where his family might be. He was formally discharged from the German army at a camp at Tunbridge Wells and decided to stay. "I had one penny and an empty suitcase. I bought a platform ticket and took the train to Haslemere because at one stage I'd been a prisoner nearby." He bluffed his way out of Haslemere station and "I walked the roads, I slept under hedges and in the end I got a job with a farmer." He bought a bicycle, then a little motorbike, then bigger bikes and "I became a mechanic at Hindhead, and while I was there Mike advertised for a mechanic. I applied, I went and Mike and the managing director interviewed me. I was scared stiff! The first job they gave me was to work on an Aston Martin DB2. It was all stripped down and I had to put it back together. Well, I'd never seen an Aston Martin before..."

Papsch illuminates something else because he retained – and retains – a pronounced German accent. "No, Mike didn't like German cars. I wouldn't know if he didn't like me as a German, but I'm sure it didn't make any difference. He employed me and he never inquired where I came from. I think he knew. You see, he was a very, very nice man. He never said any sharp or rude words to any of the boys working at the garage and I never saw him upset if something went wrong at the garage.

"There was a pub next door and sometimes we'd go in there for a game of darts. We'd go out driving and testing things and I overhauled a lot of Lancias. I used to take the cylinder heads off and I had an overhead gantry like a dentist's drill and I honed them all out, but being an aluminium head you had to be careful. I'll never forget Mike coming in one day.

Distant dialogue...

Hawthorn: Ted, you have to take some more out of there.

Papsch: I can't. There are air bubbles in the aluminium and if I take any more out they'll go right through.

Hawthorn: No, you have to, and anyway, what have you to lose? A week's wages?

Papsch: Well, I can't afford to lose a week's wages.

Anyway, Papsch "did it and we took it along the Farnham by-pass and he blew it up. I said 'I told you so' and then I had to repair it, but it was somehow great fun, it really was. Mike was just one of you.

"I had a lot of responsibility. We built up his Jaguar and that was the fastest Jag in the country. Tommy Sopwith had one, exactly the same model, but it wasn't as fast. I put 9:1 compression ratio pistons in, two 2-inch carburettors, a lightened flywheel, a semi-racing clutch. I put the battery in the boot, put on headlamps, spotlights, everything. That Jag went like a rocket. I went in it with him and that felt fantastic. Mike was extremely safe. [At this point Papsch contradicts himself, but gloriously, no half-measures.] I remember going to Heathrow with him when he was flying to the German Grand Prix at the Nurburgring and we were doing 140 miles an hour. We got to a level crossing and Mike nearly pushed the gates open with the bumper. At Staines there was a big truck in front and all of a sudden the truck stopped. The bonnet of the Jaguar went underneath – the truck was high enough – and Mike said 'that was close, Ted, wasn't it?'" Another echo of the times.

"I think it was very difficult to know Mike," Roy Salvadori says. "In his own way, apart from the fact that he could be aggressive, he could be a very kind-natured guy, very concerned with people, Jekyll and Hyde, really. Sometimes he could be very polite and well-behaved but also very boisterous, and you weren't sure which side you were going to get. A very interesting guy who livened everything up. If you were out with Michael, you'd have a jolly good evening, let's put it that way.

"The racing? None of those drivers thought they were on holiday, not possible that they thought that. They were all intelligent, and although you didn't talk about it or want to dwell on it they all realized that percentage-wise the chances were against them. One tried to get something out of life. More than anybody I think Mike felt that way. If you could have got inside Mike he may well have said that, and don't forget that from a health point of view he wasn't all that well. That's another thing which weighed against him.

"He had quite a few shunts. He had the shunt at Modena when he first drove for Ferrari and I was supposed to be driving his Cooper. I couldn't make head nor tail of the Cooper and he jumped into it and lost it on one of the corners because the brakes were playing up. He had a very big accident, very badly hurt, knocked himself about. I went to see him in hospital.

"He constantly had shunts throughout his career and he was involved in one or two very nasty ones. The accidents hurt. Basically everyone racing in those days was getting something out of it: satisfaction. That was the state of play, what you had to accept. Otherwise you weren't part of it."

In Grand Prix racing in 1955 Hawthorn did not win a single point. The organizers of the Dutch race that week after Le Mans hesitated but decided to go ahead. Hawthorn finished seventh, hampered by the gearbox. At the British at Aintree the strain began to show and after 46 laps on a very hot day he came in and handed the car to Castellotti who ran to sixth place; but in those days you only scored points up to fifth. At Monza the gearbox mounting broke.

In 1956 he joined BRM, a mistake in the way Vanwall had been. He scored points in the first race, Argentina, but in a Maserati – the BRM wasn't ready. A strange racing calendar then, the second race, Monaco, nearly four months on and Hawthorn ought to have been been partnered by a very promising young driver, Tony Brooks. But the BRMs developed valve problems and were withdrawn.

"I only sat in a Grand Prix car for the first time in October 1955," Brooks says. "I think it very likely I had not met Hawthorn before 1956. I had seen him around but not actually spoken to him."

Glimpses of a distant season...

"He turned the BRM over at the Easter Goodwood meeting (on April 2) and I turned one over at the British Grand Prix at Silverstone. This was due to my having the accelerator mechanism repaired in the pits. When I rejoined the race there had been a little more oil and rubber put down, a problem in those days. I'd been taking Abbey flat. I must have been raving mad. I noticed that the throttle was sticking slightly but I thought *Abbey is flat anyway*. So...I went in flat and because of the extra oil and rubber I needed to lift off – a quick lift – but when I tried it didn't happen: the sticking throttle. I went only about six feet onto the grass and in a decent car you'd pull back onto the track. That car was absolutely undriveable other than in the geometrical sense" – in straight lines! "You had to go round the corner like a bicycle; if you tried to do anything else such as a drift it was lethal.

"Going onto the grass was sufficient to send it spinning completely out of control, turning round and round. It hit the outside bank of the circuit, threw me out and the only decent thing it could do was to set itself on fire – the only fitting end for that motor car. I was very lucky, Mike was very lucky.

"I never really got close to Mike, I have to say. Although we were both in the BRM team it was a disastrous year and the team pulled out of a lot of races, therefore we didn't race all that often. And of course he was in the Jaguar sports car team and I was in the Aston Martin team so I didn't see all that much of him. I had no problem with him, I got on with him fine and he was a pleasant guy. I've no complaints about him as team-mate. He had a *Boy's Own* image [there it is again] of a racing driver, the complete opposite of Stirling Moss, who was a dedicated professional: you know, early to bed the night before the race. I don't think Stirling touched a drop of wine or any other alcohol at that time. Stirling was the epitome of a professional racing driver. Mike was more easy going, more the schoolboy's idea of what a racing driver should be, the flying neck scarf, the distinctive bow tie, the peaked hat with a sharp V in it – the sort of thing older members of society had read in prewar motor books. The popular press took to him in that way, the typical *Boy's Own* type of hero who enjoyed life and did motor racing as a diversion, an interesting pastime."

"Every time Mike raced he never gave up," Papsch says. "Didn't matter if he was first or wherever, he kept going. Others, I know, 'found' troubles with their cars because they couldn't stand the pace and understood they couldn't win but Mike never did that."

Another direct contradiction. Alan Brinton started covering motorsport for the – now long defunct – daily newspaper the *News Chronicle* in 1956. "I didn't get to know Hawthorn that well. He was a very convivial person, companionable with his chums, but he tended to be aloof from people like myself. I sensed he nursed apprehensions about press people." Hawthorn had his reasons for this – National Service, Le Mans 1955 – but the sharper point is that few journalists covered motorsport, they joined a tight, intimate circle, never hounded the drivers and rarely lambasted them. Mansell had daily pressures which Hawthorn experienced perhaps three, perhaps four times in his whole life, and in the Fifties it was extremely rude, if not largely unknown, to be uncivil to friends and strangers alike.

Brooks laments that when his car broke down or he had a disappointing race journalists didn't make the effort to inquire why. He would not, of course, approach a journalist himself to explain, leaving surmise and silence. One didn't do otherwise.

Brooks makes two judgments about Hawthorn. "You've asked me if they were all boozers, and boozed to compensate for the risk factor. I don't think that was the case. Mike enjoyed his pint, probably always had enjoyed his pint, that was the way he was. I don't think any driver drank to celebrate – or compensate for – the fact that they'd survived another race. Of course one was aware of the risk factor but, speaking personally, I never had to screw up my courage because if I make a mistake *here* it could really be a big one, a fatal one. I did not drive in that sort of way. Hawthorn wasn't a natural driver like Stirling or Fangio, he used to have to work at it and you could see that. In many ways it was more meritorious but he never looked relaxed at the wheel."

At the end of 1956 Fangio departed Ferrari for Maserati, Hawthorn cabled Ferrari offering his services and they accepted. He'd partner Peter Collins: they were, as someone has said, like two overgrown schoolboys when they were together and, it must also be said, exercised a devastating effect on the female of the species. However you quantify sex appeal, they had it, lots and lots of it; and it worked. The scale? That's into the big silence, too. More than an office romeo, less than an office romeo? More than a film star, less than a film star? Who knows, and who's counting, anyway?

Roy Salvadori gives an interesting view on Collins the racer. "Basically Peter, with whom I spent two or three years in the same team, didn't seem to be too ambitious. I don't think Peter ever thought in terms of World Championships."

"He was just very happy racing. He wasn't quite as aggressive a driver as Mike although, having said that, I don't mean that Mike was tough in the sense that he'd push you off or anything, but always he had a go. If you were in a race with Mike you'd know it. He wouldn't take anything from you, but he wouldn't give you anything: just a hard but clean battle and an enjoyable one.

"He was always laughing and sticking two fingers up, very much alive. With Peter, it was very much correct and proper. They were two totally different drivers, but the end result was that their lap times were pretty well the same. However, I have no doubt that Mike was the faster of the two. In temperament they were different, too, Mike boisterous, Peter reasonably quiet. If you were having a good evening with Mike it could get a little out of hand, let's put it that way. One or two drivers were livelier than the rest.

"When you take somebody's career, don't ever lose sight of who they were with. For instance, the guy that brought the most out of Mike was Lofty England, a damned good team manager. He gave Mike the opportunities and Mike responded. The person to bring the maximum out of Peter Collins was John Wyer. There's always a combination. When you think of Jimmy Clark you must think of Colin Chapman, with Jack Brabham think of John Cooper. These combinations absolutely click and they go a long way towards their achievements.

"Why should Mike and Peter Collins have stuck together? All the time at all their races you'll find they were together and you've got to have a bit of aggression in a team. It's all very well if you're driving in a 24-hour race where you can have a good partnership, but Formula One is so competitive. Take the Aston Martin team. When you had Moss in it, as we did, everybody drove quicker. If you do what you consider a good time it becomes the ulitmate time if nobody goes any quicker; but Moss would get in and sneak a couple of seconds and you'd think maybe your time wasn't so good. And you'd go quicker.

"You need some competition in a team even if it's healthy competition. I don't mean to say you're cutting each other's throats. To be truthful you don't know how fast a car can be made to go because you always feel like you're going as fast as you can. You need a yardstick, as Stirling gave us. That was slightly missing with Hawthorn and Collins. They were both happy, both enjoying themselves, not enough competition between them."

Perhaps the Championship proved that, Fangio (Maserati) winning with 46 points (40 counting) followed by Moss (Vanwall) 25, Musso (Ferrari) 16, Hawthorn 13...Collins eighth with 8.

Paradoxically, Bueb, partnering Ron Flockhart, won Le Mans in 1957 for Jaguar. Hawthorn, partnering Musso, went only to the fifth hour when the Ferrari's engine let go. Brooks, partnering Noel Cunningham-Reid in an Aston Martin, wasn't so fortunate...

"Noel brought the car in about 3 o'clock in the morning stuck in fourth. I'd had the same problem at a race at Spa and I thought I knew how to get it out of fourth. We were still in second place and the last thing I wanted was to spend the remaining 13 hours falling slowly and slowly down the field. Immediately after Noel handed the car to me I was busy looking down trying to get this damn gear lever out of gear and I went too deep into the third corner. I virtually made it round, but at the exit, instead of a steel barrier or something like that, it had a sand banking. If I'd hit that straight on it would have been fine, but as I'd nearly got round the corner the car ran up the bank and flipped, trapping me underneath. It was quite a heavy car and I lay there waiting for the next car to come along and run me over. Fortunately the next car hit the tail end of the Aston and knocked it off me. I got up and hopped away a little bit quickly."

Some short time later, a quiet farmer from the Borders, who'd accompanied a friend to Le Mans and was taking pictures for a Scottish motoring magazine, snapped the upturned Aston. His name: Jim Clark.

However disappointing the World Championship proved for Hawthorn, the season of 1957 did produce a Grand Prix which has settled into folklore, a Grand Prix of legend played out across 22 laps of the Nurburgring. Initially tactics governed it, held it hard. Hawthorn led from Collins, but Fangio attacked as he had to attack. The Ferraris would run through without a stop for fuel, Fangio's Maserati wouldn't and he'd need to gain time to cover his stop.

By lap 12, when he came in, Fangio had gained 28 seconds. That melted. The stop went terribly wrong – it lasted around 55 seconds, and before Fangio emerged his manager, Marcello Giambertone, suggested he set a trap. *Take it easy for a couple of laps to lure Hawthorn and Collins into believing they can't be caught*, Giambertone said discreetly, the Maserati pit nearby, all eyes and ears. Giambertone remembers Fangio "caught on and was about to smile. I tightened my grip on his arm and whispered 'Don't smile. Look serious. Shake your head. You're being watched...'"

On the next lap, Giambertone says, "Fangio's driving made it all too evident that his Maserati was not right. A mechanic in our pit, not in on the game, danced with frustration and let loose a flood of Italian curses. The stopwatches showed that Collins and Hawthorn, lapping together, were 38.3 seconds ahead of Fangio. I must admit that I was trembling inside. What if the tactics I had suggested proved too risky?"

The Ferrari pit held out a board telling Hawthorn he led by 45 seconds and, next lap, that had stretched to 48. Giambertone watched as the Ferrari pit held up a blackboard with a signal. "I knew what it meant. *Slow down. Keep an even pace. Fangio is losing seconds.* Guerrino Bertocchi (Maserati's chief tester) made a slight gesture to Fangio the next time he passed. Juan nodded to show he understood." The nod meant *unleash yourself*.

At that moment Juan Manuel Fangio began an assault on the Nurburgring which is difficult to quantify. Fangio himself could barely do so and has spoken of how he explored his own limits in a way he had never done before, how he "screwed" the secrets from the mighty circuit, how he couldn't sleep for two nights afterwards because the race replayed and replayed itself in his mind.

On a single lap he took 12 seconds from Hawthorn and Collins. On lap 16 he took another five, on lap 17 he cut the lead to 25½ seconds, on lap 18 he beat his own qualifying time and became the first man to go round the Nurburgring at more than 90 miles an hour, cutting the lead to 20 seconds.

"Mike and Peter thought they had it sewn up," Salvadori says, "and you must have some sympathy for them. Fangio came back at them at an impossible lick. I think everyone accepts that the two greatest drivers of the day were Fangio and Moss – in Formula One maybe Fangio had the edge, in sportscars Moss had the edge. That day Fangio was absolutely exceptional, unbelievable. He caught Mike and Peter napping and don't forget they had virtually no information to warn them. The Nurburgring measured fourteen miles so you had to wait more than nine minutes before you passed the pits and got time signals. You couldn't see Fangio: he was too far behind.

"After the pits you went round a return hairpin (a right-hand loop) so you had sight of somebody maybe up to three-quarters of a mile away – the only time you could see anyone. For a long time Fangio wasn't that close and when he did begin to draw up he closed so quickly that before they realized it he was almost with them. Fangio was so wound up it was too late. I'd been in the Formula Two race (run simultaneously with the Grand Prix), which I led and then my car broke [the suspension of Salvadori's Cooper-Climax failed on lap 11] so I watched. I have never seen a car at such angles as Fangio had that Maserati and I must emphasize the state of the signalling: the pit could give you information, but based on the gaps they'd taken *the previous lap*. The pit told you *this is the gap we recorded more than 9 minutes ago*. A few seconds later – Hawthorn and Collins gone by, Fangio arriving, a new gap being recorded – it could have been reduced by a long way, but you'd have to wait another 9 minutes to know that. There was a point at the other side of the track where teams could try and sneak a time and hold a board over the fence at a left-hander but that didn't work very well..."

On lap 19 Fangio broke the lap record again, cutting the gap to 13½ seconds. On lap 20 he took 6 seconds off that – 9 minutes 17.4 seconds. This may have been the greatest lap ever driven. Fangio's pole time had been 9 minutes 25 seconds. Now he'd cut the lead to 3 seconds. On lap 21 he flung the Maserati past Collins, flung it past Hawthorn, who strained everything on the final lap but simply couldn't catch him. Fangio won by 3.6 seconds. At the end the emotion consumed Fangio, Hawthorn and Collins each in their separate ways, and politely done it was.

This year of 1957 Hawthorn fell in love with Jean Howarth, a model. "I met him at Farnham in an hotel," she says. "I was with someone else, a friend of Mike's I was going out with. Mike, the perfect gentleman, waited until our relationship finished and then started to take me out. I wasn't into motor racing, not at all. The name Hawthorn didn't really mean much to me, just a very nice, good looking man. I modelled in London and my world lay more in that direction.

"He was extremely funny on occasions, considerate and kind. It didn't matter who he happened to be talking to, to him they were exactly the same – the

Queen of England or the dustman. He didn't distinguish between people in that way. A gentle soul, really. In the evenings down at Farnham we'd sit by the fire and have our meals off a tray on our knees. He was quite happy to stay at home and watch the television and things like that. He wasn't always whooping it up and going to parties as is so often reported.

"He was also sensitive, which he showed over his mother, an extremely difficult lady. The first or second occasion I went to stay at their home, Folley Hill, we were sitting having supper and she said: 'Mike, pass *that woman* the salt' or something like that. Mike, I think, was so upset we never stayed at the house again, we always stayed at an hotel outside Farnham where he had a permanent suite.

"I do have a feeling his mother was very suspicious. She was quite an old battleaxe. There were shops in Farnham she couldn't go into because they wouldn't serve her. If she needed groceries somebody from the office at the garage would have to go and get them. She was incredibly rude – she could be rude to people coming into the garage for petrol, so she wasn't good for Mike's business at all.

"He got on very well with her because he was a polite man. That was his way. He was not prepared to have his mother upset me so we just moved to the hotel. Of course during the week I modelled in London and Mike came up two or three times a week, but moving to the hotel was a very mature way of handling it. Nobody fell out with anybody, and in fact I didn't fall out with his mother.

"When we had the suite at the hotel we'd go down to the bar and have drinks with some chums and have dinner and then retire. I can't remember wild parties. We certainly weren't living together. I had a flat in London, and when he was in town he used to come and stay, then at week-ends I would go and stay with him.

"He was the golden boy. He flew aeroplanes, he drove fast cars and portrayed a sort of happy-go-lucky millionaire, an ex-Public Schoolboy, he had all these things, but he was just a lovely man. He had a tremendous character and he came over as a great guy. Well, he was. If he could help anybody he would. He'd go and chat with Innes [Ireland] because Innes came in slightly later. I don't think Mike would ever have been spoilt because he wasn't that sort: far too strong a character to be persuaded by money and fame. He was down-to-earth, feet firmly planted, a true Yorkshireman."

Ireland reinforces it. "I had a tuning establishment outside Elstead, Surrey, and Brit Pearce, who'd worked for Mike, came to me for a job. In my first year of competition, 1957, I won the Brooklands Memorial Trophy, and Mike, as a previous winner, presented it to me. Brit joined me just after that. His sole responsibility was working on my car because I never liked working on my own car. Mike would come over in the evenings and stand with his foot up on the wheel, pipe going, talking about this and that. He gave me a lot of useful tips about the ways of the world and the ways of motor racing – I hadn't broken into Grand Prix racing then."

Hawthorn faced 1958 and it's worth recording where he had come in the World Championship so far: fourth, fourth, third, 11th, fourth and with no points at all in 1955. Nor was he in anything like robust health. There is some unanimity over the judgment that Hawthorn made an early decision, or began to consider the decision, to retire at the end of the season: 1958 his last chance.

"Mike wasn't well and I think he knew then how bad his condition was. He wanted to try for the Championship and of course there was a great rivalry between him and Stirling," Jean Howarth says. "They were chalk and cheese really, Mike very much an amateur enjoying his racing, because he loved racing, didn't treat it as a business whereas Stirling did, and I am not sure Mike approved of that. Mike's business was his garage."

Another paradox. Salvadori is sure that "in 1958 Mike started to drive percentage races. From the earliest drives of his career he'd been absolutely flat-out, giving everything. Towards the end I don't think he really wanted to drive, he wanted to be out of it. He wasn't enjoying it. His happy period came at Jaguar. Driving with Ferrari wasn't that much fun, and in fact Peter Collins had asked John Wyer whether they could get together because he missed the atmosphere of the Aston Martin team. The Ferrari policy had always been to have the drivers at each other's throats. I can't remember who was in charge then, but the policy certainly wasn't working to any degree because Mike and Peter were buddies, they helped each other. Don't forget, too, that Mike was very experienced by 1958 and maybe he'd learned that to drive percentage races was the way to win the Championship. Well, it was in those days because the cars weren't as reliable as they are today."

Hawthorn faced 10 races, from Argentina on January 19 to Morocco on October 19. In the Argentine he suffered oil pressure problems and finished third behind Moss and Musso (like Collins, a Ferrari team-mate. Six men drove Ferraris during the season). Hawthorn set fastest lap at Monaco and led for 14 laps, but the fuel pump let go on lap 46.

Thirty-four laps later a 29-year-old Londoner's Lotus-Climax stopped, the half-shaft broken. He was called Graham Hill, and this was his first Grand Prix. He'd remember the journey down to Monte Carlo with his wife Bette in their Austin A35, covering the distance from Calais in 13 hours, a time he thought "pretty good for such a small car". He started the race last, worked his way up, "then my back wheel fell off". He suffered heat exhaustion and felt "weak as a kitten".

This was the race where Hawthorn stopped for refreshment when he'd broken down. As he wrote in *Champion Year*, "walking past the hotel near the station I looked up into one of the rooms and a lovely blonde girl looked out. I stopped and asked if she had a glass of water – not the most original of remarks, but one that lovely blondes, whose answer to most questions is 'No', could hardly refuse. She asked me to come in through the window, but I was caught by an *Autosport* reporter."

In Holland the Ferraris were outpaced and Hawthorn finished fifth, but not before the winner, Moss, had lapped him. Partnering Collins in the Nurburgring 1000 Kilometres sportscar race a week later he finished second and then went to Spa for the Belgian Grand Prix, where he finished second again. Contesting Le Mans with Collins the Ferrari didn't finish; clutch.

The French Grand Prix, fifth race of the season, was at Reims and immediately preceded by a 12-hour sportscar race which Innes Ireland had entered with his Lotus Eleven. "I put the race car on the trailer and drove it, I think, to Lydd, the airport in Kent from where you could fly vehicles across the Channel. Peter Collins was there with a little Spider Ferrari and was very windy about the people loading the cars because he said 'my clutch is about shot and if that bugger doesn't bloody well burn it out getting it into the aeroplace it might easily burn out when I'm driving it to Reims. If you're coming along behind keep an eye open for a broken-down Ferrari.' I said 'Sure I will' but it must have been OK because he got there.

"The sportscar race started at midnight on the Saturday and finished at mid-day on the Sunday. Brit, my mechanic, was there and we not only won our class, we finished sixth overall – a feather in my cap, but perhaps even more so for Brit because the Lotus Elevens, particularly with the A35 gearbox, were not well known for durability at such high speeds and I think our average speed was quite a bit over 90mph. That was motoring a bit in those days, considering Reims had two very slow corners.

"In the afternoon Mike won the Grand Prix [beating Moss by 24.6 seconds]. Mike said: 'Come along to the hotel and have some tea' – tea, mark you – so I went. I was sent to Collins' room where he was with his wife Louise. I asked: 'Where's Mike?' and Peter said: 'In the bathroom, go on, go in.' Mike lay in the bath with all his clothes and cap on, sort of giggling. They'd obviously been fooling around and he just got in the bath."

This must have been before Hawthorn knew the extent of the tragedy of the race. During the French Grand Prix, Luigi Musso's Ferrari went out of control, throwing him from it. Musso was transported to hospital where Hawthorn, Collins and Louise later went and were told he'd died.

In *Champion Year* Hawthorn wrote: "We piled into the car and went back to the hotel. There seemed nothing else to do. Everyone was depressed and quiet, just sitting around. The tragedy was heightened by the grim contrast with the fun everyone had had during the nights after practice. One night a crowd led by Luigi had somehow manhandled Harry Schell's car, a little four-wheeled Vespa, through the main door of the hotel and up the stairs to the first floor. Unfortunately Harry was on the fourth floor. They couldn't get it into the lift and so the plot, which was to drive it along the corridor to Harry's room and blow the horn, misfired. They left it outside the manager's office on the first floor and put a few flowers round it. Then they had a new idea and they went up to his room and lit long strips of newspaper which they pushed under the door."

Collins won the British Grand Prix from Hawthorn, Moss out – engine – on lap 26. (This was the race where Hawthorn took a glass of shandy. "I remember the last few laps of the race very well because I was very hot and thirsty and every time I went through Becketts the marshals on that corner were drinking beer from pint mugs and taunting me by swigging the stuff as I went through. On the last lap I signalled that I would like a drink myself so after I got the flag I kept going fairly fast until I reached Becketts where I stopped and was given a pint of shandy. Then I drove on sipping it." The donor was David Phillips, father of Ian, a former *Autosport* journalist and now marketing manager of the Jordan Formula One team. I mentioned the incident to Ian at Silverstone during the 1993 British Grand Prix – almost 25 years to the day – and he said "It's the family's only claim to fame!").

Hawthorn had 30 points from six finishes, including three fastest laps worth a point apiece; Moss 24 from three finishes. You could only count your six best results out of the 11 races – in effect five out of 10 because, although the Indianapolis 500 counted as a round of the World Championship, Formula One drivers didn't go there.

Graham and Bette Hill drove to the Nurburgring for the German Grand Prix on August 3. "I'd never met Mike Hawthorn before," Bette says. "He made a fantastic impression on me, a lovely person, great fun and saucy. I was pregnant and he was charming, absolutely charming, but they all were, you see. If you think of those drivers, there were people like Peter Collins, Mike Hawthorn,

Wolfgang von Trips, Fangio who was enchanting, Hans Herrmann, Carel Godin de Beaufort. Sometimes they had money and in lots of cases they didn't, some even had titles but they were all gentlemen, they had bearing and they were *galante*. I can't put it any other way.

"Mike offered to take Graham and Cliff Allison [another Lotus-Climax driver] round the Nurburgring to show it to them. I didn't go with them because it was a macho thing for the men, not the sort of thing women did. Motor racing was very macho, the girls there for the glamour whether you were a pregnant wife or not, but it wasn't just for those reasons that I didn't want to go round. It was a damned frightening circuit! Mike said he wanted to drive, he wouldn't let Graham or Cliff because he knew what he was doing. He took them round and they were fairly ashen-faced by the time they came back. He taught them the circuit, a wonderful thing to do for a man of his stature. He loved the sport and wanted to show these two young men how much he loved it, what you required to be at the top – to show that not only did you require a lot of talent and a lot of intelligence, but you needed to be a human being."

Brooks and Moss fled away at the start of the race in their Vanwalls, Moss plundering the lead while Hawthorn and Collins caught and overtook Brooks. Moss dropped out on lap four (magneto) and Brooks re-caught the Ferraris. "Funnily enough," Brooks says, "I had the same sort of situation as Fangio had had at the Nurburgring the year before, a battle with Mike and Peter. I wasn't allowed to practice with full petrol tanks before the race, and with full tanks without any suspension adjustments my Vanwall handled like a pig, so badly that I lost around 35 seconds (while the fuel load lightened). Hence, although I didn't pit like Fangio in 1957 I did face similar problems catching up. I'm surprised Fangio has reportedly implied he went right to the limit and beyond. I'd never do that personally because, you know, the Ring was totally unforgiving."

On lap five Brooks lay 22 seconds behind, on lap six 17. In *The German Grand Prix* Cyril Posthumus wrote: "The next few laps were tense indeed. On lap seven Brooks gained no less than 10 seconds, his smooth, clean style concealing his formidable pace. On lap eight the crowd roared because the Vanwall had lapped in 9 minutes 10 seconds and was right on the Ferraris' tails. He passed them briefly on the twisty parts of the Ring where the Vanwall excels but was repassed on the straight where the Ferraris were quicker."

They duelled.

On lap 11 Brooks led into the *Pflanzgarten*, a right-hander with a dip before it, Hawthorn perhaps 30 yards behind Collins. In *Champion Year* Hawthorn wrote that "Pete went into the dip all right, but as he accelerated out of it he seemed to me to be going too fast…he went round the corner perfectly normally, but running wide, and the car slid, drifting out. His back wheel hit the bank fantastically quickly, his car just whipped straight over. There was a blurr of blue as Pete was thrown out."

Hawthorn agonized over whether he should stop or continue to the pits, but decided against that because it would alarm Louise, Collins' wife. He'd complete the lap and do another lap when the pits should have news.

"I didn't really know what was going on because in a race you don't," Salvadori says. Salvadori now lay third, Brooks leading from Hawthorn. "I got a signal telling me who was leading, which didn't mean very much to me. I could see there had been a shunt, which itelf didn't mean very much because you'd see a lot of shunts at the Nurburgring, you expected them."

On lap 12, the lap following the crash, Hawthorn's transmission failed about three miles from the pits. He tried to coax the car towards the scene of the crash but it stopped. "Mike was walking back," Salvadori says. "The Nurburgring was so big you had to walk to a post where you'd find somebody with a motorcycle and they'd take you to the pits. As I passed him – he was walking near the side of the track – he put two fingers up, but in the Churchillian way, not a V-sign, to tell me I was now in second place, and he made a gesture to level out, *ease off, nobody's going to catch you and you're not going to catch the guy in front.*"

Hawthorn did find a motorbike and returned to the pits via the scene of the crash where he found "Pete's crash helmet and one shoe and a glove. I was relieved to see there was no blood on the helmet."

Collins had been taken to hospital in Bonn.

"We didn't know Peter had died until the evening," Salvadori says. "There was a dinner at the Sporthotel where you had to go to get your starting money. Otherwise they didn't pay you. We were due to rush back through the night to get to Brands Hatch to drive there the next day. That evening the organizer of the German Grand Prix came over to John Cooper and myself and wanted to send a telegram to Peter's parents. He asked us how it should be worded."

Hawthorn had gone to the hospital.

"Mike was devastated," Salvadori says. "I've said that Mike was tough but don't forget he was the softest guy if anybody was hurt, always the most concerned, always, always. It used to hit Mike more than anything and he was the one that really suffered. There was a softer side to Mike Hawthorn than might appear, a genuinely concerned side."

"When Mike returned to Farnham he was terribly shocked," Papsch says. "He wanted to give up motor racing, he didn't want to know anything more about motor racing, but then a lot of people said 'come on, Mike, there aren't many races left'."

"I didn't know Peter very well," Jean Howarth says. "He was different to Mike, quieter although also very much a gentleman, very sweet, very good looking. They had a lot of fun together, really a couple of comedians. Mike was more of a joker than Peter. I think Mike intended to give up anyway and Peter's death acted as the catalyst."

Three races remained, the next at Portugal on August 24. How could he go there? "He did it for Peter, he did it for the memory of Peter. He was determined to get through the season and he very much wanted to be World Champion for the memory of Peter. That is what drove him on to finish the season, but he didn't express that sort of thing, he kept that sort of thing to himself."

Moss won Portugal from Hawthorn who, on his last lap, lost brakes and took to an escape road. He stalled turning the car. He got out and pushed it back to the pavement where a spectator tried to help: outside assistance and immediate disqualification. In the fury of the moment Hawthorn lashed at him. Moss passed, doing his lap of honour, and noticed the Ferrari on the pavement. Finally Hawthorn made it limp to the pits.

That evening Hawthorn had to appear before an inquiry who suspected he'd been pushing the Ferrari on the track, which would have disqualified him: a heavy blow to the Championship. The inquiry exonerated him because Moss gave evidence that Hawthorn pushed it on the pavement and thus legally. Hawthorn kept second place.

"You want frank comment, don't you?" Tony Brooks says. "It is an absolute travesty that Stirling never won the Championship. You look at that Portuguese Grand Prix. Stirling supported Mike, Stirling said it had happened on the pavement and therefore it didn't count. Mike would have lost those points otherwise. Stirling was very, very sporting and a very great driver, one of the all-time greats, no question in my mind about that." Moss has said that "I backed Mike on a point of principle and that it cost me the Championship was one of life's little ironies."

Brooks won Monza from Hawthorn, Moss out on lap 18, gearbox.

Papsch has a photograph of the start of the race. "Mike is on the left," he says, "and as anyone can see, smoke is coming off the car because the clutch is slipping. On those cars the clutch was either in or out and you couldn't do much about it otherwise, but Mike did manage to pull away and drove the whole race like that until (10 laps from the end) Tony Brooks passed him."

That was September 7, the final race, Morocco – Casablanca – on October 19. The mathematics were simple: Moss had to win and set fastest lap while Hawthorn finished no higher than third. Otherwise Hawthorn became Champion.

The build-up, as Alan Brinton remembers, involved "a great hoohah. Would he get it or wouldn't he? Would Moss get it? The *News Chronicle* sent me to talk to Moss and then talk to Hawthorn and put a piece together. I rang Hawthorn and went to Farnham to see him. He wasn't really very communicative but the interesting thing was, looking back on it, he said: 'Shall we go out to lunch?' and I said 'Yes, that's a good idea.' He said 'I know a pub five miles away, we'll go in my Jaguar'" – the one Papsch and Hawthorn had converted into a rocket. "He put the frighteners up me, he was mad. I mean, on one or two of the roads there were blind corners on very narrow lanes and he just did not care. He *really* put the wind up me. He didn't change a lot over lunch. He seemed withdrawn. Of course he was an ill person, wasn't he?"

Moss describes the five weeks between Monza and Casablanca as "interminable". The tension reached Hawthorn and most unusually he revealed it. "Mike wanted me to be in Morocco," Jean Howarth says. "I wouldn't have gone if he hadn't invited me. He looked after me, paid for everything. It wasn't often he took me. I don't think he actually liked women at the races. He was very strange over Morocco. We always had separate rooms before races but he was very much with me the night before that one, totally unlike Mike. He wanted someone there in the bedroom with him. He was very nervous, he didn't know how the race would go. I don't know if he felt well enough.

"He had never displayed nerves to me before. Normally for five days up to a race Mike wouldn't stay with me, I didn't really see him and he didn't drink very much. People said he did but actually he didn't. In fact I'd only been to two races, the first at Goodwood where he was preoccupied with what he was doing and I stayed very much in the background. That is the way I liked it. At Casablanca I stayed very much in the background, too.

"I wouldn't talk to him on the grid or anything, wouldn't kiss him goodbye. It was just a morning's work going to the office, if I may put it like that. I never thought about the danger because if you did you wouldn't have been a girlfriend of a racing driver. You didn't want to think about things like that. If an accident happened it always happened to somebody else, it doesn't happen to your man. He didn't speak about that aspect of it, it was just there, but he was certainly different at Casablanca. I do think Peter affected him dreadfully.

"We'd go to a pub off Belgrave Square, quite a motor racing pub, and people would say: 'How many more weeks before the race, Mike?' and he'd say to me: 'If they ask me that once more...' It was getting to him.

"So I was going off to Casablanca. I was fairly naive and immature and hadn't travelled very much on my own. As models, we were always chaperoned wherever we went, Paris or Rome. In fact I flew to Casablanca with Stirling and Katie Moss, but Mike gave me a list of all the things I had to remember, like get my passport, get my money, do this, do that, ring Stirling. That's how thoughtful Mike was, the list represented a thoughtful act."

Salvadori describes Casablanca as "a good circuit, good surface, a lot of sand blown across it, but better than the majority of Grand Prix circuits." It measured 4.724 miles, some of it lined with straw bales. The race would consist of 53 laps – 250.372 miles.

Jean Howarth remembers that she and Mike "went to the Ferrari garage at Casablanca to look at the cars. It was quite a small garage. He saw his car and hit the roof because it had the number 2 on it (Collins' number at the Nurburgring). He walked straight out and wouldn't go back until they got another number for the car. He wouldn't even look at his car again."

They gave him 6.

Hawthorn took pole, Moss and Stuart Lewis-Evans (like Moss, in a Vanwall) alongside because the grid lined up three-two-three-two. Phil Hill, who'd replaced Collins at Ferrari, qualified on the second row. Hill, a pleasant American, had been given team orders to help Hawthorn, something which, he confesses, he was happy to do. Ferrari could afford to use Hill as a hare. If he finished in front of Moss it made Hawthorn Champion and the risk of Hill blowing his engine seemed well worth taking. He might force Moss to do the same, because in the dynamics of the mathematics Moss had to win.

Salvadori, on the sixth row, doesn't remember speaking to Hawthorn before the race "because it was so important and you tried not to. You wouldn't go and open a conversation because you knew they were obviously in a bit of a tizz. If you did speak you'd keep away from the subject of the race itself, have a joke and a laugh about other things. It was very serious and you let them sort their own situations out."

Moss seized the lead at the flag, but Phil Hill harried him hard until he overshot a corner on lap three and the Ferrari went down an escape road, then returned. Order: Moss, Hawthorn, Bonnier, Hill, but Brooks moved and on lap 19 passed Hawthorn, who launched a long counter-attack. Moss set fastest lap on 21, 2 minutes 22.5 seconds, 119.586mph, and "it was unlikely Mike would risk his engine going for that." He wouldn't.

"I watched the race from the pits," Jean Howarth says. "In those days you did, you helped with the timing, you were involved. The girls had a job to do or were given a job. When you were timing, if your man didn't come round right on the specific time he should have, something was wrong, his car broken down or an accident. You became slightly nervous. The atmosphere in the pit was nail-biting, but Phil Hill very much played his part and Mike drove sensibly round. He didn't want to break his car, he set out to come second. I remember thinking to myself: 'Oh, Stuart is late' and then we turned round and we could see terrible flames across the desert."

Brooks' engine had gone on lap 30. Order: Moss, Phil Hill, Hawthorn. The Ferrari pit ordered Hill to slow and he obeyed, allowing Hawthorn to move into second place, then on lap 42 Lewis-Evans' engine blew. He plunged off and fire engulfed the car.

That Sunday afternoon Papsch worked at the garage at Farnham. "There was a picture of Mike in a racing car on the wall in the showroom. During the race at Casablanca, and for no reason, it fell off and smashed the glass. If we'd told Mrs H, with all her superstitions...

"We cleaned it up and hung it again. We couldn't put any glass in it but when she came she didn't notice. We never told her because she would have been terrified. Internally she was very, very worried about him every time he went out to race. I don't think she knew to her dying day that that picture had fallen."

Moss did the only thing he could do, kept on and won the Moroccan Grand Prix, beating Hawthorn by 1 minute 24.7 seconds. Hawthorn had 49 points but could count 42, Moss only 41.

The dynasty had been forged.

Romolo Tavoni of Ferrari slapped Hawthorn on the back as he emerged from his car.

Distant dialogue...

Tavoni: Next year we will do it again.

Hawthorn: I won't be racing next year. I'm going to retire.

Tavoni: Of course you'll be racing.

Hawthorn: No.

Moss (to Hawthorn): You did it, you old so-and-so.

"That night", Jean Howarth remembers, "we went to some place in Casablanca, some night club. Mike was very happy but I can't say he went wild or got plastered because he didn't. In some ways he was very reserved and of course the accident to Stuart dampened everything. A terrible damper."

The way it was, sweet and sour, right to the last moment.

THE ECHOES OF WINTER

On Monday, October 20, 1958, Hawthorn flew from Casablanca to London on Tony Vandervell's chartered Viscount. Stuart Lewis-Evans lay strapped across a couple of seats with a nurse attending him. He was conscious, Hawthorn would remember, and very cheerful despite the pain. Roy Salvadori was on the plane but didn't see Lewis-Evans and can't remember if he was screened off. He does remember that during the journey Bernard Cahier, a respected French journalist and photographer, "said 'it's very, very serious', and that was the first time we really knew."

Moss flew back on a DC6 with a friend he'd taken from Maidstone. Alan Brinton was on that flight, and so was Lewis-Evans' father. "It was pretty obvious," Brinton remembers, "that he didn't realize how bad Stuart was. I was looking out of the window and a chap from Ferodo, sitting next to me, said: 'What a lovely sunset' and I said: 'No, no, mate, that isn't a sunset, that's an engine going white hot.' The pilot made an announcement. 'I'm afraid we're having slight trouble, we've lost an engine.' Then we lost another engine. Moss, sitting at the back with his chum, was wearing a fez and he called out: 'Oh well, does anybody know any good hymns?' We made an emergency landing at Orly, Paris, a fire engine chasing us down the runway, but we got down all right and changed to a DC4. I discovered that Lewis-Evans' father hadn't any transport so I said I'd run him home from Heathrow and we got there about three in the morning."

Hawthorn was already home by then. "There were the usual interviews and photographs," he wrote, "and I began to realize just what being a World Champion entailed. The full realization did not dawn on me until I reached my garage at Farnham. My office was submerged beneath sacks of mail; the telephone rang unceasingly. Invitations poured in asking me to speak at this dinner, be guest of honour at that function."

Ted Papsch remembers the homecoming. "We couldn't believe he'd done it, it seemed impossible after everything which had happened. He'd done something no Briton had achieved before, he never gave up and he'd done it the hard way. He was so happy but he remained friendly, he'd talk to anybody. The thought that 'I'm the great Mike Hawthorn' didn't enter his head. He wasn't Mike Hawthorn, superstar, just Mike Hawthorn. He didn't change."

Meanwhile, Hawthorn wrote, "in one week I had 27 engagements and I had to attend on my stand at the Earls Court Motor Show." Hawthorn, looking very much the businessman in a crisp, dark suit, duly posed there for photographers in front of his Ferraris.

He also had other matters on his mind. "We were going down to Farnham in the car," Jean Howarth says, "and he asked me to marry him. First of all he said he had something to tell me, and he told me about his son." This son, the result of a one-night stand after the French Grand Prix at Reims in 1953, was a closely guarded secret and Hawthorn said that only Peter and Louise Collins had known about him. "Basically they were the only people who did know. His mother certainly didn't know, it wasn't the sort of subject you'd approach his mother with. Then he turned around and asked me if I had any skeletons in my cupboard, which I thought quite funny because I was all of 22. I said that no, I hadn't. Soon after that we went up to Huddersfield where my parents lived and he asked my father and stayed the weekend. There was a very good strain of boxer dogs in Lancashire and we went over and he bought a puppy. A mile or two away from the kennels he suddenly turned to me and asked: 'Would you like a puppy?' and I said: 'Yes, please', so he turned round and bought me one. That was the sort of man he was.

"The idea was that with the Championship won Mike would take over the running of the garage. He and Duncan Hamilton were very close, they were going to start up the Ferrari concessionaire system. Maybe Mike had been given it by Enzo Ferrari. The Tourist Trophy, which wasn't doing well under his mother, would have prospered under Mike being there full-time. He was so nice to everybody, didn't matter who you were, he had time to have a chat, a glass of beer. I believe Mike gave up motor racing for three reasons. He had lost heart in it, he knew he was ill and wasn't prepared to let anybody else know and, thirdly, he didn't approve of racing drivers being married, and we were hoping to be that. It was a very responsible attitude because he'd seen too many tragedies with the wives whose husbands had been killed. Mike was the one who looked after poor Louise after Peter was killed.

"When he came back from the Nurburgring after Peter's death he was very quiet, didn't say very much, but you could see he was very sad, I suppose. Mike had a good way of disguising his feelings. I didn't know how ill he was. He kept the pain to himself. I didn't know how cross he was with his mother after the way she treated me, and his grief over Peter was very private. He kept those things within himself, but he wasn't the laughing boy I'd known before. When Peter was killed he changed quite a bit."

On Friday, October 24, members of the British Racing Drivers' Club met in the Mayfair Hotel, London, to honour Hawthorn. *Autosport* reported: "The introductory remarks were made by Earl Howe. Mike made an excellent and whimsical speech, although obviously overcome by the occasion. Stirling Moss admitted that he was most disappointed to miss the title but that he was glad it had gone to his friend Mike – particularly as he is a British driver. Sir David Eccles, President of the Board of Trade, was also present, as was the Italian ambassador." Bette and Graham Hill attended: "By then I was very pregnant and Mike tapped my stomach and said: 'How are we doing, then?'" Bette says.

The following day Lewis-Evans died. He was 28. Peter Collins had been 27, Luigi Musso 34.

On Wednesday, October 29, motorsport's governing body, the *Commission Sportive Internationale*, met at the Royal Automobile Club in Pall Mall to debate changes to the rules. "Whether," Hawthorn wrote, "this final fatality (Lewis-Evans) helped to swing the balance in the minds of the delegates we shall never know." We do know that when the announcement came that Formula One would revert to 1½ litres "pandemonium broke out...a spontaneous and genuine feeling of disgust for a decision which one instinctively felt might well be a deliberate attempt to end British supremacy in motor racing in the only way open to them, by an amendment of rules very debatably justified by the plea of making Grand Prix racing safer. Motor racing is dangerous but what is danger? It is dangerous to climb mountains. It is dangerous to explore a jungle. One cannot frame regulations to make everything safe..."

Perhaps that was it, the philosophy of a life and the rationalization of death.

On Thursday, November 6, Hawthorn went to Buckingham Palace for a 'private' luncheon with The Queen and Duke of Edinburgh. The six other guests included the Labour MP Denis Healey.

On Friday, November 14 – a dry, cold, typically autumnal day – Lotus did some testing at Brands Hatch which they also used as an opportunity to interest buyers. Lotus were beginning production of the Elite, an extremely chic looking sporty number which would take Chapman from being a man who made racing cars to a man who made production cars as well. Graham Hill, Cliff Allison, Innes Ireland and Alan Stacey were present as drivers. (Mind you, Ireland has no recollection of this and says "the only test I remember with Lotus was with the cigar-shaped F2 Lotus 15.") Peter Warr, subsequently team manager of Lotus, and a young hopeful, Keith Greene, subsequently a perceptive and engaging Le Mans team manager, also attended. Greene remembers going round "in a Standard Vanguard which Colin Chapman was driving. Hazel Chapman sat in the back seat knitting! Chapman kept up a running commentary, 'the car's not bad here, a bit heavy there'."

Two farmers from the Scottish Borders arrived late. One of them, Ian Scott Watson, was interested in buying, the other, a particularly quiet chap, was interested in driving. On the morrow the farmers were due to attend the wedding of a friend, Johnny Prentice, in Hadley, Hertfordshire, so the journey south served a dual purpose.

"By the time we got there," Scott Watson says, "everybody else had arrived, including Graham somebody – not Hill, I can't remember his other name – who fancied himself as a bit of a racing driver. The works drivers tested but in between times they let potential customers have five laps with the possibility of some more in the afternoon. That was what we were told. I had not physically met Chapman, but five years earlier I'd endeavoured to acquire a kit for a Lotus Mark 6 when they first came out. All the correspondence was signed H.P. Williams, Hazel Chapman's maiden name. However, when Colin demanded payment for the whole thing before he'd even started making it – which is what he had to do – I got cold feet and bought a Buckler instead, a total disaster. I'd had a lot of conversations with Colin and there was no unpleasantness in my deciding not to proceed. He had an amazing memory. At Brands he said: 'Oh yes, you're the chap who was going to buy a Lotus Mark 6, aren't you?'"

The other farmer was 22, he'd done a bit of racing here and there in 1956 and 1957 in Scotland and Northumberland, despite being wracked by doubts about whether he was any good, and this season of 1958 had raced a lot more in a D-type Jaguar and Scott Watson's Porsche 1600S. Of his 41 races he'd won 20.

His name: Jim Clark.

Warr had just joined Chapman after completing his National Service with the Royal Horse Artillery. He remembers his initial impression of Clark. "Part of the man was an almost embarrassing shyness and he was very modest."

"Jimmy was the last to have his go," Scott Watson says. Clark eased himself into a front-engined Lotus Formula Two car and eased it out to negotiate the club circuit. He felt cramped in the cockpit and at the first corner, Paddock, he tried to brake, but initially couldn't find the pedal and went round on the grass with the terrible thought of Chapman's wrath if he destroyed the car. This incident, he recorded, put him off a bit. In the matter of instinctive genius, the phrase *a bit* means a very short space of time.

"The pit signalling area was a hole in the ground on the outside of Paddock just above the tunnel," Scott Watson says. "We stood in there, Chapman and I, and Jimmy got quicker and quicker." Greene watched and saw that "Jimmy was naturally quicker than anybody else, he got quicker and quicker." Warr watched and saw that "soon Jimmy was quickest." The unanimity, particularly when expressed in such similar words, is worth recording and the fact that three men repeat them heightens the sense of Clark's impact.

"After he'd done four or five laps Chapman started leaping about in the hole," Scott Watson says. "I always took times, I was clicking away at the stopwatch and Chapman was clicking away at his stopwatch and he said: 'God, this bloke's quick'." Scott Watson then said words which have passed into the fabric of motorsport history: *"Yes, not bad for someone who's never been in a single-seater before and never been at Brands Hatch before, either."* Scott Watson remembers Chapman's reaction: "Chapman's face went ashen. He shouted: 'Bring him in, for God's sake, he'll kill himself…'."

Clark was wistfully amused when Scott Watson related the dialogue, rather less amused when Chapman challenged him to a 10-lap race, Chapman in the Elite, Clark in Scott Watson's Porsche. Cannily enough Clark declined because the Porsche had the wrong tyres for racing and visions of taking Paddock backwards loomed.

Clark did have a second session in the Lotus Formula Two car and got down to 58.9 seconds, although Hill had been quicker with 56.3. When Clark came in Hill took over and Scott Watson watched as "the back end broke off, the hub assembly broke off and disappeared completely. It happened in the dip up towards Druids, the car crashed heavily and it took them a week to find the hub assembly. It was on the top of a tree somewhere. If that had happened to Jimmy, he'd never have had a chance to drive for Lotus because he'd probably have been blamed. It would have been difficult to prove categorically that it didn't break when the car hit the bank, and anyway it might have put him off forever.

"Jimmy was very disappointed, however, that he'd had so few laps, and just before Hill's accident Chapman said: 'Oh well, we'll see if we can manage some more.' He had Mike Costin on test and Costin was belting round in between times with the prototype Lotus Elite. I said: 'Any chance of Jimmy having five laps in that as compensation?' Chapman said: 'Yes', and Jimmy went out, and when he came back I'd never seen him with a Cheshire Cat grin like it. The grin was ear-to-ear."

Distant dialogue…

Clark: That was bloody marvellous, far better than the single-seater.

Scott Watson: Will you buy my Porsche? If you do I'll buy you an Elite for next year!

Clark: You wouldn't, would you?

Scott Watson: I will, I'll find a way of doing it.

Scott Watson and Clark shook hands and Scott Watson advanced upon Chapman.

Scott Watson: Right, we'll have one. How quick?

Chapman: Well, how about having a go at the Boxing Day Brands Hatch meeting with it? We'll have it ready in time.

Scott Watson: Great.

Scott Watson and Clark left Brands Hatch in the Porsche and drove to Hatfield where they spent the night before Jimmy Prentice's wedding. Then they went back to their farms.

On Friday, December 5, Hawthorn prepared to announce his retirement at the BRDC annual dinner at the Park Lane Hotel. However, the *Daily Express*, long sponsors of Silverstone, were broadening their involvement and chairman Tom Blackburn would be presenting a cheque for £10,000. Hawthorn decided he couldn't compete with a news item like that and kept the announcement to the following day when he issued it through the Press Association, the national news agency taken by virtually every newspaper in the land.

Hawthorn's mistrust of the press remained. The *News Chronicle* told Brinton to get hold of him and find out what was going on. "I said 'He doesn't answer my phone calls', so they told me to go down to Farnham. I found him there and he didn't indicate why he was giving up, he didn't say anything like that. The only thing I got out of him was his nomination for a future World Champion. 'That's going to be Phil Hill,' he said."

Hawthorn's retirement involved a measure of controversy. He wrote to Enzo Ferrari telling him of it and asking if he could buy his race car. Ferrari made no reply but Tavoni told Hawthorn how angry Ferrari was – evidently Tavoni had disbelieved Hawthorn's words at Casablanca about retiring and presumably had not reported it to Ferrari. Publicly Ferrari said he respected Hawthorn's decision.

Hawthorn himself explored the reasons for retirement. He had a business to run, the sport was becoming commercial, and you couldn't be World Champion and "call your life your own." He added a poignant and compelling final reason. After the death of Collins he had no wish to continue, anyway.

On Wednesday, December 10, John Surtees, who'd won the 500cc World Championship on an MV Agusta, shared a table with Hawthorn at the BBC Sports Review of the Year at the Grosvenor House Hotel, London. Tony Vandervell and Reg Parnell were on it, too.

The *Radio Times* previewed the occasion by asking: "Who will the Sports Personality of the Year be? That is a secret until Wednesday, but whoever it is will have the satisfaction of topping a record poll. So tune in at 8.15pm and join Peter Dimmock [then a famous presenter] and two hundred sporting celebrities at a dinner in London's West End to see not only the result of the voting but many of the highlights of a dramatic year of sport." The *Radio Times* pictured Surtees in action on a bike, the Brazilian football team – who'd won the World Cup in Sweden – below him, Hawthorn below that, bare-headed in the cockpit of a car with the smile which is still remembered, Christine Truman in the genteel tennis tunic of the time below that.

During the dinner Hawthorn and Surtees fell to discussing motorcycle trials, a common interest, and agreed to go to one together. Hawthorn also said that four wheels stand up better than two and Surtees should "have a go" at racing cars. Surtees, one of the most successful riders of all time, dismissed the notion. He'd stay a bike man. Ian Black, a *swimmer*, won the BBC's Sports Personality, itself a comment on times gone by. Which swimmer would have beaten Mansell to it in 1992?

Hawthorn's suggestion of doing bike trials remains a brave one. "We were aware," Papsch says, "that he was in a lot of pain [the kidney problem]. We'd say: 'Why don't you go and see a doctor?' He'd say: 'No, everything's OK.' He never showed the pain. He was always as cheerful as anything."

"I learned later," Jean Howarth says, "that he used to have terrible blackouts at the garage, he used to lie on the floor in terrible agony. That Christmas Day was spent in bed because he felt lousy. He never complained, he never told me how ill he was feeling. I knew he was ill, but I didn't know how ill. I don't think the blackouts began until after his motor racing career ended because when they happened they lasted quite some time, so he wouldn't have taken the risk of driving a racing car.

"If he didn't want to do something that he felt wasn't right he wouldn't do it and nobody could persuade him to. He was a Yorkshireman in that sense, and in the sense that he was careful with money – didn't splash it around – but generous, too. For instance, turning round and going back to buy me that boxer was kind and thoughtful." Hawthorn suffered a marked deterioration that Christmas.

Ian Scott Watson and Jimmy Clark thought entirely about the future. "Three weeks before the Boxing Day meeting a big hype started about Brands Hatch," Scott Watson says. "The meeting was to be televised and they had trailer films about it. This little white Lotus Elite went round and round on the telly" – *Clark's* little white Lotus Elite.

He and Scott Watson caught the overnight London train at Berwick on Christmas Day and went to the Green Park Hotel where Scott Watson had arranged to meet Colin Bennett, Lotus' sales manager. "He handed the car over to us and we drove it down to Brands, the first time we had sat in the thing. At Brands Chapman said: 'It's all right, we've been doing a bit of running with it so the engine should be loosened up. You can race it normally.' Jimmy moved out for the practice and he was quite quick. I was in the pits and Mike Costin and Chapman were having a bloody great argument. I could hear them as I walked past. 'Right,' said Chapman, 'Hazel says this is to be my last race so you're going to have to let me win', and Costin said: 'What about me? It's my last, too, my wife's told me not to lose it; come on, we'll just have to make a race of it.' They argued, and I think Chapman was getting his way.

"A few yards further on stood a line of bookmakers with their boards and everything taking bets, the first time I'd seen it at a motor racing meeting. Chapman was 2:3, Costin 3:1, Jimmy 10:1, so I pulled out half a crown (12½p) and put it on Clark. I didn't tell Jimmy. I thought maybe I shouldn't...

"In the race Jimmy went into the lead, Chapman did his damndest and couldn't get past. I've a photograph of them going through Paddock absolutely side-by-side flat-out and you don't do that: Colin was trying to pass on the outside because he was so determined and he still wasn't making it, Jimmy wasn't giving an inch.

"I felt so sorry afterwards for a man called Wing Commander McKenzie in a Sprite, who'd been having a good race; he genuinely saw the pair of them coming up, tried his best to get out of the way, but tried too hard. He went sideways on the grit on the inside of Druids, Jimmy just clipped him and that let Chapman through. There was only one lap left and Jimmy couldn't retake him."

Distant dialogue...

Chapman: That was a very, very hard race. He is bloody good.

Scott Watson: Well, what can we do?

Chapman: You wouldn't fancy doing Le Mans, would you?

Scott Watson: Yes. We'll enter as Border Reivers if you can give us as much works backing as you can.

Chapman: Right.

Scott Watson: We'd like to make it all Scottish, we'll have Tommy Dickson (Lotus' Scottish distributor, garage owner, Ecurie Ecosse driver and quite a character) as co-driver.

Chapman: Right.

Clark caught the train back to Berwick while Scott Watson took the Elite to Northampton to visit his mother and then drove on home. "At the bend in the road just before you turn towards my farm the con-rod let go. I walked to the farm and phoned Chapman. I said: 'That bloody engine…'

Distant dialogue…

Chapman: Oh, you will race it when it's new and not run in.

Scott Watson: Come on, three weeks before, I saw film on television of the only white Elite in existence running round Brands Hatch; don't tell me it was my problem.'

Chapman: No, no. You're quite right. There will be a new engine at Berwick station tomorrow morning.

Chapman, Scott Watson remembers, said it with absolutely no hesitation and "from that day on we had a wonderful relationship." There would be another relationship, even more wonderful. Chapman and Clark.

On Thursday, January 22, 1959, a rainy day, Hawthorn was going to London in his Jaguar for a meeting. He didn't want to go. Jean Howarth, who was in Huddersfield, subsequently learned that "he wasn't well that day and possibly had one of his blackouts. Evidently he sat in the hall of the family house with his head in his hands, but it is a measure of him that he did go."

Papsch saw Hawthorn that morning. "He came in to the garage and filled the Jaguar up with petrol, had the tyres checked – he'd been given a set of tyres by a factory to test them. The battery was checked, the car was 100 per cent. I was in the showroom getting a new car out. Mike came through and said: 'Hello, Ted, how is it?' and I said: 'Not too bad, the car will soon be ready.' He said: 'OK, I'll see you' and then he walked out."

Near the Guildford by-pass he happened to see, and be seen by, Rob Walker en route in his Mercedes to his garage in Dorking. On the Guildford by-pass Hawthorn raced ahead and then clipped a kerb. The Jaguar spun, struck a traffic island, went across the road and clipped a lorry, then battered itself against a tree. Hawthorn, pitched into the back seat, died a few moments later.

That's an echo within The Echoes of Winter. *Motor racing is dangerous but what is danger? It is dangerous to climb mountains. It is dangerous to explore a jungle. One cannot frame regulations to make everything safe…*

There are theories about this accident, some extremely technical, some revolving around possible mud left on the road by a tractor, some even involving a blackout, some involving the tyres – on test, don't forget – which might not have given sufficient adhesion in the wet. Certainly, and Rob Walker has said this, Hawthorn ought to have been able to get himself out of a skid easily enough. An example from Jean Howarth. "Going to Folley Cottage in the Jaguar – registration VDU 881 – one time on a very icy day we were talking and he overshot the entrance to the drive and said 'Hang on'. I've since learnt what he did: a handbrake turn. He completely turned the car round and it was all frightfully controlled and beautifully done and off we shot in the opposite direction. I'd never seen that before." This Jaguar, the one Hawthorn and Papsch rebuilt into the rocket, was the one he pressed out on to the Guildford by-pass.

Postscripts, as the frost of winter gripped...

Alan Brinton: "Of course Hawthorn was mad on the road, but so were all the others mad on the road. I remember going to cover the Monaco Grand Prix, I flew to Nice and people at the airport were talking about Hawthorn, Moss and Collins. They'd arrived the day before, each had a hire car and they raced to Monte Carlo over the *Grand Corniche* – all cliffs and drops – and thought it was great fun. Compared to today, you're talking about a different mentality altogether."

Bette Hill: "Well, you see, people had fun in those days, and as it happened it was a stupid thing to do, but it was the sort of thing they did. I'm afraid they lived like that, they loved life, they were *gladiators*."

Jean Howarth: "Mike didn't want anybody to know about his son. It was an indiscretion of one night. It was just bad luck for poor old Mike that the woman became pregnant. He was killed on the Thursday, and on the Friday he was due to fly to Paris to sort out the finances for his son, getting all that straight before we officially announced our engagement. Mike was doing the gentlemanly thing, making sure the son would have enough money to live on and also give the mother something. Later Mrs Hawthorn went over to Paris to meet the mother and she tried to get the mother and son to come over to England to live, and she fell out with them – don't ask me why – but she was a real nightmare. She wouldn't have been a very nice mother-in-law.

"I don't think people truly knew how ill Mike was. He had only five years to live if he hadn't killed himself. His doctor told me that after he died, so in fact I was quite relieved that he went the way he went because he would have been in a wheelchair. The doctor was a friend of ours, his son was Mike's godson. The doctor told me Mike had only one kidney anyway – that's why he didn't go into the armed forces and Mike refused to let anyone know he only had one kidney. If he had, the world would have got to know and he wouldn't have been allowed to motor race. His other kidney was diseased and in those days we did not have kidney transplants. When I was told he couldn't have lived beyond five years I thought *thank goodness, Mike would have hated to be seen in a wheelchair, he wasn't that sort of man, he was vibrant.*"

PORTRAIT: GRAHAM HILL

These many years later you must accept two portraits of Graham Hill. The public one is well known, Ambassador to motorsport with a capital A, jaw jutting with determination to compensate for the gifts nature withheld, The Man Who Never Gave Up. It's a comfy and stirring sort of image, it is entirely authentic and very English: the driver who signed all the autographs, posed for all the pictures, but who could equally charm the Institute of Directors when he was asked to speak to them.

The public one would – and will – include mastering Monaco, itself a place which struck resonant chords in the English, becoming friends with the Rainiers, mingling easily with film stars, singing lewd songs when he was drinking with the chaps. But that was only the virility of the chaps, spiffing good fun. *Roll me o-o-over in the clo-ver, roll me over lay me down and do it again.*

The other portrait is darker, and few care to speak about it on the record although many witnessed it: the temper, the insensitivity. One time he vented this on his wife Bette in front of the mechanics and a fist fight almost broke out because someone protested and was rewarded with a virulent torrent grouped around the f-word.

This darker portrait is inhibited by considerations for Bette who, since Hill's death in 1975, has successfully brought up three children – son Damon now in Formula One himself, of course – and understandably constructs a shield around Graham's memory to the point where she laments his being "the forgotten Champion." She has plenty of evidence for that, too, and if Hill had to force his racing he did that exceptionally well. You don't become the only man to win the World Championship (twice), the Indianapolis 500 and Le Mans if you're not good. Moreover, she is herself a woman of character who knew why the anger was vented on her even when undeserved. It is a sign of extraordinary strength and can only be appreciated by a woman in love who was also a mother, backing her man completely.

I suggested to Bette that some people thought Graham a bastard. "He was [chuckle], he was. He was a bastard because he expected the same from other people as he himself gave. If they weren't prepared to do that they saw the wrong side of him. He didn't tolerate fools gladly. He was tough as old boots on me and I used to say to him: 'Graham, don't put me on a pedestal, I'm going to fall off it, I'm a human being.' He'd say: 'I know that darling, but as long as I try and keep you up there then at least you're going to make an effort.' And that is what he expected from other people."

It would be churlish to point out the chauvinism. Who was he to tell another human being they had to put themselves on a pedestal – or rather that he'd put them on one so they'd try harder to stay on it?

"He did take things out on me which were very unfair, very unkind at times. For instance, I remember an occasion which had nothing whatsoever to do with motor racing, but shows he was too soft to say no. A sculptor, David Wynne, was a friend of Graham's and, Graham being Graham, he couldn't stop buying the sculptures, so we had one in the hall, a sculpture over there, a sculpture in the drawing room, one in the garden. Everywhere you looked was a beautiful sculpture. David and his wife came to our house when we were living at Lyndhurst. We were all going to go out together. I said – I was being honest – 'it's like a David Wynne museum.' Graham had a letter in his hand. He said: 'Don't say things like that'."

He swiped at Bette with the letter.

"You know what paper does. It cut my lip, I spurted with blood which shut up the conversation straight away. I had to go back into the house and use a Kleenex or something to stop the blood. We all got in the car deathly quiet, as you can imagine. David sat in the back and laughed, then his wife laughed."

Distant dialogue...

Wynne: I've never had people falling out over my sculptures and behaving like that before.

Graham: Well, she should never have said a thing like that.

Bette: I'm only telling the truth.

Graham: You shouldn't, it hurts.

The strangest part of this episode, as Bette attests, is that "it didn't hurt David, it hurt me. I had to be extra perfect and it wasn't possible. I had to be better than I was and that's when he used to get angry with me."

Bette relates it all with no trace of self-consciousness and certainly no self-pity. She saw equally and decisively the enormous strengths of the man, she lived through more straightened beginnings than Nigel Mansell would ever know and witnessed – nay, aided – the man she married to grow into the Ambassador, big and strong and, at every turn in his life, his own man. Isn't this what's meant to make women's knees go weak, the Clint Eastwood approach? Ah well, never mind.

"If people let him down he never forgave them. If people lied to him he never forgot. Maybe he'd forgive but never forget. If people betrayed his trust they knew it. He wouldn't behave badly in front of them but he'd treat them with a little contempt. They would know that he knew. He was far too trusting. Someone once said Graham thought everyone was as nice as himself, and if he discovered they weren't he could be a bastard. And he was. He hated people who didn't conform to what he considered fair, and that summed up Graham really and truly.

"At one stage at home at Mill Hill he thought Damon had taken some money. In all honesty Damon hadn't. Damon wasn't a perfect child, but he hadn't taken it. Graham really made Damon suffer for that and then we discovered who it was" – not a member of the family – "because Graham caught them. It was a tankard with pocket money in it, 10 pences or whatever, and they were disappearing day by day. Why this person did it I shall never know, but Graham had thought it was Damon, Graham hadn't believed it wasn't Damon, and poor old Damon suffered for that.

"I stole when I was a child and my father hit me and made my nose bleed; he never hit me before or after. Money was lying there, it was a temptation, I'd wanted an ice cream so I took it." Bette recounts this to demonstrate how essentially innocent such theft would really be, coins for an ice cream or 10 pences from a tankard, and how understandable; but that wasn't the point.

"Graham had always instilled into Damon and the girls [Brigitte and Samantha] that you must never lie, you must always tell the truth. Why didn't he believe Damon? Why disbelieve *him* of all people?" When Bette posed this question Graham said he didn't know, and "of course Graham said to Damon afterwards: 'I'm terribly sorry.' Graham was humiliated."

Bette insists that she never remembers Graham lying. "Never. He was a most honest man. If the truth hurt, hard luck."

I suppose he'd defend himself over Bette's comment about the museum of statues by saying that you can say it, but not in front of the sculptor, a reasonable position; and since he is not here to defend himself, natural justice demands that all judgments on him are tempered. To libel the living is a chance you take, to libel the dead is safe as you like.

The characteristics of the man enabled him to fashion his career. Without them he'd have been another driver, another pump-and-push merchant making up the numbers at Brands Hatch in unconsequential races, the kind you could get yourself into most weekends and which lead nowhere except to more of the same next weekend. At the risk of repeating myself, you do not win the World Championship (twice) and the Indianapolis 500 and Le Mans like this, never mind get to know the Rainiers or make speeches to the Institute of Directors.

All are agreed that he was not born with the gifts of the intuitive driver. We're talking here, primarily, about Ascari, Fangio, Moss, Clark, Rindt, Villeneuve, Prost (oh, yes) and Senna. They had that, the near inexplicable ability to balance their bodies, their minds and the machines they drove and from that harmony skim along faster than all around them.

Damon says: "Mum is a very competitive person in her own right. She used to row for England and I don't know if I got my competitiveness from her or from my father. They were both competitive people. My father refused to be beaten, he refused to accept that there wasn't a way someone couldn't be beaten." Since Damon was in his mid-teens when his father died he was old enough to make such a judgment and there is too much evidence from other people to doubt that it is utterly correct. "I think Mum is right to a certain degree about the forgotten Champion. People do tend to overlook him. There's more merit in overcoming the abilities of someone like Clark through hard work. It's like a school report, isn't it? Jim Clark, A grade but U for effort; Graham Hill, C grade but A for effort."

That's the jutting jaw portrait and it is as authentic as the other one, and one was the other and the other was the one. The man was hard and soft, public and private, rational and unreasonable, just like you and I.

Graham Hill was born in Hampstead, North London, on February 15, 1929, one of two brothers. He spent his childhood in Hendon, studied engineering and did a five-year apprenticeship with S. Smith and Sons in Cricklewood, the watch, clock and instrument manufacturers. He sensed it would not be his life, although he didn't sense what his life would be. He did his National Service in the Royal Navy and bought his first car, a 1934 Morris 8 Tourer, for £110 in 1953.

He was 24, and if his autobiography *Life at the Limit* is accurate the family had never owned a car before, and the only time he'd been in one during childhood was when an uncle ran them to the seaside. Now, in 1953, the owner of the Morris inquired if Hill could drive, and he said 'Yes', and drove it home across London. He passed his test two weeks later, driving himself there and only stopping on the way to buy L-plates. Like Hawthorn, you live for the moment to see what the moment will bring. This mentality led Hill to negotiate the jungle of North London when he couldn't drive. The days of seat belts, breathalyzers and obsessive safety wouldn't come for another quarter of a century.

That year, 1953, Graham was in the London Rowing Club's eight in the Grand Challenge Cup at Henley and you should know more about Henley. It has parallels with Grand Prix racing. Many attend because it is the place to be. They position themselves in a society dance, moving from group to group in the Very Important People's Enclosure, a lawn tipping away to the Thames, drink heavily and guffaw and eye the *gels* in their pretty frocks. A few yards away the best rowers in the world slog their guts out in the grey, forbidding water, and as they cross the line they fall slack in the boats, knackered, dishevelled, spent.

Ascari didn't do this, nor Fangio, nor Moss, Clark, Rindt, Villeneuve, Prost, Senna. Hill did.

At the end of the 1953 rowing season someone suggested to him that, in an echo of Hawthorn talking to Surtees, he "had a go" at motor racing and pointed to an advertisement for Brands Hatch where you could drive a Formula Three car for 5 shillings (25p) a lap. Hill typically thought he would have a go and invested £1 in four laps. His initial impression: the car resembled a "small torpedo." He jutted his jaw (no doubt) and set off towards Paddock Hill Bend. When he came back he knew what his life would be.

If you're a certain type of competitor, needing to go to such places as Henley, exhaustion is fine and fulfilling and worthwhile, but Paddock Hill Bend with its adverse camber is the real thing. You get round it and you're into the stomach-dropping descent before the rise to Druids, you're taking it alone, measuring yourself against the machine, goading it, cajoling it, using it, pumping and squeezing it and squeezing yourself – no crew rowing with you, not their rhythm to drown in, no cox rapping the time of the strokes. No. You're into Paddock Hill Bend in a metal suitcase at the hundred and plenty, controlled uniquely by a fallible human. You, and no other. And the suitcase could break apart at any moment in any way.

"Graham did the usual thing," Bette says, "driving for somebody else at Brands for the sake of a drive and teaching people at the school there." You might wonder how somebody looking for a drive might be an instructor but – live for the moment to see what the moment brings.

The folklore suggests that in 1954 Hill met Colin Chapman and Mike Costin in a transporter at Brands. "None of them knew each other, but Colin thought Mike knew Graham and Mike thought Colin knew him. After that Graham used to go down to Hornsey, where Lotus cars were built. He asked Colin: 'Can you give me a job?' He was a qualified engineer anyway, he'd done all his apprenticeship. Colin thought: 'What does he want a job for? He only wants to go motor racing', but we were getting married in 1955 so Graham had to be reasonably gainfully employed. At the time I was earning the money in the same way it happened with Rosanne and Nigel Mansell. I paid the rent and the food and he was trying to get himself a drive everywhere." (When I mentioned before that the Hills knew more privations than the Mansells, I only meant that the privations of the Fifties were deeper than the privations of the Seventies; tough times are tough times, but some less tough than others. Ask anybody who knew the Depression of the Thirties.)

Hill joined Lotus as a mechanic, and his connection with them lasted until 1970. One of his World Championships was won in a Lotus, but the other in a BRM, Indy in a Lola, Le Mans in a Matra. That enhances the man, surely, takes us to where history places Clark: that he could drive anything. An interesting thought.

Reflecting on those early days, John Webb, who steered Brands Hatch to become one of the most exciting Grand Prix theatres in the world, says: "Graham made his name at the circuit. I remember him being so fantastic one day as an amateur that I did something which in those days we never did, call a Press Conference after the meeting. Graham was so outstanding everyone wanted to meet him."

No doubt this was the first press conference of his life. John Webb has seen too much to be able to recall details, and it would be unfair to expect him to, but no doubt Hill handled it well and maybe learnt how, if journalists come to ask you questions, they'll reproduce your answers and you can exercise a measure of control, fashion an image. I cannot prove this statement; it's only surmise, but based upon the known and sure fact that Graham Hill achieved it, and if it started here that's very explicable.

Look at it another way. Clark barely spoke in public, and thereby hangs a curiosity. Many years after Clark's death Graham Gauld sent Nigel Roebuck a tape of an interview he'd done with Clark, and this was the first time Roebuck had heard Clark's voice; Roebuck copied the tape many years further on and sent it to me, and it was the first time I'd heard Clark's voice.

When Clark did talk to people – strangers or the media – a profound self-consciousness hampered him. He rarely felt he had to give of himself. Hill cast himself, or was cast, as the Ambassador with the capital A, and carried it off superbly in all manner of circumstances. Ask the Institute of Directors, who, you can assume, have heard a speech or two in their time.

Hill raced Lotus-Climaxes and Lotus-Fords in 1956 and 1957, nagged Chapman to give him a Grand Prix drive and made his debut, as we have seen, at Monaco in 1958. He'd remember being last when the race began and because so many dropped out found himself fourth. He hadn't overtaken anyone. The car began to behave very strangely, spun, and when he stopped it he noticed a rear wheel alongside the cockpit. Interesting. That was lap 70 and he'd covered nearly 140 miles, a very long way in a Grand Prix car for the first time. As he clambered out he collapsed with heat exhaustion. *I was*, he confessed, *weak as a kitten*. Fifteen years later another Briton would make his debut at Monaco and cover 73 laps, more than 150 miles. He didn't collapse, but he emerged so weak he was *helpless as a new born babe*. Some things change by moving on. Some things don't.

Hill left Lotus for BRM (British Racing Motors, who built their own cars, engines, gearboxes and chassis) in 1960 because he was worried about the breakages, a recurring theme with other Lotus cars and drivers over the years. There will be evidence later in this book of how Colin Chapman toyed with technology in gigantic experiments, jostled with *finitely* unknown conclusions about what the technology might really do, especially if it went wrong. I hope to temper that because libelling the dead, as I say, is safe as you like; but it happened. It's not comfortable reading and we have a measure of Hill that he went back to Lotus when he must have assumed nothing had changed.

That first year at BRM was difficult, only four Championship points, and in 1961 Tony Brooks joined him. "Graham was not a natural driver, he got there by sheer work, dedication, commitment, learning the ropes the hard way," Brooks says. "He was one of the first guys who breathed, ate and slept motor racing, and he spent a lot of time at the BRM factory so that, although we had equal status in the team as drivers, he put an awful lot of effort into the technical side to try and make sure that his car was as good as it could possibly be.

"That was a substantial advantage and he had the time to do it [Brooks ran a garage business] – had the time to virtually live at the factory, hand-hone his car and the attitude of the BRM people. Graham added a political something to racing which is common today. Senna does that sort of thing, Prost does that sort of thing. In some ways I don't think Stirling tried to get into the factory to that extent. Perhaps Graham was really the first driver to infiltrate himself into the team, live with the team. As a result he put himself into a very good situation.

"I got on well with him, he was an amusing sort of guy, a bit of the *Boy's Own* type [there it is again] because he was flamboyant, but much more serious than Mike Hawthorn about his motor racing, far more dedicated, and I think that is to his credit. He was the sort of driver that I'd want to get behind me pretty quickly because he made quite a few mistakes in his earlier years, but developed his technique to a stage where he became very, very competitive.

"You might wonder why I joined BRM a second time [Brooks had started his career there in 1956]. I was still driving as competitively as ever and I was told in 1961 before signing the contract that the car which Graham would win the World Championship with in 1962 would be ready for the Monaco Grand Prix of 1961, opening race of the season. I liked the sound of it and that's why I said I'd drive it, a V8 engine, a completely new design. It looked good and my judgment in that respect proved correct, in that it did go on to win the Championship in 1962 – thanks in no small part to Graham's input into the team.

"The truth is that when the 1962 car did finally appear for the first time in practice (at Monza, September 1961) I didn't even get to drive it. Graham drove it because, as I've said, he'd successfully infiltrated himself into the team. This was a new political technique and I wasn't very thrilled. It caught me by surprise that that sort of relationship was acceptable to the team, and meanwhile I'd bought a petrol filling station near Brooklands in December 1960, and I was trying to do this, that and the other thing. I was resentful of the fact that Graham got the best equipment because, with due respect – and it is difficult to say this – I had the track record and Graham was still making his way. I was not altogether happy. However, we never had a cross word.

"We had an overweight car with a secondhand 1½-litre Coventry Climax engine and perhaps 130bhp, a glorified go-kart, and if Graham got himself as little as 10 more horsepower from his engine there was not an awful lot you could do about it. This new go-kart formula and the consequential diminution of the driver's contribution was a major factor in my decision to retire at the end of 1961 after giving BRM their best results of the year with fastest lap in the British Grand Prix (wet conditions at Aintree) and third in the US Grand Prix at Watkins Glen, my last race."

Hill stayed with BRM until the end of 1966 and four victories in 1962 gave him the World Championship. That season repays examination in some detail. BRM's V8 engine had been developed to the point where it offered 190bhp at 10,500 revs. At the first race, Holland, Hill professed himself mildly astonished that he did 1 minute 35.6 seconds in practice, quicker than the 2½-litre engines with 270bhp before the Formula changed in 1961.

Hill won in Holland, the first of the 14 in his career, from Trevor Taylor (Lotus) by a handy 27.2 seconds. BRM hadn't won since 1959, at this same Zandvoort. Traditionally the Grand Prix fraternity stayed at the Bouwes Hotel, an imposing and formal structure on the seafront in the town, and traditionally they had a post-race party. This one, Hill would remember, caused the manager consternation when some drivers tried to climb the columns in the hotel foyer. Later everyone decided to have a swim and stripped on the beach in the lights cast from the hotel. As they scampered down to the sea Hill thought it must have looked amazing, all those rows of bobbing white bottoms. Well, yes. *Roll me o-o-over in the clover, roll me over lay me down and do it again.*

A gain and a loss, no doubt, whatever your point of view, however deep your nostalgia.

At Monaco Hill was on the front row of the grid, Jim Clark on pole. At the start Willi Mairesse (Ferrari) scratched through into the lead but braked late for the Gasworks hairpin and spun. Next, Richie Ginther's throttle on his BRM jammed open and at the hairpin he hit Maurice Trintignant who in turn hit Ireland. One of Ginther's wheels was wrenched off and struck a marshal, killing him. Ginther had just missed hitting Hill's car by a "fraction". After six laps Hill took the lead from Bruce McLaren and at one point extended that to 48 seconds. Eight laps from the end – Hill struggling against falling oil pressure – the con-rod emerged from the side of the engine. He received a profound ovation as he walked back.

He was second to Clark at Spa, set fastest lap but didn't finish in France (Rouen) – or rather did finish, but ninth and 10 laps behind the winner, Dan Gurney (Porsche). Like in Monaco, Hill had led, but a fuel-injection problem hobbled him and he toured to the end. He was fourth at Aintree in the British, but won at the Nurburgring, and we'll hear a bizarre anecdote about that from Bette Hill in a moment. He won Monza and with only Watkins Glen and South Africa remaining was already having to drop points: you could only count your five best finishes. It meant Hill had 36 points in play, Bruce McLaren 22, Clark 21. McLaren would be dropping points from here on, Clark could keep whatever he got – his 21 came from only three finishes, the wins at Spa and Aintree, and fourth place at the Nurburgring.

Clark took pole at Watkins Glen, Hill took the lead, but Clark swept by and Hill could do nothing. Clark won by 9.2 seconds. It fashioned the South African Grand Prix, at East London on December 29, into a mathematical teaser. Hill took 39 points to it, Clark 30, McLaren now out of it with 24. The teaser was that if Clark won he'd move to 39 and if Hill came second he'd stay on 39 – he was now dropping second places. Clark would have the title on a tie-break of most wins, four-three.

East London, a circuit of 2.439 miles, has drifted into memory. The South African Grand Prix was held there again in 1963 and 1965 before it moved to Kyalami. The race of 1962 lives on, Clark badgered to distraction in the weeks up to it – Watkins Glen had been October 7 – by people asking him if he thought he'd win. He would have done, too. He seized pole (1 minute 29.3 seconds against Hill's 1 minute 29.6) and seized the race. On lap three he set fastest lap at 96.35 miles an hour, itself a devastating thing. Hill couldn't stay anywhere near this, and deep into the race Clark thundered out a lead reaching towards half a minute. On lap 59 of the 82 Clark noticed ominous blue smoke from the exhaust pipes. He kept a wary eye on it and pressed on for a couple of laps, then pitted because he didn't want to destroy the engine. As the mechanics worked Hill went by. Clark knew then that his first Championship would have to wait another year. Hill knew then that he'd virtually done it, and when Clark retired on lap 62 he had.

Hill would remember three aspects of the aftermath: on his lap of honour he ran over a small boy's leg and broke it, although the press of people on the track was so intense Hill didn't realize; the garland they put round his neck reminded him of a privet hedge and was so large it trailed to his feet; and "we were all very pleased."

It was, and is, a very British way of putting it.

In 1963 Hill was due to compete in the Indianapolis 500 driving a revolutionary car – "saucer-shaped," Hill described it, with small enclosed wheels. The car proved to be "diabolical" and shed a wheel. He didn't try to qualify but retreated after the car hit the wall. Weeks later *Road & Track*, the American magazine, carried a letter which called him "a coward in no uncertain terms," Bette says. "It said in effect this Limey hit the wall and left. I wrote to the magazine and cited the Nurburgring in 1962 when his race car had been written off after Carel de Beaufort was going round with an on-board camera, the camera dropped off and Graham's brand new BRM trundled, as he said, like a rabbit in a burrow. Next day Graham won the race in appalling conditions. I wrote to Mr whoever-it-was 'you have called my husband a coward and I think you should apologize for that.' It was months before *Road & Track* arrived again. I never dreamt that they'd put my letter in the magazine. Graham was sitting in the study at Lyndhurst."

Distant dialogue...

Graham: Hmm, darling, what are you doing?

Bette: Nothing. Why?

Graham: Just come here for a minute.

(Bette entered, thinking they were going to have a chat.)

Graham: Did you write that?

Bette: Yes, I did.

Graham: Don't ever write letters about me to any magazine.

Bette: They called you a coward and I am defending you.

Graham: I know, darling, I know all about it, but you never rise to that kind of bait.

"I don't agree with that, I don't agree with that at all, but he didn't see it that way, he was Graham Hill and above such things. You didn't step down to that person's level to give them the credit of a reply. It is not necessary for us to defend ourselves. We know what is right and what happened."

By 1966 Hill felt stale at BRM – it had been seven years – and rejoined Lotus to partner Clark. It produced, inevitably perhaps, tensions. "It's very difficult to be entirely objective about him," Peter Warr says. "The problem was that everybody at Lotus had been close to him because he'd started there as a mechanic when he was a struggling youngster with a lot of grit and determination. By the time he became an established Grand Prix driver – I'm not doubting that he was very good, I'm not doubting that he did an incredibly good job with BRM and then Lotus – people in the team were too close to him to be able to see him as somebody removed from them. And Graham was a devil to work with.

"He wanted half an inch up on this, two thirds down on that, adjust this, adjust that, adjust the other. He'd spend the whole of practice fiddling with the car and he'd drive the team to distraction. You'd think 'Right, we've done that, he's going to do a quick lap' and he was back in the pits. 'Can I have half an inch on the front rollbar?' Always fiddling.

"A good example was the ZF gearbox we used. It took nine months lead time to get it made and it was like a precision Swiss watch compared to your average racing gearbox, fully syncromesh. They said: 'You tell us what the engine does and we'll design the gearbox so the gearchanges are exactly right.' We'd take – I've forgotton what it was – 14 or 15 gearboxes to races because you couldn't change the ratios, so you picked the crownwheel and pinion you wanted for the top speed. If you wanted to go slower you changed the whole gearbox for a lower crownwheel and pinion, but all the time the ratios were absolutely perfectly matched to the gearbox plus, as I've said, in was all syncro, plus it was virtually troublefree.

"Jimmy coped, no trouble at all, but Graham would say: 'No, no, no, I can't hold it in third gear until that corner, I want to change to fourth and back down to third' or: 'Now, if I just had a second gear which was 200 revs longer I could hold it between this corner and that corner.' He single-handedly persuaded Colin to make us change to Hewland gearboxes, which eventually turned out to be one of motor racing's great successes, but at the time were a total pain in the ass. [Echoes of Bette Hill who says: "Graham had a very strong mind, it wasn't always right, but in many cases it contributed to being right."] If you gave Graham a box of ratios to play with he was up and down them like a concert violinist. The car was always in pieces. So it is very difficult to be objective about him – but no-one should underestimate or try and take away what he achieved. What he achieved was terrific.

"You must remember that Graham had been working at it longer than Jimmy and he'd got to the Championship in 1962, which Jimmy really should have won, Surtees got it in 1964, which he shouldn't have done [Clark led the final race, Mexico, but broke down]. That would have been Jimmy as Champion four years running.

"All these guys were rushing around like chickens with their heads cut off, working like hell, giving it their all, and there was this guy Clark out there smoother and quicker no matter what they did. Graham was a powerful personality, he came across in the social environment, a very, very likeable man, but he had to resent the fact that there was this other guy who was just quicker."

Jim Endruweit, a Lotus mechanic, follows the theme. "One hates to make comparisons, but when Clark and Hill were together at Lotus we had the two opposite ends of the spectrum entirely, Jimmy quiet and reserved, Graham hail-fellow-well-met, tell a good joke, thoroughly enjoy that sort of stuff. Jimmy would tell you what the car was doing, what was happening with the car, Graham would tell you what he wanted you to do to it. Graham was difficult, difficult.

"I'd known since 1958, when he was starting and I was starting, and, in fact, one of my first missions was down at Clermont-Ferrand, Graham driving and me doing just about everything else. I got to know him at that point and then, of course, when he came back to drive for us in 1967 it was *Mr Hill, sir*. We knew each other, we understood each other, but he was difficult because he was so demanding. He wanted to know exactly what you had done; you couldn't do

61

anything to the car without him knowing exactly what you'd done. We used to argue about front rollbars in thousandths. He'd say: 'Have you got one five thousandths different', and we'd say: 'No, we bloody haven't.' Jimmy would simply say: 'The front is doing this', and you'd have to work out what to do about it."

They were both quick of course, and we're talking relative speeds. Take 1967, Denny Hulme's Championship year in the Brabham. Hill had pole at Zandvoort, Clark at Spa, Hill in France, Clark at Silverstone, the Nurburgring, Canada, Monza, Hill at Watkins Glen, Clark in Mexico.

The tension begs a question to Bette Hill. What did Graham make of Clark? "I'm going to be pretty disloyal to Jimmy, but Jimmy didn't like Graham doing better than him. He couldn't help himself. He didn't mean it nastily, he just didn't like it. At Lotus there was no number one and number two. If Graham finished behind Jimmy in practice he'd shrug his shoulders and say: 'Well, I'm going to make something more of this in the race', but Jimmy would get down, he would really get down if he found he hadn't a time faster than Graham. We understood. It wasn't necessary to discuss it between ourselves because we knew.

"The only thing I used to tell Graham was if anything went on in the pits which wasn't to his advantage. I kept lap charts and times, and we discussed when he changed tyres and if he'd done a better lap with this tyre or that tyre. I wanted to make sure that if Jimmy was getting something on his car Graham was getting it. That wasn't the only way Graham found out, of course, because they both had their own sets of mechanics and they discussed things with Colin, but if something was around I made sure Graham knew.

"I kept both their times in two columns, and beside each had a space for remarks. I did it for practice as well as the races. They could say to the mechanics: 'What tyre did you put on, what pressure did it have?', and the mechanics would tell me, too. We were all buddies."

Across the Sixties Hill grew into an eminent Englishman, instantly recognizable by his moustache and much else, a hewn face full of character. He came to know Prince Charles well enough that Charles wrote a foreword to Hill's book *Graham*. In that foreword Charles spoke of the fun of Hill, how his "zest for life was intoxicating." That's the public portrait again.

Pat Mennem of the *Daily Mirror* remembers: "I got on all right with Hill because he made a great effort to make sure that one did. He worked at being the public relations chap very, very hard indeed, but beneath it of course you knew that a lot of the other people hated his guts, the mechanics and so on. He was a great facade man, the jovial English chap, but he was very, very difficult to deal with. If you got the people who ran his mobile home on one side they'd tell you why they didn't like him. The facade? It was a completely different image to what he really was. The car was always wrong, he didn't have any natural talent, he had to work at it. He had tremendous determination and tremendous courage, but not natural talent. Clark found it pretty easy even on a steamroller, Hill was always battling."

Alan Brinton confirms this. "Hill was two different people, the private and the public. The private one could be a bastard, very businesslike, none of the standing on tables half drunk, no fear. He had to work hard at being a public individual and he did it very well.

"For example, when I edited *Motor Racing* we put drivers on the front cover in all sorts of interesting situations and they always co-operated. Before one of his victories at Monaco we got him to go to a gaming club in London, bunny girls and everything else. He put on evening dress and posed for the picture surrounded by the bunnies, the croupier and so on. He played ball, he played ball completely because he realized that this was good for his public image. He could be a devil, too – the other side of him. I didn't see that so much, but I heard a lot about it.

"Once or twice I ghosted some stuff for him. I remember once sitting down with him at Goodwood, I'd produced the story and I said: 'You have to see it before it goes off to the printer.' We sat. 'Hang on a minute, let's go through it again.' He spent half an hour, not being critical, but meticulous. 'I think we might change this, I think we might change that.' I gave him great credit for that. He was being paid for the article, but that wasn't the point. He was going to give value. That's an insight into the man."

Late in Hill's career Derek Bell had insights, too. "Drivers in those days were brave people, totally dedicated to driving high-performance racing cars to the best of their ability. They wanted to drive against the best to prove they were the best. Graham? When you got in a race with him all he wanted to do was win.

"I should be able to remember every incident in every race I was in with those guys, but I was so awestruck to be even anywhere near them that I can't. We did the seven-race Tasman series and people at that level are very precise, they don't do stupid things. I do remember one race in New Zealand. On the front row of the grid were Jochen Rindt in a works Lotus and Chris Amon, second row Piers Courage and me in a Ferrari, third row Graham in another works Lotus and somebody else. Graham got a lot of flak because Jochen had joined Lotus, and we all knew what Jochen was like as a driver, always quicker than Graham, a wonderful bloody driver.

"We were two, two, two on the grid, but so close it would be like driving round Goodwood in Formula One cars today, narrow as hell. I watched the flag, Rindt in front and his engine going whaang, whaang, whaang, the flag fell and off we went. I sailed bang into the back of Rindt and dipped the clutch. He then moved forward and I thought 'He's off now', I let the clutch out again, bang, hit him again. I went over his rear wheel and continued up the road, no major accident. I finished the race. We were at dinner that night, Graham and me and the others sitting round the table."

Distant dialogue…

Hill: That was a bloody stupid thing you did today. What do you think you were up to?

Bell: What do you mean?

Hill: At the start. If I'd let my clutch out when you let your clutch out we'd have had a multiple crash. You'll learn that even if the flag is dropped you don't go until the man in front goes.

"Nowadays it's different, there's room, but then we were about a foot apart. Otherwise Graham was a riot, so funny, the best all-round ambassador motorsport could ever have. There is still nobody who matches him today. I'd love to think I could have achieved what he achieved in Formula One. He was the Henry Cooper of Formula One and as famous as Henry Cooper. Graham had the greatest sense of humour, the wisest wit and whenever he gave a speech he made everybody fold up."

Private and public, private and public. "Yes, there were times when you didn't go near Graham but, you see, my father was like that," Bette says. "We were four girls and we'd say to my mother: 'D'you suppose Dada' – we called him Dada – 'would buy us this or let us do this?', and she'd say: 'Don't ask now, don't touch his ears' – because you know how sensitive ears are, and it meant this is the wrong time. You did the same with Graham. I could tell by looking at him it was not the time to say: 'Oh, we've a dinner dance next week, can I have some money for a ball gown?'

"Incidentally he was as generous as anybody could possibly be. I'd say I needed a dress for some event or other and he'd ask how much I wanted, and I'd say I didn't know until I'd bought it. OK, he'd say, and he'd hand me money and say 'Give me the change.' He'd ask for the change, I never gave it to him, and it became a joke between us. We used to laugh about it."

The postscript is that Damon has been driving a Williams in 1993, so well that he took a hat-trick of victories after two near misses. "Damon," Bette says, "was as much of a clown when little as Graham. He loved life, he was fun, he used to pull his sisters' legs and he still does. He does it with me – which is a part of Graham. Damon is a tease. Graham would say: 'That's enough, young man, stop teasing the girls', and Damon would continue. He'd get a smack or be thrown out of the room. Normal for a lively little lad, absolutely normal."

"I remember him," Damon says, "as a brilliant dad, great fun, but also single-minded, a stickler for table manners and all that stuff – that we should all get up and stop watching television when he came into the house, and say 'Hello', and give him a kiss. But he wasn't a strict disciplinarian, that's not the right way to describe him. He wanted you to be well behaved when you were in public, but in private you could be yourself. I wasn't frightened of him or anything like that.

"I don't think he had it in his heart to be too hard on us. I remember him reading out our school reports. We'd all end up in tears because he'd say: 'You've got to try harder', and then it would be forgotten [chuckle], forgotten the next day. He did demand 100 per cent from the people around him, but I think we were let off the hook in that respect. He was hard on my mum. When he set out to do something he did it, and in many respects that was obvious from his home life, though generally when he was at home he just wanted to relax."

The last word belongs to Bette, if only because it is amusing in a gentle, mature sort of way. "If I saw Graham with a glamorous bird I didn't know, I would walk the other way. On occasions I turned round suddenly when he was talking to glamorous birds, I'd go to move away, and he'd grab me and say: 'Bette, come on, I want to introduce you.' They'd be princess such and such or lady so and so, and they'd be absolutely exquisitely dressed, beautiful jewellery, and I'd been sitting on a pit counter for hours and looked like the wreck of the Hesperus.

"Sometimes I'd disappear because I didn't want him to feel guilty about speaking to people, whether they were glamorous birds or anyone else. Mind you, if he was talking to Fangio I'd walk up and make sure I was introduced. If he was talking to Mike Hawthorn I'd sidle up – so it was six of one and half a dozen of the other. Inevitably Graham was always photographed with good-looking women (Brinton, the casino and the bunnies etc) and inevitably I wasn't always there.

"You go to Silverstone now, no glam birds, such a shame, isn't it? I mean, all the character has gone from it, hasn't it? I love the racing, the racing is the same and as demanding as it ever was, but it's not glamorous. That's a pity because it's what made motor racing that much more exciting…"

PORTRAIT:
JIM CLARK

"Father was a hard grafter, but he had to be because he had a tough life. He was in the First World War – I think he joined the forces under age in 1914 – and suffered attack by poison gas. He was captured and sent to Gelsenkirchen, near Essen, where he spent nine months in a German coal mine as a prisoner. He kept a diary of those nine months, but we weren't allowed to read it until we were much older.

"Because of his experiences he got on very well with all sorts of people, but he was a taskmaster. I can remember my grandfather and it was the same story. He kept peppermints in his hand, but he wouldn't give them to you, you had to fight for them, prise every finger open. It was an example of how you didn't get anything without working for it. My father went about his business quietly, but that's typical of the Scottish farmer anyway."

The speaker is Mattie Calder, the first-born to James and Helen Clark. "Father came from Perthshire and mother was a Fifer. They were married in Kilmany, near Cupar in Fife." Mattie, Susan and Isobel were born in Kinrosshire, a fourth daughter, Betty, in Fife and, on March 4, 1936 a son, James. For the rest of his life he'd be known as Jim or Jimmy, no particular significance between the two.

"Our parents were from large families, all farmers, father the eldest of nine, mother the eldest of seven – no television in those days. I suppose if Jim had come along earlier there wouldn't have been all of us! A son and heir was very much wanted, something much more traditional than it is today. We didn't come to the Borders until the middle of the Second World War, 1942. There was a great movement to the Borders then and it was a bigger farm. Jim was six." Edington Mains lay near Duns on one side and Berwick on the other, more than 1,200 acres grouped round a strong, stone farmhouse. The sisters remember their mother's brother was "mad about cars and built a little red pedal car. When Jim was five or six years old he rattled around in it." Fast? You'd better believe it.

The Borders are a distinctive region, and Edington Mains is not to be confused with England, although the border is only seven miles away (tantalizingly, however, Jim would play schoolboy hockey for Northumberland – at half-back – because of the proximity to Berwick, which is actually in England).

The Borders, whose character he'd always treasure, are rolling hillsides where dark, brooding clouds may gather, narrow country lanes decorated by the distinctive tread of tractor tyres in the mud they have shed; shorn, stone-clad villages built to withstand the winters and yet holding a distinctive charm in a sort of embrace. Here and there among the woods and pastures heavy country houses loom up drives and across manicured lawns, darkened houses somehow. The talk is of sheep and cattle, staples of survival in such a region. The men who speak of them are quiet, easy in their manners, and they respect integrity as a primary virtue.

"Jim was very straight, he'd always be honest with you, always. Even when he reached Formula One we'd think he'd have some juicy things to tell us about the other drivers, but he never did. Mother had a soft spot for him, but he wasn't spoilt and he wasn't pampered. I don't think any of us were. He was naturally a reserved person. Our father could stand up and speak about anything, but our mother never would, so in that sense he was more like her."

Oswald Brewis lived, and still lives, at a farm called Little Swinton, which is about nine miles from Edington Mains. "I got to know Jimmy through his family because I was eight years older than him. I grew up more or less with his sisters, although I saw this little lad growing up. His mother was certainly very quiet, but his father had a pawky sense of humour, that's a good word to describe it. He was – what's the other word I'm looking for? – wry, if you like, very much so. He could take the mickey out of anybody with great subtlety. I had a great respect for him in that way. He was quiet, but a very intelligent man, he didn't stand fools, and Jimmy and he were similar in that respect. Jimmy had a lot of his dad in him."

"We'd no televison so we played family games and cards," Mattie says. "One of the games was to put a book on a bottle and then you had to stand on the book, and another was walking on barrels, quite large barrels. Jim could do that. We had a pond which froze over and we skated on it. There was a card game called Pounce, where you had to pick up cards fast, and another game where you had columns on a piece of paper headed Town, Country, River, Bird, Tree; you were given a letter of the alphabet and you had to fill in each column starting with that letter as quickly as you could. (Try it yourself using, say, the letter J.) All this was general in the Borders during the war because you didn't have petrol to drive around with." (See Hawthorn and Mansell.)

Almost unconsciously Mattie Calder's words contain much more than a charming period piece of family life. The games directly demanded balance and co-ordination, mental agility, precision of thought, speed of reaction, exactly what Jim Clark would demonstrate in cars, and anyway the sisters tell a lovely tale of the day when Jim was very small and a visitor came in an Alvis. While the family chatted in the farmhouse the visitor glanced out of the window and saw the Alvis on the move, but no-one driving it. Jim was, of course, but so small he couldn't be seen.

"I would say as a family we all have quick reactions and I don't mean just driving, I mean in general. Jim was always good at sport, a good eye, competitive – as we all were, I suppose. He was very small until his mid-teens and although he then built up he remained small for his age. Our parents weren't tall, either. Jim was just a normal sort of lad."

He boarded at a prep school in Edinburgh and went to Loretto. He enjoyed his sport – particularly cricket, his touch as a batsman would never leave him – and found himself becoming more and more absorbed by reading motor racing magazines. He wasn't sure why. He proved to be no kind of scholar, and wrote cryptically in his autobiography *Jim Clark at The Wheel* that "I couldn't see what use Latin was going to be for a farmer."

There's another family tale which holds interest. "Mother went up to the school, she didn't know why, only that Jim was keen she went. When she got there he sang solo, a carol I think, so as a youngster he had a good singing voice." The real interest of course is Clark balancing his natural shyness with an understandable desire for his mother to witness his singing, and we can only guess at how difficult the balance was for him to hold.

He left Loretto at 16 and worked on the farm, initially as a shepherd. Inevitably he joined the Ednam and District Young Farmers' Club where he met Scott Watson and Andrew Cowan, who would become a leading rally driver.

"My father farmed at Duns," Cowan says, "and Edington Mains was two miles down the road. I'd known him from schooldays although I went to a local school and he went to Edinburgh. He was athletic, very good at the Young Farmers' sports day, ran very quickly, he played hockey, he shepherded his sheep: just a normal young farmer.

"Berwick and District Motor Club was one of the finest in the country at that time, extremely successful, well run, with some famous drivers in British racing circles as members. Brothers called the Stoddarts used to enter the Monte Carlo Rally in Standard Eights and I'd rush home from school and listen to the Monte report on the radio to see how they were getting on. Just after the war one of the first British circuits to be opened was Winfield – an airfield just about six miles from Berwick on the Scottish side – and the Club ran races there. The Club met in a function room over a pub called The Rum Puncheon in Berwick.

"It seemed that everyone who was a member of the Ednam Young Farmers' also became a member of the Motor Club. That's obviously why I joined, why Jim joined, in a natural progression. The Borders is all country people, a rural area, and most folk have agriculteral connections anyway. We were the same age. In those days you could apply for your driving test before you were 17. We joined the club the day after we passed our tests and got our licences. [There is, however, some confusion over this as we shall see.] Of course we'd both been driving from when we were *that* height, but tractors and all sorts, not officially on public roads."

Jim's father bought a Rover and passed his Sunbeam-Talbot on to him.

"The first time I saw him around," Scott Watson says, "I thought the bloody stupid idiot, he's not going to live very long. He drove so fast on the roads. Everybody said he was an idiot. Only when I started going in the car with him did I realized he was very, very safe, too, an incredibly confidence-inspiring driver. I'd sit beside him anywhere perfectly happily and it was sitting with him that you began to realize the natural talent everybody talks about.

"It was apparent on the open road. You'd be chattering away and all of a sudden you'd sense him easing off along a straight bit, but you couldn't see why. A second or two later you'd spot somebody coming down a side road a long way off. His forward vision was so good, his anticipation so extraordinary, that he thought far ahead all the time – but not consciously, subconsciously. He was smooth. You would be travelling fast, but without any feeling in the least bit of it being fast."

Clark also did some navigating on local rallies, sometimes for another local farmer Billy Potts, who remembers the 1955 Scottish Rally very vividly. "We were coming down through the Great Glen, it was a nice wide, open road, a grand summer's day. I said: 'Would you like a shot?', and he was just about in the driving seat before the car came to a stop. No sooner had we started than an XK

120 came flying past. I could see Jimmy's foot go flat to the floor. I was saying 'Now steady Jim, steady.' I had an Austin-Healey, and it was a pretty fast machine with all the modifications and capable of about 120, 130 miles an hour. Jim wound it up to over a hundred and after about five minutes you just had to sit back in the seat and admire a master at his work."

Brewis adds significantly to this. "I never really knew him until he started rallying at the Berwick and District Motor Club. Billy Potts drove most of them with Jimmy navigating. The first time we saw his potential as a quick driver was on the Scottish Rally when on one or two occasions Billy let him drive between the special stages. He had an astounding natural quickness."

Mind you, as Scott Watson attests, "Jimmy was the world's worst passenger ever. He didn't navigate me very often, he didn't enjoy being in the passenger seat. One rally way up in Banffshire demonstrated this, public road stuff involving a lot of map reading. We came to a section which was on four adjoining Ordinance Survey maps and we were going from one map to the other, back and forwards. It was very difficult navigating and Jimmy wasn't awfully bright at it, so he ended up kneeling on the front seat – no safety belts in those days – with the maps spread on the back yelling 'Left, right, straight on.' I thought fine until he suddenly said 'Crossroads'. No crossroads. He said 'There is, there must be.' I screeched to a stop.

"Because I was quite good at map reading it was perfectly clear we were in the middle of moorland, but supposed to be in a densely wooded area. I said: 'We're miles away.' I looked at the maps and spotted we were 12 miles off route. We'd been leading the class and really doing quite well; I turned the car round and drove it as nobody ever should have, absolutely, absolutely Harry Flatters. Because I'd quickly pictured in my mind where we had to go Jimmy didn't have to do any navigating. I glanced across at him and he was crouched down in the seat with a map over his eyes petrified, getting whiter and whiter. It was a 20-mile section, we'd been the 12 miles off it so we did 32 miles and reached the checkpoint on time. I came into it sliding sideways. He was too far gone to even grab the route card so I had to and hand it to him.

"The better a driver you are the worse a passenger you are, and the converse is probably true, which is why I enjoyed driving with Jimmy so much, but from his point of view he'd know that if a real emergency happened I might not be able to cope as well as he could."

The Berwick and District Motor Club was "a case of competing just with family cars," Cowan says. "At this stage we never bought special cars. We did it for the pleasure of the thing, handicap races, sportscar races, saloon car races, not so many open-wheelers I think. The most interesting were handicaps, just to make up the numbers. You could be racing against an ERA in an Austin Seven because the handicapping was properly balanced and properly organized."

Clark would subsequently explain that once he had his driving test he was curious to have a race, curious to see what it felt like. "He wasn't 21 and I had to sign the form so he could get a competition licence," sister Isobel says. "Mother and father were certainly not going to sign it. Father felt it wasn't productive." And of course Jim was the only son, the heir, the one to keep the farm going. Isobel signed and "that's how it began, but just for fun."

On June 3, 1956 he took the Sunbeam-Talbot across country through the solid towns of Kelso and Jedburgh to Hawick, turned left off the main street onto a contorting road into the countryside. He turned off this after three or four miles and passed under a tall, arched viaduct, ascended a track and found himself amidst two rolling hillsides cutting in a V to a stream. A farmhouse – typical of the Borders, darkened stone – lay partially camouflaged by trees. On the hillsides the detrius of the military lingered, concrete floors, Nissen huts and so forth. Stobs Camp had indeed been an army camp.

He was to take part in a sprint for cars over 2,000cc, the 'course' a ribbon of tarmac with saplings on one side and which slipped down the right-hand hillside to a small bridge at the bottom. What happened thereafter is a matter of misty legend, as you might anticipate of such a humble, pleasant, seemingly inconsequential event so long ago. Some say he was the only competitor because an elderly Vauxhall didn't make the start, some say he was beaten by a 1600 Porsche. The late and respected statistician, John Taylor (in *Jim Clark* by Doug Nye, Hazleton) records Clark as winning for the simplest of reasons. Only he finished.

Clark made no mention of Stobs Camp in his autobiography, contenting himself by saying he competed "in a number of local rallies and driving test meetings." He did however devote considerable space to an earlier event at Winfield which the Berwick and District Motor Club organized and which he won. Since he was not yet a member of the Club they withheld the victory, something which annoyed him so much he delayed joining for what he said was over a year.

Without dispute Clark's first race was at a place called Crimond, near Aberdeen, two weeks after the Stobs Camp sprint. As with so many other 'circuits', Crimond proved to be a disused airfield base which Clark would remember as wild and windswept. He'd gone there with Scott Watson to act as mechanic. Scott Watson owned a DKW Sonderklasse which he'd entered for the sportscar race and a handicap saloon race, too. Scott Walson had no thoughts of Clark racing, and Clark certainly hadn't broached the idea to him. In fact, as Clark would say, "I used to strip the bumpers off his car and mask over the headlights and so on because I was keen on racing, but never thinking I'd ever be able to get into a car because my parents were so much against it."

In the morning Scott Watson went out to practice, and when he came back said on impulse – taking pity on Clark – "OK, you have a try". "He stood there, oh, you know, chewing his finger nails. I said: 'Go on, you are far enough away from home, your parents will not hear about it. Put my helmet on. You're in the sportscar practice and no-one will realize'." Clark, excited, decided to take a chance.

He pulled on Scott Watson's helmet. "You didn't even have to wear crash helmets until 1957 or 1958," Scott Watson says. "I had a motorcycle Corker and that's what Jimmy wore." It was black with two air vents each side and a leather strap under the chin; it looked like the sort of thing girls wear on horses and, on its inside, it had printed *The Corker, made by J Compton and Sons and Webb Ltd., London E3*. It squeezed tight to the shape of the head and nipped.

"He went out in the practice session for sportscars and after five laps he was 3 seconds quicker than I had been after I'd been going round for about half an hour." This persuaded Scott Watson that he himself wasn't very good and very likely never would be, just as it persuaded him that Clark was good. "I said: 'You go into the sportscar race, you won't win anything, but you'll enjoy yourself'."

(Amusing aside: the handicaps worked on the basis of practice times and the officials now approached Scott Watson and made a very valid point. How, they wondered, had he been so quick practising for the sportscars and so slow for the saloons? They hadn't noticed it was Clark in the sportscars – same helmet – and Scott Watson wasn't about to tell them. The officals concluded that Scott Watson had gone deliberately slowly and promptly rehandicapped him. "My handicap was totally cooked after that, I was scuppered.")

Scott Watson insisted that Clark take part in the sportscar race and he did. "I can remember sitting in the DKW waiting for the race to begin," Clark wrote. "I felt I was on hallowed ground because racing to me was something almost sacred, that was not for me to touch." Terrified he'd make a fool of himself he finished last, but as Scott Watson says, "when he came back in he'd obviously enjoyed himself."

He had.

The telephone at Edington Mains rang. Isobel remembers that. "Our father didn't know Jim was at Crimond, and when one of our relatives rang and said 'Jim did well today' he said: 'What are you talking about?'" Scott Watson remembers that. "We didn't realize that by pure coincidence a whole lot of Jimmy's cousins had been at the meeting and the message reached his parents before he got home. I was hauled up before them in the nicest possible way. I said: 'Honestly, it was a little meeting, no real risk. He's very good and I'm sure he would like to have another go.' They said: 'No, no, no.'"

Clark did not race again until September 30, in four sprints at Winfield, two with the DKW, two with the Sunbeam-Talbot. He won all four. A week later he raced both cars at a meeting at Brunton Beadnell, on the Northumbrian coastline. By now Scott Watson had founded the Border Motor Racing Club.

"I spent two days with an old Land Rover and I visited every airfield on the Ordnance Survey map between the Tay and the Tyne to see if I could find an alternative to Charterhall. The Charterhall Motor Club told us we weren't to have any of our own meetings there. We weren't going to stand for that, we wanted our own meetings and eventually we found this Beadnell place, an airfield right on the side of the main Edinburgh-London railway line. It had been built during the war as a Coastal Command station, one of the first to be given an asphalt surface.

"I thought it was brilliant, a very good perimeter track, all the right shaped bends – another Silverstone. We weren't using the runways, only the perimeter. It belonged to the Duke of Northumberland but was run by a tenant farmer. We got hold of the Duke, got hold of the farmer, and said could we have a meeting on it? They granted permission.

"The RAC wouldn't give permission to run a full meeting, you had to have a high speed trial first. You did an agreed number of laps as quickly as you could and came back in and someone else would go out. You were not racing against other people. Jimmy drove the Sunbeam, he drove the DKW and he thoroughly enjoyed himself. He was brilliant at it. We were able to say to his parents that it hadn't actually been a race meeting..."

Clark competed no more in 1956, but "couldn't wait" for 1957. He raced the DKW at Charterhall (fourth), the Sunbeam at Charterhall again (eighth) and travelled with Scott Watson to Silverstone for a six-hour race, but couldn't be persuaded out onto the Grand Prix circuit. He felt he wasn't ready. By now, Scott Watson insists, his parents knew he was racing, although because Scott Watson arrived at Edington Mains with his ordinary saloon car they reasoned it couldn't be really fast, really dangerous racing.

Farming remained the core of Clark's life as it was his father's. "Jim's parents were fantastic people, great, great people," Cowan says, "successful farmers of grain and stock, sheep and cattle, very gentle and unassuming. When they went to market to buy cattle it was JC1 and JC2 – JC1 father, JC2 Jimmy – and that's how they were known when they bid in the ring. Young Jim had to buy sheep and cattle for the farm.

"The race tracks were nearly all aerodromes, old airfield circuits with usually more than one runway and a bit of perimeter. Some circuits used the perimeter, others the runway. For some reason a bit of perimeter at Charterhall couldn't be used so they ran on the main runway damn nearly a mile long. It was marked by straw bales and 5-gallon drums with a bit of sand in the bottom. The meetings there were shared with motorbike riders and you'd see the bike lads leaning over, their shoulders knocking these 5-gallon drums flying. They must have had bruises all over."

Happy, innocent days. "I acquired a Goggomobil," Scott Watson says," because I'd had a dreadful accident and my leg was in plaster for six months. I needed to be mobile somehow or other. You virtually sat on the floor in it and I found I could drive the damn thing with my leg in the plaster by shoving my body back and forward to work the pedal – you sat almost level with it. I ran it for one winter and Jimmy decided to do some driving tests, so I lent it to him.

"Before the Mini arrived, the Goggomobil was an incredible little thing, about 8ft long and 4ft wide, a rear engine, rear-wheel drive and a crash gearbox. Instead of the gearchange being normal it went first across to second, down to third and across to fourth, great fun to drive and Jimmy really threw it around. Part of the tests would be that you drove into a garage, did a three-point turn and came out again. The Goggomobil was actually so small he simply spun it round and came back out again, everybody roaring their heads off."

Autosport reported just such a meeting on May 3, 1957. "The sensation of the afternoon was the inclusion of a miniature car award, and many hardened members of the Ford Anglia brigade could just gasp in astonishment at the antics of Jimmy Clark and Ian Scott Watson sharing the latter's Goggomobil. It says a lot for Jimmy's driving when we record that he came second in the class to Jim McKay's Ford Anglia."

Scott Watson knew the editor of a Scottish motoring magazine, *Top Gear*. Scott Watson said he intended to go to Le Mans and watch the 24-hour race. The editor said: 'Take the press pass and do the report.' I said Jimmy was going and the editor said: 'Give him the photographer's pass and he can do the photos.'

"I had another friend with me, too, and from Paris to Le Mans we had a dice with a Peugeot, we in the DKW, Jimmy driving, and it was really hairy, Jimmy at his best. The third in the party – my friend – was absolutely petrified. He sat in the back seat with his hands covering his face. Eventually these people in the Peugeot came alongside and signalled to us and we stopped for lunch. They spoke a little bit of English and we had a drink with them. Then they went on for the start of the race and we decided we'd have something to eat, thinking we wouldn't get very much at Le Mans. We couldn't really speak a work of French, we just said *manger* and they brought us I don't know how many courses. The race started at 4 o'clock and we didn't get there until half past. Jimmy wasn't a bad photographer and the magazine used a selection of his and mine. We got one of Tony Brooks' ill-fated Aston Martin inverted in the sand at Tertre Rouge after crashing..."

This visit to Europe – a holiday – served other purposes. "Before Jimmy started serious racing we made a point of searching out tracks and having a look at them. I'd just got a new wide-body DKW because I'd written the previous one off. By now my leg had healed. Initially we went over to the Nurburgring, Jimmy drove it one lap round and I drove it one lap. I remember having to go down to second gear to get it up some of the hills.

"It was the first time we had seen the Nurburgring and Jimmy drove very, very quickly despite the fact there were three of us and our luggage and the DKW was still a little bit tight. He thoroughly enjoyed it although because he had passengers – us – he wasn't able to go round with quite the same abandon as if he had been on his own, and he didn't want to damage the car because we had a long way to go. We looked in at Reims and we looked in at Rouen on the way back from Le Mans. We were fascinated by seeing these places, having read all about them."

(Glancing forward, this habit of tasting tracks would assume a very sad and ironic aspect; but that was 11 years away.)

Cowan captures the spirit of the time. "You could see something in the way he drove even in those early days, yes for sure, especially in the handicap races. The big event of the year for the Berwick and District Club was the Winfield sprint – a timed event, one car at a time through a couple of bends and a chicane built of straw bales in the middle of the straight – three really quick corners. A lot of good guys used to come, good quick guys with good cars, and Jimmy could beat them with his Sunbeam-Talbot because of his commitment through the corners. He could get into anything, didn't matter what, and become the one to beat. He could make the car do just impossible things. He never tried to explain it, he was a very, very modest person who laughed, enjoyed himself in a car. I mean, this Sunbeam-Talbot was a most unlikely racing car, no special seats or anything. He plonked himself in the corner of the driving seat – he wasn't very big – and simply drove it, but he could make it talk.

"Other more experienced people like Ian Scott Watson noticed early that Jimmy was something special. The DKW which Ian had was quite a quick little car in its class, and of course in handicap races – I don't remember what it was, 800cc or something – Jimmy obviously got good handicaps. It was a two-stroke, you would wind it up and it really performed quite well. Ian obviously recognized that Jimmy was as the rest of the world saw him turn out to be and bought a Porsche – registration UUL 442 – which had belonged to Billy Cotton. It was the first quick car that Jimmy drove."

By September, Scott Watson decided Clark needed something more than the DKW, he knew Michael Burn, sales director of Frazer Nash, who distributed Porsches, and contacted him. Burn drove up to the Borders with a Porsche, bringing a journalist for the run. "There was a hell of a party and I bought the thing on a spot decision, which I took far too damn often," Scott Watson says. "Burn and the journalist stayed overnight and set off the next day to drive my DKW back down. The Porsche cost something like £1,100, quite a lot in those days and for me a very big investment, but I'd begun to think it was worth having a car Jimmy could really do something with; and anyway I wanted something a bit more interesting to drive myself.

"When Jimmy heard what I had done he thought I was mad. He kept saying we couldn't race that car but we did, and it was probably the first major turning point in Jimmy's career." Scott Watson entered Clark for three events at

Charterhall and he finished third, second and first. "Jock McBain, who ran Border Reivers, drove his Zephyr that day and suffered a comprehensive defeat by Jimmy. He got the two of us together a month or so later."

Distant dialogue...

McBain: I've decided we should get a car for Jimmy to drive in 1958. Ian, if you organize and run it under the Border Reivers banner, I'll put the money up.

Clark: Oh, I don't know.

Scott Watson: Yes, go on Jimmy, it's about time you did get something proper to drive.

"I think he was a bit surprised when Jock bought a D-type Jaguar. What I did for Jimmy, and what I feel proud to have done for Jimmy, is instilled a confidence in him in the very early days. I kept going on at him to make him believe in himself. He didn't. He had this sort of 'Oh well, really I'll pack it all up now' attitude."

Distant dialogue...

Scott Watson: Come on Jimmy, you can do it, you'll be World Champion some day.

Clark: Don't be so bloody stupid. Stop talking nonsense. I think I'll just have to pack it all in.

Scott Watson: Come on Jimmy, you can do it.

"Then," Scott Watson says, "he'd go out in a car and prove it to himself, although that was in small phases. He'd come back and say *'Hmm...'*"

Across 1957 Clark raced the Porsche four more times, won twice – once at Charterhall, his first circuit victory – and finished second twice. "I saw him in the Porsche many times," Cowan says, "and I competed against him many times. By today's standard the Porsche would be quite slow, but then it was spectacular. We'd go anywhere for a sprint or a handicap and every weekend there was something on. In the Porsche he was hairy, really hairy, but totally under control. He did that with any car, although he could drive every car to the limit and beyond if necessary.

"There are myths that on the road he was indecisive when it came to, say, a road junction. No, no, no that is not true. No, no. [However, in the last chapter of this book we shall have an hilarious contradiction to that from Jackie Stewart, no less.] Everywhere he went was flat-out, that was the only thing, and we loved it, we didn't care. I remember running into a flock of sheep one night coming home from Edinburgh.

"We'd been to the Biggar show dance and it was the middle of a foggy night. Jimmy had a Triumph TR2 or TR3 and, oh aye, everywhere was flat-out. We'd be doing well over a hundred on a long, straight stretch of road, and suddenly here were these sheep and it looked impossible to me to avoid them. He did it somehow and we got through without damaging them or ourselves, never mind killing any. That was Jim Clark, oh aye, that was his car control. Somebody like me, I'd probably have ploughed them.

"As a passenger I was never frightened. We were all the same age, you didn't know fear. We weren't wearing seat belts, that was the amazing thing. We just sat there and got on with it. His Sunbeam-Talbot was driven on the limit all the time, whether on the road or a race track and, you know, beautifully controlled."

"We'd go to London quite a lot for weekends," Brewis says, "and sitting beside him in the Porsche was quite an experience. He loved the wet, you see. It was difficult for me to cope with, I couldn't watch it, I had to get my head down.

I hate to tell you how quickly we used to go down to London. In fact I won't tell you." Well, how long did the journey take? "That's it, I am not going to say because you can work out the speed, but his average was just about the car's potential maximum." Brewis, however, sensed Clark had "a little bit left in reserve because in those situations he never drove ten-tenths, it just felt like ten-tenths to me."

The D-type Jaguar changed everything across 1958. "On Good Friday," Scott Watson says, "there was a meeting at an airfield near York called Full Sutton [now a state prison], an American base just de-acquisitioned, again perimeter rather than up and down runways, and very, very fast. The RAC ran the meeting. The idea was Jimmy would share the driving with Jimmy Somervail [yet another farmer].

"The Borders were covered in snow and ice and Somervail was supposed to provide the lorry to take the car down. He phoned and said that in this snow no way the meeting will go ahead. I rang the organizers and they said: 'It's frosty down here but no snow, it's dry and the meeting is definitely on.'

"Late in the evening before the meeting Jimmy said: 'We'll get the farm lorry.' I went to Edington Mains and Jimmy filled the radiator with water because it had been drained off (to stop the radiators freezing solid). We loaded the car onto it, reached Berwick and the damn lorry's engine seized. Jimmy hadn't realized it *hadn't* been drained after all, and when he'd turned the tap to stop the water running out he'd actually turned it on. So – what the hell are we going to do now? He said: 'I am going to the meeting.' We found a garage in Berwick which had a ramp, used that to push the D-Type onto the ground. He put a flat hat on, a pair of goggles, I jumped into the Porsche and we went in convoy all the way to Full Sutton.

"Headlamps were virtually non-existent on the D-type so I went in front to light up the way until we got to the one and only bit of dual carriageway, just north of Borough Bridge on the A1. The road was pretty straight, I waved Jimmy through because I thought the points were probably getting a bit oiled up and on the dual carriageway he would be reasonably safe. He came past me at about 120, 130, 140 miles an hour and vanished into the distance...

"We slept in the Porsche outside the race circuit because it was the first car I'd owned with reclining front seats. Jimmy went out in practice and he was bloody quick. And bloody quick in the racing, two firsts" – for racing cars over 500cc and unlimited sportscars. He was also sixth in the production sportscars unlimited, a performance Scott Watson evaluates as "quite something".

Scott Watson cast his eye further afield, to a couple of events in Spa, Belgium, attracted by the fact that Clark could drive the Porsche in the GT specials under 2,000cc and the Jaguar for sportscars over 1,500cc. Scott Watson remembers Clark as "petrified" by the very thought of this, particularly since he'd be competing against established drivers like Masten Gregory (his hero), Olivier Gendebien in a Ferrari, Lucien Bianchi in another Ferrari, Peter Whitehead (Lister Jaguar) and Archie Scott-Brown in another Lister Jaguar. Clark hadn't seen Spa before.

He shared a garage with Gregory, and the very experienced driver Jack Fairman took him round on a conducted tour in a Volkswagen, showed him braking points – which Clark didn't like, preferring to find his own – and informed him where people had been killed. The race started wet and he went well in the Porsche but fell back to fifth when it dried. In the Jaguar he was extremely nervous, felt his way carefully round and only allowed himself to exploit the car late in the race. He subsequently confessed he'd been frightened right through it – something compounded by the death of Scott-Brown, who had crashed and his Jaguar had caught fire.

Clark never liked Spa and some people say his feelings about it were much, much stronger than that.

A week later he went back to Full Sutton. "Again Somervail didn't bother to come," Scott Watson says. "Jimmy became the first person in the UK ever to win a race at an average speed of over 100 miles an hour in a sportscar. By this time Gregor Grant and Francis Penn (of *Autosport*) were beginning to recognize Jimmy, and 'Jenks' – Denis Jenkinson, the noted motor racing journalist – had also spotted him. Frazer Nash asked me if I would manage the Porsche team in the six-hour race at Silverstone. We had Jenks and Jimmy and myself and Lord Portman and Pat Surtees' father. Jimmy and I shared one car and the others all had their own. Jimmy was brilliant." However, he and Scott Watson finished 22nd, a mechanical problem, no doubt, and now long forgotten.

Driving the D-type Clark met Innes Ireland. "My father was a veterinary surgeon," Ireland says, "who used to attend to cattle and sheep at the Clark farm. I didn't know Jimmy until I raced against him at Charterhall. I wondered who the hell he was. He was driving a white D-type, a short-nosed D-type, and of course the Ecurie Ecosse Tojeiro Jaguar I had was a quicker car. I overdid the braking – my own fault, I wasn't under pressure – and the car snapped round and spun off. I still managed to win the race from Jimmy, but not by as much as I anticipated I would have done. I thought 'He's driving that old nail and he must be bloody good.'"

We've already seen what happened at Brands Hatch in Echoes of Autumn, and seen too what happened when Clark raced Chapman on Boxing Day 1958. "Those two things together," Scott Watson says, "clearly impressed Chapman immensely, but the race in the Elite more than anything else because Chapman was trying his damndest and if it hadn't been for that little shunt he wouldn't have passed Jimmy. The funny thing was that Jimmy had had the season of driving the D-type and Chapman didn't know. He remembered me, but obviously he'd not had time to look at *Autosport* or anything else. He was quite unaware of what Border Reivers were or what Jimmy had been doing in the big hairy Jaguar. I know it was very different from a Lotus Elite, but tremendous experience, in fact a sight more difficult to drive than the Formula Junior that Chapman would ask Jimmy to drive first..."

There would be time for that, but not yet. For 1959 Scott Watson bought the Elite, and Border Reivers, seeing that the Lister-Jaguar went quicker than the D-types, bought one secondhand.

Clark went down to Luton to collect it and, as he recounted in his autobiography, however cramped the cockpit area he delighted in many aspects of the car, not least on the return journey blitzing past a Ford Thunderbird, which obviously belonged to an American serviceman, at about 150 miles an hour near Huntingdon.

Brewis, who only travelled as a passenger once in this Lister-Jaguar, describes it as "hairy. Jimmy loved the opposite-lock stuff although he only did that on race tracks, and it's where he really learnt it. He loved the car because its roadholding was considerably better than the D-type's. I've some wonderful photos I took with him on opposite lock in a corner. He was very much a Fangio man, Stirling Moss he had a great respect for, and they were both magical at that type of driving."

At events here and there – Mallory Park, Oulton, Aintree, Charterhall, Goodwood, Rufforth, Stobs Camp – he'd drive the Lister or the Porsche or the Elite, and he began to win consistently. "That first year when he got the Elite – 1959 – I did return to do a bit of competitive driving in the Porsche," Scott Watson says. "The agreement was he would let me drive the Porsche when I wanted to in odd small competitions and he'd do the Elite."

As mentioned earlier, after the Boxing Day race at Brands Hatch the year before, Chapman had suggested Scott Watson should take an Elite to Le Mans for Clark to race there. Lotus provided the Elite and Border Reivers entered it. "Before we went there we did a national meeting [at Oulton Park]. The Elite was all race-prepared, but it was one of the early model bodyshells and the diff housing began to pull out of the shell. They weren't reinforced enough for the mounting points round the diff. I saw point blank there was no way Jimmy was going to drive that car at Le Mans. [He finished 10th at Oulton.]

"I phoned up Colin Chapman and said I didn't know what we were going to do but I wouldn't allow Jimmy or Tommy Dickson to take on Le Mans with it. He said: 'I'll tell you what, your entry has been accepted and we'll give you a car [another car, of course], but we want to nominate the second driver. We don't want Tommy, we want John Whitmore' – an Englishman who had raced Elites. I said: 'OK, fair enough' as a compromise, although naturally I felt sorry a bit about not being able to keep it all Scottish. Colin then said: 'If at the end of the race the car is still in one piece we'll do a deal and you can buy it.' That was the arrangement.

"The car wasn't ready, partly because Lotus had just moved out to Cheshunt and hadn't their production line running. We had an old bus which we'd converted into a transporter and we set off for Le Mans via Cheshunt to pick up the Elite. When we arrived at Cheshunt we were given a bog standard Elite, the very first one off the assembly line, totally un-race-prepared. We were also given 32 boxes of bits and pieces to convert it to racing trim.

"We had to do the whole of that in the filthy old paddock at Le Mans because we hadn't a garage booked. Jimmy and I went down in the Porsche and Jock McBain and another young farmer took the bus. We had a back-up team of young farmers, no mechanics at all except for Jock (a garage owner, incidentally). Jimmy's brother-in-law Alec Calder acted as one 'mechanic,' the rest were friends. With Jock's guidance, Jimmy and I and these amateurs converted that car in two and a half days working round the clock, and it proved to be probably the most reliable Elite there ever was! We drilled and wired every nut and bolt that could possibly have shaken loose right through the diff housing, the sump.

"Jimmy took the first stint and did very well, Whitcombe got in and did equally well. He brought the car back for Jimmy to take over and the car wouldn't restart. We looked at it: obviously the starter motor had gone. We couldn't see a way of getting into this bloody thing because of the carburettors and the manifold, but Willie Griffith, ex-chief mechanic of Team Lotus, was running an Elite for a couple of French film stars in the pit next to us. They'd retired.

"He said: 'I foresaw this.' He had a seven-jointed socket set specially made for it. We lost three-quarters of an hour, but we got it off. Of course you were not suppose to replace a damaged part unless it was one you were carrying on the car. Darkness had fallen by this time. When the starter motor came off Alex threw it onto the pit lane counter so that it rolled over the back out of sight. I said: 'You silly bugger', and picked up a new one at the back, pretended to repair it, gave it back and off went the car.

"The same thing happened again at dawn, but a French official sat on the pit counter next door and we thought he'd see what we were doing if we were not careful. We had a pail of soapy water, we pretended the starter motor was still hot and threw it in to cool it – but we'd put another one in below which I picked out. It was refitted and the Elite set off again. The official gave me a hell of a whack on the back and said '*Ah, very good acting!*' He knew, he'd seen all right, but we were a Scottish team and the French loved a Scottish team. By that time, too, relatively few cars remained and they wouldn't want to disqualify us. The Elite finished 10th overall, second in its class. That car went so quickly it was 20 seconds a lap faster than any of the other Elites."

Brewis went to Le Mans that year, one of four in a Ford Anglia, "all mechanics in a loose way [familiar with farm vehicles!]. It was a shoe-string outfit and everyone worked on the car. It was a big race with big names, but Jimmy took it fine, he never seemed to be apprehensive. He'd go quiet and withdraw into himself, but I don't think it was apprehension, more concentration. I certainly don't think he was ever frightened. Le Mans was not his kind of circuit, especially in the Elite, so from that point of view he didn't enjoy it that much. His particular skills were not required at Le Mans, but he was easy on his motor cars so we always had an advantage in that respect. That year at Le Mans was a lovely adventure by a bunch of amateurs who wanted to enjoy themselves."

Meanwhile, as Scott Watson says, "Lucas couldn't undersand what had caused the problem with the starter motors until they analyzed it and found metal fatigue. They said it could only have been caused by a vibration failure, and that in turn could have been caused by over-revving the thing by 500rpm. We discovered the mechanical rev-counter we had was reading 500rpm slow so that we'd done the 24 hours at 500 over the limit.

"Willie Griffith stripped it down for us because we had a meeting the next weekend and we found nothing wrong with the engine – perfect – so the following week Climax lifted their limit on Elite engines by 500rpm." (That next meeting, at Zandvoort, Holland, the back axle seized.)

By August Clark was paired with Masten Gregory in the Tourist Trophy at Goodwood in a Tojeiro-Jaguar. "Fascinating", Scott Watson says, "not least because Masten really was Jimmy's hero. Masten was number one and Jimmy effectively the back-up, so the car was set up for Masten and Jimmy had to drive it the best he could. He said it was set up horribly. 'I can't understand it, I'm quicker than Masten' and I said: 'Well, it doesn't surprise me', but Jimmy couldn't believe it, he couldn't get to grips with the idea that he was.

"Jimmy ran fourth, then Masten got in and went back down through the field to eighth or ninth. It was a nice sunny day and Jimmy and I sat on the grass in the corner of the paddock waiting for his turn. He couldn't face looking at the race from the pits because it was so depressing. Years later Roy Salvadori told us what happened. Going into Woodcote, Masten came past him climbing out of the cockpit. He made no attempt to brake or drive round the corner, he drove straight into the bank, comprehensively wrecking the car. Clearly from the post mortem the brakes hadn't failed and I don't know why it happened. Perhaps he'd gone into the corner too fast, panicked and decided to climb out. He was sitting on the bodywork at the back of the seat when he hit the bank. Graham Gauld got a photograph of him 10 feet in the air (Gauld says the photograph is slightly blurred, and no wonder.) He would have been killed outright if he'd still been in the car. When he landed he broke his arm." The wrecked car burst into flames and a pall of black smoke drifted from it. Fire marshals put it out although – a sign of the times – they wore no protective clothing.

Once Clark knew Gregory had no worse than the broken arm he mused that hmm...hmm...hadn't he lapped quicker than Gregory? Hadn't the event contained Stirling Moss, Wolfgang von Trips, Tony Brooks, Cliff Allison, Dan Gurney and...hmm...hadn't he been enjoying himself in amongst them?

If the man still lacked self-confidence, and maybe he did, Goodwood changed that. Retrospectively, he recognized it himself.

In the autumn of 1959, Reg Parnell, running the Aston Martin team which intended to compete in Formula One in 1960, kept an experienced eye open for potential drivers. He approached Clark who initially said "No" because he didn't think he could cope – the only time he had handled a single-seater was the Lotus Formula Two car for those few laps in the testing at Brands, autumn 1958.

Parnell journeyed to the Borders and Mattie Calder remembers "Jock McBain coming to the house with him and they were discussing the possibilities. The fact that Reg came up and said Jimmy had the potential clinched it with my father." Clark tested the Aston at Goodwood in January 1960, and as it happened Mike Costin belted round in a Lotus Formula Junior that day, too. Scott-Watson had been talking to Chapman about Clark joining Lotus in Formula One; Parnell agreed to Clark having a belt himself in the Formula Junior car and he adored it. Parnell further agreed that Clark could do Junior races in it if they didn't clash with the Grands Prix – and do Grands Prix for Lotus if Aston Martin weren't competing. They never did compete.

The matrix which held the Sixties tight had been forged: Lotus, Chapman, Clark.

"You've to remember that the time it all started Colin still raced, albeit intermittently," Peter Warr says. "Colin recognized very quickly whatever it was in Jimmy that made him really special because that was one of the things Colin could do. It may have been born out of the fact that he knew what racing cars did, particularly what they did at the limit. When Colin drove, quite a few people reckoned he was almost as good as Moss. His career stopped when he had a shunt in the Vanwall at Reims (he ran into the back of Hawthorn during practice, his *team-mate* Hawthorn, at this French Grand Prix in July 1956.) The insurance company said: 'Whoa, hang on a minute, you've got a big business, you'd better quit all this.'

"But Colin had the ability to recognize in others what he knew it took *and* Jimmy recognized in Colin somebody who understood what he – Jimmy – was talking about. It brought them very close very quickly at – what shall we say? – a technical level in terms of being able to understand what made cars quick and to describe this. What happened, of course, was that inevitably they were in a tight working relationship. Colin was a very demanding guy. He didn't demand in the sense 'I want you to do this' or 'I want you to do that,' he demanded an absolute commitment from his drivers.

"He wanted always to work on the basis that if you weren't quickest it's got to be something wrong with the car because the driver is the best there is. Very quickly this respect for what Jimmy could actually do – which was, you know, totally unbelievable – grew and grew. Again quickly, the respect became mutual and they built it into a very close personal friendship, and the better the friendship became the better the relationship became."

In Formula Junior Clark won – and won. On the weekend of the Monaco Grand Prix he took pole in the Junior race. *Autosport* reported that he "dashed into the lead and when the traffic jam sorted itself out at the Gasometer his Lotus was chased by Ashdown (Lola), Lincoln (Cooper) and Trevor (Lotus). The little cars made a brave show as they streamed up the hill to Casino; outside the famous 'money box' Geoff Duke spun his Gemini and Tim Parnell hit the barriers in avoiding him. Clark began to pull away at the rate of over a second a lap. Clark was getting round in under 1 minute 47 seconds and by the ninth lap had already 'doubled' last year's winner, Michael May (Stanguellini). With five laps to go Clark stopped at the Gasometer turn; something had happened in the ignition department."

In the magazine's Pit and Paddock section of the same issue this appeared:
ZANDVOORT – WHIT MONDAY.
Third leg of the World Championship takes place at Zandvoort on 6th June. At the time of going to press the provisional entries were
BRM: Bonnier, G. Hill, Gurney.
Cooper-Climax (works): Brabham, McLaren.
Cooper-Climax (Yeoman): Brooks, Bristow.
Team Lotus: Ireland, Stacey, Surtees.
Walker Equipe: Stirling Moss (Lotus).
Reventlow Automobiles: Reventlow, Daigh (Scarab).
Centro-Sud: Burgess, Gregory (Cooper-Maserati).
Aston Martin: Salvadori, Trintignant.
Ferrari: Von Trips, P. Hill, Ginther.

Surtees alternated where possible with bike racing. The week of Zandvoort he prepared himself to race his MV Agusta in the 500cc World Championship on the Isle of Man. Chapman decided to put Clark into the car. "Unhappily," *Autosport* reported, "the race was run in rather an atmosphere of tension: the organizers agreed to pay starting money to the fastest fifteen qualifiers but stated that twenty machines could come to the line. In consequence Lance Reventlow's Scarabs were withdrawn and Salvadori's fuel-injected Aston Martin was sent back to England. (Reventlow was a young millionaire). This was a great pity as the crowd had expected to see both the American and British marques compete." (Sign of the times: after first practice Salvadori was 4 seconds off the time Moss set for provisional pole, Moss himself tried the Aston and was 6 seconds off his own time.)

Of the 17 starters Clark, prudently feeling his way in, qualified 11th. "At 10 laps Moss was pressing Brabham really hard and Gurney was having a go at the two Lotuses [of Ireland and Moss]. Then, coming past the pits, Gurney lost his rear brakes, danced all over the road and, to the horror of the onlookers, dived over the top at the end of the straight. The American did all he knew to avoid the spectators but unfortunately the BRM collected part of the barbed wire fence and a youth was fatally injured. Everyone thought that Gurney could not possibly have survived such a spectacular accident, but the lanky Californian got away with a sprained wrist and a cut hand."

Meanwhile…

"At 15 laps Brabham led Moss by half a second, and the race average was 155.825km/h. Stacey had temporarily taken third place and Jim Clark had passed all three Ferraris and was now having a go at Graham Hill's BRM."

Later...

"Clark and Graham Hill were having a proper free-for-all. The Scotsman passed the BRM right in front of the stands only to be retaken at *Tarzan* corner. Next time round the same thing happened, but Moss had now come up and to the huge delight of the crowd overtook both of them. Clark was now seen to be having trouble sorting out his gears." The gearbox let go on lap 42.

A couple of weeks later Clark went to the Belgian Grand Prix at Spa. Practice on Spa's public roads started on the Friday from 5.30 to 8 o'clock in the evening, the organizers not wanting to disrupt daytime traffic. Spa, so daunting, so charged with danger, meant that, as someone said, "Clark was having to face up to reality for the first time in a Formula One car."

On the Saturday the Lotus of Moss broke its left rear stub axle in Burnenville, a 130 mile an hour corner. Before the corner there was a bump in the road, Moss passed over it and instantly felt the most violent oversteer he'd ever felt in his life. He had no way of knowing a wheel had come off. He thrust on full lock and dipped the brake pedal. The Lotus spun, he saw the wheel, braced himself for impact and the Lotus struck a bank. Moss passed out, but when Bruce McLaren rushed up he asked him for artificial respiration. Other drivers arrived, did what they could, found a blanket and held it as a shield against the burning sun. The ambulance took 20 minutes...

Some short while later Michael Taylor in a privately owned Lotus rounded the fast right-hander La Carriere and his steering column broke. He rode up a bank, cleared bushes and ended up seriously injured among trees. "With two accidents happening simultaneously," *Motor Sport* noted cryptically, "the organization was thrown into confusion and it was an extremely long time before the circuit was re-opened for practice."

Clark couldn't escape pondering that both these Lotuses had seriously malfunctioned, something far beyond the control of any driver and – remembering the words of Tony Brooks that you back yourself not to make mistakes – something to inspire genuine fear.

Three Lotuses remained, Ireland on the third row, Clark on the fourth, Alan Stacey on the seventh and last. A mess of a start, Clark's mechanics still pushing his car into position when the flag fell and Lucien Bianchi, sixth row but directly behind Clark, stalled rather than ploughed the mechanics. As the race unfolded Clark found he could slipstream Ireland, but Ireland spun, caught the car before he vaulted a bank, dug tremendous wheelspin out of the Lotus and, when the wheels gripped, did disappear over the bank, angry but unhurt.

On lap 20 Chris Bristow (Cooper) made a mistake on the approach to Burnenville, tried to correct it and the car somersaulted. Bristow, pitched from it onto the surface of the circuit, died instantly. The car continued, thrashing a path into an adjoining field.

Clark would write that he came "bustling down and no-one had any flags out to warn me of what was round the corner. I saw a marshal suddenly dash out on to the road, waving his arms and trying to stop me, and the next thing I saw was another marshal run from the far side of the road. I remember thinking 'Where is he going?' and then he bent down and grabbed the thing by the side of the road. It looked just like a rag doll. It was horrible and I'll never forget the sight of his mangled body being dragged to the side." Nor would Clark forget that at the end of the race his car was "spattered wth blood."

Five laps after Bristow died, Stacey was hit in the face by a bird – and birds can destroy jet engines if they're sucked into them. One report said Stacey "got onto the grass on the outside of the curve at Malmedy, hit a bank and went over and over across the road, over the right hand bank and down the hillside, the Lotus catching fire and being burnt out completely. As with Bristow's crash the driver was thrown out and killed instantly."

Clark did not see this, but became convinced that if he had he would have ended his career immediately. Habitually he kept such feelings to himself. Mattie remembers a piece of film "where he's talking about danger and he says that anyone who says it isn't dangerous is kidding themselves: 'Of course it's dangerous but I dismiss it from my mind.' I think the first shock he got was at Spa, but he only talked about that once. He said 'Spa is very dangerous, there are no escape routes, it's like racing on a railway embankment.' Jim never enjoyed Spa."

Cowan broadens the context. "Jim was always one of the boys, that was the great thing about him. He conducted himself very professionally, and it wasn't until after he died that we all realized the incredible risks they were taking. I don't think Jimmy thought about safety (in the way later generations would). For instance, I'm sure there were places that he didn't enjoy driving, like Spa, but he was still brilliant there because it was a driver's circuit."

Mennem, the *Daily Mirror* journalist who would ghost a column with Clark, gives another view. "I don't think Jim Clark had any remote idea why he was that good. He certainly couldn't tell you. He was very brave, of course. I mean, few people liked the old Spa. You'd ask Jack Brabham what he thought of it and he'd say in his Australian drawl 'I don't like it, mate', which was a long and major speech for him. Jimmy didn't seem to mind it too much, just another circuit as far as he was concerned. I've heard people say he didn't like it, but I never heard him say that. And we're talking about an era when it was dangerous, oh my God yes. Every race at Spa something terrible happened."

The real point about these views is that Cowan sensed Clark didn't like Spa and Mennen only heard others say Clark didn't like Spa. Clark chose to reveal his true feelings, as it would seem, only to his family and even then only once – except in his own book when he said he "hated" the place.

A week later he went to Le Mans, co-driving an Aston Martin with Salvadori for Border Reivers. Scott Watson, a spectator, testifies to Clark's strength of leg and the speed it gave him. "They ran across the track to get to their cars to start the race and Jimmy was always first away – the only person who regularly beat Moss at that. Jimmy would be into the car and, if it started immediately, on his way fractionally before Moss. I saw him to that twice at Le Mans, in the Elite as well as the Aston. He could just do it, he didn't have to try, he had that natural movement which just allowed him to.

"What sort of a chap was he? I was probably too near him at that time and even looking back it's difficult for me to appraise him philosophically. He was a bloody good mucker to be with, shy, and there is no doubt it came out in his biting his finger nails, this chewing away at his finger nails. He didn't really come out of his shell until about 1965, but when he was with people he knew he was a totally different person. He could become quite extrovert, always ready for a lot of fun – though not if there was anybody around whom he didn't know. He was diffident, and very diffident with the press."

Clark and Salvadori finished third at Le Mans, not bad considering the back-up consisted of friends and young farmers again. It was a wet race, which maximizes skill, and was won by Paul Frere and Olivier Gendebien in a Ferrari.

He'd finish the 1960 Grand Prix season with eight points from six races and a best finish of third in Portugal. There have been worse first seasons – and better. That third place at Oporto demands a little examination, not least because the race decided the Championship. The circuit offered tramlines and cobblestones, and in qualifying Clark made a mistake, got into a vicious slide, narrowly missed a lamp post, bounced off straw bales and minced the front end of the car.

Chapman and Endruweit worked on the car through the night in a local garage using whatever came to hand, which legend insists included tubular sections of jacks converted to repair the chassis and Araldite glue. Chapman wanted the start money, you see. "Well, ho hum, it was one of those things," Endruweit says. "Jimmy had made a fair mess of the machinery, wrecked the bodywork, tore the suspension on one side and damaged a lot of bits relevant to the front end. The rack and pinion looked more like a sausage. Privately we wrote it off, but Colin didn't – 'Can't afford to come to Oporto and not get the start money, my boy. Can we get it all together, Jim?' I said: 'One or two little problems, you know.'

"We went off to a workshop somewhere at around two in the morning, typical workshop, one 40-Watt bulb, but it did have an hydraulic press and on that we managed to straighten out the rack – bit of an eyeball job on that. We said: 'Yes, that looks straight.' The left-hand rear wishbone rear attachment – a strut it attached to – had broken out and he said: 'We can weld that back.' I said: 'Well, ho hum.' We had real old-fashioned welding stuff, a pot of something to which you added water and stirred and it gave off acetylene – it went back to the dark days of gas lamps on cars. It was the most fantastical welding kit I've ever come across and I'm not a welder, really. Colin certainly wasn't.

"We had a roll of fence wire, that's the only way I can describe it, as filler rod and I welded this thing back together. When we'd finished it all I got the most tremendous rollicking for not having a spare body on the truck. I said: 'But we don't have a spare body, there's no such animal.' It finished up a reasonably presentable car. It's very possible we used Araldite on the body. We got the car on the grid and Colin said to me: 'D'you think it'll be all right?' I said: 'Well, ho hum, yes.' He said: 'I think I ought to tell Jimmy.' So he trundled off and he had a word with Jimmy, came back and said: 'I've told him to keep out of trouble, not to get too close to anybody else in case it, you know, falls apart.' And that's what Jimmy did."

Clark drove the car expecting it to break down at any moment, but it ran smoothly to the end, lasting 2 hours 20 minutes and 53.26 seconds, or 256 miles if you prefer.

Clark spent New Year racing Lotuses in New Zealand, a trip he thoroughly enjoyed because he'd never been anywhere like that before. Spending New Year itself on a plane over the Pacific left him homesick, however.

He acted as Oswald Brewis' best man at his wedding in 1961 – "Jimmy had to make a speech and he was as bad as I was, really, he didn't like to speak in public. Although he was in Grand Prix racing he hadn't changed, but he certainly had grown up. He was still the same quiet, reticent character – not exactly shy but very reserved – but he was growing up and he had a lot more confidence, he was more worldly-wise."

He put the Lotus on the front row for the first Grand Prix of 1961 – Monaco – but finished 10th – ignition. At Zandvoort he finished third. It gives us another excuse to look at the broader context.

"He didn't go looking for trouble, but if it came to him he was quite willing to defend himself," Scott Watson says. "Let me put it this way: he would defend his honour. It was my first visit to Zandvoort, and at the end I, Jimmy's mechanic Cedric Selzer and Dick Scammell were trying to fight our way through to get to Jimmy along with a lot of the continental press. A young blond Dutch photographer started attacking Cedric – he'd had a terrible accident and wore a great big plate on his head, so a bang on that could have been fatal. I grabbed the chap's camera and was all for filling him in. I think Dick grabbed me from behind and said: 'We don't want an international incident.' I got the message and went off just after the Dutch police arrived. They were backing horses into people who had a perfectly legitimate right to be there. I thought to hell with that, and Jimmy was like me. If he hadn't been sitting in the car he'd have been getting very tensed up and ready for a sorting-out session."

In fact 1961 proved a tragic, troubled season. On the second lap of the Italian Grand Prix at Monza, in the braking area for the *Parabolica*, Clark and von Trips collided and von Trips' Ferrari rode up the banking, killing 11 spectators immediately and seriously injuring many more. Three more died later. The Ferrari beat itself to pieces as it churned back to the track, and von Trips, flung out, was dead too. There is black and white film which lasts only a second or two, but is difficult to forget: the Ferrari rotating furiously away from the bank upside-down, landing and gouging a dust storm, a piece of the car wrenched off and flung full across the track, the car itself almost disintegrating after a final rotation back onto the track into the path of other cars. Mercifully there is no glimpse of von Trips, thrown out somewhere in the dust storm. Clark would remember, in shock, how he tried to haul the Ferrari off the track; would remember how he couldn't bear to go near von Trips' body.

Clark subsequently described how he'd been slipstreaming to stay with the Ferraris and, because his handling was better, moved up to overtake von Trips. Clark remained convinced that von Trips must have gauged the Ferrari as better and wasn't expecting to be overtaken, wasn't looking. Von Trips moved onto a line to negotiate the Parabolica which brought him across the Lotus. Clark mutely beseeched him to *look in your mirrors, look in your mirrors*. Both cars were braking as hard as they could and the rear wheel of the Ferrari touched the front wheel of the Lotus.

A German spectator shot cine film – we don't need to dwell on the irony that von Trips was German – and presented it to Clark. His sisters remember that. They say "Jim played it several times on a projector and you could actually see him going in a straight line and von Trips coming into his path. An American couple who were journalists stayed with him once and he ran it for them."

Monza ended with the police looking for him, ended with Chapman flying him out as fast as possible. The season ended at Watkins Glen, which Innes Ireland won. It was the first Lotus win, too. Soon after, Lotus fired Ireland.

"I felt at the time Jimmy had something to do with it. I'd seen him in head-to-head discussions with Colin and I wasn't being included in them. I was deeply disappointed – that's too mild a word – about being out of the team because I'd gone through all the hard, difficult times with Chapman with wheels falling off and chassis breaking. The two years Jimmy and I drove together he usually practised quicker because I was never really all that quick in practice, but in races, as long as my car was running properly, I was usually in front. I didn't think I deserved to get thrown off the team. Only in later years, having seen the way Colin Chapman worked, did I realize it was just Chapman's technique [to behave like this] – but there were several years of bitter acrimony."

In 1962 Clark went to the Nurburgring in May for the 1000 kilometres race in a little Lotus 23. Brewis, accompanying him, says "one of the experiences of my life was going round the Ring with him in his own car prior to racing. Half of the circuit was completely blind, but he could remember these things if he'd been round once. It was all a bit frightening but, of course, we were young then and so it was great fun, too. In the race, a wet race, they set off from a standing start. He came round to complete the first lap, nobody else in sight. He came and went and still nobody else appeared. We wondered what the hell had happened to them all (rumour: there's been a massive crash obliterating the rest of the field. In fact, no crash, simply Clark leading by a minute and a half.) Quite extraordinary. He was in the right car at the right time in the right situation, but even so...

"He took being able to do that sort of thing in his stride. He had, if you like, an arrogance I suppose. He was completely convinced of his own invincibility. He knew he was the quickest man around so he didn't dance up and down afterwards or whatever, he expected it to happen. If it didn't, usually it wasn't his fault. Some people might have said he was a little bit too cocksure, but he had this complete belief."

He won Spa, third race of the season. He qualified only on the fifth row – he stripped the timing gear – and decided to make a "dash" at the start. Completing lap one he'd hoisted himself to fourth and by lap nine the lead.

Perhaps for the first time the true and essential greatness of Clark revealed itself. He did not just lead, he mastered the art of leading, accepted the pressure, controlled the emotion and mastered Spa at the same time. He seemed impossibly smooth through the long, lean, wooded corners, smooth round the hairpin, smooth through the dip-rise-float of *Eau Rouge* and nobody could stay near him. That's the happy part, the sporting part.

In the background tragedy, or near tragedy, stalked Spa again. On lap 26 Trevor Taylor in a Lotus collided with Willi Mairesse (Ferrari), whose car turned over and burst into a column of fire. High molten yellow-red flame licked against the wooded backdrop at *Blanchimont*. Mairesse was thrown out and so was Taylor, itself fortunate because the Lotus struck and brought down a telegraph pole.

Spectators and marshals ran down the incline, but on the track towards the accident. Smoke covered it so that approaching drivers couldn't see these people trotting towards them. Clark, meanwhile, remained so much in control that at La Source he lifted his right hand – a fleeting caress of a gesture, almost a flick of a finger – to acknowledge a photographer he recognized on the infield. He beat Graham Hill by 43.9 seconds.

He won the British at Aintree, too, but it rained immediately before the next race, the Nurburgring, rained so hard that the drivers were granted a lap each to monitor where the water lay; rained so hard they delayed the start by an hour. Clark's goggles misted and, waiting for the flag, he switched the fuel pumps off to prevent fouling the plugs. While he fiddled with the goggles the flag fell and, all in the moment, he forgot to switch the fuel pumps back on. He made a non-start at the start.

The Nurburgring's particular terrors are exhaustively documented, and perhaps in the wet sharper even than the only other place with which it could be compared, Spa. The difference between them can be expressed mathematically. The Ring had 187 corners and Spa had, well, half a dozen. If you can see 187 corners clearly as you approach them it's hard enough. One mistake, as Peter Collins made, and you're an obituary. If you can't see the 187 in the spray…

In this Clark *thought* that on the first lap he overtook 10 cars. In fact it must have been 16. That lap quite possibly stands with Fangio's in 1957 as the greatest round The Ring, different context, different judgments and skills, same result. Keith Greene drove a Gilby-BRM. "Jim was a super bloke, broad Scots accent, very nervous out of the car, chewing his finger nails and so on. The German Grand Prix was held in dreadful weather, heavy rain, water running in rivulets across the track, everything – so bad we did that complete lap before the race. I was lying about 10th, Jimmy had had the awful start and just after Adenau Bridge – a left – at a point where you were airborne, he went past me really *flying*.

"Up front, Graham Hill, John Surtees and Dan Gurney battled it out for the lead and Jimmy eventually finished fourth. After the race he said to me: 'It may have looked to you as if I was flying, but I just couldn't keep my concentration. If I'd kept on driving like that I'd have gone off. The conditions were frightening.' What he meant was he hadn't been able to keep his concentration for every moment of the race, only for most of it – and don't forget the race lasted more than two and a half hours."

Clark nursed a certain contempt for sections of the press and their worship of the winners of the races, their shallow coverage of what really happened. At the time the headlines centred around Hill beating Surtees by 2.5 seconds, which is understandable enough. Clark, fourth and 42.1 seconds behind Hill, could scarcely expect headlines – or presumably care one way or the other – but he did wish his achievement to be properly evaluated, properly set down, fully appreciated – not for reasons of vanity but only for what it was.

He considered it his greatest drive.

In October he won the United States Grand Prix at Watkins Glen. Gurney, meanwhile, had earlier in the season sounded Chapman out about converting a Lotus chassis to accept a big American engine so he could tackle Indianapolis. Gurney paid for Chapman to go to and watch the 500 race in 1962. Rodger Ward won it at an average 140.293mph and Chapman saw several aspects with absolute clarity, not least that the meaty 4.2-litre Offenhauser engines which virtually everybody used were beatable – these IndyCars had the engines at the front, so antiquated to Chapman it made him laugh out loud. Chapman reasoned that if Ford of America made an engine for the Lotus and it won Indianapolis, Ford might not be displeased. Ford thought that, too, when Chapman and Gurney flew to their headquarters outside Detroit to talk it over, but what Chapman, and particularly Clark, needed was real experience of a 2½-mile oval.

After the Watkins Glen Grand Prix they took the Lotus with its 1½-litre Climax engine to Indy for a test and it served a dual purpose. While Clark learned how to go round, the Indianapolis officials could see just what this strange little car was and if the driver could really drive. Several IndyCar drivers turned up to have a look to satisfy their own curiosity.

To be placed on trial like this annoyed Clark a great deal. He felt they were treating him "like a kid who had never raced before." But he didn't permit the anger to affect him and, anyway, the Lotus didn't have special Indy tyres, hadn't been set up for the left-hand turns. His fastest lap, 143 miles an hour, proved a great deal. It compared with the 1962 pole time of 150.370 mph by Parnelli Jones in an Agajanian 98, but Clark regularly passed through the corners 2 miles an hour quicker than the IndyCars – their real speed came in along the straights between the corners. Chapman decided a modified Lotus 25 would do nicely and work on it began at Cheshunt.

As we've seen, Clark finished second in the Championship, Graham Hill winning it in South Africa. By now Ian Scott Watson had departed. He remains reluctant to discuss this publicly, and understandably so because the split was not instigated by himself or Clark. Someone else, whom he won't name, did that. Scott Watson felt hurt to be banished from the entourage after all he'd done, and felt it more keenly because of his regard for Clark. Whatever, time healed, despite some lingering awkwardness, and the friendship survived. But it could never be quite the same again.

At the tail end of 1962, while Clark lost the Championship and Lotus worked on the IndyCar, Ford started to "think intelligently about going further into competition" with the Cortina. Walter Hayes, a senior executive, knew Chapman well and "when we decided to do a proper racing programme it seemed natural we should talk about drivers. Then came the first meeting I had with Jim Clark. Even then I had the feeling there were a number of people who didn't know too much about him."

Ford signed a contract with Chapman which included Clark racing and a separate contract with Clark to do some testing. Hayes would remember how anxious Clark was to help the motor industry.

I'm grateful to Hayes and publishers Paul Hamlyn for permission to quote from Hayes' tribute in *Jim Clark, Portrait of a Great Driver*. "When I first met him he found it extremely difficult to speak in public and was exceptionally shy about it. The great and extraordinary thing about him was this sincerity which seemed to come over. He could say things and people knew he was telling the truth because he was so patently sincere in what he was saying. You could never get him to say anything he didn't really believe. He was endlessly willing to drive people around circuits, talk about cars, he was really a tremendous ambassador for us overseas. In those early days he was a very simple young man and this was the awe-inspiring thing about him. I used to stand and look at him endlessly and ask myself 'What is it, how is it possible?'"

In time Clark created a complete folklore around the Cortina and its Lotus engine, and a generation of spectators remember. He raced it all over the place, he seemed always to take corners on two wheels – Hayes wrote that "in all his conversations he would never say what he could do or what he thought, he would always talk about the car and what the car could do. Some drivers drive as though they have to dominate the machinery but I think Jimmy drove like a ballet dancer, he had the lightest feet and hands on earth. He was a great dancer in a motor car, gentle with them, kind with them. He was a great driver because of this feeling of participation with the motor car so the driving became almost sixth sense with him in many cases."

In retrospect the World Championship of 1963 proved straightforward despite a false start. Clark retired at Monaco. After leading until the 79th lap out of 100 he suddenly slowed and could be seen gazing into the cockpit trying to work the gear-lever this way and that. It froze solid. At the *Tabac* kiosk the car coasted and by Gazometre the transmission had seized.

Peter Garnier, who wrote a study of the whole race, said: "Clark jumped out, his lead over the BRM [of Graham Hill] sufficient for him to run back round the corner and give Hill a 'slow down' signal because the Lotus was parked on the inside of the road, right at the apex of the corner. Returning to the car as Hill took the BRM through the corner into the lead, Clark found a marshal standing by who, realizing when Clark had stopped there was nothing wrong with the engine – it had still been running – tried to shove him back into the cockpit. Exasperated, Clark tried to explain, whereupon the marshal thoughtfully tried to push the gear-lever into neutral. In a fury Clark abandoned the scene and walked to the pits guarded from wellwishers and members of the press by the excitable Louis Chiron and his blue flag."

A photographer caught Clark's face in the pits, goggles hanging loose round his neck, arms at his side and his eyes strange, distracted, almost wild.

(Garnier, secretary of the Grand Prix Drivers' Association and subsequently editor of *Autocar*, found himself in an unusual situation. He attended drivers' meetings at the races where they discussed such matters as safety. These meetings could last two or three hours and he then went to the organizers to inform them what the drivers had said. A journalist, he was sworn to secrecy about who said what, which did not please some of his colleagues in the press box. Moreover, these meetings prove that, despite so much we've already heard, drivers were concerned about safety.

"I didn't find Clark shy," Garnier says, "and I find it quite funny that you say people like Pat Mennem and Alan Brinton did. He was vocal in the drivers' meetings, though the most vocal of all was Graham Hill. Surtees said little but whenever he did it was always good sense. I can still see Jim Clark sitting there smiling and laughing and talking...")

The next morning Clark caught the 6.10am Comet from Nice to London, he and Chapman raking over the Lotus gearchange, poring over drawings of it Chapman had made after the race. Clark flew on to Chicago for the Indy 500, Chapman took the drawings to the factory at Cheshunt and caught the afternoon Chicago flight. Indy was on Thursday, May 30. Clark would fly to Mosport to race on the Saturday and fly back to England to race at Crystal Palace on the Monday. Modern drivers who complain that they are always on aeroplanes might ponder that.

Clark had already given the Lotus, designated 29, some shakedown testing at Snetterton, and although the Ford engine, which gave 351bhp, didn't seem absolutely right, Clark destroyed his own 2½-litre record. He'd also tested at Kingman, Arizona, an oval, and while he still found the engine somewhat disappointing, lapped at 165 miles an hour.

Jabby Cromac, French journalist and long-time friend of Chapman, refers to Indianapolis 1963 as a "crusade" which assumed the proportions of Europe versus America and has recorded how disorganized, even innocent they were. Chapman, Clark, Cyril Audrey (the timekeeper) and Crombac all shared the same room – they hadn't known how to book rooms in advance – with Chapman and Clark in beds, Audrey on a camp bed and Crombac on the floor under a blanket. Clark qualified on the second row but many Americans wondered what Ford were doing pumping so much money into this odd little car with the engine at the wrong end and being handled by somebody they'd never heard of.

At Chirnside, Clark's sister Betty "knew mother was going to be petrified about him racing there, so I took her to Edinburgh shopping that day [the race fell on a Thursday]. Lotus had set up a direct link with Indianapolis, father rang Lotus and sat listening to the whole commentary."

Deep into the race Clark was visibly catching Parnelli Jones, a Californian, and drew up to within three or four seconds of him when he suddenly slowed. Parnelli Jones was dropping oil. Betty and mother were back from the shopping, father listening on the telephone and relaying the flow of the commentary to her so that she could relay it to mother, going about her business in the house. "I could hear someone was dropping oil."

The *Indianapolis Star* reported that "Clark's car owner, Colin Chapman, wanted chief steward Harlan Fengler to have the race leader black-flagged. That would have cost Parnelli the race. Fengler was ready to do so and even handed the appropriate flag to starter Pat Vidan. But Agajanian chief mechanic Johnny Pouelsen talked him out of it. They argued that the crack was at the oil-tank hanger and the oil had already leaked down to that level. Bitter Eddie Sachs and Roger McCluskey [two other drivers] rebutted that and said they had both spun on Parnelli's oil. The day after the race they were attending a luncheon when Sachs expressed his views a bit too forcefully. Parnelli decked him with a right cross."

Parnelli Jones won by 33 seconds, Clark finished with a broad grin and a serenade by bagpipers when he emerged from the car. He could afford the grin. Second place earned 100,000 dollars, a pretty sum, as Clark said cryptically, for turning left 800 times. Betty remembers the family were simply "glad it was all over."

"I remember," Cowan says, "when we used to talk about Indianapolis. He said he didn't like it and needed room for four or five laps until his eyes and brain and everything adjusted, and then he completely put out of his mind the speed he was doing, let everything come back to what he knew. 'You don't look at the things you're going past, you don't look right-angles out of the side of the car. Your brain speeds up, your eyes speed up, everything speeds up to make it feel comfortable.' It was like driving – well, not a tractor but certainly a Formula One car. I don't suppose he found it easy to relax while he drove at Indy, but that's how he said he tried to. He had to tell himself to forget about the top speed. He was always concerned about mechanical or tyre problems, things completely out of his control."

Things completely in his control, like Grand Prix races, he ticked off at will, and you have to face the simple fact that, his artistry aside, he made these races dull to behold. After Indianapolis he won Spa, took pole and won Holland, took pole and won France, took pole and won Silverstone. It gave him 36 points and the context is Graham Hill 13, Surtees 13. Ginther (BRM) occupied second place, but with only 14. He took pole at the Nurburgring but, dicing with Surtees for the lead, the engine began to cut out and he could do no more than finish second.

After the Ring he drove a Ford Galaxie at Brands Hatch "for fun" (he won, of course). Iain Mackay, who'd subsequently work at a high level in bike racing, was with a "small company which tuned saloon cars, Minis and what have you. You'd see Jimmy racing everywhere all over the place. I have a lasting memory of a Ford with the round lights on the back – it was like a box of cigars – and some of Clark's performances in that thing were just amazing."

(MacKay had been present at a non-Championship Formula One race at Solitude in July – between Silverstone and the Ring – "a mixed bike and car meeting. The great interest for us was that Mike Hailwood drove in the Formula One race. That proved a disaster of a thing, wet, a lot of people crashing. In the evening we went to prizegiving – they always had good prizegiving at Solitude – in a big hotel. I forget which town, but not far away. Clark sat at a mixed table with the bike guys and Mike, obviously. In the beginning Clark stayed a little bit quiet, but as the evening wore on he surprised us. I mean, he was really an entertaining man, a lovely man. Everyone had a few drinks – wines or a few beers or whatever – and he opened up. He went a bit wild, everyone did, it was one of those evenings. He was fondly thought of by the motorcyclists after that because he was so nice, so full of fun.

"I keep drawing parallels with Mike. In my opinion they both had very distinctive styles, not only on the track but off it. They were just genuine people, no side to either of them. Clark did win an awful lot of saloon car races, but not always easily. That's when he fought. He was a real fighter, too, a fighter, a real Scotsman in that respect. I remember him as much loved in the paddock, much appreciated because of how genuine he was.")

That month of July *Autocar* reported: "Jim Clark's Indianapolis Lotus 29 was recently tested at Milwaukee, a one-mile oval used by the Indy cars, and lapped in 32.65 second (110.3mph) – compared with the existing lap record of 34.09 seconds (105.62mph). Encouraged by this performance, Colin Chapman has entered Clark and the 'Lotus-powered-by-Ford' for the remaining two Championship events – at Milwaukee on 18 August and Trenton on 22 September."

At Milwaukee Clark found the Lotus so nimble it could nip inside the American monsters on the corners and he lapped everyone except A.J. Foyt. Mr Foyt, doyen of Indy, all-American folk hero and a considerable presence, was not lapped because Mr Clark, shepherd, farmer and former rookie, judged it would be impolitic to do that. Mr Clark certainly could have lapped Mr Foyt. A couple of days later, testing at Trenton, the steering broke on the Lotus...

And he came to Monza for the Italian Grand Prix on September 8, Monza using the combined road and banking sections. The banking proved so dangerous in qualifying the police said the safety of spectators could not be guaranteed and the meeting was confined to the road circuit. The race? Slipstreaming and slipstreaming, cars moving in shoals, the order constantly changing, but eventually Clark and Gurney (Brabham-Climax) lapped everyone, and when Gurney dropped out with fuel feed problems Clark cantered it. He had 51 points, Ginther next on 24.

Autosport reported that "the scenes at the end were indescribable. Whilst Clark was being mobbed, hundreds of spectators invaded the track with cars still circulating – fortunately slowly. This was disgraceful, and no credit to the heavy-handed Monza police who stood by helplessly. Then, after a jubilant Clark, Chapman and Spence [the other Lotus driver] did a victory tour in the winning car, the new World Champion was whipped away by the police to quiz him regarding the accident of two years ago. Not a very nice way to treat a visitor who has just become the World's Number One driver."

Clark had arrived at the Lotus pit to be confronted by a happy melee, Chapman elbowing his way towards the car. Chapman clambered on the back clutching the trophy and clung as Clark eased round a lap of honour, pausing to pick up Spence who'd stopped out on the circuit 13 laps from the end with oil pressure problems. When Clark returned with his passengers to the pit the melee had become so intense he took refuge in a necessary and useful sanctuary.

Alan Brinton says that "in anticipation of Clark winning, Dunlop had fixed up a little caravan in the paddock for any interviews to take place. I waited there for him, he managed to get inside through all the policemen and excited Italians, he shut the door and we carried out this interview with the howling mob looking in through the window, rocking the caravan backwards and forwards."

By chance and by a few moments, Brinton missed an official approaching Clark to say the police wanted to talk to him about the 1961 accident with von Trips. Clark walked to the race organizer's office where he was expected to sign a summons to appear at the local magistrates the following morning. He protested he couldn't read Italian and anyway had made prior arrangements to fly home with Jack Brabham on that following morning. He protested further that he'd already participated in a lengthy inquiry the year before, and what more could he add now? They said he could leave Italy if he gave them the name of a lawyer to represent him.

He went back to the Hotel de Ville, a favoured haunt of drivers and journalists not far from the track. He bumped into Brinton, staying there with his wife and two sons. "I'd done all my writing, done my work, got back and we were in the foyer. I was just going towards the bar and this quiet little man came up. Jimmy. He saw us and said: 'Could I buy you all a drink?' I said: 'This is Peter and this is Ian', and he said: 'What would you like? Orange squash?' He was by nature kindly, thoughtful and, I mean, here was the new World Champion. Absolutely amazing." The real measure of Jim Clark is that, the legal threat of the crash having risen again so sharply with unknown, perhaps alarming consequences, he still behaved entirely normally.

It is a theme taken up by Peter Warr. "What he achieved and no-one else managed to achieve was that he stayed the same guy all through his career, as approachable and chatty and – dare one say it? – ordinary to talk to right the way through. Now in point of fact what you got to know when you got to know him better was that underneath there lay a determination which was very dominant in his character, but which he didn't allow to show.

"He had an amazing ability to transmit what he wanted to do and say without ever to my knowledge anyone thinking 'Oh, he's a bit of a prima donna, he's a superstar' because in his own eyes he never was. He saw himself as a guy who did something he loved doing and recognized that he could to it quite well. He had real difficulty coming to terms with why he was so good. He didn't know. It was just something that had been given to him and so, from that point of view, he was the most genuine person you could ever possibly hope to meet.

"He'd pop into the office and ask you what to all intents and purposes seemed the most mundane questions, like 'Do you know what's the time of the last train back up to Scotland?'. You'd think *surely he's got somebody to take care of that for him*, but he hadn't, and that was part of his enormous appeal: that he was just a regular guy."

(Example: Mattie says: "He didn't realize he was famous. I remember flying to London with him and people were gazing and he said: 'What are they looking at?' and I said: 'At you!' And: "Did he change at all? I remember going to London with my mother and we actually walked past him because he was so smart in a suit instead of his usual green sweater!" This seems to be the only concession he made to genuine fame.)

"I suppose," Warr says, "in a way part of the mythology comes from people not being able to reconcile the personality they saw and met and talked to with this guy who was just so much better than anyone else in a car. If you take any sportsman who has reached this standing in almost any field, be it soccer, athletics, cricket, whatever, they always have – and have had to have – a bravado and brashness which announced to the world that they were who they were. Jimmy didn't do it. That's what captivated people about him.

"All the little anecdotes you hear helped to build up the stature and the standing he had in everybody's eyes. There are hundreds of people who say 'this guy Jimmy Clark came up and offered to buy me a drink, he said please can I buy you a drink?' Even in those days it was unheard of, superstars were superstars, albeit at a different level of intensity and media exposure, but even so…

"What did Clark have? All the ingredients to be best, physical attributes, reaction time, the understanding of the car, great skill and experience, plus the burning desire which never showed except funnily enough off the track. I remember a party we had at Colin Chapman's house when he lived in Hertfordshire. This happened around Christmas and Hazel was intensely house-proud, her house was beautiful with, I remember, very expensive wall lights up the stairs.

"It all got a bit out of hand and people had had a lot to drink, including Jimmy. Bets were laid on who could get up the stairs to the landing on a pogo stick. People tried – they were jumping and falling and all Hazel's lights were knocked off the wall. When Jimmy got onto the pogo stick he went bomp-bomp-bomp straight up the middle to the landing, so of course that spoiled the game.

"Then somebody got out what used to be called a woggle board, a log with a plank on top. You put a foot each side and balanced on it. The deal was a fiver to anyone who could stand on it with his drink for 30 seconds without spilling it. People tried and went crashing to the floor, banging into the furniture. Jimmy got on and stood there for about a minute and a half and then asked in his quiet way: 'Could somebody please pass me another drink?' He was so competitive but it didn't show until you got him in a scene like that, which in one sense was totally unimportant, but in another sense he had to win – and also he had the balance to do it, on the pogo stick, on the woggle board (and despite drink having being taken).

"If you say *well, OK, what about so-and-so, didn't he have it, didn't he have the attributes?*, you might get the answer 'Yes', and *so-and-so, didn't he also have the attributes?*, you might get the answer 'Yes', too, but what they didn't have was the personality which went with it, and that made the man who everyone worshipped."

Scott Watson remembers something else, equally relevant. "When Jimmy won his first World Championship a man called John Milne, who owned a whisky company and a couple of very good restaurants in Glasgow, put on a super party to celebrate. It was in one of his two restaurants; he had the Provost of Glasgow, a lot of influential friends and a lot of the motor racing types. The party was absolutely out of this world.

"I got quite drunk, to be quite honest – or maybe I ate too much caviar! – and I ended up unconscious in the loo. Somebody picked me up and laid me on a settee until we were ready to go home. They virtually carried me and put me in the back of Jimmy's Galaxie. It was a November night and I came round about 20 miles this side of Edinburgh. My mind cleared and I could see his shoulders working. I heard him say to Graham Gauld: 'God, this thing winds up a little bit', because it wasn't his car, he'd borrowed it. They heard my drunken voice from the back – first time they'd heard I was awake – say: 'It's probably ice!' Great guffaws of laughter. Further on Jimmy realized it was sheet black ice. He hadn't noticed it himself because we were in amongst trees at the time, but at the top end of a village he saw it was, whereupon he gave a demonstration of how to drive on ice. It was frankly unbelievable.

"He was still pressing on in this 17–18ft long 7ft wide Galaxie doing about 90 miles an hour. I didn't feel any fear and I'm sure Graham didn't either. I woke up completely and watched his absolute confidence in his driving. How could he do that? It was very difficult to know. Even knowing him as well as I did, you could only judge him against your own driving ability, and mine wasn't all that great. The more you sat with him the more you saw he had extraordinary reactions, far, far quicker than any other human I've ever met, allied to an anticipatory sense which nobody else I've ever known had, either. You put the two together and add the physical attributes and perhaps that explains it.

"He was actually a very athletic chap. He didn't particularly look that, but he was – he played hockey for Northumberland, don't forget. He could move extremely quickly. The two of us were exactly the same height – 5ft 6in – but his legs were 3 inches longer than mine. His legs were comparatively long and extremely powerful. As I've said, running across the track for the Le Mans start he'd always be first away."

For the rest of his life Clark would have to accommodate his fame whether he liked it or not. "When he made it," his sisters say, "we were amazed." Cowan noted that Clark's parents "obviously loved his success, but in just a nice way. And the only thing Jimmy would be impatient about was…well, he didn't suffer fools gladly, that's for sure. If people were becoming a nuisance he would tell them so in no uncertain terms. He was that type of guy, and as he became more famous he was being pestered more and more, people trying to befriend him for reasons other than that he was a genuine hero. But on the whole he handled it very well.

"The Berwick and District Motor Club dinner was somehow magical. It'd be a Friday night, Jimmy was World Champion, he'd arrive with Graham Hill, Jack Brabham, Dan Gurney, he'd have said to them 'Come on, we're going to the Berwick dinner.' I compare that with the drivers of today in Formula One. They hardly speak to each other. If they come within three feet they hit each other. Of course they're not all like that, but in the old days they'd come up and enjoy themselves. Brilliant. They stayed at Edington Mains with Jim and, you know…brilliant nights."

The question of what Clark had won't go away. Speaking on BBC Radio Scotland's tribute to him in 1988, Bernard Setright discussed what happened when he – Setright – became involved in testing Grand Prix tyres. "These tests were to make tyres work at their best, a delicate matter of balancing pressures and shapes and suspension settings, but the fascinating result was how the superiority of Clark showed up compared to all the other drivers.

"We measured the wear of each tyre, and each make of tyre, at the end of a race and calculated from that how much longer the tyres would have lasted. In this way we found out how much of each tyre each individual driver was using. Jack Brabham was a great oversteerer who would use up his back tyres faster than his fronts – he and people like Graham Hill would use the backs 50 per cent faster. Gurney, driving the same car as Brabham, would use up the front tyres faster.

"In Clark's case it was entirely different. He had such balance he used the four corners of the car to the optimum. The result was that had he gone on and on with the same set of tyres he'd have used up all four at exactly the same time. The difference was a matter of 1 per cent at all four corners. He had a sensitivity to the way the car behaved, a sensitivity to what the surface allowed and an awareness of what he himself could do, which bordered on the incredible, when you come down to differences like 1 per cent."

Maybe that's it. Maybe that's only part of it. Maybe the whole of it remains as inexplicable as genius itself, something for psychologists and anthropologists to trawl through, examining the family tree, studying physical reports, gauging eyesight, co-ordination, desire, self-confidence, self-control, opportunity. Maybe, maybe not.

PORTRAIT:
JOHN SURTEES

Two men stood side-by-side holding their motorbikes ready. They faced a grassy hillclimb stretching some 100 yards up the side of a valley. The place, near Farningham, Kent, was this day in 1947 like so many others, natural and slightly informal. One of the men, Jack Surtees – medium height, broad shoulders – had a look of absolute determination in his eye. The other man would be famous by association, because his brother Ted kept goal for Spurs. He was called Harry Ditchburn. The meeting has long gone into memory although, the two men standing poised, this was its climax: a shoot-out, Surtees and Ditchburn emerging to contest the final.

At the signal they pushed the bikes forward, vaulted on and accelerated up, up, up. The 596cc Norton which Surtees rode moved some distance and the engine began stuttering, came to a complete halt. Ditchburn continued alone to the top and won. Jack Surtees strode back, faced his son John and gave him "a clip round the ear."

Charlie Rous, then Jack's sidecar passenger and later a noted writer on bike racing, watched this happen. "John was only 13, but that didn't matter. Jack clipped his ear because John had got the bike ready and not switched on the fuel tap."

This story is important for several reasons. It demonstrates how close John already was to bike racing – indeed, born and raised in it – and the standards his father expected. Jack could be hard, and in time so could John. Rous has no doubt that father shaped son. "The great difference between Jack and Mike Hailwood's father Stan was that Jack had no real money. He worked from a very small premises at Forest Hill in South London where he sold motorbikes, so obviously he had a few quid, but everything was done on a shoestring in his racing, every penny earned.

"This was the way they were. They did everything themselves, they didn't employ the super-tuners or anything. John did an apprenticeship at the Vincent factory, but essentially taught himself. What did shape John was his father's very strict way of carrying on, watching the pennies no matter what he might have in the bank, self-reliance, complete dedication. He hasn't changed to his day. *There's only one way to do something the way I want it done and that is to do it myself.* And he can. That is the point, you see. He could do it with bikes and he could to it with cars as well. When he had his own Formula One team he literally built the cars himself."

No understanding of John is possible without direct reference to Jack and

John's mother Dorothy. "She was just as much interested in bikes as Jack," Rous says. "Dorothy was an expert sidecar driver – not in racing but on the road – a superb motorcyclist and car driver. John was born a natural. Without question he inherited his father's ability and his mother's, he was quite extraordinary from the word go."

"What sort of a chap was Dad?" John Surtees muses. "Oh, Dad was a wonderful character. He had a reasonable degree of temper, but a great big heart. He would always be a sucker for someone's sob story. If he had a couple of shillings in his pocket and some kid came along he'd give them to him. He was a good dad, a good friend as well.

"He'd had a pretty tough time early on, he could be militant about things. He grew up in the sort of environment where his father had been at Sainsburys and tried to form some sort of shop floor representation, tried to start a union. That led to trouble. Dad ran away because of this and he and his brother were taken in by the Salvation Army. Dad and brother joined up under age, went off to France for the First World War and his brother got blown up driving an ambulance. Dad came back, then he went off as a driver for the commission which carried out the original investigation into establishing a Jewish state in Israel.

"After he left the army he found himself in the same position as so many others, no jobs. Eventually he became a bus driver. He met and married my mother and opened up a little motorcycle shop. I came along in 1934. By the time the Second World War started he had another shop which dealt partly in motor cycles and repairs and partly in cars. He was called into the army again – at Catterick – and on one of his trips back home he fell asleep on his bike, had a hell of a crash, smashed himself up a bit. He was invalided out of the army. I remember going along with him when he took the shop in Sunderland Road, Forest Hill.

"Immediately after the war he picked up an old Ford V8 with the big dickie seat. We went to our first race meeting with myself, my brother and sister sort of stuck in the dickie seat with the racing Norton and combination sidecar on a tow hook – not in a trailer or anything. And off we went to Cadwell Park with a toolbox in the sidecar. This was The Surtees Racing Team, Dad starting his riding career again, everything on a shoe-string because he had nothing. We had a great time, camped, got flooded out…"

Jack had ridden from the Thirties (against among others Stan Hailwood) and at Catterick helped train dispatch riders, an idea fostered by Graham Walker, father of Murray. Now, back in competition, he met Rous in 1947 when Rous was 17. "My father was a friend of his and bought one or two bikes off him. I started grass track racing at Brands Hatch in 1947, and a year later I became Jack's passenger in his sidecar. I was called up to do my National Service in the Royal Air Force, but got home at weekends whenever I could and raced with Jack through most of 1949. On the odd occasion when I couldn't get leave or weekend passes John went in the chair in my place. I can't say for sure, but where a grass track meeting took place and the programme gave C. Rous as passenger it could well have been John."

Surtees confirms this, although he says "it only happened on the odd occasion from when I was 14 and my first race on a bike at 15."

Rous expands on it. "Everyone says Mike Hailwood was so young when he started, and that's true, but so was Surtees. In fact Surtees started under age.

The ACU [Auto Cycle Union] frowned on anybody racing before they were 16 – it was banned, as a matter of fact – but at grass tracks and things like that controls were more relaxed."

A hard school, certainly. "John wasn't a crasher because if he did he got a good telling off from his father. *Motor bikes are not made to fall off*, Jack used to say, *and that is that*." Surtees himself recounts how he once fell off at Clearways, Jack strode there and yes, gave him a "quick clip round the ear." Surtees smiles as he recounts this so many years later.

"In 1950, for his own racing Jack bought a 1,000cc Vincent, spanking new, and he wanted to race it the following weekend," Rous says. "He took young John to Brands one mid-week day because you could test for as long as you wanted. John did about 200 laps just going round and round and round, and this was a 150 mile an hour machine.

"I had a BSA Twin road machine and his father had an identical bike in his stock. One evening we were working at their home – they lived near Croydon – and something was needed from back at the shop at Forest Hill. John was 16 and he'd only just got his licence. We climbed on our respective bikes and rode to Forest Hill. I've never forgotten it. He out-rode me so completely that it was astonishing. We had a bit of a lads' dice, nowhere near the sort of traffic on the roads like now. In corners and round bends he simply rode away from me. Maybe I exercised more caution because I was older, 20, and I'd been riding for four years, but I remember looking up and saying: Good God, what a rider this is."

Surtees confesses he "doesn't really know" about being a natural, but qualifies that. "I didn't think so much of riding, I was more interested in tinkering with the bikes. You'd have a trial bike, you put it together and it seemed a very natural thing to get on it and become part of the bike. Dad in his own way took it for granted I would ride, Mum took it for granted, I took it for granted. First I learnt on bicycles and when I could get motor power I got motor power. I wasn't a natural there because I rode them too fast and fell off. I went down to Brands Hatch with an old Triumph, went around and said: This is what I want to do."

Surtees made his debut at a place called Stokenchurch, a grass track near High Wycombe at the side of the main Oxford road. "Jack had the Ford V8 lorry, maroon, like a big box," Rous says. "John had been entered for the meeting and we took two or three bikes. Jack asked me to ride them and then asked which I thought best. I selected one. Jack said: 'Go up to the line with him and make sure everything's OK.' I did that and the race started. Jack climbed into the back of the lorry and sat there until the race ended. He couldn't bring himself to watch. And he was a hard man, tough. The important thing about the family was that they were extremely close-knit. If you talk to John even now he refers to everything as *we did this* and *we did that* and he means the family, really. I suppose for the short period I was connected with them I became one of the we's.

"I acted as Jack's passenger for the last meeting at Brands Hatch on the grass in 1949. It was then laid out as a road circuit about a mile long. At the first meeting at this 'new' Brands I again acted as Jack's passenger and John rode a 250 Triumph so he took part in the first heat and thus the very first event at the circuit. It followed the original grass track and went round anti-clockwise: down the straight to Clearways, around a kidney-shape, along the Bottom straight. Dingle Dell didn't exist, you went into what used to be called Paddock Bend and came up Paddock Hill. Next time you go to Brands, if you look down at the foot of Paddock Hill – in the dip there – you'll see a bit of old tarmac on the right. That's the original circuit and it shows you how narrow it was. In that first race John diced for the lead and through inexperience came off.

"Geoff Duke and Mike Hailwood rapidly became established in their careers and went straight into world classics and got into works teams comparatively quickly. Duke started in 1948 and was only just beaten for the 500cc World Championship in 1950. He joined the Italian team Gilera and very rarely did you see him in races in this country, just the Grands Prix. That was the way you were held by a factory. Norton, AJS, all the works teams didn't want their riders taking part in ordinary Brands Hatch-type meetings because they could hurt themselves.

"Surtees' first full season was 1951, but in minor English meetings, and he continued for the best part of five years with that type of racing. You name the English circuit, he was the champion, the record holder and everything else until he joined MV in 1955. I often thought he should have had a works ride a lot earlier, but his career was probably planned to some degree by his father: bringing up a fast rider slowly. Whether John chose that too I don't really know but he was so young – in 1950 only 16, in 1955 only 21. By then he'd become a world-class rider and a year later 500cc World Champion.

"Before he moved up to that, from say 1952 onwards, he reached the stage where frankly he never lost. Surtees' dedication to racing was such that he was never a popular rider. He made races look too easy. He'd leave the starting line like a rocket, build up a tremendous lead and perhaps break the track record on the last lap, by which time he was already out of sight of everyone else. That did not endear him to the public (who like to see dicing and racing, of course). He didn't care at all. He had only one object, to win. The crowd didn't exist."

To have the full measure of the Surtees family, Rous recalls John's marriage to his first wife, Pat, in Winchester Cathedral. "Her father was mad keen on motor racing and Jimmy Clark was the chief usher for them, I was the chief usher for the Surtees side. Jack asked me to do it. The unusual thing was that John wore top hat and tails, the morning suit. All the bride's family did, and all the people on their side, too. Jack particularly requested that I wear an ordinary lounge suit, an ordinary collar and tie, and that's how all the people on the Surtees' side were dressed. Why? Jack didn't have, and John doesn't have, much time for pomp and circumstance. In fact he hasn't any time for it at all. They were very, very down to earth people.

"I didn't know Clark because I didn't cover car racing, only bikes, but curiously, he had an office at the bottom of Fleet Street – I don't know what he did there, perhaps used it as some sort of base – and one day I was walking down Fleet Street and he was walking up. 'Oh, hello, how are you?' he said. He remembered me from the wedding. 'Got time for a quick one?' I said I had and I added 'Let's nip in here.' We had a drink in the little alley beside the *Daily Express* in a pub called The Poppins."

Across his career John Surtees rode and drove a long road. The machiney alone tells you that: Vincent, Norton, AJS, EMC, REG, NSU, MV Agusta; Lotus, Cooper, Porsche, Vanwall, Lola, Ferrari, Matra, Honda, McLaren, Chaparral, Ford Capri and the car which bore his own name. He won races in or on virtually all of them, which remains deeply monumental, not to mention running his own Formula One team.

He won the 500cc race on the Isle of Man three years consecutively and averaged 102.44 miles an hour the third time. No man had done this before. He won the German Grand Prix at the Nurburgring, car racing's equivalent to the Isle of Man, two years consecutively and the second year qualified at 98.43 miles an hour. No man had gone so fast there before.

Along the road there would be Championships, risks and experiments, heated words, hardened memories, at least one savage crash. The man who did all this sits these days in his office in Surrey, white-haired, a merry twinkle in his eye, and still believing that in almost all circumstances he was right. He's always regarded life itself as a raw challenge and accepted the challenge full frontal. This explains why he accepted to drive for Honda in Formula One and why he pushed and pushed Honda; and you'd scarcely think of Honda as a company which needed pushing. It did and it got the push, all right.

"Me launching John's career in cars? Let's put that into perspective," Ken Tyrrell says. Tyrrell had worked in the family's timber business, tried racing in junior formulae and realized nature did not intend him to do this. What he could do was run a team, as he still does. In 1960 he had Formula Junior cars.

"John was obviously thinking about turning to cars and I read somewhere he had been driving the Aston Martin Formula One car, which was never any good." Surtees had in fact tested an Aston DBR1 sportscar at Goodwood in October 1959 and the F1 car in January, although he found it a disquieting experience, the car "nervous." A broken chassis was diagnosed. Interestingly, Surtees took his MV Agusta team-mate John Hartle with him and Hartle drove it, too.

Tyrrell says: "Because I saw he'd been driving it I called him up and asked him: 'How would you like to come and drive for me?' He had to do some motor racing in order to be able to do Formula One. You can't just go straight in. As a result of that he came down to Goodwood and got into my Formula Junior car. He was a natural, absolutely, and that was clearly evident immediately. You didn't need to be an expert to see it.

"He was able to throw the car around, something that motorcyclists don't do. In fact a little later, I think at John's suggestion, I gave Bob McIntyre [a legendary and lamented Glaswegian rider] a test down there. Bob came down with a young Scots fellow who pranced around, walked around on the balls of his feet making a general nuisance of himself. I didn't find out until a couple of years later that that young man was Jackie Stewart. He'd come down because he was a mate of Bob's.

"So Bob drove the car and he was useless, absolutely bloody useless. Jackie said quite rightly to me afterwards – he wasn't Jackie Stewart to me then, just this little Scots fellow – 'Bob's problem is he's never had a car which can be driven properly. The only vehicle he ever drives is his Bedford van with his motorbikes in.' Bob didn't know what it was to have an excess of power which made the back end come out, that sort of thing. And if a bike starts to move around you fall off it."

Surtees remembers it. "Ken is a person who gets wound up and goes off at all sorts of tangents, but basically he has a logical make-up, he can put two and two together. I think he thought there was nothing to lose, here's another rider who's very high in racing, might as well give him a go, too."

What were the differences between bikes and cars apart from the obvious? "First of all I was accustomed to racing and accustomed to being on racing tracks. I hadn't ever been to Goodwood before, so it wasn't like say Brands which of course I knew intimately. I'd had fast road cars, a couple of Aston Martins, a Porsche 356 which I skated around in, a BMW I used from 1957, but they weren't racers.

"You are immediately aware of vision. You are not up there on top of a bike and so you have to acquire a judgment of *widths*. Secondly, noise. In a front-engined car, particularly at low speeds, you get a great deal of mechanical noise which you don't experience in the same way at all on a bike. The noise passed beside you on a bike and flowed away. Third, heat. This heat would be in the cockpit, which you certainly don't experience on a bike, and with front radiators you had hot air all around you.

"In the car I followed the same principles of lines as I cornered. The big thing was getting used to slower corners. The faster corners – apart from having a steering wheel and using your foot on the throttle instead of your hand – were approached in the same way technically, in the way you held the balance, the feel of the road, the line of the corner. Not much difference, really, even in relative speeds. OK, you probably got a bit of understeer, but you naturally correct that.

"Slow corners were so different from a bike because of the braking power of the car and how you can brake right to the apex. The amount of power you can get onto the road with a car is that much more than a bike because you start putting the power on before the car is out of the corner. So in the car I was exploring different limits. In a chicane, if you'd given a bike full power you'd have been in the trees. The biggest aspects to come to terms with were these slower corners and slower circuits."

No matter. Surtees was literally into cars. "What John undertook was to drive whenever he could," Tyrrell says. "His father stood behind him all the time and what a pain in the backside his father was. 'Don't sign anything, don't sign anything', he kept saying, but I didn't really need John to sign anything anyway! He first raced at Goodwood on Easter Monday and he came second to Jim Clark. John has always been a bit of a difficult bloke, you know, but he never caused me any trouble. The one race where he could have done really well – the British Empire Trophy at Silverstone – I think he must have had a commitment with his bike which clashed. My other driver was Henry Taylor, and Henry won Monaco – the traditional supporting race to the Grand Prix, then Formula Junior and almost the same as the Formula Three which it later became – and Henry won the British Empire Trophy. By then the Cooper with the BMC engine wasn't very competitive and we'd bought ourselves a Lotus with a Cosworth engine. Henry led from start to finish, which John could have done."

Both Clark and Surtees would remember that Goodwood race on Easter Monday with some clarity. Moreover – and this is rarer than you think – when they subsequently wrote about it they both agreed what had happened. Clark, incidentally, hadn't driven for Team Lotus before.

They arrived at Madgwick together, Surtees took the lead, Clark, who knew his Lotus had better handling, slipstreamed, overtook Surtees on the second lap at Woodcote. Surtees – inevitably – attributes this to his own mistake. On the fifth lap Surtees retook Clark, the crowd reportedly savouring every moment of it, and Clark responded by retaking him. During the race Clark hammered out a new Formula Junior lap record and Surtees, briefly down to third place, rallied strongly and finished second.

Tyrrell understandably can't remember how many times Surtees drove for him in 1960 (in fact six) but Surtees approached car racing like a man moving urgently. He'd drive five Formula Two races and in one of them, at Brands Hatch, he and Geoff Duke crashed!

He tested, too, for Lotus and Chapman offered him a Formula One drive as and when he was available. It's difficult to believe now, but Surtees competed in, and won, the World 350 and 500cc bike Championships in 1960 and concurrently (so to speak) drove four Grands Prix as well as Formula Junior with Tyrrell and Formula Two. This is his schedule up to his Formula One debut in the International Trophy at Silverstone on May 14:

March 19	Formula Junior	Goodwood	2
April 2	Formula Junior	Oulton	R
	Formula Two	Oulton	2
April 18	500cc	Cesenatico	1
April 25	500cc	Imola	1
April 30	Formula Two	Aintree	4

At the International Trophy (Lotus-Climax) he dropped out with an oil leak. On the same day he finished second in a Formula Junior race. Thereafter:

| May 22 | World 350cc | Clermont-Ferrand | 3 |
| | World 500cc | Clermont-Ferrand | 1 |

He made his Grand Prix debut at Monaco on May 29. On the second day of qualifying *Autosport* reported that "practice began at the unearthly hour of 0600hrs, when the crackle of exhausts awakened the entire Principality. In the Junior section Jim Clark (Lotus) bettered Henry Taylor's time by no less than 3 secs, and Trevor Taylor by 2 secs." (This was the race Henry Taylor won – Clark seventh with ignition problems.)

Reporting on the Grand Prix qualifying, *Autosport* offered this lovely paragraph: "Saturday evening's training produced the expected scramble to qualify. Soon it was obvious that the 16 would all have to be under 1 min 40 secs. At one time Innes Ireland was not in the list so Stirling Moss sportingly undertook to show him the way round" – although in his second Grand Prix season Ireland hadn't competed here before. "It was quite a spectacle! Moss pointed out proper lines, braking points and where to tramp on the loud pedal – meanwhile sticking up two fingers in what looked like a rude gesture. He was merely indicating 'use second gear here!'"

Surtees qualified on the second last row of the grid, 1 minute 39.0 seconds. Moss, on pole, had 1 minute 36.3. Ireland, learning fast, put his Lotus on the third row.

Autosport offered another lovely paragraph. "Just before the off, to the astonishment of the crowd, what looked like a world famous Field Marshal [Montgomery] was seen in the pits area. Gendarmes were not quite sure what to do but breathed a sigh of relief when the military figure was revealed as Peter Kavanagh doing one of his well-known impersonations." Moss won the race, Surtees dropped out on lap 18 when the transmission failed. Thereafter:

June 15	World 350cc	Isle of Man	2
June 17	World 500cc	Isle of Man	1
June 25	World 350cc	Assen	1
	World 500cc	Assen	R
July 3	World 500cc	Spa	1
July 16	British GP	Silverstone	2

From the third row of the grid Surtees worked his way up to second, finishing 49.6 seconds behind Brabham. This must be seen as an outstanding performance and more. If the car people wondered about a biker they wondered no more. Maybe that dry, overcast July day the great double really began. Thereafter at Solitude he took the World Championship:

July 24	World 500cc	Solitude	1
	Formula Two	Solitude	R
Aug 1	Non-Champ F1 cars	Brands Hatch	6
	Formula Junior	Brands Hatch	4
Aug 6	World 350cc	Dundrod	1
	World 500cc	Dundrod	2

Dundrod stands as only the second 500cc race of the season Surtees hadn't won. The R at Assen on June 25 represents a crash, although only after he'd broken the track record. Now, in the Ulster Grand Prix, he finished 20.4 seconds behind Hartle (Norton). Thereby hangs a tale. Of it Peter Carrick wrote in *Great Motor-Cycle Riders* that "the racing withdrawals of Gilera, Guzzi and Mondial gave MV Augusta a clear field in 1958, and John Hartle, riding alongside John Surtees, responded well. In five of the seven rounds in the 350cc class he finished second to Surtees and notched two second places and one third in the 500cc series, finishing the season as runner-up to World Champion Surtees in both classes. On the Isle of Man that year he went into the record books, along with Surtees, by lapping the TT course at more than 100mph.

"Hartle remained with MV until the end of 1959, but it was not altogether a happy relationship. Surtees' role as premier rider for MV unfortunately overshadowed some impressive performances by Hartle, but in too many races he was impeded and frustrated by crashes or mechanical breakdown. Even so he finished second to Surtees for so long he finally decided to break away and in 1960, with few if any works rides available, he was back again on his own Nortons."

Rous gives the background. "Hartle came from Chapel-en-le-Frith and was a year or two older than Surtees. When he was called up to do his National Service they sent him down a coal mine because he'd been working in that industry. Hartle had an unfortunate physical problem. His bones were extremely brittle, a lack of calcium or whatever. If he fell he was almost sure to break one and they took a long time to heal. For an ordinary person the break would mend in three months, with Hartle it might be nine months. He was a very good rider, but always in the shadow of Surtees. He seemed a very good team man, but never a winner. In fact he did win a 350 TT on the Isle of Man, but only because Surtees broke down. In his career Hartle came and went, his career went up and down like Tower Bridge because of his various injuries.

"When he and John were riding for Norton they were in some Swedish resort, an inland place with a lake. Surtees went in off the jetty and mustn't have realized the depth of the water. Because of the purity of the water he couldn't float and found himself in extreme difficulties, went under for the third time. Hartle rescued him and, if Hartle hadn't, quite possibly Surtees would have drowned."

Surtees confirmed this. "John Hartle and Jack Brett [another Norton team-mate] were both good swimmers and they made it look so easy. Although I had rarely attempted to swim in my life it looked inviting, and in I went straight to the bottom. It was fresh water with virtually no buoyancy and I sank about 20 feet. No matter what I tried I couldn't get to the surface. John Hartle's sure hands got me up in the end. There is no doubt that he saved my life that day."

| Aug 14 | Portuguese GP | Oporto | R |

Alan Brinton had found Surtees "a very withdrawn individual. I knew nothing about motorcycle racing and I first met him when the *News Chronicle* ran a series of competitions on motorsport. Surtees was pulled in as the judge, so we went up to the Dorchester, two or three of us, had lunch with him and decided who'd won the prize. He'd got his arm in a sling, he'd fallen off a bike. He lived near Bromley in a very ordinary sort of house, I think with his parents. Portugal was his third Grand Prix. I was due to fly down there from Heathrow. I rang him and said: 'Come on, don't let's waste our money, I'll pick you up and we'll go to the airport together.' He said: 'Oh, good idea.' So I picked him up. He was not very communicative.

"In the race Moss had some trouble and called into the pits. Surtees led by a long way, overdid it, put his wheels in the tramlines and went off." Surtees explained that he'd had difficulty adjusting to the slow corners, but the line for faster corners was all but identical to bikes. Oporto spread tramlines and cobblestones and plenty of slow corners. Overall he revelled, studiously ignoring mutterings from established drivers about *who did this kid think he was, anyway?* This kid thought he was going to be World Champion, a feeling he, but not they, knew well. He crashed because petrol leaked onto the sole of his driving shoe and as he braked his foot slithered from the pedal. Instead of continuing up an escape road he tried to turn into the corner and ran into a kerb.

"We came back to Heathrow," Brinton says. "I'd a Mini-Cooper and I let him drive it. I said: 'Do you realize you might have made a little bit of history at Oporto yesterday? All right, so you went off but you were leading by a mile and this is only your third Grand Prix.' He said: 'Yes, yes, I suppose it was.' It hadn't gone to his head." To him Oporto did not represent a culmination, a proving, but part of the beginning. Thereafter:

Aug 27	Formula Two	Brands	R
Sept 11	World 350cc	Monza	R
	World 500cc	Monza	1
Sept 17	Formula Two	Snetterton	R
	Formula Junior	Snetterton	4
Sept 24	Formula Junior	Oulton	R
Nov 20	US Grand Prix	Riverside	R

Surtees departed Lotus amidst some typical Colin Chapman confusion. Chapman said he wanted Surtees to stay for 1961, Surtees said he'd like to partner Clark, but what then would happen to Ireland? Chapman assured Surtees that everything was arranged with Ireland, Ireland began to phone Surtees asking vehemently what are you doing taking my place from me? When they both faced Chapman to clarify the situation Chapman said he'd be running a second works team and Ireland would be in that. Surtees, unhappy about a situation so vague, did what he would subsequently do to another famous team when he found himself in an untenable position: made his own arrangements.

"When I drove with Jimmy in 1960 I expected to stay with him in 1961," Surtees says. "In fact I chose him to stay with me. Chapman gave me the option of Innes or Jimmy. He was already the works driver for Formula Junior and Formula Two. I took Jimmy because, one, I liked him and, two, I thought we knew and complemented each other in the team. Actually I believe I was quicker than Jimmy. I didn't think I could get on with Innes [two strong and dissimilar characters] because I judged our partnership would have a negative effect on the team. I was a new boy, I didn't know enough about car racing, but I thought Innes was a bit from the old school, which frankly resented people like myself and Jimmy coming in. It happens every generation and every generation must learn to live with it, but the fact remains it had happened and brought some ill-feeling, and I did think it was negative. When Chapman said 'either or' I said 'Jimmy'. What Chapman might have done in any case (disregarded Surtees; made *his* own arrangements?) I don't know. I'd like to have known..."

Surtees' bike career over – even he couldn't do a *full* season of both and he had nothing more to prove on bikes – he looked around for a Formula One drive. The choice proved very limited. BRM had Graham Hill and Brooks, Ferrari had five drivers, Porsche had Bonnier, Gurney, Herrmann and Beaufort and Lotus was now closed. The Cooper team remained. He joined: a mistake. It happens. From 1961 he took but four points; Enzo Ferrari approached him towards the end of the year but, although Surtees flew to Italy and met him and went on the subtle indoctrination of a conducted tour of the factory, he nursed uneasy feelings. For 1961 the CSI, the sport's governing body, had limited engine capacity to 1,500cc. The British teams protested this, took comfort that their protests would be upheld. Ferrari, meanwhile, immediately started work to meet the regulations and produced the beautiful shark-nosed Tipo 156. In it Phil Hill won the Championship from his team-mate von Trips.

At the factory Surtees sniffed complacency, knew the British teams would be catching up in 1962 and profoundly felt he wasn't armed with enough knowledge of car racing to surmount Ferrari politics. He'd need a solid base to do that. He'd vivid experience of Count Agusta of MV in bikes and sensed the same feudal kingdom mentality of Enzo Ferrari. He declined Ferrari's offer of a contract, but artfully enough not to preclude possible negotiations in the more distant future.

Surtees had a Lola for 1962, finished second in Britain and Germany and Ferrari contacted him again. This time Surtees said 'Yes'. He had the base of three seasons.

"Clark wasn't like Surtees," David Benson says. "Surtees was absolutely cold-blooded when it came to the racing. You could upset Surtees about strange things, things you'd written about him, but I've never met a calmer man before a race. Jimmy bit his nails, Surtees went cold. I remember at Silverstone and the *Daily Express* International Trophy meeting, Surtees on the front row in the Ferrari and I was walking about on the grid. He called me over. I wondered what he wanted to talk about so close to the start – no warm-up lap in those days and the minutes ticking away until they'd all clear off from the grid. He pointed to the rear-view mirror on the Ferrari, a streamlined thing, and said: 'I've just got the agency to distribute those. Can you do a piece about them in the *Express* because they are ideal for road cars.' That's the way he thought so close to a race."

(This must have been only partly motivated by self-interest. Surtees had a keen and perceptive interest in road safety and would write in a Silverstone programme in these mid-Sixties, addressing himself to the ordinary motorist: "I believe in taking the simple and surely commonsense precaution of wearing safety belts. There can no longer be any argument as to their effectiveness or value. Drivers of sportscars or other fast machinery are expected to be reasonably knowledgeable on most topics connected with motoring but it is this section of our community that has often displayed considerable lack of awareness of the benefits of using seat belts. Remember the best drivers do make mistakes." Surtees wrote this more than a decade before the wearing of belts became compulsory; and who else promoted the subject with such vehemence in the mid-Sixties? *Grand Prix* drivers weren't all wearing them then.)

This man could cope with Ferrari, the whims of Enzo and the frustrations of Scuderia Ferrari, separately or together, as they came. Surtees made that clear at his very first race, a sportscar 12-hour event at Sebring. His team-mate Willy Mairesse had, according to Surtees, tried both cars before Surtees arrived and decided Surtees' felt more comfortable – important in endurance. Surtees made his feelings known. The team manager, Eugenio Dragoni, fudged the issue and Surtees departed the circuit enraged. They had to talk him out of catching the plane home.

Push John Surtees, you get pushed back.

He won his first Grand Prix at the Nurburgring in August, itself a feat. Clark and Lotus had stretched, as we have seen, a tight net over the whole season thus far. Surtees was in no sense intimidated by this or by Clark. Surtees accepts that often enough Clark had superior machinery, but Surtees would compensate by absolute bravery. And "the Ring allowed you to equalize the mechanical advantage that Jimmy enjoyed most of the time, to put it bluntly. You had to pull up every possible thing in your favour. In many ways the Ring was very daunting, and to put it all together over that distance was a wholly different thing, changing conditions, wide variations and, strangely enough, although it had a lot of slow corners it had an awful lot of quick corners, which I normally favoured."

At the Nurburgring Clark took pole (8 minutes 45.8 seconds), with Surtees alongside (8 minutes 46.7). Clark's engine wasn't firing properly, Surtees made a poor start and Ginther (BRM) led. Moving into the second lap Clark attacked Surtees and that forced them both past Ginther at Atzenbach, over at the back of the pits. A great duel unfolded, the touch-skill of Clark against the determination of Surtees, who broke the lap record on lap two, Clark clinging, forcing. Clark led as they crossed the line to complete lap four, but repeatedly the Lotus fired on only seven cylinders. Surtees drew away and won by 1 minute 17.5 seconds.

Clark continued the season imperiously, although Surtees took pole at Monza. Clark won. Thereafter...Clark pole and winning Mexico, Clark pole and winning South Africa. Surtees did not finish any of these races: engine at Monza, piston at Watkins Glen, disqualified after a pit-stop push-start in Mexico, engine at East London. Final 1963 points:

Clark 54 (73), G. Hill 29, Ginther 29 (34), Surtees 22.

That might mean little for 1964. It is in the nature of Formula One that dominant situations are permeable and impermanent. A new season, a new chance. Of the three leading contenders for the 1964 World Championship,

Surtees also competed in five rounds of the Sportscar Championship, including Le Mans where he finished third; Clark spread himself to Formula Two, Indianapolis, the wonderful tightrope walks with Ford Cortinas; Graham Hill spread himself to Formula Two, a Ferrari in the Targa Florio, a Ferrari at Le Mans where he finished second...

A flavour of that. All three went to Sebring for the 12-hour race on March 22: Surtees third, Clark 21st, Hill out when his gearbox failed. A new season and who knows? While Hill contested the Targa Florio on April 26 Clark drove a Formula Two Lotus at the Nurburgring.

Dickie Attwood was, as he says, "coming up through the ranks at the time. Formula Junior suddenly became Formula Two, and in order to give the younger guys like myself a bit of experience they brought in what they termed graded drivers, Jimmy among them. We moved round like a circus and I think I came to know Jimmy as well as anybody in racing: an ordinary bloke who just happened to be a brilliant driver. Most drivers, if the truth be known, are very shy.

"I remember the race at the Nurburgring, on the South Circuit, a really good five-miler, and Jimmy cleared off into the lead, me second. I put everything into one lap. I knew to myself I'd got everything absolutely correct, a few hundred revs quicker than I had been before coming out of every corner, using all the circuit. Well, I thought, at least I've got fastest lap. I waited for the prizegiving that night and, you know, Clark fastest lap. I'd done everything, I couldn't have done more and he was still quicker. He almost didn't have to try. It was really annoying, actually. At the end of practises at all these races the question was always *what has Jimmy done?* He was the barometer the other people went by and they all knew it."

This was the man Surtees intended to beat.

On April 12, Surtees won a non-Championship race at Syracuse (Clark was at Oulton Park that weekend winning in a Lotus Cortina, a Lotus 19 and a Lotus Elan). On May 2, Hill came second in the International Trophy at Silverstone – Surtees dropped out (fuel pump) and Clark went out, too.

Clark set off to qualify for Indianapolis, which meant he missed the first day's practice for the opening Grand Prix, Monaco. Surtees, armed with a new V8 Ferrari, struck out fastest time, although he complained about the gearbox. A tight session, Jack Brabham 0.1 second behind Surtees, Graham Hill 0.2 behind Brabham.

"I met Jim at Nice Airport," Andrew Cowan says. "I'd been practising for the Alpine Rally in a Ford Mustang. Jim flew in on the Friday morning from Indy, I picked him up and drove him straight to Lotus, just opposite the pits. They rented a shop with a house above it. I dropped him in the back street, parked the car and went to the Lotus pit. Eventually Jim came out wearing his ordinary clothes, sat and watched the Formula One practice. His car sat there. He went back across and put his overalls on. He never spoke to people. When Jim moved into the build-up he ignored people. He jumped in the car, he did four laps, set fastest time, slowed down, came in and went straight to the hotel. He was tired, you see."

That lap, 1 minute 34.0 seconds, was a record (although unofficial because lap records are only set during races). Brabham almost shaved it – 1 minute 34.1; Graham Hill and Surtees on the second row.

"On the Saturday morning Jim was a bit fresher and we had a chat," Cowan says. "Jackie and Helen Stewart were with us – he was driving a Formula Three

Tyrrell. We were all in the Lotus pit, final practice for the Grand Prix going on. Nobody beat Jim's time and he only went out for the last quarter of an hour, did some 10 laps and that was him ready. Jackie raced in the Formula Three event. Jim, Helen and I stood in the trees in the centre. I'll never forget this: Helen Stewart almost picked the bark off one as Jackie won. Jim was absolutely thrilled for him, thrilled, thrilled, thrilled, yes."

J Stewart	(Cooper-BRM)	42m 35.0s
S Moser	(Brabham-BMC)	42m 52.0s
M Bianchi	(Alpine-Renault)	43m 13.9s

(Chauvinistically, *Autosport* said: "Stewart went on to another unchallenged victory while Continental cars and drivers encouragingly filled the minor places.")

The Grand Prix: *Autosport* reported that "following the antics of Louis Chiron with the flag of Monaco, the field got away to a perfect start, with Jim Clark slightly in front of a tightly packed and jostling group headed by Graham Hill and Jack Brabham. Up Ste Devote they swept by, in a glorious crescendo of sound from fifteen V8 engines and Bandini's lone V6. Down past the Tip Top to Mirabeau, and Station corner, on to the promenade and then through the tunnel it was a tremendous spectacle. Clark came through the chicane in a vicious slide, appearing to bounce off the straw bales, hurled the Lotus into the notorious Tobacconist Kiosk, and was leading the pack as they shrieked past the pits and the Royal Box to start the second lap. The order was Clark, Brabham, Graham Hill, Gurney, Surtees, Ginther, Arundell ..."

Clark drew away from Brabham across the first five laps but something was wrong with his car. Sparks churned from it. The rollbar virtually disintegrated and *Autosport* reported that "there had been a moment or so when Chiron threatened to have him black-flagged. However, the Lotus seemed to be unaffected and the excitable Monegasque was persuaded not to take any action."

Surtees had already been into the pits complaining about the gearbox – he felt the gearchange wasn't right – but rejoined quickly. He went as far as the tunnel before the Ferrari stopped altogether. Clark pitted on lap 36 to have what remained of the rollbar removed, letting Gurney into the lead, Graham Hill second. Clark broke the lap record, Hill responded by breaking it, too. Gurney dropped out, gearbox, and needed treatment for burns from hot oil. Reportedly a pretty nurse cut away the pants of his Dunlop overalls. Hill led Clark by 5 seconds and increased it to 14.4 after 80 laps – 20 laps left. Eventually Clark stopped – oil pressure – leaving Hill a clear winner from Ginther.

A week later Clark and Hill contested the London Trophy at Crystal Palace, and as the programme noted: "Today the new Formula Two cars are racing in the South of England for the first time. Indeed, until this weekend there had been no British race exclusively in the class. One of the arguments in favour of the new class is that it gives up-and-coming drivers the chance to race the world's best in identical cars. Today just such a chance has arrived. World Champion Jim Clark and the man he dethroned, Graham Hill, will need every scrap of experience and skill to hold the challenge of men like Mike Spence, Richard Attwood and Alan Rees who are well acquainted with the tricky Palace circuit from their Formula Junior days. Although he had a couple of practice laps in the Renault Alpine at Pau, this will be Graham Hill's first taste of Formula Two racing." Denny Hulme had a Brabham, Brian Hart a Lotus, Jochen Rindt a Cooper. Interestingly Hill won his heat, Clark only second in his, and neither won the final; Hill second, Clark 10th.

At Zandvoort for the Dutch Grand Prix, Gurney (Brabham) took pole, Clark and Hill alongside him on the front row, Surtees behind. Surtees had a new car, the gearbox problems cured. The race proved straightforward, Clark leading all the way and winning, Surtees moving up from fifth to a strong second, 53.6 seconds behind Clark.

A week later Surtees and Hill contested the Nurburgring 1000 kilometres, Clark being at Indianapolis (where he retired, suspension.) Surtees ought to have won at the Ring, but his Ferrari lost a wheel late in the race and Hill was disqualified for a refuelling infringement.

At Spa for the Belgian Grand Prix, Surtees had fuel-feed problems in qualifying, battled into the lead – he held it for a single lap – and retired; more fuel-feed problems. Gurney, leading and within sight of victory, ran out of fuel and Clark nipped past McLaren to win the race. At Le Mans Hill finished second in a Ferrari, with Surtees third.

"The only time the Ferrari Formula One team tested was after Le Mans," Surtees says. "Before that very little would happen – all the attention focused on the sportscars because it attracted a lot of sponsorship. If you won Le Mans money came in and it helped to sell the road cars. Afterwards we'd get a bit of movement. If you look at the records after Le Mans the car's performance starts to improve purely because of the concentration on it."

Not immediately. Surtees has described the French Grand Prix at Rouen as a "fiasco" for Ferrari, the team arriving so late they missed the first day's practice altogether. That day Clark did what contemporary accounts describe as an "almost unbelievable" lap of 2 minutes 9.6 seconds, 7.3 faster than Hill's record set the last time the cars had been there in 1962.

At this meeting Clark tried Lindsay's ERA, covered three laps and "shook everyone" by getting down to 2 minutes 48.7 seconds, which someone described as "a really splendid time for such a veteran machine." Endruweit remembers that. "One of the attractions of the meeting was a vintage car event, more of an exhibition drive than a race. The ERA was an incredible old machine. Somebody came along and said: 'I would be awfully pleased if Mr Clark would give it a try.' Off Jimmy trundled in it and the bloke was understandably nervous because he didn't want the hell beaten out of the thing. Then Jimmy went quicker and put up a faster time than the owner had ever dreamed of, brought the car back and the car wasn't sweating, you know. Jimmy had this tremendous empathy with machinery and that is one of the things I was most impressed by: how he could get into a totally strange machine and drive it extremely well, hardly trying as it were, and he'd had no previous free laps, never seen a car like this before."

Surtees put the Ferrari on the front row, Clark on pole. Clark took the lead and on lap two Surtees gave a "distress signal", and after three laps the Ferrari "lay forlorn" in its pit while mechanics tried to find the trouble. Surtees restarted on about five cylinders.

At 10 laps Clark led Gurney, and Surtees was back in the pits, his race over. Clark broke the lap record three times, then, on lap 30, he cruised into the pits, his engine gone. Gurney won from Graham Hill, which gave a Championship table after four Grands Prix: Clark 21, Graham Hill 20, Ginther and Arundell 11, Gurney 10, Brabham 8, McLaren 7, Surtees 6.

(Lindsay won the Golden Age race with a fastest lap of 2 minutes 50 seconds. Compare Clark's time, above. In the Formula Three race Stewart won on aggregate by 1 minute 16.6 seconds from his team-mate Warwick Banks. *Autosport* described him as "a natural who has demonstrated in less than three months he has already outgrown Formula Three racing.")

Surtees felt depressed, no matter that he keenly anticipated the British Grand Prix (dubbed the European Grand Prix) at Brands Hatch as a homecoming, stirring memories no doubt of the very first heat of the very first race there on a bike. But – who could stop Clark? Before the meeting Clark described a lap which Brands Hatch carried in the race programme, and it's worth reproducing verbatim.

"In dry weather we should be lapping at well under 1 minute 40 seconds. As I run my finger over a map of the circuit I find that there are 20 places where something interesting is happening, and where for a driver the difference between doing everything just right and not-so-well can mean that fraction of a second which loses places on the starting grid, or even positions in the race. Brands Hatch being what we call a medium-speed circuit, we shall probably be using only four of our five speeds and on that basis this is how it will go:

"I shall be coming past the pits in fourth and approaching our first 'point of interest', the area before Paddock Hill Bend. Here I shall be braking heavily at a point where there is quite an undulation in the surface, and with the brakes still on I shall be going down to third and then possibly second before accelerating through the second part of the bend. I come in from perhaps a bit left of centre to clip the inside edge just before the final drop into the dip.

"Here there is a sudden change of camber which has to be watched if the car is not to 'grass' on the left side coming out of the bend. When going really fast at Paddock you feel quite a bit of G loading at the bottom of the dip. It is one of the trickiest corners on a British circuit.

"Assuming there is no-one trying to come up on my right side, I keep well over to the left going up the hill, then brake hard and simultaneously drop down to first for Druids Hill Bend. By keeping it reasonably tight coming out of the turn I can reduce the amount of S-bending necessary to be properly lined up for the first part of Bottom Bend.

"For this, I have to be well over to the right side of the track, and I take second gear before making the left-hand turn. There are black and white marker stones on the apex of the bend, and I aim to keep close to these, giving me plenty of track to the right for accelerating on to Bottom Straight. This part of the course is badly named because, as any Brands Hatch driver will confirm, it is really a long left-hand curve and you cannot see the first part of South Bank Bend until you are about half way along it.

"I should get third briefly here before going down to second again when braking for South Bank. The line here is quite different from that used for racing on the short club circuit. We have to keep over to the right much later so as to flatten out as much as possible the second half of the bend – it doubles back uphill under the footbridge. Anyone who fails to cut right back across to the left side for the second apex usually finds that they have to back off to prevent themselves running out of road on the right, and of course this loses valuable time on the climb up into the new loop.

"Now I am entering the fastest part of the course and I shall be up into third again by the time I take the right-hand kink just before the brow of the hill, and fourth as I drop down again under the second bridge. You get a curious sensation here on a Grand Prix car because at one point it seems as though the bridge has fallen onto the track and you are driving straight for it, but of course the track drops away in time!

"With the car well over to the left I have to brake quite hard and drop down to third for the fairly fast uphill right-hander, Hawthorn's Bend, for which I try to cut across comparatively late so that I do not stray out too far as I come out of the bend. This is a corner which gives me a lot of satisfaction when I take it well, and where valuable tenths of a second can be saved.

"The next right-hander, Westfield Bend, is slower than Hawthorn's, although not as slow as it looks as you approach it. By keeping well over to the left in the braking area, I can drop down to second and then cut across to go through quite fast, remembering that there is a rough patch coming out which needs watching when accelerating hard.

"Speed builds up quite quickly now as the gradient is sharply downhill, and I am back in third before I clip the right-hand edge of the track in the dip at Dingle Dell. By holding my line there, the Lotus automatically comes back on to the left-hand side of the track as we go uphill again towards Dingle Dell Corner. This needs a lot of concentration, first because you approach it blind, second because you have to brake heavily, and third because the track suddenly flattens out as you are still braking and the back end tends to become a bit light. I drop down to second for this one, and the short straight from here to Stirling's Bend becomes in effect an 'S' as I pull the car back from the left to the right side of the track before braking heavily again.

"Stirling's Bend is one of those tight left-handers that seem to go on for ever, and it is essential to turn in late if you hope to come out at any speed and still stay on the track. It is a borderline case between first and second gear, and even if I use first I need second again immediately I am out of the turn and heading slightly downhill towards the third footbridge just before rejoining the short circuit at Clearways.

"This is another tricky point, because on the Grand Prix circuit Clearways becomes a fast corner, for which I hold the car in third, and if you run too wide on the entry you have to fight to keep the car from taking to the grass on the outside. The big problem here comes in matching your speed and braking as you emerge from under the bridge to the precise moment when you have to lock over from the left to the right side of the track.

"I aim to be pretty close in going over the 'hump' then let the car come out again towards the centre for the next part of the bend where I am back on full throttle. Even on the final run-in to the start-finish line there is no time for relaxation beause there is quite a pronounced dip just at the start of the pit area (where I get fourth) which can unsettle a car if it is not correctly placed. Finally, just to let me know one more lap has been completed, I get another 'dip' just across the line as I accelerate through another undulation.

"Well, there it is. About 100 seconds' worth of concentrated driving during which 20 different sets of circumstances have arisen on average one every five seconds, each demanding something different from the chap in the cockpit."

Instructive? But yes, not least how precise, clinical and unhurried it seems, although he doesn't mention speeds. Drivers don't think in those terms, only revs and gearchanges. For the benefit of spectators, however, Brands Hatch offered their own guestimates: 90mph at Paddock Hill Bend, 115 at Pilgrim's

Rise, 50 at Druid's, 90 at Bottom Bend, 120 along Bottom Straight, 90 at South Bend, 150 on the straight, 110 at Hawthorn's, 110 at Westfield Bend, 75 at Dingle Dell, 70 at Stirling's Bend, 120 at Clearways, 135 crossing the start-finish line.

Clark took pole with 1 minute 38.1 seconds and in the race set fastest lap, 1 minute 38.8. which translates to 96.561 miles an hour. Brands measured 2.65 miles. Breaking the chronology and peering towards the distant future, in 1986 Brands measured 2.614 miles. At the British Grand Prix, Nigel Mansell set fastest lap, 1 minute 9.593 seconds, which translates to 135.191 miles an hour. I mention this only because it raises an eternal and maddeningly frustrating question: if Clark had driven then, had driven a 1986 car, what would he have done?

That aside, Clark's 1964 lap destroys the mythology that he just drove. As you can see, he foresaw, calculated and understood what he was doing every yard of Brands and why. The intuitive gifts allowed him to build monumental laps, but build them on his reasoning.

In qualifying, Surtees suffered a surfeit of dramas again. His V8 Ferrari hadn't arrived, so he took Bandini's V6 and Bandini didn't get a run on the first day – a session enervated by an offer of 100 bottles of champagne by the London *Evening News* to the fastest driver. Surtees, fifth, mourned a lost opportunity, and so doubtless did Clark and Hill, third and fourth. Gurney – 1 minute 38.4 seconds – became the toast of the paddock, or toasted the paddock, anyway.

On the second day, Surtees had the V8 and did 1 minute 38.7, worth the second row, while Clark, as we have seen, took pole. By 9 o'clock in the morning of race day ominous rain eased and an estimated 40,000 people were already inside Brands being 'entertained'. Military bands played, and then came a demonstration of modern battle tactics with armoured cars, helicopters and the troops of Eastern Command. *Autosport* reported that "unprepared folk jumped high in the air when the RA gunners suddenly blasted off a 25-pounder near the tunnel. The wind changed direction and people in the tribunes disappeared behind a choking smokescreen."

Breaking the chronology and peering towards the distant future again, at Brands Hatch in 1986 soldiers in British, American and German uniforms refought World War Two at Clearways. I happened to be sitting next to Nigel Roebuck and could see that the 'entertainment' revolted him, as indeed it did many others. Someone wondered what Christian Danner, a pleasant German driving for the Arrows team, made of it. "Nothing like the restful crack of gunfire to help the lunch down a treat," Roebuck wrote. "Eventually – mercifully – they ran out of bullets or something, and then they all trooped off again. Extraordinary."

Some things change crossing the Bridge of Time, some things don't.

On July 11, 1964 when – mercifully – the RA gunners stopped blasting off their 25-pounder, the flag fell and Clark took the lead, Surtees fourth at the end of the opening lap with Gurney and Graham Hill between. Gurney moved on Clark, but Gurney's engine let go and, as he cruised, Hill went by and so did Surtees, who beat the record on lap four with 1 minute 39.6 seconds.

The race evolved into two distinct struggles, Hill attacking Clark for the lead, Brabham attacking Surtees for third place. On lap 16 Brabham spun, settling one struggle. The vast crowd watched fascinated as Hill maintained his attack lap after lap, never more than half a second behind Clark. The impetus of this became so strong that by lap 35 they'd moved past everyone except Surtees, who realized that to try to catch them would be risky, and circulated steadily around the 1 minute 40 seconds mark. Hill made a thrust on the final lap but, the crowd on their feet, Clark held him, Surtees finishing 1 minute 20.6 seconds distant. Clark 30 points, Graham Hill 26, Ginther, Arundell and Brabham 11, Gurney and Surtees 10.

The drivers did not flee Brands Hatch in helicopters, they played a cricket match at Farningham the following day against a local side and it raised £250 for Oxfam. The drivers' team embraced Clark (captain), Paddy Hopkirk, Stewart, Hailwood, McLaren, Sir Gawaine Baillie, Sir John Whitmore, Surtees, Peter Jopp, Les Leston, Innes Ireland, Graham Hill, Jo Bonnier, Attwood and Amon. You may have noticed that traditionally a cricket team comprises 11 and the Drivers fielded 15...

Jo Bonnier, a Swiss-domiciled Swede, had certainly never played the game before and quite possibly had not heard of it either, but this did not prevent him from taking what one contemporary account describes as "a tremendous catch". Mattie Calder saw the match and remembers how good Hailwood was, and how "Jim hit sixes all over the place". Someone else (alas, I don't know who) claimed Clark made 65 and saw the ball "quicker than anybody else," which says a great deal. Hill would remember how Bonnier held a cricket bat like a baseball bat, would remember how after the match they all went to a restaurant called The Contented Plate to celebrate Amon's birthday.

A week later Clark won the Solitude non-Championship Grand Prix from Surtees. Hill didn't finish.

"So," Surtees says, "we did some testing, we did some development work, started to get the car racing properly. Well, we got it working pretty well for the Nurburgring" – potentially a crucial Grand Prix. Only four remained after it. Qualifying was marred by a crash by de Beaufort, whose Porsche went off at Bergwerk. Head and spine injuries subsequently proved fatal.

Surtees took pole from Clark, but Bandini seized the lead and held it to the South Curve where, in a surge, Clark, Surtees and Gurney went past him. Into the North Curve Gurney had his Brabham inches from Clark's exhaust, Surtees wheel-to-wheel with Gurney. Somehwere out there on that opening lap Surtees took Gurney and as they crossed the line to begin lap two lay no more than half a second behind Clark. At the South Curve he nipped out and took Clark and further on Gurney did, too. Gurney, in superb form, took Surtees, but Surtees wasn't unduly concerned. He'd find whatever he needed from the Ferrari. Ultimately he didn't need to.

Gurney duelled Surtees, Hill duelled Clark and at the end of lap five the Ferrari held the Brabham by inches, both over 10 seconds in front of Hill, who gradually pulled away from Clark. The crowd reportedly "gasped" as Gurney overtook Surtees on the inside of the North Curve, but – the two cars fleeing over the rise after the North Curve – Surtees drew alongside. On lap seven Surtees battered the lap record with 8 minutes 45 seconds and led Gurney by 3 seconds.

Clark's engine failed, Surtees cranked up the record to 8 minutes 39 and Gurney drifted away from him, water temperature beginning to rise – Surtees thought that must have been through the Brabham gathering a stray newspaper which had blown onto the track and blocked the airflow to the radiator. Surtees was strong, had been all his life, the Ferrari had become strong, and he beat Hill by 1 minute 15.6 seconds. In retrospect this result was pivotal: Hill 32 points,

Clark 30, but Surtees now 19. In the background Enzo Ferrari threatened to boycott Monza because Ferrari hadn't been allowed to test there, a delightful piece of Ferrari spite, and rendered more amusing because of the team's indifference to testing until after Le Mans.

Rindt made his Grand Prix debut at the next race, Zeltweg, a rough and ready – well, primitive – airfield and not to be confused with the Osterreichring, used for the Austrian Grand Prix from 1970. The Osterreichring, too, carried a Zeltweg dateline, but nestled into foothills some miles away. *This* Zeltweg was laid with concrete sections and the cars rumbled and bucked across them. (In practice Ginther shed a wheel and it flowed full into a spectator area, striking the flank of a saloon car.) It had a long start-finish straight, a curve to a peardrop-shaped right-right bringing them back to another long straight which ran parallel to the start-finish and was linked to it, at the end, by two 90-degree rights. Straw bales offered the protection and a London double-decker bus had a scoreboard on its roof to show the crowd the first four cars.

In Rindt's biography Heinz Pruller wrote that "photographers were at the airport as the top drivers arrived and tried to arrange the classic, handshaking photographs – Rindt and Clark, then Rindt with Hill – but Jochen was determined to avoid being obtrusive; he didn't yet feel like master in his own home, but more like a guest in his own country. The drivers' briefing was held in English and Jochen missed a point. When he asked, one of the English drivers turned round and suggested 'don't worry, just follow us.'"

Hill took pole on a four-wide front row, Clark next to him, then Surtees and Gurney. Surtees took an early lead, Graham Hill dropped out on lap five – distributor – and three laps later Surtees stopped. "I'd passed the others and, a bloody thing, the front suspension broke. You'd never expect a Ferrari suspension component to actually break, a chance in a million that it did." At that moment he thought the Championship had gone. Gurney led Clark by more than 12 seconds after 25 laps, but on lap 40 Clark coasted into the pits, a driveshaft broken. Zeltweg's sectional concrete claimed its victims.

Bandini survived to win from Ginther, with privateer Bob Anderson in a Brabham third. Anderson had ridden motorbikes at World Championship level, which gave the race an unusual dimension. Surtees and Hailwood (eighth here in a Lotus) had, too, of course, and Siffert (Brabham), who retired here after a spin, had been Swiss bike champion before he came to cars. No change in the Championship: Hill 32, Clark 30, Surtees 19.

A week later Clark, Hill and Surtees contested the Tourist Trophy at Goodwood. In midfield in the race Surtees found himself boxed when the car in front swerved to avoid a crash ahead. He struck a bank, the impact so great it knocked him out. "Innes Ireland got himself into trouble with the Aston Martin and took me off. I went to hospital with concussion." That was August 29. The Italian Grand Prix at Monza would be on September 6. Surtees underwent medical checks – concussion is a strange, unpredicable condition – and flew to Monza.

"That was a drama. BRM launched a protest that I hadn't had time to recover, that I couldn't be fit. The Ferrari team manager Dragoni said: 'We can't do anything about that', then he said: 'I tell you what, Signor Marghiere – seconded to the Cape Canaveral rocket centre to study the effects on the brain and things like that – is at Milan University. He can carry out tests, say you're fit to drive and they'll have to accept it.' Luckily this was Italy [Surtees chuckles: What Italian, professor or merely *tifosi* wouldn't sign a health certificate for a Ferrari driver going for the Championship, and at Monza?]. Off I trundled into Milan and I was stuck through all these machines, put through everything else and Marghiere said: 'He has some little bruising, but nothing that will impede his driving. Yes, he can drive."

Surtees took pole...

(The Monza police, notorious for their brusque insensitivity, "rudely handled" Enzo Ferrari during the Saturday session.)

At the flag Hill, on the right of the three-car front row, dipped the clutch and nothing happened. The BRM didn't move. Instinctively he whipped his arm up hoping the surge of cars behind would see it, he *felt* the surge: noise, dust and smoke. Nobody hit him. Hill, pushed from the grid to the pits, watched the race helplessly. Gurney led lap one with Surtees attacking and slipping through on lap two as McLaren and Clark were poised to try and get the lead themselves. A slipstreaming race of many fleeting combinations, but unravelling when Clark's engine let go on lap 28 and Gurney's engine started to fail. Surtees, imperious, beat McLaren by more than a minute and Monza surrendered to emotion. "A very good race, a very good race," Surtees says crisply. Hill 32, Clark 30, Surtees 28.

Monza did not conclude with a cricket match, but a lively party at the Hotel de la Ville culminating in a pitched battle of wrapped napkins between the Cooper, Lotus and Brabham teams. Later Dan Gurney's Fiat 600 would be discovered perched on a flower-bed in the middle of a roundabout.

Between Monza and the United States Grand Prix, Clark drove at Albi, Oulton Park, the non-Championship Canadian Grand Prix at Mosport and Trenton in New Jersey. Hill, who took his family on holiday, drove at Oulton, Snetterton and Montlhery.

Surtees spent time in Italy urging Ferrari to put their full weight behind the effort at Watkins Glen – Enzo, as ever, locked into a dispute, this time with the Italian Automobile Club over whether the Ferrari Grand Touring car had been produced in sufficient numbers (minimum 100) to qualify for the races. Enzo took flight into one of his rages, said none of his racing cars would compete domestically again and would never compete abroad in the famous red again, either. At Watkins Glen they ran in white livery, a historical moment.

A fascinating race of move and counter-move, Clark on pole and Surtees on the front row, Hill on the second, Clark leading, Surtees through at the Esses. By lap nine Clark lay within a second of Surtees, pressured, retook the lead. Surtees found the Ferrari a couple of hundred revs down on the straights. Hill took him. Clark's engine started stuttering and banging and he pitted. On lap 56 of 110 a pit board ordered his Lotus team-mate Mike Spence, comfortably fourth, to come in and give his car to Clark – a gamble, and controversial and cunning, too. Clark could not score points in Spence's car – the days of Fangio and car-hopping had long gone – but what he manifestly could do was take points from Surtees. If Clark passed Hill and Surtees he pushed them back and they received less points. Damage-limitation by Clark, in fact.

On lap 68 Surtees missed a gear and plunged off the circuit onto the grass, churned dust. "There was a little bit of a dice going on," Surtees says, "I was having a go at Graham Hill. I went off at the end of the straight." Surtees rejoined, but Gurney had moved by into second place, although Dan stopped a lap later – engine. At 70 laps Hill led Surtees by 17 seconds, Clark a minute behind and soon enough the engine on *this* Lotus trailed away. That was lap 92, Hill and Surtees holding station, risking nothing.

On lap 101 Hailwood's Lotus laid oil all over the right-hander before the start-finish straight. Cars "waltzed" through it and Bandini (Ferrari), who'd retired just after half-distance, scampered down there and began to fling cement dust on it in case Surtees waltzed completely off. Innes Ireland scampered up to help, but officals ordered them away. Hill tip-toed through the oil and won by 30.5 seconds from Surtees.

Mathematics exercised everyone before the climax, the Mexican Grand Prix, because a driver could count only his six best finishes. Hill now had seven and so dropped his two points from Belgium, which left him with 39, Surtees 34, Clark 30. The mathematics became more subtle: Clark could still take the title if he won the race, Hill finished no higher than fourth and Surtees finished no higher than third. Hill and Clark would share 39, Hill gaining 3 points, but having to drop them because he'd finished fourth in Holland. Clark would have it on the most-wins tie-break, four-two. Hill had to win and even this would be worth only 6 points – those nagging 3 from Holland would have to be dropped. Hill's maximum total: 45. If Surtees won he became undisputed Champion, no further mathematics necessary. If he finished second, with Hill not in the top three, he won it, too.

Question to Surtees: Did you speak to Bandini before the race, because the way it shook out he could really help you?

"Oh, we used to talk about things, bits and pieces, but we had no arrangements in a team like Ferrari, particularly the way things were with Dragoni (not the world's greatest team manager, let us say). You concentrated on yourself. I had a good relationship with Bandini, and obviously you said: 'Come on, if you are around maybe we could do some slipstreaming down the long straight.'"

Ferrari had taken four cars, supposedly two with V8 engines for Surtees, a flat-12 for Bandini and a V6 held in reserve. "The engine which had the most power of the lot," Surtees says, "was the V6 like we'd had in 1963, but it wasn't reliable enough at the power it produced. The V6 was going into the Ferrari Dino and so they made the V8 which was to be for a similar project. Ferrari had a commercial application in his mind for the V8. Then people said: 'We'd love a 12-cylinder' and Ferrari made it, and that was the emotional side of Enzo as well as the practical.

"I tried the 12 and the 8 in practice, but the big worry was that the 12 tended to use a lot of oil, and with the banking and the G forces we thought we might have oil problems. There was also fuel consumption although, strangely enough, because the circuit was at altitude, this didn't prove too bad. Ferrari said: 'No, no, you must use the 8,' thinking of playing for safety – in the latter part of the season the 8 hadn't been giving troubles. It didn't always run particularly well, but it was a strong engine. Ferrari said: 'We know very well the 12 is a bit quicker, but the 8 is more secure.'

"We went through practice trying to get the mixture right, we needed a very fine mixture setting at that altitude. They were able to do it with the 12 because it had the Lucas injection, they weakened it away up at the top and its performance leap-frogged over the 8 – we were trying to get finer and finer settings, but with injection pumps originally made for 2½-litre engines. You can see from the practice times we struggled, but Mexico could often be very hot, a very rough circuit, and I knew anything could happen."

Clark took pole from Gurney, Bandini and Surtees on the second row, Hill on the third. The bumps on the circuit gave Hill a sore head, a sore neck and a sore knee. The Mexican Grand Prix is mythological. At the start Hill, hauling his goggles down, broke the elastic and sat helplessly fiddling with them. That cost him a bag of places. Surtees gave the Ferrari full power, it responded, almost immediately staggered forward misfiring, nearly stopped, fired again. "We'd gone on weakening the mixture and weakening the mixture, looking for performance, and the thing wouldn't run smoothly. I flapped along for a while before frankly it started to boil and then it got cooking, running better and better." By then Clark had long gone, and they crossed the line to complete lap one with Hill ninth and Surtees 10th. Next lap Hill picked up a couple of places, but Clark commanded the race and on lap five led Gurney by 5 seconds. Surtees, biding his time, moved up to eighth.

At lap 10 Clark paced himself from Gurney, who drew away from Bandini. Hill reached Bandini on lap 11. Hill took him and imagined if he stayed there he'd be Champion even if Surtees came by and won the race. Hill was mistaken: that would have given Surtees 43 points, Hill only 40 (four gained here, the dreaded three from Holland discarded). Certainly if Clark won and Hill stayed third and Surtees seventh, Hill had it – but on lap 16 Surtees, who'd wrestled with Brabham for six laps, got by and was coming hard.

Lap 21 of the 65: Clark 7 seconds from Gurney, Gurney 12 seconds from Hill, Bandini swarming Hill, Surtees 4 seconds behind this pair and being harried by Brabham. On lap 31, one of the mathematical permutations was settled in a moment which remains, at least within the elderly confines of the sport, a matter of some doubt. It involved the integrity of Bandini, and since Bandini is not alive to defend himself, I'm going to give different versions of what happened.

Hill, in his autobiography, wrote that Bandini started to challenge him and made "one or two wild attempts to pass going into the hairpin. On one lap he dived straight in underneath me [inside] and I had to move out to give him room – it was a bit of a desperate effort and as I was coming out of the hairpin his front wheel hit my back wheel and spun me round into the guard rail."

Autosport reported: "Bandini was fractionally behind and on a slightly tighter line as they came through the hairpin. As they began to exit, the Ferrari started to slide wide and its front wheel hit the right-hand wheel of the BRM. The BRM spun round and went into the guard rail backwards."

Hill reflected after the race that while others might say Bandini did this deliberately – it not only took Hill out of the race but lifted Surtees to fourth, and if it had taken Bandini himself out would have lifted Surtees to third – Hill did not believe this.

Surtees reflects that Bandini never indulged in "dirty tactics" and points out that Hill and Bandini shook hands afterwards. "I came up to this battle. To start with it all carried on normally. At the banked hairpin the standard procedure would be to go up the outside and dive into the centre. I believe signals were going out to Hill of me getting closer and closer and *Hill was racing me rather than Bandini*" – never mind that Bandini lay between them. "I saw the whole thing getting more desperate, big locking-up of wheels, diving for things. Bandini tried to get past several times coming up the inside to this hairpin, and each time Hill got across and would start blocking him. What then happened was a Prost-Senna situation where each of them did not quite get it right. I think

Bandini had actually stolen the corner, Hill tried to close the door, they touched and that was it."

Surtees also points out that at this precise moment Clark, leading the race so easily, would win the Championship unless Surtees could reach second place, which meant not only passing Bandini – who'd set off after the crash – but Gurney as well.

Hill limped a lap and a half with his exhaust pipes buckled by the impact against the guard rail at the top of the hairpin banking, moved to the pits where the mechanics "broke off the end of the pipe" and he chugged out again, chugged towards the end of the race. He'd finish it two laps behind.

Clark cruised. We do not know when the second climactic moment of the race came – seven, eight or 10 laps before it finished. Again, the only man who can tell us is not alive to do so. What is certain is that at the hairpin Clark noticed oil and clearly not from the Hill-Bandini crash so long ago. He'd have noticed before if it was.

The next lap Clark varied his line through and next time round after that noted the oil lay on the line he'd taken before. It was his own. A rubber oil pipe had split, and although he backed off that wouldn't help. He could run only as far as the oil pipe would allow: when it broke completely he'd stop.

That happened crossing the line to begin the last lap. As he slowed, passing the pits, he raised both hands from the cockpit in a gesture of despair and Gurney stormed by into the lead, Bandini second, Surtees third.

By definition mythology is never clear. If those positions were maintained Hill became Champion, 39 points against the 38 of Surtees. Hill insisted in his autobiography that the Ferrari team, realizing this, "rushed out in front of the pits and stood in the road frantically waving to Bandini to slow down and let Surtees go by." Hill confessed that he did not see this (presumably someone told him later) and did not know the positions. "Unfortunately for me Bandini understood – it was pretty obvious because they were standing in the middle of the track – and he slowed up and let Surtees take second spot."

Autosport, who did not have their regular correspondent, Gregor Grant, at the circuit, reported that as Clark slowed "the Ferraris were over a minute away and their pit had time to get a signal ready for Bandini to let Surtees through into what might be second place."

Motor Sport, who also did not have their regular correspondent, Denis Jenkinson, in attendance, reported that "Gurney went into the lead with Surtees second, Bandini dropping back as had been planned previously."

Hill, chugging, only knew what he had seen, Clark's Lotus in trouble.

No lap charts were published then, and both *Autosport* and *Motor Sport* are vague – not so say evasive – about the order of the Ferraris as they crossed the line to begin the last lap. Why should this be important? Because if Surtees had taken Bandini all the talk of mechanics waving in the road becomes fiction. Surtees would already have been past him and into the all-important second place, anyway. Surtees (in an earlier interview with the author) was adamant he saw nobody in the road and saw no signals.

Surtees, bless him, can't remember a precise moment almost 30 years earlier. He's not sure whether he overtook Bandini on the second last or last lap. "I think it was coming into the last lap and it would have been either coming into the big banking right curve or slipstreamed him down to the bottom of the straight and picked him off there. Let's be very practical: I was close enough to him to do that

– he had the anticipated oil problems with the flat-12 – and I don't doubt he would have let me past if he had had to, anyway. None of us in the race was really aware of the Championship situation – it was such confusion." Bandini would, however, have been aware that Surtees' chances could only be improved by finishing in front of him, not behind, regardless of everything else.

Surtees also reasons that Bandini would act honourably because "he would acknowledge I was the quicker of the two of us, he wasn't the type of man to try and gain petty things and deprive me of something. If it had happened at the beginning of the race he'd have fought tooth-and-nail. We had nothing in our contracts about number one and number two drivers. You establish that by being fastest in races and testing."

Dan Gurney crossed the line after 2 hours 9 minutes and 50.32 seconds, Surtees 1 minute 8.94 seconds later, Bandini third, Spence – who'd toyed briefly with the idea of pulling up behind the slowing Clark and nosing him to the finish – fourth, Clark not running but classified fifth.

They decorated Surtees with a truly vast garland and, his eyes seemingly set in ovals from his goggles, he gave Stirling Moss an interview, went to the prizegiving, where he received a Longines watch (worth more than he'd got for the Championship) and set off to have a quiet dinner.

There are a couple of little tailpieces to Mexico. The first: John Blunsden and Alan Brinton produced a publication called *Motor Racing* and clearly they wanted an interview with Surtees when he got home. Brinton remembers that "we went down to his place, Grey Timbers it was called, and Surtees said: 'Look, I am World Champion and I want to make a good job of it.' He was virtually asking: 'How do I go about this? What should my attitude be? I must try and be ambassador to the sport and so on.' John and I did talk to him along those lines. Whether he took our advice or not I don't know. He seemed to have the feeling that the people in car racing were rather stand-offish, he didn't find them as matey as the motorcycle crowd where everybody mixed in. He was a complex character, but a very, very gutsy driver, for all that…"

The second is also a question. How would Ferrari have reacted if Bandini had truly finished in front of you and cost Ferrari the World Championship? "It might have served a purpose, actually. It might have got Dragoni out of the team." Big John Surtees was laughing when he said that, a very naughty laugh indeed, even all these years later.

THE ECHOES OF SUMMER

1965

The fifth issue of a publication called *The Motor Racing Register* appeared before the start of the 1965 season, a hardback book costing 15 shillings (75p). It gave extensive details about fixtures, records and rules, temporal in nature and of only marginal historical interest. The final 110 pages are much more interesting, containing as they do a *Who Was Who in 1964: Some Personalities in British Motor Racing*.

Here, listed in alphabetical order, are the leading drivers with biographical details, including in many cases their home addresses and telephone numbers. Thus you could write to Peter Arundell at 5 Middleboy, Abridge, Essex (Theydon Bois 3501) or Jim Clark at Edington Mains, Duns, Berwickshire (no phone number), Graham Hill at 32 Parkside, Mill Hill, London NW7 (no phone number), Jackie Stewart at Clayton, Milton, Dumbarton (home Dumbarton 2990, work Dumbarton 2465), John Surtees at 97 Foxley Lane, Purley, Surrey. The studied remoteness rested in the future and would have been inconceivable...

By now Clark and Chapman had become synonymous. "There was never a cross word, never a tantrum between them," Warr says, "and what's more I don't honestly think Jimmy ever considered driving for anybody else. He was completely satisfied. They never had a contract. Jimmy would come up and say to Colin: 'Well, what's the deal for next year?' and Colin would say: 'We're going to do this, we'll build this car and have a go at that' and Jimmy would say: 'Well, yes, that's all right', and away they went.

"What you had was a situation where the rest of the world were wetting themselves to get their hands on a talent like his, and yet strange in a way because I don't think anyone ever made a serious attempt to poach him. That is a measure of the relationship. Other teams knew that this link, this bond between them, was so close no way you could get him. Take a comparision with today (late 1992). Senna is with McLaren and there's no doubt that Frank Williams has had the most enormous go at trying to whittle him away into his team. That would never have happened with Jimmy because, although it was something someone like Frank might have wanted to do, he wouldn't have tried. He'd have known the impossibility of it before he started."

On January 1, driving the Lotus 33, Clark won the South African Grand Prix at East London by 29 seconds from Surtees, Hill third at 31.8 seconds. *Autosport* reported that "Hill, in a last desperate attempt, began to close up on Surtees, but the Ferrari got down to 1 minute 28.2 seconds as compared to Hill's best of 1 minute 28.5 in the closing stages. Out came the chequered flag, which was duly presented to Jim Clark, before officials realized there was still another lap to go. Fortunately Jim had been given a last-lap signal by Colin Chapman and decided to keep on motoring. Thus he had the unique experience of being flagged twice.

"The scenes at the finish were chaotic, with Clark being jostled by hundreds of eager wellwishers who, somehow, had invaded the track. Even the presence of alsatian dogs and efforts by officials to form a rope barrier were to no avail and Jim received his trophy and laurel wreath virtually hidden from view among a mass of humanity."

Clark toured Australia and New Zealand between that January and early March, winning 11 of 15 races and heats: a driver at the height of his powers wielding the right machinery. The whole of 1965 lay at his mercy.

Eoin Young had met Clark on previous visits. "Ford lent him a Zodiac, the Mark IV with the long bonnet. I'm not at all sure he'd ever been to Mount Cook. I'm sitting there thinking 'Well, he doesn't drive that fast,' then I looked over his shoulder at the speedo and it was right off the clock. Then I thought 'Well, we'll see once we get off the tarmac and into the mountain roads, we'll see what he's made of.' He did the same speed on the gravel."

Distant dialogue...

Young: Just a minute, have you been up here before?

Clark: No.

Young: How can you drive like this on these roads?

Clark: It's just like home.

(When Young finally reached Scotland some while later he realized it was just like that...)

At the Race of Champions at Brands Hatch on March 13 Clark crashed chasing Gurney and destroyed the Lotus, a lapse so rare it remains something people remember. Denis Jenkinson described the crash. "Down the hill they came together, Clark determined to get the lead back, but now Gurney was on the better line and through Bottom Bend there just isn't enough room for two cars abreast and Clark understeered himself off the road onto the grass. All along Bottom Straight he worked to get the Lotus back on the road, but he failed and struck an earth bank behind the pits. The car leapt the bank in a shower of dirt and crashed on its wheels, and Clark stepped out with a minor bruise."

This March day, incidentally, Clark held two lap records at Brands Hatch, for touring cars over 2,000cc (the Ford Galaxie) and for touring cars between 1,301 and 2,000cc (the Ford Lotus Cortina). In qualifying for the Race of Champions he did 1 minute 35.2 seconds which, *Motor Sport* noted cryptically, "made the existing record of 1 minute 38.8 seconds look silly."

Clark had to make a decision whether to run at the Indianapolis 500 or the Monaco Grand Prix. Logistically both could barely be accommodated, Monaco on the Sunday, Indy on the Monday. Clark cannily reasoned that Lotus were committed to Indy because of their contract with Ford, and the Grand Prix cars might, across this one weekend, receive less than full attention. He took a plane to Indianapolis and qualified on the front row.

Graham Hill took pole at Monaco, led the race until lap 25 when he came fast out of the tunnel and saw Anderson's Brabham limping towards the chicane. Hill braked hard, saw he couldn't get through, lifted off and steered the BRM down the escape road. He climbed out and pushed the car back to the circuit, costing him half a minute. Stewart, Bandini, Surtees and Brabham moved past. Hill, angry, set off in pursuit. Stewart spun on lap 30, recovered, and on lap 34 waved Hill through. Brabham led, Bandini and Surtees scrapping amongst themselves behind him. Brabham broke down on lap 43 – engine – and Hill moved on the Ferraris. As he caught them he noted "frantic" signals from the Ferrari pit telling them to stop scrapping and fend Hill off. On lap 53 Hill took Surtees, then tracked Bandini, exerting enormous pressure.

Autosport reported: "The excitement was tremendous as Hill hounded Bandini. The Italian was keeping surprisingly cool, driving really well and naturally anxious to avoid any repitition of the Mexican incident (the Grand Prix of 1964 when Bandini crashed with Hill). All eyes were on the bitter struggle going on in front. Hill, chin jutting out and inscrutable as ever, was driving ten-tenths, never putting a wheel wrong and getting the utmost from his splendidly prepared BRM."

On lap 58 Surtees hammered out a new lap record, 1 minute 33 seconds, and Hill responded by equalling it.

"It was obvious that Bandini would have to give way sooner or later. Winding the flat-12 to the limit he set a new record on lap 63 with 1 minute 32.9 seconds. Two laps later Hill equalled this and next time round he went down to 1 minute 32.7, having taken the lead at the Station from Bandini. Programmes were waved and the Londoner was cheered all the way round the circuit. This put Bandini on his mettle and the young Italian gave his car the stick to equal Hill's new record and once again get close to the back wheels of the BRM. Hill responded with 1 minute 32.5, which was immediately equalled by Bandini on lap 67. Not to be outdone, Surtees did the same on lap 69. The crowds could hardly contain themselves. All restraint was thrown to the winds and the yelling and cheering was just like a football match."

Hill judged this, his third consecutive Monaco win (and thus an authentic hat-trick) as good a drive as at the Ring, 1962; and both in their different ways the best of his career. On the Monday he and Bette stretched out on the beach warmed by the sun of the Med and Hill experienced a "tremendous feeling of peace, serenity and fulfillment."

As he lay there, at 4 o'clock in the morning at Indianapolis a cannon sounded to open the gates of the Speedway. From 8.30 the showbiz hard-sell razzle which Clark disliked so much, all of it striking discordant notes within him, gathered in a great unstoppable swell: bands, drum majorettes in skimpy silver lame costumes holding have-a-nice-day smiles, ranks of uniformed marchers carrying obscure flags, military drums beat-beat-beating; a cannon announcing the launching of multi-coloured balloons to float free, a waft of a breeze spreading them towards a blue but hazy sky; unstoppable dignitaries touring in saloon cars, waving and waving like it was an election campaign.

Of Indianapolis Clark once said: "If I had taken notice of half the tales I had heard I wouldn't have gone out there in the first place. I had to listen to it all – the boasting, the predicting – for a month. It became tedious, wearying, but there is an old saying we have in Europe. When the flag comes down the ballyhoo ends."

It ended at 9.53am local time when the track president, one Tony Hulman, mouthed the traditional incantation: "Gentlemen, start your engines." They growled around him, rising and rising, and the 33 cars moved off to start the parade lap to the rolling start. They followed the pace car, three abreast, gently, gently feeling their way round the four turns.

The track commentator, voice rising (you'd better believe it) said: "They're rounding the fourth turn and approaching the starting line watching for the green flag to start the race. The pace car pulls into the pits. The race...is...on. Clark leads the pack." The pace car peeled hard left and at that instant the 33 were moving fast.

A contemporary account caught the initial frenzy nicely enough. "With a thunderous roar the multi-hued field, glittering in the sunshine, swept down the pit straight past the wildly waving green flag and the race was on. Clark and Foyt accelerate side by side in the lead, but it is Clark's green Lotus that noses ahead of Foyt's gaily-painted blue and white car into Turn One..."

There's a great purity about oval racing, a clean symmetry.

Clark led after the first lap, which he covered in 59.45 seconds, an average speed of 151.380 miles an hour. On the second lap Foyt overtook him, although legend insists that Clark permitted this so that Foyt could set, and take the risk of setting, the pace. Foyt, shrewd himself, slowed and Clark immediately retook him on lap three. Foyt clung and at the end of that third lap the two cars crossed the starting line together. On the fourth lap Clark had Foyt full behind him, but began to move away, and at the end of the eighth the duel had been decided, Clark six car's lengths ahead. He'd only lose the lead when he made his pit stop, an extremely brisk one anyway. Chapman had designed a special petrol feed nozzle and a contemporary account describes the pit stop as "fantastically fast, under 25 seconds."

At the 50-mile post Clark had averaged 151.833mph. Thereafter, running smoothly and consistently:

100 miles	149.334mph
150 miles	152.489mph
200 miles	151.574mph
250 miles	152.185mph
300 miles	152.301mph
350 miles	151.100mph
400 miles	151.145mph
450 miles	150.996mph
500 miles	150.686mph

Foyt went out on lap 116 – transmission – and when the race ended at 2.18pm Clark had led 190 of the 200 laps. Chapman, in a sweatshirt and sunglasses, sprang onto the pit lane wall and prepared to salute Clark with both hands raised. The commentator said: "While Parnelli Jones and Andretti battle down to the wire, Jim Clark crosses the finish line to win the race with the comfortable lead of two minutes. It's the culmination of three years of effort by car builder Colin Chapman and he dances down the pits like a ballet artist as Jim Clark drives a triumphant road to the winner's circle, Jim Clark the first European to win the Indianapolis 500 since 1916."

Despite throttling down towards the end, he averaged that 150.686mph, destroying Foyt's record of 147.350 set the year before.

Another contemporary account said: "The finish came surprisingly quickly, too quickly for the starter, who forgot to give Clark the white flag indicating the last lap. Then having received the chequered flag and completed the cooling-off lap, Clark and the Lotus headed for Victory Lane where the traditional glass of milk was thrust into his hand."

Autosport reported that "as the Flying Scot, oil and sweat stained from the race, came along Victory Alley the Scottish pipes began to wail – heaven knows where they came from! – and the huge crowd of almost 350,000 people cheered. The end of a fantastic drive by a fantastic driver."

Yes and no. In Victory Lane, Clark, tightly hemmed by a mass of photographers and interviewers, said: "No race is easy when you're out there driving it. I'll admit, however, that I expected more of a competitive race." This is polite-speak for whatever happened to those fearsome Yanks?

Clark went to Mosport a week later where he raced a Lotus 30 – it retired – and two days after that won both heats of the London Trophy at Crystal Palace in a Formula Two Lotus. A week after that he went to Spa and the Belgian Grand Prix.

"Clark was so quiet, and not only quiet but shy to the point where it was painful," Brinton says. "For Spa he and I always stayed at a place called the *Val d'Ambleve*, a lovely hotel set in its own grounds on the far side of Stavelot. I then edited a publication called *Ford Competition News* with John Blunsden, a monthly newspaper, and the obvious thing was an interview with Clark. D'you know, we sat in the garden there for between two and three hours. He went right through it and told me the whole story of how he'd won Indianapolis. Can you imagine a driver today being prepared to do that? He remembered it in great detail. Drivers do, you know. Nor was it a question of money, no, not at all, he just did it."

Mind you, Clark won $166,621 (however did they calculate that?) at Indianapolis, which translated at the time to £56,168 – of which £9,500 were lap prizes; and this when £5,000 a year represented a plump annual wage in Britain. Nor would Clark always be so content to co-operate in an interview, as Brinton discovered after the Belgian Grand Prix...

A stinking wet race and Clark moved into a large lead although Stewart (BRM), second, amazed everyone by how he handled Spa at his first race there. Andrew Cowan, spectating, remembers it well and offers a penetrating insight into how Clark's mind worked. "In the rain Jimmy disappeared and left everybody, then he started getting pit signals that Stewart in the BRM was up to second place and, of course, Jimmy was backing off in these terrible conditions.

"Sometimes Jackie put up a faster lap than Jimmy, and Jimmy found himself in a dilemma. He didn't know what to do. He felt Jackie was inexperienced and he didn't dare back off any more because if he did that Jackie would have been getting messages *'you're catching Clark'* and start taking risks. So Jimmy began to drive flat-out all the time, taking the risks himself to make sure Jackie didn't take them. He explained that afterwards. Jimmy was scared in case Jackie got carried away with himself. I can remember the end of that race, too. Jim came in and said: 'Ooh, that was really something.'"

Meanwhile, back at the *Val d'Ambleve*, re-enter Brinton. "I did a series of broadcast tapes for a petrol company on the story of each race. They lasted about a quarter of an hour, they were copied and sent to radio stations worldwide. You always had to interview the winner, invariably Clark. He'd glimpse me coming with my tape recorder and say: 'Oh, no, Alan, look please.'

"I saw him over dinner and I said: 'Look, we've got to do this' and he said: 'Later, later.' He was so shy. Finally it was getting late and I said: 'For crying out loud, where's he gone?' Answer: He'd gone to bed. I knocked on the door and said: 'Look Jim, I'm going off early in the morning and I've got to do this.' There were two beds in this large room, one a double bed and the other a sort of divan across the end of it. I said: 'Who's in the big one?' and he said: 'Oh Peter Arundell. We spun for it and I lost the toss.' This was Jim Clark, who'd already won the World Championship in 1963, was leading the current Championship and had just won Indianapolis.

"I said: 'Come on now, let's do this interview', and I asked him the obvious questions, and he hummed and hawed and messed about. I said: 'Don't worry, we'll try it again, and he said: 'I can't do it, I can't.' I said: 'Don't go to sleep, I'll come back in 10 minutes and I'll write you out a short script.' I did that and he read it out in a rather stilted way, but it was the best we could do. He had this awful shyness with a microphone."

Clark won the Championship at the Nurburgring on August 1. The stark statistics of this Championship have a monumental eloquence which scarcely need expansion:

South Africa:	pole, led all 85 laps, fastest lap.
Monaco:	absent at Indianapolis.
Belgium:	front row, led all 32 laps, fastest lap.
France:	pole, led all 40 laps, fastest lap.
Britain:	pole, led all 80 laps.
Holland:	front row, led 70 of 75 laps, fastest lap.
Germany:	pole, led all 15 laps, fastest lap.

The Nurburgring he lapped in 8 minutes 24.1 seconds, which stood in direct comparison with the time of Surtees in 1964, 8 minutes 39.0; or putting it another way, Surtees averaged 98.30mph on his lap, Clark 101.22. Clark evidently said in his usual economy of words: "I'm glad I clinched the Championship at the Nurburgring. I've always wanted to win a major race here." The points tables had a monumental eloquence, too, at season's end: Clark 54, Hill 47 but 40 counting – only your best six results did that – Stewart 34 but 33 counting, Gurney 25, Surtees 17.

At a race like the British Grand Prix, as Oswald Brewis attests, Clark "looked for familiar faces and people he could trust and I knew him very well by then. I could cope with him and whatever mood he might be in. For example, you didn't speak to him at all before a race and it was something you had to be very careful about.

"That's where I got on so well with him, because I knew him and how he reacted, how he withdrew into himself progressively as the race came closer. Oh yes, you could tell that. People who rubbed him up the wrong way were made very much aware of the fact. He didn't speak much and you certainly wouldn't speak about his racing unless he brought the subject up himself. I never did. Quite often I shared a room with him and we had very interesting discussions. We'd put our books down when we'd finished reading last thing at night and that was the time when he would open up."

This Silverstone, Graham Hill beat Clark for provisional pole on the first day of qualifying (by 0.2 of a second). "We shared a room, we'd gone off to bed, we were talking as usual, and he'd been given second fastest time. He said: 'You know, that was wrong,' and he turned out to be correct. I'm not sure that they officially corrected the times, but it was accepted Jimmy had been quicker, and he knew he had been. He'd probably said it to Chapman when the session finished, but we'd been talking all night at dinner with friends and he hadn't said a word about it."

In fact Silverstone proved the only Grand Prix Clark might have lost up to and including The Ring. He led by half a lap from Hill but had oil problems, and on right-hand corners – Silverstone is basically right-handed, Woodcote, Copse, Becketts, Stowe, Club – to prevent whatever oil remained from vanishing he switched the engine off and free-wheeled through them. Hill got pit signals telling him *Clark's in trouble, Clark's in trouble*, Hill attacked, set a new lap record on the last lap – which explains why it's missing from Clark's table above – but Clark got home by 3.2 seconds.

Jim Endruweit of Lotus remembers that. "It illustrates the feeling Jimmy had for cars. He was leading, he roars into the corner before the pit straight, comes ripping round this corner and suddenly no engine noise from the car, all terribly quiet. It's towards the end of the race, the tension is high in the pits. We're having heart failure. Just as suddenly the engine comes back on again. Jimmy is low in the cockpit and all we see is a little thumb sticking up over the top of the screen (the thumbs-up). We said: 'What the hell is he up to? He seems to know what he's doing, but we don't.' After the race he explained. 'I was coming round and I noticed the oil pressure had dropped. As I moved around the corner I shut the engine down until the oil pressure straightened up again and went on.'

"He figured out this only happened on the corners. I can't tell you if he did it on every corner, but he certainly did on the one before the pit lane straight. He knew where he was, knew how much Hill was taking from him and still won, even though by a fairly close margin. It did illustrate a tremendous feeling for a car, and yet he was not a bit mechanically inclined. Put a spanner in his hand and he wouldn't know what to do with it."

On September 18 the rally driver Roger Clark contested the Gold Cup race at Oulton Park. "I did quite a season of various sorts of racing to get my driving better for the tarmac sections of rallies. Boreham Ford's factory built a racing saloon car because I think there was a bit of rivalry, you know, to prove you didn't need to be Lotus to build a racing car. So they sat me in it and I did the Gold Cup. I was in front of Clark (in the works Lotus) and Graham Hill (in a Lotus-BRM) – not easily, but I was in front of them. They were panting along behind me with a chap in a big Falcon right up their chuff. Clark didn't say a lot. He might have had to explain why this bloody rally driver was in front – but he didn't have to because a halfshaft broke. Really it was good fun, light-hearted. If I'd won it would have been very interesting." But something much more interesting would happen to R Clark; he'd be asked to teach J Clark how to drive a rally car.

A week after Oulton, Surtees drove a Lola at Mosport, Canada, and Stewart had a Lola there, too. Evidently Stewart wasn't terribly happy with his car and asked Surtees to take it out and have a look. Surtees crashed, the car flipped, and he didn't remember anything for four days. He ruptured his kidneys, broke his pelvis and for a while his life lay in danger. He came back to London tightly swathed in bandages. He'd be racing again the following April...

1966

Any season may change the character of motorsport unexpectedly. Part of the fascination is that you can never tell where or when. This season a new 3-litre formula was introduced but, without question, a spate of crashes at Spa in June constituted the more fundamental change. We'll come to that in a moment because there had already been other crashes, real ones at Indianapolis and simulated ones during the making of the film *Grand Prix* directed by John Frankenheimer. This film, the story of a season shot with on-board footage which remains classic material, blended real drivers with actors – notably James Garner and Yves Montand. Frankenheimer explains: "Steve McQueen was making a movie at the same time to be called *Day of the Champion*. It would conflict with ours and there was a big fight over who got the drivers. McQueen got Surtees, Stewart and Clark, and they were under contract to him. Surtees and Stewart came around to us, but Clark never did."

Initially Frankenheimer had Graham Hill, Bonnier, Spence, Phil Hill and Ginther. The fun began when Frankenheimer's operation reached Monaco to shoot over the Grand Prix weekend. It was, he says, "most difficult because if we'd had an accident in Monte Carlo, if we'd done anything in Monte Carlo, the picture would have been over. Nobody wanted us. Horrendous. Monte Carlo in those days was controlled by both Aristotle Onassis and Prince Rainier and they hated each other. So when Rainier would close the road for us, Onassis, who owned from the Casino on, would open it to traffic. We'd be coming with race cars up over the Casino turn, there would be a traffic light and we'd have to put on the brakes. We alienated everybody in Grand Prix racing because of the traffic jams we created. Colin Chapman missed a whole practice session because of us. Graham Hill was a great help. Graham and I became very dear friends."

(Hill, who "baulked" at playing the part of Billy Turner and insisted on the character being called Bob Turner, attended the premiere of the film in New York and London and wondered why his appearance on the screen provoked roars of laughter.)

Stewart won the real Monaco Grand Prix, first round of the season, from Bandini with Graham Hill third. Clark's Lotus jammed in first gear and subsequently he retired after 61 laps – suspension failure.

A week later Clark, Hill (a late entry driving for an American millionaire) and Stewart contested Indianpolis, a race which *The Star* called "the most fantastic, confused and incredible 500." Nobody would dispute that.

Bette didn't want Graham to drive there but hadn't told him. Graham didn't want her there "because he said it wasn't a place for a woman. The lavatories didn't even have doors on them until Graham first went. I can't remember his exact words but he said it was indecent and degrading, and anyway the next day they were putting doors on. It wasn't called the Brickyard for nothing. It was a Brickyard."

Bette would have to be content with watching it in a Hammersmith cinema. John Player had organized special showings in cinemas across Britain and they attracted a total audience of 25,000. Bette was just arriving at Hammersmith when a journalist told her of a massive accident on the first lap. Worse, inside she faced a blank screen: a great irony because Amerian television screens and photographers' lenses were full of it.

A driver called Billy Foster struck the rear of Gordon Johncock and 16 cars became enmashed, rotating at wild angles, boring into each other, wheels and debris scattered like leaves on the wind. Astonishingly, only A.J. Foyt received any injury – he cut his hand clambering over the safety fence – and one spectator was hurt by a flying wheel. Hill would remember trying to weave a path through like a dodgem car.

"We didn't know who had been injured," Bette says. "We all milled around for quite a while. You can imagine it, everyone saying: 'Oh my God.' I was with the Lestons, Denny Hulme, the usual London bunch, and we were supposed to be having a good night out. I only found out Graham was all right when the screen came on and they showed the shunt, showed Foyt climbing up the railing hurting his hand. We watched Graham come through the melee, a talented thing to do, brave, sensible. The others crashed into each other, but Graham saw a gap – the sort of gap he had seen on so many occasions in races – and got through it. Brilliant, brilliant. Somebody else with the same sort of sense and intelligence followed him through, although I never found out who."

The wreckage took an hour and 23 minutes to clear. At the restart Clark led despite spinning twice, Stewart overtook him and led from laps 147 to 192 when a scavenge pump failed. The order had been: Stewart, Clark, Hill. The race commentator bayed "these foreigners are certainly doing a good job." Hill passed Clark and Bette could "hardly bear the suspense. Towards the end I found I was saying to myself 'Stay there Graham, you can win this one.' I could see by the set of his jaw. The lap scorers and scoreboard had all gone crazy in the confusion." The commentator kept baying *Clark's in the lead, Clark's in the lead*, because he seemed to be, a lap in front of Hill, but Bette (with all her lap-charting experience) knew he couldn't be because of those two spins and subsequent visits to the pits.

Clark saw pit signals *you're in front* and Hill saw pit signals *you're in front*. The confusion remains of CinemaScope proportions. Hill took the chequered flag, but on the podium the whispers began that perhaps he hadn't won. Hill's reply: "No way, mate, I drank the milk!" Chapman, meanwhile, remonstrated with the officials. Clark struggled through to Hill, tugged his sleeve and inquired who had won. Hill, obligatory girl on each arm, gazed at each in turn, then the melee of people and said: "Well, if I haven't I don't know what all these people are doing." The result would be confirmed later and fashioned the second leg of a unique Triple Crown, Hill World Champion in 1962, winner of Indy in 1966 and in 1972 winner of Le Mans.

"Graham," Bette says, "enjoyed Indy because he enjoyed all the American hype. He loved Americans. That was the fun side of Graham, you see. He liked all of it, the rookies having to do it under certain times, the introductions the drivers got, all the showmanship. I tell you also that the Americans enjoyed Graham, they loved him because he was a showman. He really did enhance their races, he chatted up the birds and the girls loved that. He enjoyed being fun."

And now we come to the Belgian Grand Prix, which would have such far-reaching consequences, would change Formula One. Dark clounds gathered over Spa, but no rain fell. At the start a crisp, ominous announcement was made in the press box – *rain falling at Stavelot*. Surtees, on pole, would remember the rain beginning on the opening lap, would remember saying to himself *be careful*.

Surtees reached Burnenville, the long 150mph right sweep out in the country, and stayed off the racing line because rubber laid there during qualifying might be slippery on a surface now glistening. From experience he knew, too, that light rain at Burnenville might well mean heavy rain at Stavelot, the hard right where the cars turned for the long run back to the start-finish line.

Going towards Burnenville, Jack Brabham was on the wet and his car flicked sideways into "a terrific slide – it was fantastic." He skimmed away towards a house. As the car reached the lip of the road it suddenly stopped sliding. He had no idea why. He estimated he'd missed the straw bales and some concrete posts by inches.

Stewart, coming hard, would remember he just missed Brabham "by a miracle," would remember giving "a slight sigh of relief".

At Malmedy – just after Burnenville – the cars pitched full into the water. Bonnier spun and collected the Lotus of Spence. Both cars went off. Hulme and Siffert crashed. Hill picked a path through what he'd remember as all these spinning cars and pressed on towards the Masta kink, midway between Malmedy and Stavelot. Masta, Hill thought, "didn't look right."

Stewart, reaching Masta, found a river of water across the road. He saw Rindt spin clean through Masta and then aquaplaned himself, would remember spinning, battering some railing down. He struck a post. Hill's BRM spun and he thundered down the road backwards "at fantastic speed", he went off and came to rest against a straw bale in a ditch. As Hill struggled to restart his engine he saw Stewart trapped beyond the railing but in the same ditch. Hill scrambled to Stewart and saw he was in pain, saw the petrol tank had split, the fuel soaking Stewart. Hill feared an inferno at any instant; he stooped and hauled at Stewart, who murmured about a pain in his shoulder. Hill realized the only way to get Stewart out was to remove the steering wheel because it pressed hard against Stewart's leg.

Bob Bondurant in a privately-entered BRM lost control and his car turned over, finishing on the grass on the other side of the road. Stewart, semi-conscious, gazed across and saw blood coming from Bondurant's lips and wondered "why he looked so sorry for himself, after all it was I who had crashed." Bondurant sprinted to Stewart's BRM and Hill said they needed tools. Hill set off to find a toolbox – some reports say he got spanners from a spectator who had some in his boot – returned and removed the steering wheel.

He and Bondurant then lifted Stewart out and took him to what Hill would remember as a small farm building nearby. He stripped Stewart to prevent the soaked overalls burning his skin any further and then ran towards a marshal's post. No ambulance had yet come, so Hill phoned and returned again, reaching the building at the same time as the ambulance – a converted bus.

The nurses in it, who Stewart reasoned must be nuns, tried to cover his nakedness with the soaked overalls, but Hill stopped that. He thought they were more worried about their embarrassment than Stewart's condition. Stewart would remember "slowly and with gentle care the nuns began to dress me. At least I think they were nuns. And I think they were dressing me. If, that is, they were there at all. You see, I cannot be sure."

Meanwhile, Surtees had completed the first lap followed by Brabham, Bandini, Ginther, Rindt and Ligier – then, silence. *Autosport* reported that "the seconds ticked away and still no-one appeared. Eventually Dan Gurney turned up, 1 minute 50 seconds behind the leader, motoring very gently. Rumours grew that there had been an almighty shunt, but over the PA came little or no reassuring news apart from a brief announcement that Bonnier and Spence had collided, gone off the road, and were unhurt."

The nurses put Stewart in the ambulance and it moved to the pits. Louis Stanley got in it and so did Stewart's wife Helen. Some reports say the nurses laid Stewart on a bed, some on the floor of the ambulance, while Stanley sat on a chair. Someone, probably Stanley, told him – using sign language – that he should be careful not to upset Helen. Stewart said to her: "Helen, this is very good experience for you." He was as concussed as that.

Moving in and out of consciousness, Stewart held a bizarre conversation with Stanley, wondering if Helen was all right, wondering where they were going; this conversation culminated with Stanley insisting that if Stewart insisted on calling him by his Christian name he should use Louis, not Lou.

The ambulance headed towards the town of Verviers, but the driver lost his way...

In the pits an executive of Exclusive Jet Aviation reacted fast, phoned Paris and had a Lear flown to Liege, the nearest available airport to Verviers. At 7 o'clock that evening Stewart was taken from the hospital, put on the Lear and 35 minutes later it landed in London. He was in St Thomas' by 9.30pm.

The full impact of the race – which Surtees won despite an inspired drive from Jochen Rindt – was in no sense apparent at the time. The *Autosport* editorial began: "With only 15 starters and eight eliminated before half a lap had been covered, last Sunday's Grand Prix of Belgium was pretty poor value for spectators." Gregor Grant began his report: "In one of the most disappointing Grands Prix ever staged ..."

The full impact came later and would become controversial. Stewart resolved to launch a campaign for safety and did so, risking and receiving taunts of cowardice and other such madness. Whenever you watch a Grand Prix today, the Armco, the run-off areas, the sand-traps, Formula One's own doctor Professor Sid Watkins ever poised in a waiting car, fire marshals in flameproof clothing who know their drill and react fast, in-course medical centres, each driver's blood group known, helicopters ready, think only of the Masta kink, June 12, 1966...

At Le Mans, Surtees left Ferrari after a bitter argument over whether he took first stint or not. Enzo Ferrari was scarcely a man to compromise and neither was John Surtees. All unknowing, this would lead Surtees to a strange, quasi-romantic venture with Honda.

I wondered what sort of relationship Surtees had had with Bandini. "Oh, super. He virtually cried and pleaded with me not to leave Ferrari when it all came to a head. I said to people in the team: 'Look, you will kill the lad because the sort of responsibility he'll face – an Italian in a Ferrari car – isn't on.' I knew the sort of pressure which existed. As much as we were governors of our own destiny, if you drove for a team like Ferrari it wasn't quite like that.

"There was a policy of keeping people a little bit at odds with each other. You'd have journalists writing stories trying to get the needle going between Bandini and myself, a policy which the team followed. Actually it didn't achieve that, and on the whole I had as good a relationship with Lorenzo as I had with any other driver."

The 1966 Championship belonged to Jack Brabham, who finished with 45 points (42 counting), Surtees on 28, Graham Hill fifth (17), Clark sixth (16), Stewart seventh (14). Before we leave 1966 two stories, one brief, one to be examined at some length.

Maurice Hamilton, today a leading writer on motorsport, was a young fan and on a practice day at Oulton Park, few people around, he approached Clark for his autograph. "As Clark signed, my pen ran out, but the interesting aspect was that Clark seemed more embarrassed than I." Clark completed his signature although all he did was cut grooves. Hamilton later traced ink into these grooves and has the autograph still.

On the morning of Saturday, November 19, 1966 Jimmy Clark took breakfast at the Excelsior Hotel, Heathrow, with Andrew Cowan. "He was nervous about it, he really was nervous about it. Yes, oh aye, you could tell that. He didn't know how to take it and he wondered if he would be competititive. He was nervous about possibly not being competitive." The minutes ticked away to the start of the RAC Rally.

The scope, danger and demands of this event – strewn across six days and 55 special stages, without pace notes – stood as a daunting examination of professional rally drivers. Clark came to it as a virtual stranger to the intricacies of muddy tracks, forests, banks and ravines, shingle and shale and stone, a lot of it surging at him in the night. It is true Clark had rallied a bit in the Fifties, but only locally and, anyway, the Fifties were a long time ago. "Lots and lots of good drivers competed in the RAC," Cowan says, "so he wasn't going to go straight in there and lead, but he hoped he'd be in the top 10."

The story of how Clark got into the rally is almost as interesting as what he did on the rally itself. Barrie Gill, then motor racing correspondent of *The Sun*, persuaded that newspaper to co-sponsor the rally with Lombank. Gill understood the mechanisms of publicity and so did Stuart Turner, who at that time worked for BMC.

Brian Melia, a very experienced rally driver, worked for Ford. "I was down to do the race as a number one with my own co-driver and suddenly out of the blue Stuart Turner got hold of Graham Hill and put him in a Mini for the RAC and of course the newspapers splashed it. Henry Taylor, Ford's competition manager, said *What are we going to do about this? There's only one thing. We'll have to get Jimmy*. I was dispatched to Snetterton where Jimmy was testing the Lotus IndyCar. I drove Vic Elford's rally Lotus Cortina up there – Vic had gone off on a previous rally on the first stage but not damaged it, so I had a fully prepared rally car which had done about five serious miles. My instructions were not to come back until I'd persuaded Jimmy to do the RAC.

"I'd never met him. I stood there for most of the day kicking my heels because he was tied up with the IndyCar. He'd do two or three laps and come in and talk to Colin Chapman, go out again, and eventually he stuffed it into the bank and that was the end of the day. I'd been chatting with him between times, and anyway he knew I would be there because obviously Henry had talked to him, Henry knew him. I asked him: 'Are you interested?' When he stuffed the IndyCar everybody was about to pack up and go home. He said 'Come on' and jumped into the Cortina. In those days, because of the rough stages, rally cars ran for the most part on tyres we called nobblies, a mud tread if you like.

"As you came out of the pits there was a nice, wide right-hander at the top of the pit straight. He hammered out screaming up through the gearbox, went round the corner on these bloody nobblies, and he was used to going round it in a Cortina set up for racing with wide slicks. We went off through the cabbages – people grew crops round the edge of the circuit – we powered across through these cabbages, mud flying all over the place. He had no idea how a rally car handled at all. We got back on the circuit and I suppose he was a bit embarrassed, but we took it as a big joke. I'd been through worse things and I don't think he expected me to be as calm as I was.

"He'd found the limitations of the car on that first corner, that was the thing. From there on he was fine. We did two or three laps and it was decided then to go down to talk to Henry about it. Henry lived towards Malden, in Essex, a nice big country mansion type of place. Jimmy said: 'Fine, we'll drive down there, but I'm taking the Cortina', so I had to drive his Galaxie, which seemed as wide as a room, first time I'd driven anything that size. I followed him and left them to it. The outcome was that yours truly lost his drive in the RAC! It was too close to the Rally to build a car for Jimmy so my co-driver was dumped and I came in as navigator/co-driver with Jimmy in my car."

Henry Taylor decided to enlist Roger Clark, who'd rallied for a decade and was a leading exponent of the art, to give Jimmy Clark an introductory session. "I got the job of familiarizing him with what it was like driving in the forests, the general feel of a rally car as opposed to a racing car," Roger Clark says. "Both Jimmy and I were closely connected with Ford, we'd been to quite a few Ford functions and things like that. Obviously we were in two different branches of the sport so we didn't see a lot of each other, but it wasn't as if a total stranger showed up.

"The army had a place near Bagshot where they did endurance testing on tanks, tank transporters, any military vehicle which is likely to be used on rough roads. It was a genuine forest and quite tough. We used it for all the Escort and Cortina development, basically as a suspension test, and we'd spend days there.

"When Jimmy came we kept it private. If he'd made a balls-up the press would have made a meal of it, not what we were looking for at all. The time we spent together was just with the team, and my job to instruct him how to do it. Jimmy showed up, put his overalls on, put his helmet on. We talked about what the differences were before he got in and the new sensations he would feel. I spent as much time as I judged necessary to demonstrate where we were going and what we would be doing and the type of driving we used.

"I drove first, with him as a passenger, and I gave a running commentary, *I'm doing this, I'm doing that*. Jimmy was calm and collected and perceptive and never a problem. Within an hour of watching me, then getting in and doing it himself, he was driving very competently. He didn't take long to get the feel of it, get his confidence. We swopped around so I could show him different bits – braking, the way you set the car up in corners and this sort of thing, then he'd try it. He picked it up naturally, and by the end of the day he was quite quick, to say the least.

"Obviously you've got a much less responsive car than in Formula One in all sorts of ways. Steering? Roadholding? It's less responsive wherever you go. You're on a surface which has less than half the grip of tarmac, you need a new appreciation of what you can get out of it – basically very slippery roads. I think he was amazed at how quickly you could go if you knew how to go about it.

"The slip angles of the car off tarmac are three times what they are on tarmac, your anticipation is different because the steering responses and so on are much slower, caused by the lack of grip. You're floating the car above the surface, if you

131

like, you're using its inertia to help it into the right position. It's slower than a racing car although that is relative because you're driving within the same percentages – 100 per cent round a track, 100 per cent through a forest.

"Rallying wasn't totally alien to him. I mean, a motor car is a motor car whether it's on tarmac or loose surface, it still points the same way, it still does the same things, makes the same noises: it's just different grip levels with the tyres, a rougher road, this sort of thing.

"You didn't have to show him anything twice, he picked it all up very quickly, which was super to see, in fact a privilege to see. Once you'd pointed him into the little realms he'd never been to before, demonstrated them, talked to him about them, it came just like *that* to him. When we'd finished he said: 'Thank you very much' in that quiet way he had. 'Cheers, see you at the event.'"

Roger Clark also gave the same lesson to Graham Hill, although he can't remember if it was 1966. That is not the point. The comparison is the point. "Graham was always good fun, I got on very well with him. I knew him on the same basis as I knew Jimmy, but in the car it was a different ball park. Graham had to work at it. He couldn't grasp the new set of circumstances that easily, and although he wasn't at a loss he wasn't at ease, he hadn't got this natural flow with him. It took a lot longer to sink in than it did with Jimmy. You showed Jimmy something once and he'd copy you. Graham wouldn't be able to do it first time, he'd probably have to do it five times before he got the gist, a much slower learning curve *although he did get there*. [Author's italics.]

"I had the feeling Graham was not as *fine* as Jimmy, more – how can you say it? – clumsy with the car. If you wanted him to turn right he'd turn right [demonstrates exaggerated hands churning a steering wheel] whereas Jimmy would caress it round [holds finger tips to a steering wheel]. Graham felt frustrated because he couldn't grasp it immediately, but everyone knows Graham's character, he was a gritter, he'd learn in the end."

Jimmy Clark received a second lesson, this one conducted by Melia. "We went to a place down in Kent. Somebody whose name I forget built trials cars and owned some land Brands Hatch way. We were offered the use of the land, it was autumn and not much time left. I went down to look at it and very little really resembled a rally stage, perhaps a couple of hundred yards over the whole terrain.

"It was almost scrub land, overgrown and with very young trees, saplings, just room for a tractor. Extremely narrow. The possibilities of getting a car sideways before a corner were very limited, although it had one or two open stretches. Of course you need to link these to do a sensible test and it was only half a mile, you hardly got into top gear. I patrolled it, put arrows up and made the best of it because to chuck somebody cold into the RAC Rally...well, he needs everything he can get. The idea was for him to push a rally car to its limit on the loose, but this was very Mickey Mouse, a bit of a morning out. I'm sure he learnt something from it, but not a great deal. Everything was disjointed before the rally. I saw him for a couple of hours here, a couple of hours there. I didn't think there was any real point in talking tactics."

Jimmy Clark rang Cowan, "and he said to me: 'What do we wear, Andrew?' because in those days all we wore were the blue Dunlop overalls. I said: 'Normally just a tee shirt, maybe a sweatshirt and a pair of trousers.' He couldn't come to terms with the fact that professional rally drivers turned up in a sports jacket and flannels. You didn't *have* to wear a tie, although some people did ..."

Jim Porter, who subsequently would run the RAC Rally, gives the background to the real action. "For the driver the event was completely 'blind' and remained so for a number of years thereafter. So far as the route was concerned, you didn't even get the route book covering the whole event until the day before the start. The first rally I did in 1961 we got it at lunchtime and we just about finished it at midnight to start the next morning – that was putting the route onto maps so you knew whether you were going north, south, east or west. Brian would have been in the same boat – 12 hours to put the whole lot on maps and then away you go. You really had no clue whatever what lay round the next corner.

"For the last few years you've been allowed to make reconnaisance runs over the special stages, albeit slowly, for the 10 years before that you had some sort of instructions which told you what was going to happen at the various junctions, warning arrows so you knew if you faced a hairpin or a flat-out left bend or whatever, but in the era when Clark drove you didn't even have that. You were given your route map and you weren't much wiser. It got you to the starting line in a forest and what happened between there and the finish remained totally unknown until you'd driven through. You didn't know where the hell it was going.

"I remember most of all that Clark was a very unassuming character, not at all what one would expect from a Formula One driver. Very quiet, very reserved, very much aware that he'd entered an unfamiliar world. He wasn't making any noises about how good he was going to be or making noises about anything else, just sort of quietly accepted it and got on with it. And that's impressive."

After breakfast at the Excelsior – it served as the rally headquarters – Clark went down to his Lotus Cortina where Melia waited for him. *Autosport,* noting that the car park where the rally began must have been the coldest place in Britain, reported: "The starting ramp has now been accepted as a regular feature and a huge crowd turned up to watch World Champion Jack Brabham flag off the first crew. Graham Hill, accompanied by Maxwell Boyd, caused great amusement when he engaged reverse gear on his Mini-Cooper S with Brabham yelling: 'Hey, this way, cobber!' Jim Clark pretended to be about to take the wrong turning out of the start area – which would have been difficult with a co-driver of the calibre of Brian Melia."

This innocent fun, created as it would seem for the attendant televison cameras, belied a great deal, not least that Hill and Clark would take the rally very seriously indeed; nor that they would be in against the leading names, Timo Makinen (Mini-Cooper S), Roger Clark himself (Lotus Cortina), Paddy Hopkirk (Mini-Cooper S), Erik Carlsson (Saab), Bengt Soderstrom (Lotus Cortina) and Cowan (Hillman Imp). In all, 144 cars competed.

The rally moved down the M4 and went through nine special stages before halting at Bristol Airport. "Jimmy had absolute luck," Melia says, "because he'd had three *monumentals* by the time we got to Bristol. I remember the first vividly. We climbed to a great big left-hander. He shot straight on and stood on the anchors because we'd left the road – and a good job. If we'd kept on we'd have gone over the edge of a ruddy great drop. The other thing which certainly concerned me early on was his hanging the tail of the car out. He was used to a wide sweep of tarmac – on a rally there isn't that sort of room – and he hung the tail out on the grass a time or two. I thought: this isn't going to go on very long before we meet something a bit solid."

Stage One (Bramshill Forest): R Clark 4m 33s in the lead, J Clark fifth with 4m 38s; Stage Two (Wareham) R Clark 4m 00s, J Clark still fifth with 4m 07s.

On Stage Three Melia remembers being on a "long, long left-hander with a road coming down to join the road we were on" – forming a triangle where they met – "and I had an impression there'd been trees in this little triangle, but now chopped down." Clark got it wrong, went off and Melia thought "there's got to be a tree stump or something, but he missed everything and finished up on this other road."

This dropped Clark out of the top eight, but on Stage Six (Haldon) he finished fourth, and the next stage (Porlock Hill) second behind Makinen, although 10 seconds slower. *Autosport*, meanwhile, reported that the Hill/Boyd Mini-Cooper S "came in for attention from the BMC mechanics. It had shed a gear wheel on the ascent of Porlock and this had later punctured the sump, which was not repaired."

Quantocks was the last stage before Bristol Airport. "He lost it going downhill on a cambered road with a bank on the left and a drop on the right," Melia says. " We finished up in a ditch, there was a bowl where they'd been taking a tree out, we hit the stump and it stopped us – which didn't do the suspension much good. We got to the supper halt and the lads fettled the suspension. We'd done very little damage so the car was 100 per cent.

"Then we went into Wales. I knew Wales pretty well, knew the forest stages, I'd reached familiar territory. From there on our rally just took off. I could talk him through a lot of the stages and, as I did that, he started to get the drop on it all. From there on it was...magic.

"Bearing in mind my history as a rally driver, I *knew* how to drive as quick as Jimmy, but obviously I didn't have the talent to put it into practice. Jimmy was driving like I drove, but much quicker! You can cite two contemporary drivers, Vic Elford and Roger Clark, to illustrate the extremes in technique of travelling fast on a rally stage where you don't know what's round the corner. You've the guy who goes balls-out into the corner (Elford) and hopes the corner is what he's guessed it's going to be. If he guesses right he's faster than anybody and he goes on and on, guess-guess-guess-guess, and suddenly he's caught out and he's in big trouble. He's fastest in the rally until he gets there, and then he's out of the rally.

"Roger's technique was that of going to a corner throwing it sideways, and once you've got a car sideways, if the corner turns out to be a slight one fine, you're back on the power. If it goes tighter, as you take your foot off you've so much side reaction to the tyres the car basically stops sideways, you're controlling it and you can point it in any direction you want. It is, however, inherently slower than the guy who guesses right.

"Between those extremes is an optimum. Jimmy drove in the way I'd tried to do for years. By that time he'd had his scares and I was managing to talk him through the corners. I couldn't do that with all of them because there is just so much you can remember about 20 forests in Wales. One fir tree is a bit like another fir tree. He was using the optimum method very, very quickly."

On Stage 11 (Brechfa) Clark was sixth, but he won Stage 12 (Towy) with 6m 25s – Makinen fifth, 6m 40s – and won Stage 14 (Myherin). It surely demands to be set out:

J Clark	(Lotus Cortina)	5m 15s
V Elford	(Lotus Cortina)	5m 24s
T Makinen	(Mini-Cooper S)	5m 28s
Tony Fall	(Mini-Cooper S)	5m 29s
B Soderstrom	(Lotus Cortina)	5m 32s
Hakan Lindberg	(Renault)	5m 32s

"By the time we got out of Wales," Melia says, "Jimmy had picked up 99 per cent of rallying and was going much quicker than anybody around him. My knowledge helped him to settle in, if you like. We came out of Wales and the time we'd lost down south – because we limped off Quantocks – we were pulling back hand over fist. In the car it was less frightening than other people I've been with because he was so obviously in control, just a joy, it really was."

Don't let's side-step the essence of combat. "I only saw him," Roger Clark says, "in the standing time during service points. I can't remember saying more than 'Hello, how are you doing, what's happening, what's your position?', because at that time he'd had no serious problems with the car. You know, you come in and do your own thing. When the flag drops you're not very interested in other people. I wasn't surprised that he was doing well because he was so easy, so natural, but you can't put experience into the chap's head. That comes the hard way."

It does, and would.

Reaching the Lake District Hill went out. The earlier loss of a gearwheel tooth proved too much. In the Lake District David Benson of the *Daily Express* travelled along in a celebrity Triumph 2000 driven by the race and rally driver John Sprinzel. "We had a fast car, overdrive in all four gears, it could pull 130 miles an hour in overdrive top and we were going very, very fast, climbing on a narrow road in the dark. Jimmy's lights came up behind us, we moved over and let him by. The road twisted and turned going down to a lake and then went up the hill the other side. We weren't hanging about, and that Lotus Cortina just disappeared. You could see a dab of the brake lights, a dab of the brake lights, the car going round a bend, a dab of the brake lights. He must have put a mile and more between himself and us before he vanished over the top of the hill."

Melia contemplated percentages. Clark had mastered 99 per cent of rallying, but Melia remained "bothered because I knew that every now and again the 1 per cent would come up and it was a question of where it came up. If it arrived *here* he'd get out of it, but if it arrived *there* he might not. I've an idea Timo Makinen led, although we were taking time off him and I thought: we can win this, yes."

That rested on the 1 per cent.

"There was a stage on the hillside overlooking Peebles. I remembered a critical turning on this stage, but I couldn't remember if we'd be approaching it from the direction I'd approached it from before (the 'blind' rally again). Anyway, the corner's there whichever way you're coming. Whether you approach it uphill or downhill is another matter.

"In fact the corner was a junction, a very, very tight junction, pretty narrow, poor visibility and at the sort of speed you were doing, once you saw it it was too bloody late. You finished up at the hairpin – a hairpin so tight it was a five-point turn or whatever to get round. I'd been with other people a number of times and the best we'd managed was to arrive at this thing all four wheels locked, stick the car into reverse, come back to it. This junction really was as tight as that.

"I remember describing it to Jimmy. I said: 'We are going to reach this, but I don't know where or when.' I tried to give him a picture of it verbally and warned him I'd shout *left!* We were going uphill at a hell of a rate, I suddenly saw it coming up, I shouted *left!* and he went round it as if he was on rails: a combination of knowing what to look for, reacting to me shouting and realizing it was there. He stood on the brakes because he knew what he was going to do, changed down, off the brakes, round it and away – absolutely smooth, that was the thing. Let me put this into context. In rallying on corners you're fighting for half a second here, half a second there. That junction was worth *15 seconds* to us."

Deep into Scotland, at a stage called Loch Achray, the 1 per cent played its hand. "We came down a long straight dip and at the bottom – as they do in forestry roads, to get water from one side to the other – they'd put a culvert under the road, laid the hard stuff on top and rolled it: it wasn't a hump or anything, just slightly proud if you know what I mean. Further on the road snaked round a rock face. I could see it all coming, but you can't tell the guy, you can't get it out, you can't explain it, but you *know*. Right up to the last minute I could see exactly what was going to happen.

"The car lifted only slightly on the suspension but lost adhesion and we went barreling towards the rock, hit the door on his side. If the snake – a kink, really – had been less, he'd probably have scraped the door but got through. He was annoyed with himself, simple as that. We didn't remove the door (although badly stoved in), we carried on.

"The difficulty proved to be steering the damn thing because it couldn't go round corners in that state. We had trouble at one corner and Jimmy stalled. It wouldn't restart. The suspension had come up and ripped the cable to the starter. The only way was by getting right down under the engine. Jimmy did that and got the starter motor going, but it wouldn't pick up. I jumped into the driver's seat through the passenger door and revved, revved, revved. I drove from there with Jimmy in the passenger seat. "We came to a big open hairpin and I tried to get round on the limited steering lock. I didn't want to stop in case it stalled again, so I took a big wide sweep and if it had been another 2 feet wider we'd have made it. As it was we went off."

They pushed it back on and crawled to the end of the stage, losing some 45 minutes. The service crew rebuilt the right-hand front corner of the car, made the door "a little bit better, so we could get in and out, and we went to the start of the next stage.

"Jackie Stewart had come to one service point. Jimmy introduced him – 'it's Jackie, you know.' Jackie said to me: 'You must be bloody mad going out with this bugger!' Jackie also said: 'I'm going to watch you on such-and-such a stage. We were three-quarters of an hour late and he must have thought we'd already gone through by then. He stood in the trees with a camera and I remember waving to him. You can imagine his comments afterwards."

Clark was undeterred, and three stages after Loch Achray finished fourth, then fourth in the stage after that. They reached Glengap, and they reached the 1 per cent again.

Melia charts the background as dispassionately as he can. "The Scandinavians used to come over and show the British how to drive, they talked about *yomping*. Erik Carlsson *yomped* his Saab, landed on one wheel, landed at all sorts of angles. One time I decided to have big balls and keep my foot down. It's a bit hairy because the whole point of driving is keeping contact with the road.

"Once you're off the ground I thought the car would keep going in the same direction and all you had to do was keep your foot down. I frightened myself in a big way on the RAC one year, a long straight, a few bumps along it and I thought *I'll be a Scandinavian, here we go* and the car bounced and bounced and bounced and it doesn't bounce straight. Eventually I jumped off the road onto a bank – trees on the other side – and straddled the bank. I realized then it wasn't just a question of being brave, because not only does the car not come down straight, but it twitches every which way. That's what caught Jimmy out.

"It was at night and you could see a long way ahead in the headlamps. On a long straight he kept his toe down and the car started to jump about at 90 miles an hour, four wheels off, land, four wheels off, land. It dug the right-hand front wheel into the soft stuff at the side of the road and over it went, flipped. It rolled as a ball would roll, offside to roof to nearside, and kept on rolling like that in sequence and then it hit a bank. That translated the forward momentum into rotational momentum.

"It must have gone over at least three times in the air and did it much more quickly than it had been doing it before. We cleared a 7ft dyke and landed the right way up in a bog 60, 70 yards from the road. Jimmy's first thought on coming down was that he'd blown the engine and we wouldn't be able to get back into the rally. He said that while we'd been going over: 'I was definitely trying to keep my foot off the throttle so I didn't blow the engine.' He couldn't know whether he'd managed to keep his foot off – however desperately he tried as we rolled bang-bang-bang. That was his reaction as we sat in the car after it had landed. He didn't say it in retrospect, he didn't have time to collect his thoughts and make that up, he said it because he'd tried to do it.

"In those days rally drivers didn't think like that, engines were unburstable, you revved it until it wouldn't go any further and *then* changed gear. A racing driver had a rev-counter which told tales, it was different, and he reacted like that. I mean, he wanted to get back in the rally even as it was going over and over and over. But we were stuck in the bog, out. Something like that brings two guys together. He feels disappointment for me, I feel disappointment for him."

When Melia and Clark looked around they discovered "we didn't just clear the ditch where we'd gone off. They'd planted saplings and you could see where we had mown some down, but others weren't touched. We'd cleared them altogether. We walked back, but we had no idea where we were so I got the map out and said: 'Well, I reckon we're roughly here, which means closer to the end of the stage than the start, let's walk that away.' We got the torch out, but it's difficult to read a map and walk in the pitch black at the same time – you start falling over – so we linked arms, he held the torch and we walked out of the forest like that.

"I expected a quote professional driver unquote like Jimmy to have a busy schedule, etc, etc and be off and away. But he insisted on staying with the team right the way through to the end of the rally."

Melia's wife Dorothy remembers "being in a filling station at a motorway service area and people recognized him. They came up for an autograph. Freezing cold, early hours of the morning, we were all tired, but Jimmy was still very polite, none of your *oh, no, groan*. He signed. In the last stage of the rally – Sherwood Forest – we watched together. I kept pillows in the car so that, when you climbed trees to get a better view, you could take them up and sit on them. Jimmy and I ended up having a pillow fight up a tree…"

In the RAC Rally of 1966 Clark had been as high as sixth. Makinen dropped out and Soderstrom won it.

Postscripts, beginning with Clark himself, who said he drove the RAC on a "trial and error basis" and found his main problem was slowing the car properly for corners. To do that in a racing car required braking slightly at an angle, in a rally car the angle was much more pronounced. He had to feel to get this balance right, feel to have the car so he could "flick" it, feel when to be back on the throttle.

"For Jimmy to get to sixth was a hell of a feat, yes," Roger Clark says. "Whenever they have come together in competitions, the rally driver has been further ahead of the race driver on rallying than the race driver has been ahead of the rally driver on circuits." Jim Clark virtually reversed that. "I think Jimmy was one of the best natural drivers ever against all comers in any discipline. He could make motor cars do what other people couldn't. I got the impression that he felt for the limit of the rally car and he found it. It's an instinct and, no problem, he did it."

Except the 1 per cent, of course.

Cowan says: "I didn't see Jimmy after the rally, but subsequently he talked about it all the time. He loved it, he absolutely loved it. He would have done more of it. That's the type of guy he was."

And Hill? "It would have been easier for Graham in a rear-wheel-drive car than a front-wheel-drive," Cowan says. "The Mini-Cooper was so difficult to drive. A rear-wheel car you can make oversteer by sticking your foot on the power and flicking the steering wheel, a front-wheel-drive it's done under braking conditions, you've got to set up oversteer before you get the power on. He hated it, he thought we were mad and he didn't know how we survived." And how did Jim Clark cope with making the transition? "It wasn't such a transition, he was coming back to his roots, coming back to the way he'd been brought up driving Land Rovers in a grass field. It used to be fantastic fun sliding a tractor, and he did it the same as we all did, so it wasn't so difficult for him.

"The thing that Jimmy could do, he could make that tractor slide at 15 miles an hour and he could make a Lotus Formula One car do the same at 180 miles an hour. It came from the guts. A lot of people can make a tractor slide on a grassy hill, but you start trying to do it on slick tyres at 180 and make it look easy and natural."

Tony Mason, who navigated for Roger Clark when he won the RAC in 1972 and is now achieving semi-cult status on the BBC by reporting on rallying, was in 1966 "a total unknown. At the Excelsior Hotel Jim Clark came over and asked if he could buy me a drink. He was the nicest guy I have ever met. What he did on the rally has never been repeated." This is a delightful tribute and one which could be repeated many times, but I've not quoted it for that reason. Clark confided to Mason that "after the car had rolled the second time he began to analyze what he had done wrong." This amazing man left the road at 90 miles an hour in the dark and as the car battered itself across a field he thought *I must get my foot off the accelerator to save the engine* and simultaneously *how did I make the mistake?*

Racing drivers are not like you or I. Most racing drivers – past, present, future – are not like Jimmy Clark.

That Christmas he sent out his Christmas cards, a photograph of the Lotus Cortina rounding a corner on the Loch Achray stage of the rally, and yes the driver's door is stoved in. On the inside of the card he'd had printed *Car built by Ford, coachwork by Clark.*

To Brian and Dorothy Melia he wrote: "And we didn't even have FF. All the best, Jim." FF? Their personal shorthand for Full Frottle. "You spend a week in a car with a guy and you get to know him pretty well," Melia says. "It's something that just sort of clicks, in terms of somebody says something and"…and it goes into the shorthand of the relationship. It also begs a question: if Clark judged he didn't get full throttle, what might he have done if he had? Crashed more heavily? Blown Soderstrom and Makinen and the rest back to wherever they came from?

To Cowan he sent the same card and wrote: "I told you. It's the same as circuit racing, only the scenery is different."

The 1967 RAC Rally was cancelled because of foot-and-mouth disease, something Clark would surely have understood, and in any case there is no suggestion he intended to take part in it, however much he told Cowan he'd love to do more; and the 1968 RAC Rally was seven months too late, however you care to measure that.

A final postcript, late 1992, and I'm interviewing Peter Warr who says: "You were talking about the RAC Rally and Jimmy lifting his foot off in mid-air. Well, I had the same experience with Johnny Herbert at Monza when I was at Lotus and I tested him in a Formula One car three days before his shunt in Formula 3000. He told me what the car did while it was in the air after he bumped the kerb at the chicane. It's the same thing Jimmy had: a mind that can concentrate and absorb even in those circumstances."

In January 1967 Clark moved to Paris to escape the punitive British tax laws. He moved into Jabby Crombac's flat, Crombac protected him from unwanted intruders – mainly journalists – and he acquired a taste for French food, particularly sea food. There is contradictory evidence of Clark in Paris. Some say he became cosmopolitan, more worldly. "In a way," Brinton says, "he was a very sad person in the last couple of years. He didn't like to be having to live abroad. I noticed that sadness, oh yes." Others felt the Borders would always be his spiritual home, but not, perhaps, his temporal abode. These contradictions will be more fully explored in the chapter Bridge of Sighs, although we'll have a sharp contribution or two within a couple of paragraphs.

Pat Mennem ghosted a column with Clark for the *Daily Mirror*. (Evidently Clark had fallen out with the *Daily Express* after the von Trips accident when, returning to Edington Mains, he found an *Express* newshound on his doorstep; and subsequently when he won the *Daily Express* International Trophy race one year he put the cup itself on the Aga cooker, risking it melting. When someone pointed this out he said: 'Leave it there.') "He was going from Paris to Indianapolis," Mennem says, "and because he lived in Paris he came on a 'local' flight to change for the intercontinental flight. He had some time to spare at Heathrow. I was in the office at Holborn when he rang and said: 'Come up and have a drink.' He was obviously a little bit tight by the sound of his voice – tired and emotional, as they say."

Distant dialogue…

Mennem: Are you going to come out through Customs? The moment you do that it will count against your permitted number of days in Britain. You know I can't come through to you. What are we going to do?'

Clark: Well, I want to talk to somebody.

Mennem: I can't see how we could do it.

"In the end we decided it wasn't possible, I didn't meet him and he went off. He loathed France, well he loathed living in France, he loathed Indy, he couldn't stand the ballyhoo there. When he lived in Paris the things that really fascinated him, the things he wanted to know, were whether they had put parking meters up in Duns, for example.

"Ghosting a column with him? Terrible. He was always busy, very hard to nail down. I remember once at Silverstone I said: 'We've really got to get down to it, do it now.' This was the day before the British Grand Prix and he'd been putting me off and putting me off and putting me off. Eventually he said: 'Right, we'll go to my car' and we did, his little Lotus Elan. I sat next to him, we were in a very confined space and he was so wound up the tension transmitted itself to me. In the end I was shaking so much I practically couldn't write anything down.

"He was a very, very pleasant young Border farmer with this great aptitude to drive who was more or less led astray by Colin Chapman. Chapman planted his values, which were those of an alley cat, weren't they? He imposed those values on Jimmy Clark, who wasn't naturally like that – but, you know, he was told not to say a word, squeeze everybody for everything all the time. It wasn't his nature.

"I went up to Edinburgh with him once and we went shopping. It was market day and we met some of his farmer mates, all these farmer chaps chatting to him, and they never mentioned motor racing once. They were totally disinterested in motor racing. Sheep were the great thing. In his own element he was simply a charming man. He took me out to lunch, the only Grand Prix driver I think who ever did that…"

We must balance Mennem's words with those of Walter Hayes who, in tribute to Clark, wrote: "He was terribly unbusinesslike. September arrived one year and there were still no contracts signed with anyone. We would tell him what we would like him to do and he would tell us what he wouldn't do, and we would then agree how much we thought we ought to pay him. Then he would say "fine", and it was never referred to again. One became very protective and felt one had to take care of this young man because he didn't know to ask for more." Hayes expanded on this by saying that the first year Clark drove for Ford (the Cortinas and the promotional work) they paid him £1,500 but mid-way through the season Hayes thought – and told Clark – it wasn't enough. Clark replied: "Why not?" and dismissed the subject. (When I mentioned this during my interview with Clark's three surviving sisters they were not remotely surprised and thought it entirely typical.)

Cowan puts Paris into perspective. "He got on very well with Jabby Crombac, one of the journalists he had most respect for, and they were great mates. He actually didn't spend a lot of time in Paris, but I know he looked forward to coming home when his term there was over. I think he was allowed back only 10 days a year. I do know that after the British Grand Prix he was on a plane and out the same night. He didn't stay over because that would have counted as an extra day. He spent as few days as possible for the Grand Prix."

(Crombac, incidentally, has recorded how Clark in Paris spent a lot of time with his advisors and a lot of time poring over the motoring magazines, where any mistakes annoyed him. The habits of a lifetime. If you are exact in what you do you expect that of others).

1967

Graham Hill joined Clark at Lotus – Hill coming home, as it were – but, shifts and currents, the Brabham car bestrode the year, Denny Hulme (driving one) winning the Championship from Jack, Clark third, Surtees and Amon joint fourth, Graham Hill joint sixth with Pedro Rodriguez. That is a quick and easy summation and you could write it about any year.

You need, always, to keep an eye on the background which will be the foreground any minute now, other shifts and currents. At Zandvoort for the Dutch Grand Prix Cosworth introduced their DFV engine, something to seize and reshape Formula One racing. The story is well enough known – Chapman and Walter Hayes as the moving forces of the project, Keith Duckworth and Mike Costin as the creators of the engine.

"Practice," Duckworth would remember, "went fairly well. Jim was trying to get used to the car. The engine came onto the power very suddenly and went an awful lot quicker than the drivers were used to."

Mennem observed closely. "They placed a block of wood behind Clark's head because when he put his foot on the accelerator the car shot away at such a speed he slid from the pedals. He could brace his head against the wood. How do I know? I saw it, I was there, yes, cigar in one hand, gin and tonic in the other..."

Hill went quickest on both the qualifying days, Clark third row of the grid (1 minute 24.6 seconds against 1 minute 26.8). "I remember very, very clearly", Bette Hill says, "that Graham had done all the testing for the engine because Jimmy was a tax exile. Graham worked hard at it. We went to Zandvoort, two of Jimmy's sisters with us and Sally Stokes, Clark's girlfriend, and Graham got pole. Jimmy was furious, he was angry.

"We had to tread very, very carefully as to what we said or did during dinner that night and, in fact, his sisters said to me they were so glad Graham didn't tease Jimmy about having pole. I said: 'Well, that's not the sort of person Graham is. He knows how Jimmy feels because he knows Jimmy inside out.' Graham would have taken it slightly differently if the situation had been reversed, because Graham was probably a better loser than a winner. Jimmy sulked. He didn't like it at all. Fair enough, I suppose. In one way it's understandable but in another way it isn't in a sportsman. You don't begrudge someone their success."

In the race Hill led until lap 11 when he retired with, as Duckworth says, "the car making clankety-clank noises. I went immediately to the car to find out why and ignored the rest of the race because I was more interested in finding out. It became fairly obvious we'd lost some teeth from the gears driving the cam and I worried the same thing would happen to Jim, but it didn't."

Clark beat Brabham by 23.6 seconds, although Duckworth occupied himself totally with the problems of the noise. "I was near Jim's car as they restarted it to drive it back along the road to the garage after the race. It had an enormous rattle and teeth were missing from its gears. The difference proved to be that the teeth next to each other had fallen off Graham's car and it had lost drive, but on Jim's there was a tooth missing and then another and it managed to drive across the gaps – obviously a close run thing."

"The thing that always riled me," Bette Hill says, "was that Graham was out in the lead a long way ahead with the engine he had been using for testing and it blew up and Jimmy went on and won. All the record books say *first time out for the Cosworth, won by Jim Clark*. No credit is given to Graham. If anyone deserves the credit it is Graham, together with Mike Costin and Keith Duckworth. Jimmy wasn't even in the country to do the testing work, but he is in the record books, which hurts – hurts me and I knew it hurt Graham, but he was too big a man to make an issue out of it. He was big enough to go and congratulate Jimmy. If it had been the other way round Jimmy would have sulked off, he would have gone away. I know so, I know so because that was Jimmy's way. He didn't like defeat."

Melia wasn't aware of this, although he sketches his own background. Because he worked for Ford he'd been delegated to handle the Autolite plugs which the Cosworth would use – Autolite, Ford's American plug division. "Holland was my first Grand Prix and I couldn't contribute a great deal as the new guy. Anyway it went like clockwork and Jimmy won, no trouble, but the problem occurred in Belgium, the next race. Cosworth had been testing the engines in Northampton and there were about three or four sets of Autolites in the country. They were using them again and again.

"I came in and faced the problem 'we need some plugs' and decided on 2,000. The plugs were made in the States, low-volume stuff, they'd make a batch and not another for 12 months, and suddenly this guy in the UK wanted 2,000! It didn't happen overnight, it took me 18 weeks to get them. Meanwhile, the Cosworth people were putting the old ones in, putting the old ones in and stretching the threads. Nobody knew much about Autolite – they thought it might have been a spotlamp! Champion was the spark plug. The rumour got round that these Autolites come loose, you'd better tighten them whatever you do.

"The Lotus guys picked this up and were screwing them in. The neck of a 10mm plug is thin, you've a ceramic inside, your metal shell is relatively thin. If the plug gets stretched at that narrow point it breaks the internal seal, which means the heat can get up past it. That's what happened in Belgium, a disaster for us. Jimmy led by whatever (around 20 seconds) and his engine packed up. It blew the ceramics out of a couple of plugs and everyone said they should have used Champion, a proper racing plug, instead of these newfangled Autolites. By that time we'd new ones, but the Lotus mechanics had been told to screw them in tight. One ceramic had gone completely out and we reckon to this day there's a Belgian in the woods somewhere with a spark plug through his heart. We never did get it back.

"I had a fortnight to put things right (in time for the French Grand Prix), I bought some torque wrenches and gave two to the team. I said: 'There they are, they're pre-set and you can't alter them,' and I kept the adjusting key…"

Clark broke down in France, but it was crownwheel and pinion not plugs, Graham Hill the same after setting fastest lap. Clark, however, won the British at Silverstone. A cherubic 16-year-old, who lived near the circuit, witnessed it and became captivated. He'd already met Clark at Duns years before because "my uncle was a farmer at Greenlaw, just south of Duns, and a friend. They raced each other round the Borders, raced each other over to Carlisle. Nowadays one would be accused of being dangerous, of being a lunatic, but in those days everybody raced everywhere and you had Charterhall and Ecurie Ecosse and all those good old boys. People in the Borders were proper people." The speaker is Lord Alexander Hesketh, who one day would himself amaze Formula One. He found Clark "a charming man, charming", and because of him and the Borders folk "my car never had a Union Jack on it, it always had a St George's Cross and a St Andrews Cross."

Sixteen-year-old Hesketh hadn't seen Clark drive before and never would again. "I wanted to view all parts of the circuit at Silverstone and spent the weekend walking round. The point about Clark was that you watched him come round a corner in the middle of the road and everyone else climbed over the kerb. You thought *this Lotus with Clark in it is a very slow car* and then you'd hear the announcer say 'Jimmy Clark, a second a lap quicker than anybody else'."

Oswald Brewis still went to the Grands Prix "and Jimmy seemed to like my company. He was a tax exile then and went straight back off to Paris on the night of the race. I saw quite a bit of him that weekend, but I didn't have a chat with him after the race." Brewis never saw Clark again.

As we've seen, Denny Hulme took the Championship in a Brabham from Jack Brabham, Clark third. There's little point in dwelling on it.

1968

The Grand Prix season began in South Africa on January 1, Clark beating Graham Hill by 25.3 seconds. He took the Lotus to New Zealand and Australia for eight races, won four, had a second and a fifth and retired in the other two. On March 31 he drove in a Formula Two race at Mountjuich Park, Spain. Jacky Ickx remembers that. "I tried to overtake Clark in the hairpin, I was obviously too fast, I braked too late and hit him. Afterwards I went straight to him and I said: 'Really, I'm sorry about it' and he said: 'OK, you're sorry and that's OK one time – but not two times.' It was a gentleman's sport."

The mechanic Dave Sims looked after Clark's car. "Mountjuich was a disaster. On the grid Ickx decided to put new pads on the front of the V6 Dino, which they did. He told them he'd had a vibration from the front brakes on the warm-up lap. For some unknown reason the mechanics put new, unbedded pads on. First corner Ickx went straight into the back of Jimmy, totally out of control, no brakes. It wasn't Ickx's fault – but unbelievable the mechanics did what they did. And Graham Hill's engine blew up. A disaster."

Melia, speaking quietly, says: "I'm stuck for words to describe Jimmy Clark's personality. Forget about his talent. As a friend he was a tremendous guy. Absolutely. I saw the talent on the Formula One circuit looking after his spark plugs, and socially as well because when practice finished different groups would go out for meals. He was great fun in those circumstances, full of life, genuine as you could wish for. Four of us had dinner the Sunday night after the race in Spain. There was an actor on another table – I can't remember his name although I can see his face now – one of the old film stars living in Spain. He came across and they had a chat and Jimmy signed his autograph. I remember the evening as nice, pleasant, the race over. Next day he left Barcelona for, I assume, Paris. I used to drive to races carrying about 2,000 spark plugs. I woke up the next morning and headed home for the BOAC-500 mile race at Brands Hatch." Melia never saw Clark again.

"A guy called Mike Gregory was on Graham's car," Sims says. "We loaded the truck up that Sunday night, just the two of us, and got going because Barcelona-to-Hockenheim was a fair run in those days." Hockenheim, the following Sunday, would be the next Formula Two race.

They reached the circuit on the Wednesday and "we had to do an engine change on Graham's car and a rear-end change on Jimmy's. We did that, but as the days went on it got colder, foggier and wetter. We got troubles with the heating unit freezing up and it kept breaking the metering unit belts."

Sims and Gregory hadn't been to Hockenheim before and certainly Clark hadn't driven a race there before, although Scott Watson remembers Clark "saying something about he wasn't particularly looking forward to it, he didn't like the track', so I think he must have looked in there sometime, the way he did when he happened to be passing circuits. It's very close to the autobahn. I said: 'Why aren't you going to Brands?'"

The question endures. The entrant Alan Mann originally approached Clark to drive a Ford sportscar in the BOAC 500. The Ford, sleek and sensuous in its shape – the bodywork appeared pure as a unfolding ripple – was to make its debut. Because Ford actively backed the car, Clark felt a moral responsibility to accept the drive, but evidently Mann did not confirm it and Clark assumed he'd changed his mind. Clark would go to Hockenheim instead.

Bette Hill, close to the situation, offers another version. "The saddest thing about it is that neither Graham nor Jimmy needed to be in that race at all. They were both going to do the BOAC, but because Lotus had entered the Formula Two race at Hockenheim the authorities there threatened to fine them and disqualify them from the Championship if they didn't honour their entry, so they had to go and take part."

In the Brands Hatch programme the preview to the race included this: "Ford of Britain have chosen to run their brand new 3-litre Grand Prix-engined prototypes for the first time ever in the BOAC 500. With Denny Hulme, Bruce McLaren, Mike Spence and a driver yet to be nominated they have an excellent driving force." Clearly this preview went to press early. The later page for the entries must have been kept open longer. It includes:

GROUP 6 PROTOTYPE SPORTS CARS – 2,000cc to 3,000cc

| 33 | Alan Mann Racing Ltd | Jack Brabham | Mike Spence |
| 34 | Alan Mann Racing Ltd | Denny Hulme | Bruce McLaren |

The BOAC was a major event attracting 36 entries and five reserves including Ickx and Brian Redman in a Ford GT40, Bonnier in a Lola, Jackie Oliver and John Miles in a works Lotus Europa, Rindt and Herrmann in a Porsche, Siffert in another, Elford in another, Attwood in an Alfa Romeo. The start: noon.

Towards the back of the programme a full-page advertisement proclaimed FI Stars and Cars! and beneath that a photograph of Clark in a Lotus, then *At Silverstone on April 27th for the Daily Express Trophy. Tickets: £1 entrance, children 5/- [25p]. Free car parking.*

On Friday, April 5 Clark went to a dinner party. On Saturday, April 6 he went to the small Parisian airport of Toussus-le-Noble, much favoured by racing drivers, and flew his Piper Twin Commanche to Germany, a great convenience because he could use it after the race to move quickly to Zandvoort where he'd do some testing on the Monday.

The Formula Two race at Hockenheim was clearly so ordinary that Chapman did not break his family holiday in St Moritz to attend it. Chief mechanic Endruweit, who also travelled to Hockenheim, says: "Chapman didn't normally go to Formula Two meetings. He kept himself, if you like, for Formula One and I did the rest, which was Formula Two, sportscars, you name it. If there was nothing else on I'd do Formula One and he'd do Formula One, if there was something else on he'd do Formula One and I'd do the other. That's how it worked."

Derek Bell, a young driver in a Brabham, happened to be staying at the same hotel as Lotus in Speyer, a small place not far from the circuit. He'd been woken early that Saturday morning by the distinctive sound of a racing engine and sensed the mechanics were trying to cure a misfire.

"Yes," Sims says, "we had an intermittent misfire. We woke a lot of people by starting the car at 2 o'clock in the morning. We worked in the garages underneath the hotel because Hockenheim had no garages of its own, no paddock. It meant that each evening we had to load both cars into the transporter and take them back to the hotel. It was hard."

Clark arrived and, Sims says, "didn't like Hockenheim, Graham didn't like it and Chris Amon didn't like it either. None of the established drivers liked it." During practice on that Saturday – Clark missed the first of the three sessions, the metering problem – "he wasn't happy. The car just did not handle going fast in the wet, it would not work for him, and this at an horrendous, dangerous track, trees just off the apex of corners. They didn't go down well with Jimmy at all. He said it was more dangerous than the Nurburgring – so much quicker. Hockenheim had no chicanes then, it was flat-out – imagine three Woodcote corners – and no margin for error anywhere. You didn't use the brakes except coming into the stadium complex.

"We weren't happy, we still had the small misfire. It didn't hold the car back and never got any worse, but wasn't running 100 per cent smoothly. A lot of it was the metering unit icing up, the weather was freeze, freeze, freeze, we kept putting boiling water over it from kettles."

After the Saturday practice Bell went back to the hotel and "there was my hero sitting at a table saying: 'Come and have a cup of tea with me.' We sat and took tea."

The chronology ticked. Sims and Gregory were able to leave the cars safely at the circuit on this night, the eve of the race. By then, security had been put in place to guard all the gathering of cars.

"The team went to the track and left the drivers to follow later on," Bell says. "We left about 9 o'clock. Graham and Jimmy said: 'Do you want a lift?' and I said: 'Why not?' There's me with Graham Hill, who I had the greatest respect for, who I adored, and Jimmy of course, my hero, very softly spoken. There he sat, ordinary, and he'd twice been World Champion."

Distant dialogue…

Clark: Don't get too close to me when you come up to lap me.

Bell: Why's that? You're joking, aren't you?

Clark: No, I've this misfire, the car is quite dodgy and it could suddenly cut out in the middle of a corner. Don't get too close.

At Hockenheim they dropped Bell off at Brabham – have a good race, Clark murmured – and continued to their own pits. "We did a morning warm-up," Sims says, "the same cold weather, the session delayed because of the fog. Nobody was happy at all. Everybody just wanted to go home. It really was a strained atmosphere, weird, strange. Jimmy said: 'Right, look, just keep me in touch with the race, don't expect me to go charging round. Keep me informed what is going on and we'll take it from there. The car isn't happy and I am not happy with the car, the tyres have no grip whatsoever.' He went and talked to Graham and Chris Amon and they said the same, horrible, slippery, absolutely no grip. We got the one minute signal and Jimmy said to me on the grid: 'OK, see you later, keep me informed'."

Those were the last words Clark spoke.

Sims moved to the pits and prepared to use a clipboard to keep Clark informed…

The Formula Two race would be run over two heats. At the flag for this first heat the cars churned spray and Clark, seventh on the grid, drifted back.

Hill's Lotus performed no better than Clark's, although each time he reached the infield – the part of the track which uncoils like a snake amid concrete grandstands and snaps hard right to the pit lane straight – he glimpsed Clark up ahead. However, because Clark exited the infield long before Hill did, and because the infield was slow, Hill did not see Clark move past the pits and out along the ribbon of track into lap five. When Hill reached the sweeping right-hander – where today the first chicane is – he noticed skid marks leading into the trees. He thought that whoever left those would be in "serious trouble." He did not think of Clark, who he imagined had already passed the point, long gone into the distance.

Bell moved past the pits and out along the ribbon of track urging the Brabham towards some 140 miles an hour into that sweeping right-hander. Glancing left he saw someone had "gone off in a big way," although, like Hill, he had no way of knowing who.

What happened on lap five of heat one of the Deutschland Trophy seems clear. Clark's right rear tyre punctured. The centrifugal force generated at 140 miles an hour by a car travelling straight ahead physically holds the walls of the tyre outwards so that the driver cannot sense the puncture. As he turned into the right-hander, gravity dissipated the centrifugal force extremely quickly. The tyre collapsed.

A marshal, who saw it, said the Lotus appeared to "break away at the rear end" – pitching it hard left. Clark caught and corrected that instinctively, something virtually instantaneous to it happening, but as he did the car broke away to the right. Clark caught and corrected that but the laws of physics governed the car, not he. It broke to the left again – the decrease of speed minimal – and shrieked across a narrow grassy strip into trees. It struck a tree sideways.

Endruweit, in the pits, says: "Jimmy didn't come round, you didn't see him and you thought 'God, he's gone missing.' Next thing there is a kerfuffle – an ambulance moving from the paddock area. You knew something had happened. There were a couple of young German ladies who had attached themselves to us for the weekend, the way they used to, both quite decent girls. I knew one of them, lovely girl, a photographer, and I was using her as an interpreter. We went along to the organizers' place and I said: 'What the hell's happened to Jimmy?' And they were very loath to say, they wouldn't say."

Sims "waited and waited in the pits and, of course, you didn't have the communications then that you have now as soon as someone goes missing. No monitor, no radio, nothing. Then a Porsche came by – a road car, might have been the pace car. The guy in it said: 'Come on, there's been an accident.' I jumped in and said: 'What's the problem?' He said: 'A Lotus has gone off, Jim Clark.'

They didn't stop the race and we went out onto the track in this Porsche, a bit scarey in among all the racing cars, and I remember it was a bit dark. The racing cars didn't slow – no yellow flags. When we reached the scene there was nothing. So I asked myself: what's happened here? You know, you can't see anything. Then I did see an ambulance parked in the shrubbery. [Bell remembers seeing this, too, as he passed in the Brabham, and somehow it confirmed his fears, although he still didn't know it was Clark.] You must remember I was fairly young then, 25.

Distant dialogue...
Sims: Where is the car? Where is Jimmy?

Someone: He is in the ambulance.

Sims: How is he? Is he having a check-up?

Someone: I am afraid he is clinically dead.

Sims, moving into shock: Yes, yes. Pardon, but where is the car?

"I had ignored what he'd said, *no, I thought, he's got his German and English mixed up*. Then I saw where the car was and I asked where the rest of it was, the engine and gearbox weren't there. I said: 'What have you done with them, what has happened here?' I could see the monocoque and it had gone a sort of banana shape when it hit the tree, but the force of hitting the tree ripped the engine and gearbox out. They went on in to the woods and sat there 50 or 60 yards away. Then I started to realize. I said: 'Well', and this man said: 'I have to tell you again he is clinically dead but we are flying him to Mannheim.' I didn't look in the ambulance. They had closed the doors. (Someone pointed out where Clark's head had struck the tree and it was 15 feet up.)

"At that point I didn't know what to do. I hadn't got a phone, people were coming through the woods – spectators – people were picking up pieces. I said: 'First of all, don't let anybody touch anything, for goodness sake stop people pinching stuff.' I said [probably to the man in the pace car]: 'Get on to your people in the pits and tell them to give Graham the arrow to come in.' Graham had gone past, he didn't notice what was happening. Then I said: 'You'd better get me back to the pits fast to speak to Graham to find out what we do now.'"

Endruweit, still at the organizers', listened to "chit chat" in German flow back and forth between officials and the photographer. "'Right', she said, 'come with me', and we leapt into her car. She'd found out what hospital and we went ambulance chasing, if you like, to I don't know where. I just left everything. I thought I'd be away half an hour. In fact I was away four hours."

Sims, returning to the pits, was in a state. "It's my fault the number one, the greatest driver has just been killed. What do I do? Run away? What do I do? Where is the chief mechanic, where is the Old Man? We got Graham in and I said: 'Look, Jimmy is dead, they want somebody to go with him to Mannheim, what do I do?'"

Hill wrote in his autobiography *Life at the Limit* (which was unghosted) that "my reactions at the time were a bit odd – I don't think I really took in what had happened. It was as if someone had told me it was a fine day – I heard what they had said but I didn't twig what it meant. It took a while to register that that was the last time we were going to see Jimmy."

"Without Graham," Sims says, "I don't know what would have happened, he was an absolute, unbelievable pillar of strength. He went and saw the organizers and told them we were going to take our truck out there and pick everything up. 'First thing we will do that,' he said, 'and I'll come with you.' So me, Graham and Mike Gregory went in the truck and with the help of some marshals we loaded every scrap into the truck. We had to do that for the inquiry there would have to be, then we went back to the paddock."

Endruweit reached the hospital and "I kept saying: 'What's happened, what's happened?' and they wouldn't tell me. Nobody would say anything. I was sitting around and sitting around, dependent entirely on this young lady. Eventually, after a considerable time, they said: 'Sit down, Mr Endruweit, have a drink' (brandy) and I thought: Hello, this is not good news. At that point – only then – did they tell me that Jimmy had been killed. The only thing we'd assumed was that he'd been seriously injured and they were doing something fierce to him in the hospital, it was touch and go and they were going to say 'great' – they'd saved him – or say something else.

"They asked me if I'd make a formal identification so we trolled off down and I did that. Jimmy wasn't marked. In essence he'd hit this modest tree, you know, 4-inch diameter, that sort of size, a young tree, and it had taken the rear suspension off. It was explained to me, in the hospital I think, that he had gone sideways into the tree and had a lower cranium fracture. In other words, the base of his skull – about the base of his crash hat – had taken the impact against the tree. And that was it."

By now Sims and Gregory had driven the truck back to the hotel and "the delayed shock was coming in," Sims says.

Endruweit, in the hospital, said: "'I need a phone' and they took me to some vast room where there was one. I rang Chapman because I knew where he was. He'd left me a contact number at the something-hotel in the morning. I got through and I said: 'Look, I need to speak to Colin Chapman', and they said he'd gone out for a walk. I said: 'For Christ's sake go out and find him.' They actually did go out and find him. I absolutely had to speak to Jimmy's father because it was the right thing to do, and by then obviously it was known about. This news, which I had been given quarter of an hour previously, had become common knowledge back in Britain. I broke it to his father with great difficulty. How do you do that? His dad took it in his dour Scots fashion, I suppose. I couldn't tell you whether he knew or not by the time I phoned him. All I was able to say was he'd been killed instantly, he wasn't damaged and things like that. Colin rang."

Hazel Chapman remembers Chapman repeating everything Endruweit said twice.

"He was totally shattered and, I suspect, in shock," Endruweit says. "When I'd spoken to him he jumped in his car and drove like a maniac" towards Hockenheim. Endruweit returned to the hotel and "met up with Graham again – he'd taken control of the other half of the operation, if you like." Endruweit presumably informed Hill that Chapman was coming and Hill in turn informed Sims with the words "we'd better not to anything else until he arrives."

Derek Bell heard an echo of what Clark said – *I've got this misfire, the car is quite dodgy and could suddenly cut out in the middle of a corner, don't get too close* – "that is what he said to me and I still believe that is why he died. I came round the lap after and saw the ambulance there. The car had disappeared, gone, there were no guardrails worth talking about. My car had a clutch problem so I stopped early and that's when I was told.

"Racing drivers were looked upon much as playboys, only wealthy people did it. Well, people didn't realize that Jimmy and Graham and the likes of me struggled and scratched because we had no money at all. When my family told me I was doing this stupid, dangerous sport and you could get killed – in those days somebody got killed every month and it was a cruel sport – I'd say: 'But Jimmy's never broken the skin on his body. I'm not as good as him, but if he hasn't, why should I?' It acted as my safety valve, kept me going. Then he died."

At Brands Hatch Brinton heard an announcement over the public address system and "the crowd went silent. The announcement was simply that he had had an accident." Jochen Rindt heard the truth in the pits and it devastated him.

"Jimmy," he would say, "was the one I was with most frequently and we were pretty close friends, as much as this is possible in motor racing." Bob Dance, chief mechanic on the Lotus Europa team, could have gone to Hockenheim but chose Brands instead. He remembers the announcement and recalls "we were aware that he'd died before the end of the BOAC although I can't be sure who told us. It became pretty common knowledge and it didn't just affect us, it affected everybody."

Nigel Roebuck knew Clark was dead two hours into the BOAC 500. "The BOAC, you see, started at noon and Jimmy had been killed in the morning. The race was going through a boring period and I went off to Chater's, the bookshop, which used to be behind the Clearways grandstand. I was looking through one or two books and the guy in the shop said: 'Have you heard about Clark?' and I said 'No', and he said...

"I returned to the grandstand and told the people I was with and it spread, people heard. In the pits afterwards I said to Brian Redman that he seemed cheerful – but he hadn't heard. I don't know whether Ickx knew or not. I talked later to John Wyer (running the J W Automotive Engineering team, and thus Ickx) and he said: 'No, no, we didn't tell them.' Whether Ickx had found out some other way is possible, of course."

Eoin Young had travelled to Brands with Bruce McLaren. "I first heard," Young says, "when I was walking along that inside pit lane to the tunnel with Mike Spence and he was dumbstruck. He'd heard because his car was out by then. I said: 'What's the matter?' and he said: 'Jimmy's been killed.' I drove back with Bruce, I had my tape recorder on, and he did a whole column on Jimmy. Within weeks Spence was dead, too."

Brinton learned later that Clark had been killed. "I heard it in the press room. The news soon got around." It did not reach Brian Melia. "I can remember exactly where I was, I can remember the actual point on the road. We were in traffic trying to get out of Brands and it came on the radio. [Pause.] In Grand Prix racing there were a hell of a lot of prima donnas and fair weather friends even then, oh yes, some people I wouldn't wish to call friends. If they'd got a problem and you could help they'd fawn over you, next race they'd walk down the pit lane straight past you. Jackie Stewart wasn't like that, Jimmy Clark certainly wasn't like that."

John Watson, later the leading British driver of his generation – post-Hunt, pre-Mansell – was "driving home from Belfast in an MGB, blue with a black hardtop to be more precise, on the way to my family home just outside Hollywood. The road went uphill, I was in a speed limit and I heard on the radio he'd been killed: unreal, almost as if somebody had put a cold rod through me. I'd never met Clark, I knew him only through reading the motoring magazines and seeing him on television. I was racing my Formula Two car and to me it was unbelievable that somebody immortal suddenly wasn't there. I waited until I got home, hoping to hear a further report which would contradict what I'd just heard. It affected me more subconsciously than consciously: you could be alive and you are dead, in the space of a millisecond life can go, go as quick as that.

"Driving a racing car is a wonderful, exhilarating and fulfilling experience, particularly if you do it well and achieve a level of success, but you have to think of it in another way also. The thing which is giving you that fulfillment, that pleasure at any given point on any race track, can be gone in that millisecond, bang, history, you are dead. That quick. I am sure you are familiar with death in many other areas. In motor racing you are aware that the dangers are very present and you take every possible step to make sure you don't go over the line, but when something happens beyond your control – a mechanical failure or whatever in Jim Clark's incident – it is frightening because it illustrates almost more clearly than anyone can put into words how fragile we are and how vulnerable we are."

Niki Lauda would write in his autobiography: "Clark died in a shunt exactly one week before my first race. I can remember it to this day. I was watching a race in Aspern (an aerodrome in Austria). Just as the race finished it came over the PA system that Clark had been killed at Hockenheim. The news went through me like a knife and I was very depressed: what a shame, I thought, he'll be missed, the world will be a poorer place without him. I had no sense of drama about his death, no feeling of awesome tragedy. It never crossed the mind of a 19-year-old that the weeks, months and years ahead would be just as dangerous for me."

Bette Hill says: "We were living at our lovely home Lyndhurst, in Hertfordshire, and I'd put the television on just because I was interested in the BOAC and thought there might be news of it. I'd walk past the TV now and again keeping an eye on it. Suddenly there was Jimmy's face on the screen and they said he'd had a serious accident at Hockenheim, been taken to hospital. They believed his injuries were serious. Damon was standing beside me and I said: 'Pray it's not true'."

Ian Scott Watson sat at home and the phone rang, the *Daily Express* in London. "I can only assume David Benson had given my number because I knew him quite well and he had the number. The *Express* said: 'Look, we don't want the family to hear it on the news and Andrew Ferguson (of Lotus) probably won't have time to ring everybody to warn them because he's gone off to the hospital.' I was so taken aback, so mortified I didn't think I could face phoning the Clarks. I thought I'd phone Alec Calder, Jimmy's eldest brother-in-law, but there was a lawyer who was very friendly with Alec and looked after the Clark family. I phoned him and he said: 'Leave it to me.'

"Within five minutes the phone rang again. Border Television said they'd just heard and would I be prepared to come down to the studio immediately to do something for the 6.30pm news. I said I'd do that because I thought it would take my mind off it for a couple of hours. I jumped in my Elan and went flat-out to Carlisle where Border Television is. I got back home and I still couldn't believe it."

Cowan drove from Aberdeen to Stirling. "I had just competed in the Granite City Rally, a round of the British Championship, I was in a rally car and it didn't have a radio, but one of my service crew up ahead did have a radio and he heard the newsflash. Jim Clark had been seriously injured at Hockenheim. He pulled me in, stopped me and told me. I drove into Stirling to a friend of mine, Logan Morris, also a rally driver. I was going there with my girlfriend, who was with me in the car. I pulled up at the door outside and Logan stood there at the window absolutely expressionless. I knew then."

That night everyone knew. A sonorous, decorous voice came from every radio. *"Ten o'clock. This is BBC Radio Four, the Home Service. Here is the news read by Roy Williamson. The racing driver Jim Clark has been killed in a crash on a German track. President Johnson surrounded by a strong security guard attended a memorial service in Washington."* Williamson moved through the headlines and then began the bulletin proper. *"Jim Clark, the former World*

Champion racing driver, died this afternoon when his car crashed on the Hockenheim track in West Germany. He was 32. The accident occurred when his car, a Lotus-Cosworth, coming out of a bend at about 170 miles an hour zig-zagged along the track, skidded, then somersaulted and crashed broadside into a wood. The car was wrecked. Debris was scattered over a wide area. An announcement at the track said Clark got into a skid caused by suspension failure. Officials have been trying to establish the cause of the accident. Clark was taken from the wreckage severely injured and died on his way to hospital."

"I went home to my farm that Sunday night and that was desperate, everywhere frozen, Duns deserted," Cowan says. "The milkman was the first person I had contact with the next morning. I went to the door and the milkman came up making his delivery. He got out and stood there with tears streaming down his face. No word was spoken."

Late on race night Hill phoned Bette. They could, she says, do no more than "commiserate with each other. Everyone was totally and utterly devastated. Here was this young man – with the emphasis on the fact that he was a young man, he had everything going for him – and if it could happen to him everyone else was equally as vulnerable, if not more so."

Sims, Gregory, Hill and Endruweit sat in the hotel in Speyer and, Sims estimates, "Chapman arrived around one in the morning. He looked at me."

Distant dialogue…

Chapman: What the hell have you done?

Sims: I haven't done anything.

Chapman: What happened, what on earth happened? I can't believe this is going on.

Sims: None of us can.

Chapman: Right, I want that truck out of here right now, get it to England now.

Sims: But the police have sealed it, they've told us not to move it and they're coming back at eight in the morning.

Chapman: You have got to go, but don't go through any borders whatever. Get out and do it and that is an order.

Sims and Gregory walked to the truck, Chapman accompanying them. Chapman seemed calmer then, but he asked Sims again: "What happened? What went wrong?" "It couldn't have been a mistake by Jimmy, he wouldn't push himself to that point, he was not stupid. He'd go over the top of ten-tenths, but know he remained fully in control. He'd never take a car to the point where he could no longer control it – even the Old Man said something must have gone wrong with the car.

"So we left him, Graham and Jim, and set off in the early hours of the morning up the autobahn. We decided to get off that when we were up near Belgium and the Ardennes. We had a map and we found a track. It had a border post with just a swinging gate, nobody there. We went through and must have been across before 8 o'clock, before the police reached the hotel in Speyer. We drove through little villages and once we were on a farmer's track. Eventually we reached the main road and headed for Zeebrugge. I was surprised the German police didn't put a guard on the truck and I was surprised we weren't picked up going out of the Hockenheim area, but no police cars, nothing, very weird.

"We got to the docks at Zeebrugge, a boat leaving in 15 minutes, and in those days you could go straight ahead, say: 'Let me on, let me on,' give them cigarettes or something. They'd get you on for that. The guy on Customs pointed to the truck (which had Lotus written all over it)."

Distant dialogue...
Customs official: Jim Clark?
Sims: Yes, Jim Clark.
Customs official: I want to see.
Sims: No, you can't.
Customs official: OK, you don't get on the boat. I want to take photographs.

"This is the guy," Sims says, "who is going to let me on the boat. I said to myself: what are we going to do now? We had no choice so we let him take photographs of what was left of the wreckage of the car. I think he took them for himself, not for any official reason. At this point we hadn't even got Jimmy's racing shoes out of the car, they were pinned behind the pedals. I mean, Jimmy's Rolex watch was still jammed beneath the master cylinder. We'd left Hockenheim so fast we hadn't had time to extract all that stuff.

"When eventually we left on the boat it was a Godsend, but when we docked in England the British police were waiting – I don't know if the Belgian Customs telephoned ahead or even the German police, who would know we had gone by then – and they escorted us all the way to the factory, but we were not allowed to take the truck in (and onto private property.) The truck stayed outside the gates for two days, the police kept watch on it and then they said: 'OK, it's all yours.'"

Hill flew his own plane from Germany to Elstree that Monday and when he landed a friend came over and said: "What about poor old Jim?" Hill would remember "I continued filling my logbook, without looking up, and said 'yeah...it was terrible.' That probably seems abrupt; it wasn't meant to be but it was all the emotion I could afford to show. I was terribly upset over Jimmy's death but, as a racing driver, I couldn't allow my emotions to come through. If I did I would have been lost and unable to cope."

"The next week was horrendous because the press didn't leave Graham alone, didn't leave us alone," Bette Hill says. "Then everyone went to Scotland for the funeral and we had photographers with cameras up our noses. They don't really think about grief, they want to get their pictures on the front pages and it's hard to take when you've been that close to someone. We were as close to Jimmy as we would have been to a brother, I suppose, Graham did rallying with him, they grew up in motor racing together. Graham was a great fun man so wherever Graham was Jimmy was. He enjoyed Graham's company as a result of that and together with Innes Ireland – more or less the trio – we travelled together.

"Dan Gurney came over and cried his way through the funeral, but Graham was so strong. With Innes and Dan and one or two of the other drivers he had to lower Jimmy's coffin into the grave and that's tough, that's very hard to take, especially with someone you like, someone you love."

Clark was buried in the churchyard at Chirnside. "I'm not a person who is very demonstrative at funerals," Ian Scott Wason says. "I sometimes feel embarrassed in that when I'm not crying I don't feel I should be. It was the one and only time that I did. I realized I was getting pretty near to breaking down at Jimmy's funeral. It was a very moving ceremony. Suddenly the whole thing was beginning to come to me."

Sims suffered a private agony. "Night after night I asked myself if the accident had been caused by something I didn't do. You put your head on the pillow and the race check would go through your brain, and you'd be ticking the check list off. Strange, but I never really talked to anybody about it because it would have opened up too many things so I just didn't. It wasn't fair to his family to talk about it. I didn't want to hold my hand up and say I was the last person to talk to Jimmy Clark so I didn't."

Over two years later Heinz Pruller, journalist, television broadcaster and biographer of Jochen Rindt – *The Story of a World Champion* – sat with Chapman at the Earls Court motor show and felt able to broach the subject. "This entire motoring racing business," Chapman said, "is a question of feelings of triumph one moment and utter despair the next. One has to learn therefore to control one's feelings; if one doesn't one just goes mad. One simply has to be without pity: the line between success and disaster is very, very thin – the difference between the driver who walks away after an accident and the one who dies is just as thin. When someone is killed in one of my cars I accept responsibility, but not blame. We are all to blame, the whole of the Grand Prix circus; we must accept equal blame."

Peter Warr ponders the question *was Chapman the same after Clark's death?* and says "not really. Two things happened. First it took him a long time to get over it. You've got to remember that 1968 was a terrible year because Jimmy crashed in April, Mike Spence was killed at Indianapolis a month later, and in July Jo Schlesser was killed in a Honda at Rouen. A terrible year. It did take Colin a long time to get over Jimmy, partly because there was this intensely close personal relationship between them. Colin vowed at the time never to get as close to a driver again because of the pain it would cause if something happened. I could see that in him.

"Graham Hill held the team together and in 1969 Jochen Rindt came on the scene. Jochen wasn't the sort of personality or character Colin could have got near anyway, a foreigner, young, very bullish and all the rest of it. His interests and Colin's weren't the same. When Emerson Fittipaldi became number one after Jochen's accident Colin was getting to the point where he could feel a sense of the generation gap. Here he had a guy driving for him young enough to be his son. These new young lads, good though they were, were employed race drivers as opposed to friends."

Chapman decided to instigate a most exhaustive and impartial inquiry, despite what Lotus would do themselves – Dance says the wheels of the time didn't have safety bolts and thus a tyre would "deflate down into a well." Lotus conducted tests, blowing tyres up, deflating them, timing that, trying to measure it all. Chapman asked Peter Jowitt, Senior Engineer of the Experimental Aircraft Department at Farnborough and an RAC scrutineer, to take on the independent inquiry. Jowitt put together a logical, painstaking and scientific account of what had happened. I'm indebted to it for the paragraph I've used to describe the accident earlier in this section.

Jowitt was no friend of Chapman, was surprised to be asked, and felt he had to revise his view of the man because "he must have known that he could expect nothing but the unvarnished result of the investigation, but he was absolutely determined to have the truth, no matter how hurtful." To summarize Jowitt: he placed great emphasis on the marshal who'd seen the car weaving and then found an "oddly shaped cut in the tread of the rear right-hand tyre." The cut had penetrated the tyre and no part of the wreckage seemed to have done it. Clark therefore had a puncture, but balancing the speed of the track and the rate of deflation – particularly since when the car moved directly ahead centrifugal forces held the tyre out, masking the puncture – even the "unearthly skill of Jimmy Clark" could do nothing.

In the last instants of his life Clark became a passenger.

Some suggest that he may have picked up a piece of metal from the surface of the track the lap before. In *The Legend Lives On* (PSL, third edition) Graham Gauld writes that during the Saturday practice a driver called Walter Habegger broke his crankshaft and that could have left something on the track; further, Gauld writes that in the stadium complex Clark was observed to slide but catch it on a left-hand corner and the exit from the complex is a hard right – throwing the loading onto the left rear tyre, not the right rear. Gauld reasons that Clark would attribute the slide to the wetness of the track surface. Whatever, he surely accelerated past the pits, the speed rising and rising, totally unaware of the danger.

"Jimmy's death shook Chapman as much as you can shake any living person," Sims says. "To him, Jimmy was immortal, nobody could even think about it. You heard of other drivers being killed or injured, but not Jimmy – not injured, let alone killed."

Bette Hill insists that the immediate aftermath demonstrates the character of her husband. "It only made him more determined because he had to uphold Lotus. It was a terrible time. We had Mike Spence killed at Indianapolis. We said *not another one*. A ghastly year, a hell of a year but things like that only made Graham stronger. Colin virtually gave up and didn't want to go anywhere.

"Colin didn't have any brothers, you see, so Jimmy was his brother, and not only that, Jimmy more or less did what Colin told him to do. Graham didn't. Graham had a very strong mind, it wasn't always right, but in many cases it contributed to being right. On occasions he and Colin came unstuck, they didn't agree, but – with regard to Colin – Jimmy was much more of a yes man because he preferred it that way. He liked to have it done for him and he trusted Colin implicitly because of Colin's dedication to him.

"Graham knew that Colin would give preferential treatment to Jimmy, we all knew it, Colin knew it, Colin knew that we knew it. There is nothing to hide in that respect. I'm not speaking badly of the dead – all three are not here to answer, which is bloody ridiculous – but they would agree with me.

"Chapman was totally and utterly shattered. As a family the Chapmans were shattered. To the little Chapman girls and Clive, Jimmy was the bigger brother, to Hazel and Colin he was their brother. He'd been around with them so long, the beginning, the middle, the Championships, everything. It makes a big hole in your life. It's something you learn to live with, but you never get over. I don't think Colin ever got over Jimmy dying.

"Graham had to pick up Lotus by its nuts and bolts and put it all together again. Had he not the team would have folded. Chapman did not want to go on, he did not want to go on, the mechanics didn't want to go on, but we were into a Championship and the next Grand Prix was Spain (on May 12). We couldn't afford for me to go everywhere – Graham had to pay for me and himself – but he said: 'Would you come with me?' I think he felt he needed some support.

"We had to resurrect motor racing, people had to start living their lives again. You don't forget, of course, you never forget, but the Spanish Grand Prix was coming on so shortly afterwards." A couple of days before Hill flew to Jarama, Spence was killed, May 7, a month to the day after Clark.

"So we went to Jarama. A couple used to go around the races and they thought they were Jimmy's official timekeepers. Looking back it's quite funny, but at the time it wasn't. There I was sitting on the pit counter with my hook in front of me to record the times. I'd taken my own little stool, which I always did. This particular person insisted that she was the official timekeeper. I said 'I don't give a stuff whether you are or not, this is where I'm going to sit. There's only one car – Graham's – and I'm taking his times. Find yourself another slot.' She called me a very unladylike name and Graham, who had enough on his plate, turned and said: 'Don't talk to my wife like that'.

"It's so terrible, isn't it, that within such a short space of time after Jimmy's funeral people wanted to get in on the act? Graham said to her: 'Just stay away from it.' He told me to 'do what I want you to do', which is what I did. When Graham went out and got going fast, people started creeping into the pit, which I found incredible. They didn't respect what was happening and the tension was great anyway. I mean, we were scared. I was terrified – a Lotus had crashed, they hadn't found the reason for it, Graham was doing it alone in a Lotus."

In the one and a half hour morning session on Friday, May 10 Pedro Rodriguez (BRM) went quickest, Hill a mere 0.3 second behind.

"You could see it as Graham started to do well. The mechanics lightened up, almost as if they'd had a drink. Afterwards Graham took them all out for a meal, which was important psychologically. *These are my men, these are the people I work with, these are the people who are helping me*. He was stronger than ever and whatever he felt inside he didn't let too many people know. The mechanics knew because they talked to each other. Jimmy's name came up in conversation, of course it did. People patted Graham on the back and quite honestly that was the wrong thing to do, that made it more emotional."

Hill qualified on the third row of a tight grid, Amon (Ferrari) on pole with 1 minute 27.9, Hill 1 minute 28.4. It didn't mean much across 90 laps and 190 miles.

"We phoned Colin the night before the race and told him what position we were, and he said: 'Well, all right.' Then on race day King Carlos was introduced to all the drivers and all their names were flashed up in lights, a lovely thing, like a carnival. Graham had a job to do and was damn well going to do it. We all started to smile again. And of course he won the race, tremendous..."

Amon led comfortably, but on lap 58 his fuel pump let go. Hill held off a dogged thrust by Hulme (McLaren) – at one point Hulme drew full up behind Hill and attacked very hard, then Hulme had gearbox problems and Hill won by 16 seconds.

"Other people would have retired after Jimmy's death," Bette Hill says, "other people would have said: 'My friend is dead, I'm not going to carry on motor racing', but Graham didn't. It was up to him to keep at it. Graham had a reputation for *applicability* and Damon has it, too: you don't give up. We don't as a family give up."

Sims adds to this. "Graham totally held the team together. I think he even controlled the Old Man to a point behind the scenes, something that has never been made public. Graham did a lot of team planning after Jimmy's death, he sat down with the Old Man for long hours and he did a lot of work."

Two weeks after Spain, Hill won Monaco, Chapman back in attendance. Life, whatever it was or was not, moved on. Hill slogged the rest of the season out. The driveshaft went in Belgium. An Italian, Ludovico Scarfiotti, had driven a Cooper-BRM in Spain and at Monaco, but wasn't in Belgium. On the day before the Belgian Grand Prix he practised for a hillclimb and was killed. That was June 8, a month and a day after Spence, two months and a day after Clark.

Hill spun in Holland and chugged to the end nine laps behind the winner, Stewart, then the driveshaft went again in France. During the race Jo Schlesser was killed in a Honda. That was July 7, two months to the day after Spence, three months to the day after Clark, and a month and a day away from Scarfiotti. Hill's driveshaft went again at the British and they came to the Nurburgring, August 4. The conjunction of the calendar – April 7, May 7, June 8, July 7 – was near enough to make many drivers openly apprehensive, among them Stewart, who evidently wandered round asking *What are we doing here?* A whisper passed up and down the pit lane. *Who's next?*

Sims "got all sorts of press in German after Jimmy's death, an account of this, an account of that. Because it was Jim Clark everyone had their own view – the *Daily Mirror*, the *News of the World*, all that sort of nonsense. I got a lot of phone calls and that put me into my shell really. The Old Man called me in and asked me what I wanted to do. I said I'd take advice. He said: 'The world is still going to go on. I want you to go to a race meeting straight away. Next weekend you are at the Nurburgring.' That was it, back in Formula One with Graham."

There were three accidents in qualifying – Elford, Beltoise, Amon – but the race passed safely enough. All 20 who set off returned at the end and the order seems almost irrelevant: Hill second, anyway.

He lost a wheel at Monza, came fourth in Canada, came second at Watkins Glen, came to the last race, Mexico, with 39 points, Stewart 36, Hulme 33. By the second lap Stewart led Hill, Hulme third – but he broke down on lap 10. Deep into the race Stewart's handling went and Hill won by 1 minute 19.32 seconds. A vignette of the tumult at the end of Mexico: a strong and tall and handsome man densely surrounded by wellwishers, heavily garlanded and sipping champagne; and within arm's reach Chapman ticks off an interview, turns, cranes up to Hill, and Hill touches his arm – an extremely masculine gesture meaning many things, but primarily we did it. Chapman is smiling. Many, many thought they'd never see that again.

Bette Hill insists that Graham is the forgotten Champion. Maybe. What he did between April 7 and Mexico November 3, 1968 entitles him to be remembered forever; and by so many he is…and will be.

PORTRAIT:
JACKIE STEWART

Swiss taxi drivers are not a species to be unduly impressed by wealth. I'd caught the train to Nyon, a pleasant place a handful of stops from Geneva, and showed the driver the address I had written on a piece of paper. He moved away from the station, climbed for a while and nosed his way along a road, checking off the numbers until we came to the one on the piece of paper. He turned into a long drive and we found what seemed to be a minor chateau spreading in front of us. "This can't be it," the driver said, "this can't be a private house."

It was.

The small, neat Scotsman had come a long way from Dumbuck Garage, Milton, Dumbartonshire; all the way to here. The interior as well as the exterior of the house proclaimed as much, one wall a montage of photographs of Jackie Stewart with celebrities, all manner of European royalty, The Beatles and so many more I can't remember them. If you reflect that people who've met one member of our Royal Family once are apt to bore you with the details for years afterwards the montage was extremely impressive. Moreover, no doubt scattered around the world are other people's montages with the owners delighted to have *Stewart* posing with *them*.

Jackie Stewart is no ordinary man and was no ordinary driver, either. He once told Benson of the *Express* "that he could differentiate between what was threatening and what was not. Stewart said 'If we are talking in the street and a car backfires I wouldn't flinch because I would recognize instantly that it was of no immediate danger to me.' I believe him, just as I believe normal people duck and say: 'What the hell was that?'"

Whatever gifts Stewart was born with – his father raced 500cc bikes at the Isle of Man TT in the Thirties and finished sixth in the Senior race, his mother handled potent road cars superbly – he dissected, examined and drew conclusions. Here is Benson discussing precisely this. The *Express* had Stewart as a celebrity columnist. Such columns are ghosted by a journalist and widely dreaded within the profession because all too frequently the newspaper has been seduced by the possibilities of the celebrity's name; the celebrity himself either has little to say beyond the banal or won't say it for fear of the repercussions.

"I'd do my report of a Grand Prix and then interview Jackie afterwards for his view from behind the wheel, and the paper ran the two pieces side by side. I always used a tape recorder because with Jackie that was the easiest way. He spoke effortlessly and had an absolute recall of a whole race, every part of that race, where he was, where the others were. Now think of a race of, say, 80 laps and Jackie led from start to finish. You can imagine how boring that might be, particularly if you're clearly in front, but no, he had absolute recall of it."

Almost unbelievably this man of such articulation is dyslexic. He is articulate *about* dyslexia and once confessed that he couldn't write down the alphabet in the correct sequence if you gave him a lifetime to try, but so what? He is an example of how you overcome it and has taken care over the years to speak about the problems of dyslexia, how you recognize it in others, how parents can cope.

Like the photo montages, there must be, I assume, people scattered all over the world who have taken comfort and heart from Stewart's words and made their lives more complete than they might otherwise have been.

The road to Nyon began on the road from Glasgow to Dumbarton in 1926. The Stewart family were country folk and Stewart's grandfather, evidently, found employment as a gamekeeper on the estate of a wealthy industrialist, Lord Weir. Stewart's father Bob regularly fished with Lord Weir and that day in 1926, on their way to some fishing, Lord Weir pointed to a small petrol station with a couple of hand-operated pumps and said it might have a good future. Motoring would increase and it was the first petrol station outside Glasgow. Lord Weir offered to help Bob buy it, but Bob, no doubt grateful but proud in the way of the Stewarts, said he'd find the money himself and around 1928 he did. He married – Jeannie – in 1930 and a year later Jimmy was born.

Bob was humorous and good at business. He survived the war by setting up a taxi service when no new cars were available for sale and petrol was strictly rationed, but people from the big tankers landing in the Clyde needed transport. Although a disciplinarian he was such a good man that Jimmy feels "he was more like my best friend than my father." When Jimmy began racing in 1953 he had Bob's full encouragement, though most definitely not Jeannie's. Whenever Jimmy returned home from a race "I found my mother consumed by nervous exhaustion. That was what made me finally stop my career. I had to decide that the family came first." As we've seen, Jimmy had had a bad crash, too, severely injuring an arm at the Nurburgring in 1955, and if he'd kept on he risked permanent damage.

By 1953 the garage sold Jaguars and obtained a C-Type for demonstrations. Jimmy sent it down to Lofty England who, he says, "breathed on it, although not to the point where a normal motorist couldn't handle it. The car could be docile if you wanted it to be because after all it was a registered road car." Jeannie, evidently, handled it as she'd handled powerful Rileys before, no problem. She never, however, raced.

While Jimmy competed, Bob brought Jackie Stewart, eight years younger, to a lot of the races. Jimmy took him, too, so "at an early age he'd been all over the place, Silverstone, Goodwood, Snetterton, even Le Mans in 1954. Because of the age difference, and because he was such a little lad wearing wee shorts, it was as if I had my son with me – I was a full grown man and a racing driver. I was naturally protective towards him."

Stewart himself nursed notions of being a footballer, but took up clay pigeon shooting. Inevitably he'd been behind the wheel from an early age. "I first drove a car when I was nine at my father's garage. It was particularly enjoyable when winter came and there was snow or ice around. I'd slither and slide around and try and control it. When I was 12 Jim was already driving racing cars. I followed him around with an autograph book trying to get the great names of the day. I was always in awe of these drivers and dreamed one day of becoming one, but I never thought it would happen.

"I don't know if the dyslexia spurred me on. I think all it did was depress me. School was the unhappiest days of my life. I have the deepest sympathy for any person who has children with it, any person who has it, or indeed any other learning disability. I work very hard for dyslexia because of the pain and suffering a young person gets from his or her peers – although many more young men than young girls have it.

"You're held to be dumb, stupid, thick, because you can't read a sentence, you can't count correctly. In most cases you're a pathetic case at school, so you can get an inferiority complex which is very large and can be very damaging in the long term. It can cause terrible problems. I got over that, although I haven't got over dyslexia. I still have it and I don't mind talking about it. I don't mind admitting I don't know the alphabet, but it doesn't matter really because I'm good at other things. That's what is important: you can be good at other things.

"It wasn't until I was 21 that I first drove a racing car. That was a late start, absolutely, because nowadays if you're not into karts at 12 or 13 you're not going to make it. In those days it wasn't the same, and for me the timing was pretty right because before that I was clay pigeon shooting for Scotland and Britain, and that gave me experience of competing, which was extremely useful."

He only narrowly failed to make the British team for the Olympic Games in Rome in 1960. Jimmy remembers that Stewart came to a point where he'd done the clay pigeon shooting and had to decide what to do with the rest of his life. As Bob had encouraged Jimmy, so Jimmy encouraged Jackie. A customer and friend who owned a Marcos came into the garage one day and offered Jackie the chance to compete in a couple of speed tests, Jimmy put his weight behind the idea and the career began.

Jeannie, however, "closed her mind completely" to this and never acknowledged that Jackie drove until the day he announced his retirement. "I think Jackie was right to race despite this," Jimmy says. "He had his own life to live, no matter that I had made a different decision, and the point is he was an absolute natural from the start. He opened people's eyes to what he could do very, very quickly."

(Intriguingly, Stewart remembers his first sight of Jim Clark "when Clark was going to a Rest and Be Thankful hillclimb. He came into the garage. He had a TR2 and was filling it up. Everybody said 'that fellow over there is the big hope for the future, he's going to be a great driver.' And there he was, a sort of meek and mild man. I'll never forget he was wearing a dark blue round-necked sweater, as he was always to wear.

"He was the first person that I identified with as having skill in excess of everyone else. He drove in a different way to that which was characteristic of Grand Prix racing at the time. It had always been in my mind, I suppose, that Grand Prix racing was fast and furious. Jim Clark never really drove in a style like that. He had a finesse which I later tried to develop for myself – but it was Jimmy who highlighted it to me and showed me that that clearly was the way to go.")

So: Stewart's first race was at Charterhall in 1961 in the Marcos, a car with a wooden chassis. He was placed in all the four meetings he entered that year, drove four times again in 1962 and won three, retired in the other one.

He met Ken Tyrrell, as we have seen, when he went to Goodwood with Bob McIntyre so that McIntyre could have a test drive. In 1963 Stewart joined Ecurie Ecosse and won regularly: 14 of them and two second places. That year Tyrrell ran a young American, Tim Mayer, who would be killed in Australia a year later. Tyrrell happened to be at Goodwood some time after and, chatting with the track manager Robin McKay, the name of Stewart came up. Legend insists that that night Tyrrell rang Dumbarton but got Jimmy Stewart, not Jackie.

Distant dialogue...

Tyrrell: Does your brother want to become a Grand Prix driver? How serious is he?

Jimmy: He's taking it very seriously.

Tyrrell: Well, tell him I'll give him a test drive if he'll come to Goodwood.

Stewart went, Tyrrell explained what was what, and what you did with what was what, Stewart clambered into Tyrrell's Formula Three Cooper-BMC and drove the first lap of his life in a single-seater racing car. He was good. The partnership developed and matured quickly, which is how, while Graham Hill was winning the Monaco Grand Prix in May 1964, Stewart was winning the Formula Three race.

"For some reason," Alan Brinton says, "I went to the little pub where Bruce McLaren and one or two other people were staying. It was past the Mirabeau down a road off to the left. I went in – I think it must have been to see Bruce – and in came Stewart, very, very shy, apologetic. He wanted to have a word with Bruce, by then of course an established Grand Prix driver. He wanted a few tips on the corners and how he should approach it and so on.

"Looking back, this represented a glimpse of the future. Here was a man who would be three times World Champion and was prepared to come along, seek out Bruce and ask for his advice. Stewart hadn't the same instinct as Clark in a racing car, but he was able to communicate far better. Clark could jump into a three-wheeler and do tricks whereas Stewart would say: 'No, no, I think we ought to have a fourth wheel.' That was his approach."

"In debriefs – the awful word they use nowadays after practice and which I prefer to call analysis – Stewart was thorough. Clark would say: 'Jack it up a bit, I was getting some understeer' and that's about all he'd tell them. Stewart was different, and I think I did glimpse that in the little pub at Monaco: meticulous in every way, a great exponent of smooth driving and the right way to do things, no histrionics, no anything else."

That season of 1964 Stewart won Formula Three races at Snetterton, Goodwood, Oulton, Aintree, Silverstone, Mallory, Rouen, Reims and Zandvoort as well as Monaco, *and* in Formula Two in a Lotus-Cosworth at Snetterton.

He shared an apartment in London with Clark and they dubbed it the Scottish Embassy. "We lived there happily," Stewart says, "with me in Formula Three and driving for Ecurie Ecosse and all sorts of other cars, as well as against Jimmy in Lotus Cortinas. I was very much Robin and he was Batman, which is what everybody at that time started to call us. Of course to live with somebody, to share doing the breakfast, share bathrooms and confidences and all the things that one does, is a nice way to get to know them. Jimmy was always very protective about his privacy. In many ways he was a secretive man regarding his money, his career and his girlfriends. I mean, terribly secretive."

Stewart made his Grand Prix debut in South Africa the following year with British Racing Motors, who between 1963 and 1965 were very strong indeed. *Autosport* reported that late in the race Bandini, Stewart and Surtees "were travelling in close company. The Scotsman waved Surtees through, but Bandini was not so obliging, leading to a certain amount of fist-shaking by his Ferrari team-mate." Eventually Surtees got through. "Stewart's engine spluttered and almost stopped as the Scotsman fiddled around to get fuel through from the pump. He was apparently successful because the motor soon picked up and sounded as healthy as ever."

He finished sixth and, at that moment in the history of modern Grand Prix racing only 33 other drivers had taken points in their first race. You can get lucky with a lot of retirements to achieve it, but this didn't happen to Stewart. Of the 20 who started 15 were classified at the end. What carried much more significance was that at the next race, Monaco (Clark was at Indy), Stewart qualified on the second row – in front of Surtees – and slotted into second place behind Hill as the race began. Hill drew Stewart with him away from the rest of the field and when Hill stopped – he thought his engine was on fire – Stewart led the race for five laps. Hill recovered, returned and Stewart waved him through – they were both BRM drivers. Stewart finished third. At the Belgian Grand Prix at Spa, the race after, he finished second to Clark: we've already heard how Clark speeded up to convince Stewart he couldn't catch him. In France Stewart finished second to Clark, at Silverstone fifth, in Holland second to Clark. This extraordinary sequence only ended at the Nurburgring.

Travel back to 1950, the dawn of the modern era, and consider Juan-Manuel Fangio. He was on the front row for the first race at Silvertone but didn't finish; took pole and won Monaco, took pole but did not finish in Switzerland; was on the front row and won Belgium, took pole and won France. This is not an attempt to compare Stewart with Fangio or even equate the beginnings of their Grand Prix careers, merely reach towards a context. In 1950 Fangio was 39 and had been driving competitively for 12 years; in 1965 Stewart was 26 and had been driving only since 1961. Travel on to 1980. Prost, albeit in an uncompetitive McLaren, came sixth on his debut in Argentina, fifth in Brazil two weeks later. This is still regarded as a genuine feat. Prost did not, however, score points again until the British Grand Prix at Brands Hatch – four races after Brazil.

You can expand the context, and this is much more relevant. Fangio totalled 24 wins in his career, it was Clark who beat that with 25, it was Stewart who beat Clark with 27, and Prost who beat Stewart on his way to more than a half-century. It can be no co-incidence that these drivers who started so strongly went on so strongly and finished so strongly.

Moreover, at Monza on September 12, 1965 Stewart won his first, itself a genuine feat so early. He concealed his natural delight. Monza, he would say, was not a particularly demanding circuit. True it required the smoothness, true it required courage to outbrake opponents into the corners, but that aside he judged Monza a place where a rookie might expect to win.

Incidentally, towards the end of the race, Graham Hill, closely followed by Stewart, went onto the marbles at the side of the track, costing crucial time. Stewart became extremely concerned that as the rookie he'd be blamed, even though Hill admitted the mistake. Stewart appreciated, and treasured, Hill's honesty. In *Life at the Limit* Hill explained that with all the slipstreaming, as team-mates they had a system of passing and repassing each other, and it was pointless to "chop" Stewart. Hill says he moved aside to give Stewart room, fully intending to keep the system operating and get past him again in a moment, and that's when he reached the marbles. Hill "fumed", but presumably at himself.

BRM lost competitiveness in 1966 despite Stewart winning the first race, Monaco. Spa and the crash followed. This remained a potent topic he'd return and return to. In late 1992, when he was promoting the second edition of his book *Jackie Stewart's Principles of Performance Driving*, (Hazleton) he'd say: "It's a good read because it relates to my motor sporting days as well as what I know about cars today, and how I can pass on some of the things we found out in racing to help someone driving a normal car. In fact the principles which I used are the same in road cars, it's no different. You must be very gentle, very persuasive with the car, you try and make yourself the ideal chauffeur. That's what you want to be.

"Originally when I raced there weren't seat belts, that's correct. We're talking about the mid-Sixties right through to many people not wearing seat belts in 1966, 1967, 1968. I wore them from 1966 because I went to Indianapolis and drove there and it was compulsory."

He stayed with BRM for 1967 and became the team's number one driver, Hill having departed for Lotus. Unfortunately, BRM lost reliability as well as competitiveness and Stewart endured a miserable season, ninth in the table with only 10 points. He successfully drove Tyrrell's Matras in Formula Two and Tyrrell happened to go to the Dutch Grand Prix at Zandvoort to watch. He saw the Cosworth engine's first triumphal running, saw Clark win with it and saw, all in the moment, that he had to have the engine.

Tyrrell quickly persuaded Matra to commit themselves to Formula One and placed an immediate order for three Cosworths at £7,500 each. Stewart had already been to Maranello in June – after Zandvoort, as it happened – to have a chat with Enzo Ferrari about 1968. He took with him misgivings about how Ferrari treated their drivers, although, like every other visitor down the years – see Surtees! – he emerged extremely impressed by the factory and the facilities.

He insisted on a contract and had one worked out with his lawyers, then heard that Ferrari had made an offer to Ickx because, Ferrari said, Stewart was asking too much money – typical Ferrari wheeling and dealing amongst Enzo's inexplicable moods. Ferrari claimed it was all a misunderstanding, but Stewart, his fears confirmed, did not pursue the matter, and in any case Tyrrell beckoned with the Cosworth engines.

Stewart liked the team, rated it and, weighing everything carefully, decided the risk would be worth the taking. Large tracts of human endeavour are littered with such moments. Chances come unexpectedly, they seem a risk, you examine the proposition as logically as you can and, taking a deep breath, sign. Only in retrospect is the full significance revealed, not least that it was no risk at all.

He led in South Africa, but Clark overtook him and won. He crashed in practice for the Formula Two race at Jarama, breaking a bone in his hand. It didn't seem to be serious, but proved agonizing. Within days Clark had died at Hockenheim. Stewart drove Monaco in the agony, had a special plastic sleeve made for Spa, but ran out of fuel, then won Holland and was placed in France (third) and Brands Hatch (sixth). Tyrrell, who finds extreme difficulty concealing his feelings, bubbled about the Championship. In those circumstances, an arm in agony or not, Stewart certainly wouldn't be missing the German Grand Prix at the Nurburgring.

Those three days at the Ring are difficult to describe properly, the overhanging atmosphere of the sequence of deaths – Clark, Spence, Schlesser all killed early in the months before and now this race due on August 4; the sheer, unconcealed and unconcealable danger (Stewart once pointed to a small wall-mirror in the chateau at Nyon and said before he went to the Ring he'd gaze into the mirror and wonder if he'd ever gaze into it again); the brooding pine trees which could make it so sinister; the weather which could be anything...

Those three days it rained like a bitch.

Hill described the days as "the most miserable" of their kind anyone had ever seen. You'd go out, he said, and climb into what seemed to be cloud. *Autosport* described it in more detail. "The ever-changeable Eifel weather made a mockery of practice. In theory there were three practice sessions, two on Friday and one on Saturday. Friday's morning session was reduced to a fog-bound farce, while the afternoon session had to be called off because of lack of visibility."

On Saturday it rained and the mist was still thick around the circuit, and it looked as if there would be no practice that day, but towards the end of the afternoon the mist lifted slightly and the organizers decided, after consulting the GPDA (Grand Prix Drivers Association), that the cars could go out after all. The organizers were concerned the drivers might not race. The AvD (*Automobilklub von Deutschland*) then decided to run a further practice session on the Sunday morning. Conditions for this were no better. The visibility had improved, but the track was virtually awash after heavy overnight rain and it still continued to fall steadily."

Stewart, wearing the plastic sleeve, would take his place on the third row of the grid although, after what had passed for 'qualifying', the grid itself scarcely represented any car's true potential. On the Sunday morning he had to be ordered out for that additional practice by Ken Tyrrell, who pointed out that unless he did he wouldn't know where the water ran deepest across the track, where it might be drier; and anyway reports came in of the water dragging mud onto the track. You needed to see where that might be. Of the 21 entrants for the race only 12 ventured out. The leading times:

Stewart (Matra)	9 minutes 54.2 seconds
Hulme (McLaren)	10 minutes 16.0 seconds
Beltoise (Matra)	10 minutes 17.3 seconds

Hill and Bonnier toured the circuit in a road car, and when the organizers asked if it was possible to race they said that on balance they thought they could. They did not relish it, but – they'd race.

At the flag Hill took the lead, Stewart third. Stewart knew – they all knew – perfectly well that the leader holds a tremendous advantage: no rolling ball of impenetrable spray coming back to him from cars ahead. To put yourself in that position is another matter altogether, requiring not just speed and skill but, at some instant, judgment and absolute nerve. By Adenau (seven kilometres from the start) Stewart was past Amon, by *Schwalbenschwanz* (19 kilometres) he led.

What followed remains one of the greatest sustained pieces of driving, not just by Stewart, but by anybody else. Crossing the line to complete lap one he led Hill by 8 seconds. Hill felt helpless in the face of it; and was. A lap later that had become 34 seconds, by lap three 37 seconds and it grew through 59 seconds to 90 seconds at half-distance, lap seven. Far, far back, Hill battled to hold Amon off in a different race altogether. Stewart hammered out the fastest lap on lap eight – 9 minutes 36 seconds – and extended the lead to 1 minute 52 seconds.

With three laps left he pushed that to over 2 minutes. *Autosport* reported that on lap 12 Amon's Ferrari "spun wildly on the slippery surface, finishing up on a grass bank completely undamaged." In the spray Hill did not see this and spun himself in the Esses after Hohe Acht, "stalling the Lotus in the middle of the road. Glancing nervously over his shoulder, expecting Amon's Ferrari to come hurtling out of the mist at any moment, the Londoner got out of the car – which had refused to start on the button – turned its nose down the hill, engaged the starter and gear at the same time and rejoined. This series of manoeuvres cost Mr Hill a minute and probably gave him a few grey hairs."

On the final lap, "Stewart came up to lap Jackie Oliver (Lotus) just before the Adenau forest; he didn't see the Lotus until he was almost on top of it and suddenly saw the wing emerging from the spray ahead; he had to brake violently and gave himself a nasty moment." Stewart ran safe to the end after that and "as the Matra appeared over the brow, hats shot into the air in triumph."

Stewart beat Hill by 4 minutes 3.2 seconds. Nursing his arm he stood under an umbrella, Ken Tyrrell peering into the gloom watching and waiting, waiting, waiting for Hill to appear. Yes, a long wait.

That margin of 4 minutes 3.2 seconds assumes a context of its own, one curiously ignored by all the record books I've come across. It was vastly the largest margin of any race since 1950, beating the 3 minutes 29.7 seconds by which Tony Brooks beat Roy Salvadori at the Ring in 1958. That improved on the 3 minutes 13.9 seconds by which Stirling Moss beat Fangio at Pescara in 1957, Moss reportedly so far ahead he stopped on lap 12 (of 18) to take on oil and have a drink. Until Stewart, these seem to have been the only races decided by margins in excess of 3 minutes. Some sources say Giuseppe Farina won the Belgian Grand Prix at Spa in 1951 from Alberto Ascari by 3 minutes exactly, although timekeeping was much more rudimentary then, and another source suggests 3 minutes 9.0 seconds.

Only three other races had finished with the margin over 2 minutes, and even a minute was something of a rarity. Interesting, too, that the big margins were all set on long circuits, the Nurburgring (14.17 miles) twice, Spa (8.749 miles) and Pescara (16.055 miles).

Stewart's win at the Ring brought him to within 4 points of Hill in the Championship and four races remained. Starting around the time of the German Grand Prix, and particuarly at Watkins Glen and in Mexico, Stewart began consciously to develop the mechanisms of complete self-control, every aspect of it, not just in the race but in the days before it. He'd liken it to a balloon, how you slowly deflate it until what remains is *flat*. In time the self-control would be extended to cover every aspect of his life, too.

People called him a clinical driver. "Yes, I think that's one of the best compliments they can pay me because that's what I tried to do. Emotion is very dangerous, it's something very colourful, and of course it's sometimes very enjoyable in certain circumstances. In other circumstances it can be very danger-ous indeed. Most things which people say spontaneously or in anger they wish they'd never said. If they exercised more control over their emotions they probably wouldn't have said it at all. You've got to be very careful to harness it correctly. If you're driving a racing car that certainly is one of the most important issues – and incidentally, driving a car on the road. If you let your emotions take hold of you, suddenly you grow horns and behave like a complete wild man – or a wild woman."

When Stewart mastered the mechanisms he became an extremely difficult driver to beat in any conditions on any circuit. The mastery would be achieved in 1969. "I very much contrast Jackie with Jimmy Clark," Brian Melia says. "I had a lot of time for both of them, two super guys, but in a way I admire Jackie more because he got to where he was by ruddy hard work, even the PR image he developed. The Grand Prix drivers got involved in the Springfield Boy's Club in London. In those days Jackie was no public speaker, even at places like that – he did a workmanlike job, but it certainly wasn't his forte by any stretch of the imagination – but he worked at that and developed it.

"I remember him telling me about being successful in the races. Having got practice over with, he said, one of the most important things is getting the start right. *No point in saying to yourself: we'll start and then I'll settle down and sort it all out.* We discussed the way he disciplined himself, how he detached himself from whatever was happening around him and sat there in a world of his own. He'd fixed on what he was going to do at the first corner. Say he'd be on the front row of the grid: he had his wits together, everybody else had white knuckles and were gung ho. Jackie had sorted it all out, cut himself off, controlled his nerves, controlled his adrenalin. Jimmy Clark didn't have to think that way and that's why I'm contrasting the two."

In his own selflessly honest examination of himself, Stewart judged he wasn't mature enough to handle being World Champion in 1968. Hill, of course, was hauling Lotus along after Clark's death, something Peter Warr describes as a "tremendous feat, gutsy, sort of holding the team together and motivating it." Justice demanded that Hill should have the Championship. Time ebbed away for him, Stewart had it all in front of him.

At Monza neither finished. Hill was fourth in Canada, Stewart sixth, Stewart won Watkins Glen from Hill, and at Mexico – where they could each take the title, Hulme also nursing a distant chance – Hill won, Stewart falling away with fuel pressure problems. There are few monuments in motor racing, a severe rationing of commemorations, the very occasional plaque (and only then, like Clark's at Hockenheim, to mark where a fatal accident took place), barely a statue; perhaps the people within motorsport are running headlong towards the future so hard they distrust the past, even their own; perhaps they don't care. Life's about tomorrows, not yesterdays, you're only as good as your last race, that sort of mumbo-jumbo thinking. Certainly sentiment is distrusted.

For what Graham Hill achieved between April 7 and November 3, 1968 there ought to be a monument, and it ought to be placed at Silverstone where every driver of today and tomorrow can see it, to give them the perspective of what they are doing and what can be done. Where should it be? Beside the new bridge which is still somehow the Bridge of Time? Yes.

Stewart would be 30 during the 1969 season and the Tyrrell team would have the experience of 1968 behind them. It created a platform, strong and sure. Stewart stormed the start of the season, winning South Africa from Hill and winning Spain from Bruce McLaren, but you can't pass across that race so quickly or so mutely. By now exaggerated rear wings were in fashion and Melia holds a revealing memory of Barcelona.

"Chapman was a real bodger. I have a certain amount of disgust for Chapman. He very nearly killed Graham Hill at Barcelona with the wings. Chapman started messing around with the wings and the car gained more and more time, and it was only a question of when he went too far. That's what he did, and Graham was lucky to get away with it. When this was going on in the pits during practice, me being an engineer, it sickened me. I was disgusted, I walked away from it. Chapman was like a little kid, you know: *Stopwatch! Another .2 of a second with that setting, do a bit more. Stopwatch! Another .2 of a second.'* Stuff the driver, he's expendable ..."

On lap nine, and travelling at more than 150 miles an hour, Hill lost control of his Lotus and it beat itself to pieces against the Armco. Hill, shaken but otherwise unhurt, surveyed the wreckage which he estimated spread back 200 yards. Extremely concerned about his team-mate Rindt, he watched Rindt's car pass and noticed his rear wing starting to crease. According to Hill the mechanics came up and he dispatched one back to the pits to tell Chapman to signal Rindt in. He himself ran towards the hairpin in the hope that Rindt, travelling more slowly there, could see the frantic signals he intended to make.

However, Rindt would tell Heinz Pruller: "I tried for several laps to communicate with Graham by means of hand signals, but as I didn't get any response I assumed that I was in no danger. Nor did the pits give me any signals."

Stewart tried to signal to the Lotus pit.

Pruller takes it up: "Then Dave, Hill's mechanic, ran across, on Chapman's instructions, to find out what had happened. When he got to Hill's car, Dave thought he could see the beginnings of a fracture in Rindt's rear wing, but he couldn't be sure: it could have been an illusion. Hill had the same suspicion. He sent Dave back to the pits to warn Chapman: he should order Jochen in...but it was too late."

The precise chronology is mildly contradictory – where did Hill go, what lap did he get there (he crashed on lap nine, remember, Rindt not until lap 20, some 14 minutes later)? Any historian faces mangled chronology, the questions only the dead can answer, the garbled memories, and here they are, Hill trying to communicate with Rindt, Rindt trying to communicate with Hill, everybody trying to communicate with Chapman, including Stewart. But the image becomes terribly, terribly clear: one wing had cracked up, another wing cracked up.

There's a photograph of Rindt deep into his crash, the car airborne and tilted forward, the front left wheel bent shockingly sideways, the nose impacted so hard it is folded full back under the car. Helplessly it churned along the Armco towards the carcass of Hill's car which lay abandoned alongside the track. It struck the carcass. Hill watched helpless as Rindt went over it – the effect like a catapult – rose and flipped, landed upside-down. Hill ran there and organized the people around to heave the Lotus onto its wheels. Petrol seeped and flowed everywhere, and momentarily Hill feared a holocaust. A cigarette butt cast casually down by any of the large number of people milling would have done that. Hill clambered onto the Lotus – it was almost bent double – and pulled as hard as he could to free the steering wheel, which itself had folded into Rindt. Then he helped haul Rindt, bleeding profusely, out, helped him onto a stretcher.

As Stewart passed, he saw Rindt still in the cockpit but, mercifully, moving. "For me that was good enough, but suddenly I couldn't see Graham any more. Instead I saw a marshal draw his finger across his throat, which presumably meant someone had been killed. I was afraid it might be Graham because I had seen him kneeling by his car before Jochen crashed." (Hill must have been examining it to see what had caused his accident, but even Stewart couldn't deduce *motives* at high speed.)

Stewart took no pleasure from the victory; quite the reverse. He estimated it was in its way the worst race he'd been involved in, and he felt he'd "stolen" it.

The next day, Jochen was back home and dozing when he mumbled to his wife Nina: "I always wondered what Jimmy felt at Hockenheim. Now I think I know: nothing."

Stewart's reaction during the race was to control both his feelings and his emotions. They could be released, but only afterwards. He would always know what he was doing and precisely why. The discipline is not heartless but *necessary*. Otherwise go and do something else, like run a garage on the road from Glasgow to Dumbarton.

At Monaco a vast, angry row broke over the wings, and they were banned after first practice, itself a decision bringing acrimony – some in favour, some against, some better placed to exploit wings, some better placed to run without them. Stewart led at Monaco until the driveshaft broke on lap 23. He stormed Zandvoort – Spa was cancelled because the organizers refused to comply with driver demands over safety. He stormed France, too. He won Silverstone by a lap from Ickx, was second at the Nurburgring despite a gearbox which did everything except give him all the gears all the time.

Monza, potentially the Championship decider, proved thus. To the enthusiast all races are wonders to behold, to the casual spectator some are extremely exciting and some are processions. This Monza satisfied everyone, a thriller as thrillers should be, slipstreaming and jousting and jostling, Stewart nursing the predetermined tactic of having a 'hot' fourth gear in case he needed that for the flight to the finishing line from the slipstreaming pack. Four cars – Stewart's Matra, Rindt's Lotus, Beltoise's Matra and McLaren's McLaren – jousted and jostled into the horseshoe Parabolica curve last time round, Stewart momentarily unbalanced (in his mental processes) by attacks from Beltoise and Rindt, all relative positions suddenly fluid; Stewart went wide deep into the Parabolica, held that swiftly and surely, then surged and stormed to the line. Their race times:

Stewart	1 hour 39 minutes 11.26 seconds
Rindt	at 0.08 of a second
Beltoise	at 0.17 of a second
McLaren	at 0.19 of a second

"I have many happy memories. Obviously when you win the World Championship for the first time it's always full of excitement, although, as I've said, I used to try and remove emotion from the performance. I suppose it wasn't until a couple of days later that it dawned on me that I'd got this silly title of World Champion [chuckle]."

There are anecdotes to thread into the tail end of the season. In the race after Monza – Canada, at Mosport, 60 miles east of Toronto – Stewart crashed, or rather Ickx crashed into him, but that's not the anecdote. During the Grand Prix meeting, Melia says, "We were in the Holiday Inn and not only were all the residents in there trying to eat, but half of Ontario as well. I sat at a big cosmopolitan table, various trade people, press people, hangers-on and one or two young groupies who chased round the circuits. Jackie got up from a table way over in the corner, came across and said: 'Come on, I'd like you to meet somebody.' He took me over and introduced me to Edsel Ford. Jackie had no reason to do that, he just took it on himself, and it was a very nice gesture." Presenting people to people was already a Stewart trait.

At Watkins Glen, Hill crashed in bizarre circumstances. He spun on oil, the car stalled, he climbed out and push-started. When he levered himself back in he couldn't re-do his seat belts because the cockpit was too narrow. He continued with them undone. The rear tyres were worn and as he flowed past the pits he gesticulated so they'd be ready for him to come in next time round. Along the straight a tyre deflated, Hill lost control, the car went into a bank and he was flung out.

"In that shunt," Peter Warr says, "Graham broke both his legs very badly. Colin could be very cold and calculating and worked out very quickly that Graham was never going to be the same again. So he did a deal with Rob Walker to take him on the next year..."

It comes and goes, this maddening business of motor racing. Hill's career as a front runner ended on Chapman's decision, and yes, no sentiment really, no passengers. Hill drove another six seasons and never finished higher than fourth. Rindt won the Championship for Lotus in 1970 and never lived to see it. Thereafter Formula One found itself into the Stewart era. Nobody should have been surprised. If you can dissect, analyze and dismiss a backfire from gunfire on a city street and remain motionless,what chance have the others?

It brought much to him, not least the Nyon taxi driver who truly believed no private individual could live in a place like *that*.

THE ECHOES OF AUTUMN

The year 1970 remains shaded in the black of mourning, Bruce McLaren killed privately testing his CanAm car at Goodwood in June, Jochen Rindt killed during qualifying for the Italian Grand Prix at Monza in September, his Lotus thrashing itself to pieces at the Parabolica. He became World Champion posthumously.

Stewart had a disappointing season, joint fifth in the Championship, while Surtees and Hill clearly neared the end of their careers. Surtees already ran his own team and Hill would do so.

Derek Bell drove for Surtees in 1970. "I had a great respect for John on motorbikes and in cars. I got an offer to drive for him in Formula One through Tom Wheatcroft (of Donington). I'd had my two years at Ferrari and I came back to do Formula Two, led the European Formula Two Championship the whole year only to be beaten by Clay Regazzoni at the end because he was with a works team and I was a privateer for Wheatcroft.

"Tom said he'd an engine from Lotus and how about driving in the United States Grand Prix? You can imagine, an ex-Lotus engine, you're going to get a real bucket of nails. We stuck it in John's second TS7 car and I finished sixth, the car right up there, wonderful, just like driving a Formula Two car with 400 horsepower – a glorious thing to drive. I really flew in it 'til a bolt came loose and I had to back off, but I thought *I'm going to finish the Grand Prix in the points* and I did.

"John built great cars. The only trouble was he offered me Formula 5000 and I said I can't go back to Formula 5000, let Mike Hailwood do it. Mike did it and went on to drive really well in Formula One. That's one of the mistakes I made. I'd achieved something already, I'd been to Ferrari, been to Porsche as a sportscar driver and all the rest, and suddenly John wanted me to compete in a domestic championship and I didn't want to: 5000 seemed to involve so many has-beens, apart from Mike on his way up. I could have had that drive and, yes, I made a mistake.

"I got on well with John. I will say John honestly thought his car was the best and I will also say he blamed it on the drivers that we didn't do better. For example, in 1974 in South Africa [third race of the season] Carlos Pace put the Surtees on the front row. By the time we got to Brands Hatch in July for the British Grand Prix, Pace had got out of the drive to join Brabham, I stepped in and couldn't qualify the car. I ended up being there because I wanted to drive anything and I would drive anything. You never know, it might just work. Jochen Mass got out of the drive, too, towards the end of the season.

"John would try anybody, tried every driver he could and I don't think he really admitted there was something wrong with his organization that didn't make the car work. I never talked to him about it because it wasn't something you brought up. His view, I'm sure, was *the car started so well in South Africa so, oh well, it's the drivers*. I remember coming back from Austria, where I hadn't qualified, and I sat there with the chief engineer, I said *let's go through it. The shockers are bad. Why don't we go to Goodwood for a half a day, run round and round and round and cure the problem?* What happened? John would go to Goodwood and do a 1 minute 9 seconds. *Nothing wrong with the car at all*, he'd say. Of course there was nothing wrong with the car at one-nine, but at one-seven it was more difficult to drive.

"I did once say: 'Let's go to Goodwood, I won't charge you, let's sort it out.' OK, they said, we'll go to Goodwood. I didn't hear a thing. At the end of the season somebody phoned me up and said I should be at Goodwood, Surtees is there testing new drivers. Instead of sorting the car out long before, Surtees thought: let's put another driver in to make it quicker.

"I remember a flight going across to Austria – I know John had a tough time, it was all to do with budget, we all know that, but he wouldn't really admit it. The chief mechanic was with me on the plane and he was wearing gym shoes, dirty white gym pumps. Nowadays everybody wears trainers, but not in 1974, and I thought: this is the chief mechanic.

"I asked why we couldn't just have the car as it had been before? Why can't we run it the same as it was at Kyalami? My argument was that it worked there, let's make it work now. Nobody seemed to heed me. I was, I suppose, not strong enough. These days drivers would go mad."

If 1970 remains shaded in black, 1971 remains brightly coloured tartan. Across it Stewart exercised almost complete control; almost because Mario Andretti, now with Ferrari, won South Africa from him by 20.9 seconds. Stewart took Spain and Monaco, the latter flag-to-flag as they say. He spun in the wet at Zandvoort, 11th, but ticked off victories in France and Britain.

There's a revealing insight into Surtees centred around Silverstone, 1971. Charlie Rous, who'd partnered Surtees' father in sidecars, recounts it. "I admired John very much. He is such an introverted sort of person and I was never with him over a long enough period of time to become very, very friendly, but every time I see him, even now, his eyes brighten up and he always says: 'Hello, Charlie, how are you? Lovely to see you.'

"I'd not bumped into him for a great many years and he'd established his own Formula One team. I was working for the *Chronicle and Echo* in Northampton, and they sent me over to Silverstone to do the Formula One report. I was walking through the paddock, a huge transporter stood there with Team Surtees written on the side of it. John happened to come out of the thing and saw me about 100 yards away and started waving like mad, waving for me to come over, which I did. He said: 'How nice to see somebody who I really know'."

The revealing part is that, as with Hailwood, Surtees only really felt comfortable with the bike fraternity, where all forms of pretention were regarded with derision and disdain.

Stewart won in Germany, but dropped out in Austria on August 15, although he took the Championship there because the only men who could catch him, Ickx and Peterson, had troubles of their own. Ickx was out on lap 32 – engine – and Peterson, wrestling the handling of his March, finished eighth. No driver would win the Championship this early until the Hungaroring, on August 16, 1992.

Stewart rationalized his craft in 1971. "The basis of motor racing is to compete against the elements that are competing against you. In my particular case the first element is speed, the second element would be the car and the third would be track.

"The whole idea is to eliminate speed by trying to produce a slow-motion activity, to crank down the speed so that I can see the corner coming very slowly as if I were going along watching a movie and suddenly the projectionist turns it into slow motion. I see it coming up very clearly with great detail. This gives me enough time to brake, to change gear, to engage the weight-balance of the car from one wheel to another. The car in many respects is an animal, almost a woman. It behaves in a very strange way; sometimes it can be very co-operative, it can be very wonderful, at other times it can turn on you in the middle of a corner."

There's a revealing insight into Graham Hill at Mosport, second last race of the season. It could serve for many more such moments, perhaps many thousands of such moments. An 11-year-old Canadian motor racing fan called Peter Dick had a paddock pass, the paddock being a long tent where work on the cars went on and a simple knee-high rope separated spectators from it. "I'd recently finished reading Hill's autobiography *Life At The Limit*, and when I saw him enter the area where his car/team was I crossed the rope and spoke to him. I was a dorky-looking kid and I nervously told him in my high, pre-pubescent voice that I loved the book. He sat down with me on some tyres and had a little five-minute chat. He took time out and was very friendly, warm, and to this day I remember his smile."

Surtees, whose team won the European Formula Two Championship with Hailwood in 1972, drove his last Grand Prix in Italy, on September 10, but retired in all senses of the word on lap 20, with fuel vaporization.

Stewart finished second in the 1972 World Championship to Emerson Fittipaldi, Lotus, but took the title again in 1973. Ends, beginnings and a great interlocking at Monaco, on June 3, 1973. While Stewart was winning the race – his 25th, equalling Clark's total – a lanky 26-year-old, who'd put a Hesketh March onto the ninth row of the grid, ran seventh (or was it sixth?) until the engine blew five laps from the end. He was called James Hunt and he was so exhausted he could barely get out of the car. Hesketh, or more properly Lord Alexander Hesketh, had decided that Formula Three races were damnably difficult to win, Formula Two races were also damned difficult to win, so Formula One would undoubtedly be easier.

A paradox. Hesketh would win a Formula One race, but not for another three years. Hunt would drive 92 Grands Prix, seven of them at Monaco, but would never win there. Neither had Hawthorn, Clark or Surtees. Hill, of course, bestrode the Principality – a book on him bears the title *Mr Monaco* – and had won it five times, including three years consecutively, but would never win it again.

A further paradox. Hunt's successor in the dynasty, Mansell, raced karts this year of 1973 and wouldn't step into a single-seater racing car for another three years. He'd drive 181 Grands Prix, 12 of them at Monaco, but never win there.

After Monaco Stewart had a lean run: fifth in Sweden, fourth in France, lapped and 10th at Silverstone before he won Holland to move past Clark's total. Hawthorn drove 45 races for three wins, Holland was Hill's 154th race and he'd won 14, Surtees' career spanned 111 races for six wins. Clark had rapped out his 25 from only 72 races, Stewart had taken 94 for the 26.

At Monza Stewart fashioned a very great drive to come in...fourth. A nail sliced into his left rear tyre and he pitted on lap eight, losing a minute and emerging 20th. "Jackie once told me," Benson says, "that it took him a long time to realize you didn't have to be in pole position to win races. Certainly in the latter half of his career he wasn't on pole that often, but by God he knew how to go round the circuits, where he could make up time.

"Jackie was an absolute master at the Nurburgring, but that Italian Grand Prix at Monza – and I am sure Ken Tyrrell will agree with me – was something else; he gained a second a lap on Peterson and Fittipaldi, who were at the front, and 2 seconds a lap on everybody else in the race. And you could only gain time at two places on the circuit, the chicanes."

Peterson won it from Fittipaldi, Stewart only (in context) 33.20 seconds behind. He once confessed to me wryly that he felt the only reason the Tyrrell team kept holding out pit signals showing him gaining was to keep him "interested". In a racing car, any racing car, Jackie Stewart was always interested...

Watkins Glen, the final race of 1973, would have been Stewart's 100th. It was John Watson's second. He'd made his debut in a Brabham at Silverstone, and Bernie Ecclestone, who owned the team, ran a third car for him in America – Reutemann and Wilson Fittipaldi in the other two – as a reward for his work during the season.

After Holland Stewart had won Germany, so he came to Watkins Glen with a career total of 27 victories, an allcomers record which would stand for two generations.

On the morning of Saturday, October 6, 1973 Stewart's team-mate Francois Cevert lost control of his Tyrrell in the fast Esses, touched Armco on one side of the track, was flung across and hit the Armco on the other side with immense force. He was killed.

Watson remembers: "Suddenly everybody came into the pits and that awful eerie silence descended. Cevert had had a huge accident on the very fast section which is actually a bridge over the access route to the pits, and very quickly it became clear that he had been killed. I was walking around like everybody else thinking 'We can't go out and practice, we can't do this and we can't do that'. After about 20 minutes or so Bernie Ecclestone came up to me and said: 'Right, back in the car.' I said: 'I can't, I can't go out, it's disrespectful.' Bernie told me something which I'd always remember and try to live by.

"The driver, Bernie said, was doing something which gives pleasure and fulfillment, and when the thing went wrong it went wrong in the space of a second and then it was finished. Up to that point the driver was more alive, more fulfilled than any ordinary person could ever understand. It is very sad, but you shouldn't reflect upon it sadly. It is always sad when someone gets killed, but it is not something you should be negative about. You shouldn't allow it to draw you down.

"Of course, you knew there were risks, and this knowledge was your own mental crash barrier, if you like. In the incidence of Cevert, whatever caused the accident – mechanical failure, simple driver error or whatever – in the space of a second you went from being one of the most liked men in motor racing to being a posthumous racing driver. It is an awful transition in the sense that the driver might have been standing in the pits laughing two or three minutes before, but I did always remember those words from Bernie, and I have tried to make my emotional state remember them, because since then, of course, other drivers have been hurt, injured, killed.

"Once you are in a car you tend not to be thinking about those things so much, but it is a process you might think about standing around in the pits. 'Oh, wasn't it terrible' or 'that corner is too dangerous, we're going to have to do something about it.' But, you know, we were all taking the same risks, mine no bigger than anyone else's, Jim Clark's no bigger than anyone else's. We are all equally vulnerable."

Stewart and Tyrrell withdrew from the United States Grand Prix. Watson's engine went on lap eight, Hunt set fastest lap and finished second to Peterson.

One week later Stewart announced his retirement at a press conference at the Carlton Tower Hotel, London, which drew 300 journalists and photographers. The decision, highly secret, had been taken as long ago as April. Facing a thicket of microphones, Stewart, neat as ever in a suit and tie, his long Sixties-style hair hanging full over his collar, said: "I couldn't be happier than I am now. I don't have a mark on my body from racing. I've never had an accident that drew blood, and the two bumps which I did have were minor ones of their type.

"Part of the reason is that I've driven for some remarkable people, and I could not have achieved what I have done with any other team. Ken Tyrrell has shaped my personality in racing and he's given me all the knowledge and experience which have made me what I am today." More quietly and with obvious sincerity, he spoke of the "difficult time for us all" after Cevert's death.

Bette Hill wrote in *The Other Side Of The Hill*: "Francois was the loveliest thing that ever happened to me at a race meeting. He had a terrific warmth about him which came from within – and I think he was probably the most handsome man I have ever seen. Whenever I was at a race meeting he made me feel as though I was the only woman around. When he hugged and kissed me his incredibly blue eyes weren't wandering everywhere else looking for a better bet."

Graham Hill had started his own team in 1973, using a Shadow and backed by Embassy. He failed to win a point. In 1974 he ran a Lola, or more correctly a Lola derivative, which became known as the Hill GH1. He was evidently a prickly team manager, so prickly that one interview I'd arranged with a former member of the team had to be aborted because the interviewee felt he couldn't compromise if he gave it and risked destroying Hill's legend. Better to say nothing.

Deep waters.

In 1975 Hill failed to qualify for the Monaco Grand Prix: a day of great pathos. Bette wrote: "I stood there waiting anxiously for the qualifications to be announced. I wrote each one down – first Graham was in, then out – and after I'd written down the last name and car I ran all the way to the pits at the other end of the quay. By the time I got there I was out of breath and I fell into the Revcon hospitality wagon where Graham and Ray Trimble, the team manager, were sitting.

"I said: 'I'm sorry, darling – you're not even first reserve.' 'Aren't I?' said Graham, so surprised and sad. The whole day he was so quiet. On race day the crowd made up for everything – they gave him a fantastic reception and cheered and cheered and cheered."

A couple of months later Hill announced his retirement on the eve of the British Grand Prix. He'd concentrate on running his team. On November 29,

1975 he flew his plane back from a test session at Paul Ricard and it crashed near Elstree, killing him, his promising young driver Tony Brise and four other team members.

In an editorial tribute *Autosport* said: "Above any of his tangible successes both on and off the racing circuits, we must thank him for being a true, fun-loving British gentleman. A man who commanded respect in any company and who, through his motor racing exploits, represented Britain proudly and with dignity throughout the world."

That's one portrait of the man, and an authentic one. The other portrait lies with the aborted interview, lies in the deep waters, and can perhaps be allowed to remain there now.

Howden Ganley drove 35 Grand Prix races between 1971 and 1974, and the last word on these Echoes of Autumn should go to him. "I was very lucky I raced in the era when I did. I raced with John Surtees and Jackie Stewart and Graham Hill initially, although Graham was fading a little bit. At Hockenheim during my first year I had a big dice with Surtees in the Jochen Rindt non-Championship Grand Prix, and later in the year another at Oulton Park, so you were driving with and against proper people.

"And we were on the old circuits, the old Nurburgring, the old Monaco. I did sportscars as well, so I drove Spa in its original form, and that was just fantastic. Wheel-to-wheel with Surtees? It was no problem, those guys really played straight. You never had any of this push-and-shove stuff you see now. People were a lot cleaner then. I guess there wasn't the money involved, wasn't so much at stake. It was a bit more gentlemanly." Indeed it was.

PORTRAIT: JAMES HUNT

(This chapter was written before the untimely, unexpected and shocking death of Hunt from a heart attack at the age of 45 in June 1993. I've thought long and hard about rephrasing the chapter, but have decided to leave it alone, except for some additions which Richard Williams of the Independent on Sunday *has very kindly allowed me to use from his interview with 'Bubbles' Horsley. I would have been happy for Hunt to have read the chapter, and I would, I hope, have stood by every word. That's why I've left it alone. There will, however, be many tributes to Hunt's memory in* The Bridge of Sighs *at the end of the book.)*

Maybe even the deception deceived. Any Public Schoolboy found himself expected, as a species, to be at ease with the world, confident anywhere in the world, an inspired amateur who wouldn't take life itself – never mind banging around in racing cars – particularly seriously. *Chaps* didn't. *Chaps* romped and raunched and played pranks and ruled India; *chaps* might no longer be expected to sing *Roll me o-o-over in the clover* because that had gone, but they'd certainly be expected to distantly remember the words and understand that that was what *gels* were for. Hence the deception. In truth, the Public Schoolboy was – and is – as varied and vulnerable as anyone else, and they come in all shapes and sizes, including the meek and humble. How many hated the damn schools, hated the prehistoric rituals, the petty privileges, worked their nuts off for exams and wished they'd been at a Comprehensive or Grammar School because those schools had better academic facilities and they'd be home for mum's cooking?

The facade too often demanded they be something else, demanded they be *chaps*, and the facade made little space for them to be anything else. The facade demanded it of James Hunt, and at moments he was and at moments be certainly wasn't. Sometimes he seemed to be wielding the facade like a tool, showing up at airports in plimsolls and no socks, and jeans, and no money and no passport.

Sometimes he'd make a *chaps'* quip, *ha ha*. A Dutch girl journalist once had a liberated idea for a series of features. She'd seduce celebrities and write about what happened. She seduced Hunt (no great feat of itself) and wrote that he wasn't very good. Someone asked Hunt for his response. "*She* wasn't very good."

Ha, ha.

At important moments, particularly contemplating the racing car he was about to get in and immediate mortality, Hunt could be a very hard person, introspective, wretching the race out of himself, pressing down on himself in a most professional way. They compared him with Graham Hill, a talented grinder. Hunt the inspired amateur is strictly in your mind.

It is true that, far from being a Battle of Britain pilot born a generation too late (another tedious caricature and one too many couldn't resist), he vomited before races. No doubt the Battle of Britain pilots included the meek and humble, and how many vomited behind the Nissen huts when the bell rang and they were supposed to be running like hell towards their Spitfire, mortality imminent? I know that disturbs their facade, but it must have been so because human nature is so, and always has been.

Born to middle-class parents, Hunt went to Wellington College in Berkshire, an establishment known as a feeder for nearby Sandhurst and the military, although that need not be your course. You didn't have to. It was easier if you did, but never mind.

Hunt's parents expected him to take up a profession; they thought perhaps medicine. He declined, dropped out into a basketful of sporadic jobs selling ice cream, stocking supermarket shelves, being refused the important position of bus conductor because he was too tall; and all to buy a Mini and race it. In time he bought a Formula Ford *on hire purchase*, and by 1969 he raced in Formula Three.

David Benson first met him "at Crystal Palace in F3, a very close Championship won by a guy called Dave Walker. James ran his own car with bits of sponsorship from Coca Cola. At Crystal Palace three cars came round the last bend in line abreast, Walker just ahead, Hunt and a bloke called Dave Morgan. Morgan and Hunt touched, Hunt careered off to the outside, Morgan careered off to the inside. James jumped out of his car, looked for a gap in the traffic, ran across the track, picked Morgan out of his car and thumped him.

"There was an inquiry, they disappeared into the Stewards' office and this went on and on. I waited outside. Eventually they emerged, Hunt had been cleared and Morgan suspended. I thought: *everybody saw that bugger get out of the car and thump Morgan and he's the one who got away with it. This must be a bloke to get to know*. I followed him in Formula Three, watched him, and so on. I had a Triumph 2000 which had taken part in the London to Mexico Rally and was doing rallycross. I had an appointment to go to Lydden Hill in Kent to do some driving, and I asked James to come. He appeared with John Hogan, then working for an advertising company, and one of his accounts was Coca Cola.

"The car was set up for two people, huge rollcage, everything. Hogan climbed through the rollcage and sat in the back and off we went to Lydden. James took it out on the circuit as a trial run and afterwards drove it back to London. I remember being very, very impressed by how smoothly he drove. That to me is always the quality of a top racing driver. Smoothness. The gearchanging was that, his progress was that, he never took a chance, and he spotted cop cars long before I did.

"He was a bit like a man without an anchor. He lived in a little room in South London somewhere, a flat perhaps, always short of money because everything went into his racing. I'd invite him round to my place in the mews in Mayfair for parties and he'd come, but he looked like a hippie."

Others noticed, including Alan Brinton, who found Hunt difficult to understand. "I don't think he really liked motor racing very much. He was always scaring himself. Even on the way up in the sport he was well aware of the dangers, so why he did it at all I don't know. A foolish young man as a driver, wasn't he, in his younger years? Hunt the Shunt and hippie, and unthinking about his public profile. It may have been a rebellion against his parental class. Perhaps he was determined to show he was something rather different.

"We had an incident when he was in Formula Three. He won a Grovewood Award – and I always had advance knowledge because I produced the press handouts for John Webb. To do this I sent out a little form to the drivers asking them where they were born, their first race, and so on, prior to the awards. About a fortnight before the awards. Hunt got into the news because he tried to walk into the RAC clubhouse in Pall Mall without wearing a tie. They stopped him. The story appeared – racing driver not being allowed in – with a mention that he was going to get an award.

"I went up in flames. He'd broken a confidence, he wasn't supposed to say anything. I got him to my office and gave him a good dressing down. Those awards helped a great deal in drivers' careers as a stepping off point. I said it was serious and he risked not getting it – we weren't actually going to take it off him, but he didn't know that. He apologized and said he'd never thought of it."

Publicity, whether Hunt thought of it or not, would pursue him with varying degrees of ferocity and enormity throughout his racing career, and deep into the potentially tranquil years beyond it.

In 1970 he contested European Formula Three, living in a tent and surviving purely on winnings. Dark and wonderful tales endure: siphoning off petrol from parked cars, hitch-hiking, borrowing money from passengers on cross-Channel ferries for *food*. Through 1970–1972 he crashed a time or three and perhaps inevitably became known as Hunt the Shunt. The alliteration proved so irresistible that it didn't really matter that he didn't crash *that* much.

In 1971, however, Hunt did have a bad one at Zandvoort in a March, covering a lot of the track upside down with the surface grinding his helmet. "I saw him at Monte Carlo after that," Benson says, "and it had taken them a long time to get him out. He had all his fingers bandaged.

"He never really changed, always wild, loved wearing jeans, running around barefoot, Biblical haircut, long golden hair. He did look like a hippie, but this wonderfully articulate Public School voice coming out from somewhere in the hair. He was a very huggable sort of guy – but very fast in a car. Hogan said to me: 'The trouble with James is he's a frustrated Spitfire pilot,' and that was it, that really summed him up."

In 1972 Hunt drove for March, didn't feel they were putting their backs in, and left after a row – "a fiasco" as he puts it – at Monte Carlo. Meanwhile, another Formula Three team meandered, but I do them a monumental injustice by calling them another Formula Three team. The pillars of it were Lord Alexander Hesketh of Easton Neston Manor, Northamptonshire and Anthony 'Bubbles' Horsley, a friend.

"Bubbles persuaded me that we should go into Formula Three and he knew a guy building this car called a Dastle in a barn outside Guildford, mainly filled with straw. We went to see this car and for 1972 Formula Three it was quite sophisticated; it had inboard front discs, which was considered quite sexy. Apart from that it was uncompetitive in every other way and Bubbles hadn't driven for three or four years, no, more than that, six or seven years. He got behind the wheel and scared himself very badly," Lord Hesketh says.

Horsley fills in the background. "Alexander and I had a Formula Three team which was, you might say, ill-conceived, and done for reasons of boredom to fill weekends. I was the driver. I'd driven in the Sixties, but I was well past my sell-by date."

"We went to Monte Carlo," Hesketh says, "and I think we just about scraped into qualification and tottered round. The next race was at a place called Chimay, in Belgium, which I think has now been closed down. It was a seriously good track, a baby Spa: a triangle in three villages run by Baron Chimay, who was 60, completely car mad, and had an E-type Jaguar with no windscreen. He'd blast it round the track.

"The circuit must have been 2½ miles long with 40ft of Armco in its entirety, a lot of straw bales and not much else, but it was a regular feature on the old Formula Three round. I turned up and Bubbles said that he was no longer number one driver, he was team manager, and we'd got a new number one driver called James Hunt. I'd never heard of James Hunt. He was a complete mystery figure to me. There was this gangling, blond, long-haired, knock-kneed youth smiling very nicely and rather pleased to be in the drive. We went from there."

"We met James," Horsley says, "and because of his natural character and the attractiveness of his character one instantly became friendly with him. He'd lost his drive with March and we sort of fell into each other's arms."

Not quite yet. As Hesketh says: "He couldn't drive for us at Chimay, he had some contract with some terrible team, one of those awful racing deals where I don't think his car even turned up. Some dreadful figure stood there saying *your contract says this* but, I mean, such is life. Then we went to Silverstone and he took the lead backwards. He was on the front row of the grid, he got banged up the backside by the car behind him, spun round and came straight into the wall in front of me."

Horsley remembers it slightly differently. "He drove for us, and what was very illuminating was that after the first race one suddenly realized 'My God, here is a real talent' – not just a raw driving talent, but actually a mental attitude towards achieving success. That stood as a complete contrast to his then reputation of happy-go-lucky playboy Hunt the Shunt.

"He just wasn't like that at all. He was good at motivating the team, fantastic at attention to detail, talking through all the problems. He would take criticism. He and I had some quite stormy areas of our relationship. We had times of being cool to each other because we criticized each other's performances very strongly, and in ways that aren't always pleasant to hear.

"He was very serious about succeeding. He was driven by a desire for success. It had been tough for him to get going. He'd had to beg, borrow, steal, whatever to get cars and drives in the early days because he had no money at all. Underneath he had this complete determination to succeed, but on the surface the image was always smiling, although he wasn't at all gung-ho. Not a Hooray-Henry, never had been. It's difficult to say. He never believed the bullshit of it, that never got to him. He never thought 'I'm a God,' or started to believe in all the glamour and all the crap that goes with that side of it. He was very happy to cruise up and down the pits looking at the girls, but he never allowed that side of him to get to him."

He took advantage of it, though? "Of course. Who wouldn't? What he didn't like were the sycophants who would appear and hang on because it was James Hunt or Hesketh Racing. He could spot them a mile off. He wouldn't be rude to them. He just wouldn't bother with them. I think because of that James was very honorable, a very decent guy, a very nice human being, which is quite rare in this business."

Hesketh says that "we sort of struggled through that season. He was owed money by March and they settled with a Formula Two tub, but quite an old one. It was supposed to be a 722 – because they always numbered their cars like that – but I think it was actually a 712 and he did rather well in that."

He did. Take Oulton Park on September 16, the fifth and last round of the John Player F2 Championship (calculated on the five British F2 races of the season) – "a big race in those days, Ronnie Peterson, James and Niki Lauda, those three fighting all the way for the front. I think Ronnie and Niki were March works drivers in the new car, and so that was very satisfactory."

Motor Sport said that although Peterson won, "only inches behind at the finish was his Austrian team-mate Niki Lauda. There were several surprises in this closely fought race. Former F3 driver James Hunt challenged the works cars for much of the race and this was a battle for the lead once Jody Scheckter's McLaren had retired from first place with broke transmission. In the closing stages Hunt even snatched the lead from Peterson, only to spin and eventually finish third. The fastest lap and a new F2 record went jointly to the three leading Marches and John Watson's new works Chevron B20. Watson, after a slow start, was closing on the leaders when the Chevron struck engine trouble. John Surtees retired on the start line and Graham Hill finished last of the 10 finishers after losing several laps with fuel pressure problems."

"In Formula Two", Horsley says, "we were having the most terrible time at Pau in the south of France. James had fallen off and bent the car in first practice, crinkled the monocoque, so that was that. The previous two meetings had been bad. Basically we were going backwards. We thought 'we've got to do something quickly or this will end in tears.' Yet at the same time we knew the ingredients were there. We'd driven together, but I realized my talents lay in the management side, so we decided to put everything behind James and give it a real go." To emphasize Hunt's progress, he was fifth in a round of the European F2 Championship in Albi, France, and eighth in the final round at Hockenheim – Lauda ninth.

"Bubbles and I went off to London," Lord Hesketh says, "and we said: 'OK, we go racing again next year, and the choice was a March with a BMW engine – and no-one knew what the BMW engine was like, no-one had seen a BMW engine – or the winning car of 1972, which was Mike Hailwood's Surtees with a Hart engine. Brian Hart is a great man, but it just happened that that combination which won everything in 1972 was in no way competitive with the March-BMW which came." Hesketh and Horsley had gone for the Surtees-Hart.

Autosport caught the overall mood by saying: "James Hunt made a startling entry into Formula Two at the end of last year with an old March. This year with sponsorship from Hesketh Finance and a new TS15 he promises to be a leading challenger. Almost certainly his car will be the most gaily painted on show and the team personnel have been kitted out to appear like American footballers."

Hesketh remembers: "Mallory Park was the first race of the season, a very cold, wet day, and these BMWs came out and were 1½ seconds quicker than anything else, and that was it." Over two legs Jean-Pierre Jarier won by almost a minute from Hailwood (Surtees-Ford) and inevitably set fastest lap. "So," Hesketh says, "we'd got these cars and they weren't much cop."

Undaunted, Hesketh got his hands on a Surtees car which had been "resting for some considerable time with a clapped out DFV in the back, and I mean clapped out – rev-limited to 9,000 or even 8.8 – and some very dicey old

Firestone tyres on it." Hesketh entered this package for the Race of Champions, a non-Championship Formula One event, at Brands Hatch. Hunt finished third and would say that if he hadn't been learning how to drive a Formula One car as he went along he might well have won.

"That was great," Hesketh says, "we said 'This is it, Formula One is where we are going to.' We threw all the Formula Two stuff away and went off to see the Chicken of Bicester, as we used to call Mr Max Mosley, at March and we rented a tub off him. Bubbles said: 'The thing is, they won't sell us the latest gear if we go quickly'."

"We knew James could do it," Horsley says, "and Max Mosley was running March and we sat down and did a deal. We discussed with him the possibility of a March Formula One car. That really sowed the seeds. After the Race of Champions we concluded the deal with Max and we hired the March. We didn't own it that first year. I think we paid five grand for the season. We bought the engines – four at about six grand each. It wasn't a lot of money. We did a deal with DAF and we had a truck. It wasn't the money-no-object that people thought it was."

Hesketh says: "We spotted Dr Harvey Postlethwaite, lured him out of the March factory, and he was the first person in Hesketh racing who actually got paid in real money other than an IOU."

"At Goodwood we were testing and Surtees was testing," Horsley says. "This was before we'd ever gone and done a Formula One race. We did a few laps to bed everything down and we knew Goodwood well. Surtees had given us all the right gear ratios and so on, and the car was pretty well set up. James did a few laps, came in and said: 'It doesn't seem to have an awful lot of power' – a telling remark in that the power of a Formula One engine did not cause him any problem. He said: 'I expected it to be more powerful.' We said: 'Go out and do a few laps in anger.' He did, and was going nearly a second quicker than Surtees. OK, John Surtees was near the end of his career, but nevertheless it was a real indication. We departed from March [meaning the factory] not only with a hired chassis, but with two of their best people, Postlethwaite and Nigel Stroud. Then it changed. With the arrival of them and Beaky Sims [Clark's mechanic] we suddenly looked like real people."

"We wandered about and we went off to Monaco," Hesketh says, "where we qualified, and we thought that was great, too. [Hunt on the ninth row of the grid, but with Carlos Reutemann and his Brabham and Graham Hill in a Shadow behind him.] We were running sixth and we broke down about two laps from the end and finished ninth" – Hunt's engine dropped a valve.

"James had never driven a race like it in his life, a big, big difference from doing a Formula Two race, and he couldn't get out of the car. He was absolutely, completely, physically wrecked. He was like a baby. He could barely stand up and, you know, he was fit, he'd always been fit, and he'd lost something unbelievable like 10 or 11 pounds weight. He was just like a new born baby, he couldn't do anything.

"We missed the next race because I think we'd forgotten to get an entry (Sweden) and the next entry we could get was for the French Grand Prix at Paul Ricard. We wandered off down there and very nearly got black-flagged because our airbox kept coming off. The first thing Harvey Postlethwaite did was a different airbox, the first of those mean, straight, high ones, and on a fast track worth about 15 horsepower. James came sixth – a World Championship point.

"From there we go to Silverstone and James goes very quickly, a guy who's come from nowhere and we're on the fifth row of the grid, far higher than you'd expect. On the first lap Jody Scheckter comes through on cold tyres, spins, wipes out the entire race. The accident went on and on. Everyone walks away apart from Andrea de Adamich (Brabham) who got broken ankles. Funnily enough, the crash cost us the race. James nearly had his head chopped off by Scheckter's wing which had parted company with his car. It took our airbox with it and we only had that one of these special Harvey Postlethwaite airboxes. Tremendous kerfuffle, the race restarts and very quickly it's a four-car race – Denny Hulme, Peterson, Revson, James. And James set fastest lap, very significant, it was only the guy's third Grand Prix, so very significant in a big, fancy field, and if he'd had that airbox, which was worth several hundred rpm…

"You can always look back and point to races you should have won, races you would have won, and I'm not saying we were unlucky because it's true you make your own luck but it's quite interesting that there were occasions in James' career which if they'd gone right for him would have made his record look really outstanding. How many drivers in a car which is not even a works car get out there and, in their third Grand Prix in a private team, set fastest lap and get points for finishing fourth? Doesn't happen. He's now got points in two out of the three races."

Thereby hangs a tale of Silverstone, recounted by Horsley. "The serious side of James wasn't really known or didn't appear, as it often doesn't, because of course the attractive side for the media was the good-looking, happy-go-lucky, seemingly amateur approach – by God, taking on and beating all these rather dull and boring professionals. He probably wasn't one of the greatest test drivers, although certainly in the top 15 per cent. He had very good memory recall about practice sessions.

"After the final session he came back to the circuit at about 9 o'clock at night and we were all packing up to go home. When you think you start at five or six in the morning they're long, hard days. He said: 'I've just remembered that in my quick laps at the end I think I buzzed the engine and a valve touched.' That showed he'd remembered. A lot of people might have said: 'I can't go back and ask them to change an engine now', but he did. The guys weren't best pleased – they wanted to get to their beds – but we worked 'til two in the morning, changed the engine. When we stripped it down there was a bent valve. He was absolutely right."

And another Horsley memory, replying to the specific question about his happiest memory. "It's all a sort of jumble. I think the first year with the March at the British Grand Prix, where we were suddenly running right with the leading group with a few laps to go, and in fact we could have won it. We finished fourth, but it was nose-to-tail on the last lap. The raw joy of everybody. 'My God, we actually can do this.' It was a very incident-packed day. From that moment on we were really taken seriously. But the thing I remember most is the voice. We always called each other the same name, Mucker or Dad."

At Silverstone Watson made his Grand Prix debut in a Brabham, though he'd first seen Hunt in Formula Three in 1971. Circa 1972–73 he judged Hunt "a very energetic young person, extremely fit and highly competitive, very fast, tremendous self-confidence – certainly from the outside. He epitomized the English Public Schoolboy, an almost ideal product of that system. James wasn't a racing driver because of family involvement, he just arrived in it, did it well, and enjoyed what he got out of it. He was very, very quick, especially in the March in 1973: a very simple car, relatively easy to drive, and with a small, compact team having fun. I found it difficult, however, to understand how a racing driver in what I call the modern context could afford to be so relaxed away from the race track."

"The next race, which is Holland, it's Stewart, Cevert, Hunt nose-to-tail all the way through and finished like that with Gijs van Lennep sixth in an Iso-Ford, a great big fat thing, the car not the driver," Hesketh says. Because the German Grand Prix at the Nurburgring followed only a week after Zandvoort the team decided not to go, but they did go to Austria, where Postlethwaite had done a lot of work on the car aerodynamically.

Benson observed that. "Harvey knew what he was doing, Harvey was breaking new ground. I don't think he ever designed as well again compared with what the opposition were doing then. A lot of it was aerodynamics, relatively easy minor modifications needed to get a car competitive in those days, and it was competitive." In Austria, however, the fuel metering went on lap four.

"Italy? Big, big crash in practice, end of chassis, so we can't start, then we go to Canada which was Niki's race and the last great BRM race, I think" – Lauda led for 17 laps before the transmission broke. "In the wet that BRM V12 was so smooth it tore away with it," Hesketh says. Hunt finished seventh. "Then we went to Watkins Glen, a very good circuit for the March, but a very tragic meeting because that's where Cevert got killed and Stewart didn't race because of that." (Hesketh's otherwise excellent memory fails him just this once – "because of Stewart's withdrawal we were on the front row of the grid, first time we'd been there, alongside Peterson." Forgive Lord Hesketh this slip. During the hour I spent with him he consulted no notes or record books, just spoke; and anyway Hunt was nearly on the front row: Reutemann took the place alongside Peterson, 1 minute 40.013 against Hunt's 1 minute 40.520, and over 3.376 miles that isn't much, is it?)

Hunt drove a strong race, pressured Peterson, was never more than a second behind, and in the rush for the line only failed by 0.688 of a second, and that isn't much either, is it?

Autosport reported: "As the pair of them slid around the last corner for the last time they were locked tighter than ever before, and as they flashed under the jumping lavender figure (the man with the chequered flag) the gap was 0.688. Greeting them both were a wild cluster of pit crewmen who had vaulted the barrier onto the track, Hesketh and Lotus people alike, with Chapman's cybernetic cap flying about them all."

"So – we finished the season with a second place [and Hunt eighth in the Championship with 14 points, two more than Ickx in the Ferrari]. There you are, you've got a guy who's considered a joke before the season and he scored points in Monaco, Britain, Holland and America – he's progressing, sixth, fourth, third, second. It's a pretty outstanding record in a car which never achieved anything with anyone else driving it. We did a bloody sight better than Jarier and Pescarolo" (in the works Marches), Hesketh says.

The imagery of Lord Hesketh, the ancestral home, Bubbles Horsley and Hunt the Public Schoolboy – not to mention Hesketh's mother, who wore a black eyepatch and sold team tee-shirts at Monte Carlo – seduced and overwhelmed the British media and thence the Great British Public. Foreigners looked askance and uncomprehending at this amazing group, and so did the people within Formula One. The memory of that amuses Lord Alexander Hesketh enormously.

"Well, I was in it to win a Grand Prix. The *romp* was really to bait the others and tune them up. The principal object of the exercise was to build cars and go fast and win. It would be the same if you did it today. I still think it is possible. You'd have to multiply the numbers up a bit, but it remains possible. The fact of the matter was, it was incredibly hard to win a Formula Three race and we never did. We picked the wrong car for 1973, the Surtees with the Hart engine rather than the new BMW, and we couldn't win a race in Formula Two. In Formula One the competition was actually less.

"The point is that in Formula One they're all tremendously grand, you know. It has to be said. They'd never believe it if you said it to them, but they were actually rather pompous, the people who ran Formula One. It may have been pomposity coming from the Goldhawk Road and it may have been pomposity coming from the motor trade, but they were saying: 'Oh well, you know, these young boys, they don't know what they're doing, this is a grown-up sport for real men and professionalism' and all the rest of it. We said: ' OK, if they don't take us seriously, fine.' If you happen to be a bit of a student of history, as I am, it's always an advantage not to be taken seriously, anyway, so…"

To which Horsley says: "I think Alexander really wanted to win with an unsponsored image of amateur-but-deadly-serious to prove a point that you can do it and have fun, but still be good at it. Motor racing was beginning to change then, the marketing men were beginning to be there with their briefcases. Initially we were considered far too flippant and that we didn't take it seriously at all. That was the image that came across. We were all personal friends. Nowadays you so often see the driver and the team owner in conflict, and the sponsor comes in and says various things and it's in the boardrooms, almost like hostile takeovers. We had the air-conditioned motorhome and all that, but it was more like open house."

Benson, who had the awkward task of covering motor racing for the *Daily Express* and giving them the imagery whilst never losing sight of the real perspective, says: "Hesketh and Hunt were wonderfully exuberant to be with, they had a devil-may-care attitude. They played down what they were trying to do, but they had a very serious intent. Bubbles was a very, very good team manager, very much better than he was made out to be, and Harvey knew what he was doing, too. James was lucky that Hesketh picked him up and put him into Formula One, lucky that it attracted attention because it was Lord Hesketh, a private team, Bubbles and the helicopter pad – a lot of fun.

"Hesketh had a Rolls-Royce and at one time used it as a support vehicle. He'd tow the Formula Two car to the track on a trailer and he had a special stripe painted along the Rolls-Royce, truly from *Boy's Own*, but really happening. The team were competitive and that was the joke: they were extremely serious. They had a good team of mechanics and, of course, they did have this extraordinary bloke called Hunt, fast and fearless in his driving."

"We were quite happy to go along as a sort of dissolute bunch of layabouts, if that's what they wanted us to appear to be, you know, more money than sense and everything else," Hesketh says. "The truth of the matter is that if you look back – and there's nothing like 20:20 hindsight – the satisfaction I get has nothing to do with any year that I ran the car, but that James became World Champion, and became World Champion in a very significant way.

"When he drove for us the cars were typically always very fast on fast tracks, but never particularly competitive on slow tracks. Today we would have been constantly uncompetitive because all tracks are slow tracks. The great days of Silverstone, Woodcote Corner and so on have gone. James drove some seriously good races. There are a lot of drivers who are rated and who have never driven a seriously good race.

"Then you have Harvey Postlethwaite, the Doc, everyone said a rather vague, misty-eyed fellow. However, he went on to become the first Englishman to be a chief engineer at Ferrari. You don't have his career if you are not without talent. Bubbles I think produced an amazing team considering everyone said we were rich. Our budget was always infinitely lower in comparative pound for pound compared to our rivals. In 1973, excluding girls, champagne and entertainment, we did our racing for under £90,000. Now I know the value of the pound in your pocket has gone down, but, to put it in context, a DFV cost, I suppose, about £15,000. We did the season for the price of six DFVs.

"Admittedly James was earning nothing, Bubbles was earning very little, the Doc was earning very little and the mechanics didn't earn a great deal. We had the smallest transporter in the paddock, a 10 or 12-ton DAF, and we ran one car and one and a half chassis." Well, yes and well, not exactly. Hesketh contradicts himself in the way you would expect, gloriously and hugely. "I had a helicopter and an aeroplane because the other teams had them. We stayed around after the races because we had nowhere to go in them. We'd never admit to that so it was pointless having them." Only, I think, Lord Alexander Hesketh could have spoken these words.

Horsley says: "In 1973 we were all really earning sort of baked beans. James was on a percentage of prizemoney, probably very, very little money. It might have been a £2,500 retainer because he went out and bought a Ford Capri with it, and he got the best music system he could because his music system was always very important. He always walked round with what seemed like a studio with him, and he'd set it up in his hotel room and you always knew which hotel room he had. You never had to ask. I think he spent all his 1973 retainer on the Capri."

"We took a decision in the summer of 1973 that we couldn't run a March the following year because if we were going to be quicker we had to build our own car," Hesketh says, "so we built our own car. I remember we finished it on Christmas night, well Christmas morning. I remember firing up the engine – must have been about one o'clock in the morning – in the stables which we'd converted." In a manger, I suppose, if that's not blasphemy. Horsley says: "When we started building our own car the price obviously escalated considerably because we needed much better facilities, more people. I think 1974 cost around £200,000 – £220,000, three times more than the previous year. James' earnings went up to £10,000 or £15,000, which is not a lot."

The Hesketh wouldn't be ready for Argentina on January 13 or, as it proved, for Brazil on January 27, so the team used the faithful old March 731 until the Race of Champions. Lord Hesketh did not journey to Argentina, but reports told him "James took the lead, got over-excitement and spun off, so that was the end of Argentina." The reports were true, at least in that Hunt took the lead and spun.

"We went to Interlagos and we had to take the March because we had a terrible problem with getting the fuel tanks to seal on our car, and it arrived on the day of the race. So we had to do it with the March, which didn't like

Interlagos. A crappy race and we finished a lap behind. The next morning we set the new car down and went round 2 seconds a lap quicker than pole, put it in its box again and sent it back to England."

The Hesketh didn't finish the Race of Champions or the South African Grand Prix – driveshaft on lap 14 – then "we won our first race, the *Daily Express* International Trophy, a big race in those days and the opening of the European season. It was our easiest. We did three laps and qualified with a 1 minute 16.2, a completely new record, Ronnie Peterson second on the grid then everyone else. We only did about six laps in practice and went home and no-one got near us. Come the race day, and the first thing James goes round in the morning warm-up and he runs over a hare at high speed down Hanger Straight, which completely destroys the front of the car.

"We get to the start, the flag drops and the gearshaft comes off in his hand – its mounting had fractured. First time round he's dropped from first place to 16th and we said: 'Oh God, it's too much.' He drives the race of a lifetime, nothing but blood and gore on the palm of his hand; he slammed his hand into the gearstick and drove like that. He overtook Peterson at Woodcote with two wheels on the grass at 165 miles an hour. The rest is history and we all went wild and said this is fantastic.

"Then we had a very, very tough season because we had to learn how you run a racing team when you've built your own car. The car proved quick, but we suffered reliability problems, we had all sorts of learning how to do it, so we finished in exactly the same place as the year before, but from nearly twice as many races. Very frustrating because there were circuits where we weren't competitive, circuits where we were, but things always kept breaking."

Spa, Hunt running at the end but three laps behind; Belgium, rear suspension on lap 46; Monaco, driveshaft on lap 28; Sweden, Hunt third; Holland, accident on lap two; France, accident on lap one; Britain, rear suspension on lap three; Germany, gearbox on lap 12; Austria, Hunt third; Italy, engine on lap three; Canada, Hunt fourth; USA, Hunt third. The Championship: Fittipaldi 55, Regazzoni 52, Scheckter 45, Lauda 38...Hunt eighth on 15.

During this season, incidentally, Hesketh gave an interview to Eoin Young for *Autosport* during which he said: "I pay for the way I live at the moment, so it's my funeral if it goes under. A lot of people want to make a lot of money to store it away. I want to make a lot of money to be able to spend it. I like spending to create something which is entirely my own, and this is why I have the racing team." Young is a character who savours characters and clearly wallowed in the possibilites of such an interview. He informed his readers that Lord Thomas Alexander Hesketh, 23, ran away from Ampleforth College, Yorkshire, when he was 15, went to a crammer to get three 0-levels and – Young's phrase – "was more interested in life than learning." He sold used cars in Leicestershire, spent time with an investment banking corporation in California, and worked in ship-broking in Hong Kong. If you need ingredients to fuel imagery, here they are, and Bubbles of course, and Master James, and building a Grand Prix car in stables...

Thence, 1975.

"We were building a new car which was not really very new – new in the sense that it had a number of innovations which were new for Grand Prix racing, the first car which had side radiators which used differentials to pull the air through so there was no drag. It had very low drag on the front, very quick on a fast circuit. We were by now short of money, which made it more difficult," Hesketh says.

"We couldn't get a sponsor. It strikes one as odd, but there you are. We were finishing with tremendous results [of them more in a moment] the whole way through that season. People kept saying: 'We don't want to sponsor you because you're too famous, as a team you've too much personality.' I mean, today you could sell that, but then they were seriously talking bullshit about the product. You could say: 'Well, wasn't that all very disappointing?', but I wasn't disappointed. James went on to fame and glory and everyone else did, too.

"We started off 1975 in the Argentine where he led all the way until 10 laps from the end, then made a mistake and spun and Emerson got through. James finished second. We went to Brazil and I can't remember where we finished [sixth, and from the fourth row of the grid]. South Africa was a terrible race [Hunt, sixth row of the grid, dropped out with throttle linkage on lap 54] and Barcelona was, well…"

Hunt, second row of the grid, had an accident on lap seven. "Barcelona was, well, the first Grand Prix where we were a mile in front. He led for six laps then failed to understand the oil flag and flew into a piece of Armco. Monaco, funnily enough, we should have won. We used a tactic which was Bubbles' idea. Nobody brought cars in if a track was wet, but Bubbles saw that, with all those big tyres going round, tracks dried out quickly. We brought James in way ahead of everyone else. He was lying fourth, I think, and Firestone sponsored a tyre change award. I know teams do it today in 6 seconds, we used to do it in 14, which in those day was very quick. And we took 58 seconds, we just screwed it."

Everything came true at the eighth race, Zandvoort: Hunt on the second row and the team did what they'd done at Monaco, came in early for dry tyres. He held off Lauda, the first time he'd handled such pressure from the lead, and won it by 1.06 seconds. Nothing would be the same again.

"In 1975 we were seriously competitive, we led five or six Grands Prix and won Holland – we should have won a lot more. At the start of the season James kept coming off the track. He was so surprised to be in front that it had a traumatic effect on him. At Barcelona, for instance, he forgot what oil signs looked like, which was quite important as he went through the oil. In the second half of the Championship we were really humming, James fourth in the Championship and we fourth in the Constructors,' significant in the sense that we were running a one-car team so we were scoring at theoretically two-thirds the rate. Your number one car is always going to score far higher than your number two car."

Nor did Hunt's wife Suzy do anything but make the imagery even more delicious. A London model, she really looked better than a model (if I may be impertinent), her face full of character rather than that rigid, posed look which models so often have and you can't tell one from another; she was closer to a Hollywood presence, or perhaps European aristocracy.

On the track the car ran strong and sure, fourth at Silverstone, second in Austria, fifth in Italy, fourth at Watkins Glen. By then Hunt was leaving to join McLaren. "We said to James: 'This is it, we haven't got the money, we can't be competitive next year.' So off he went to McLaren. No point in being sentimental about it," Hesketh says. "The fact was the money had run out. We'd been in cash difficulties really for the whole year. If you look at it the other way, we had an apprentice every year from the local Comprehensive school in Towcester, and the first of those went on to be Niki Lauda's preferred number one mechanic. Everyone from the famous to the least famous did very well, a great endorsement of the team.

"I'm essentially a romantic. I am a believer in the *amateur* [French pronunciation]. I have always had grave doubts about the supremacy of professionalism for a number of reasons, one of which is if we made a mistake we really didn't mind about it because it didn't affect our self-assessment of our technical worth. We'd say: 'OK, we made a mess of it, we'll try something else. This is the policy, this is what we are going to do, we'll battle to the end, etc, etc', which is a great advantage. It means you can be much more flexible.

"We weren't dealing with any egos at all, also a great advantage. That included James, oh yes, absolutely. The only problems we ever had with James were quite the reverse, they were about doubts. He ground it out of himself and he had moments of real worry about whether he had the ability to do it. No, I wasn't involved in that because I've always taken a very cavalier view of life. I met him, I hired him, his nickname was Superstar, and as far as I was concerned he was going to be World Champion, only a matter of time when this event happened. Bubbles had to deal with the difficulties of James facing up to going faster and believing he was better, and all of that."

Horsley says: "1975 was a strange year because the money ran out in the spring, so we rather lived hand-to-mouth for the rest of the year and we rented out the second car to pay-drivers and we did funny deals with odd people for money. There were some shipping people who put a sea-horse on the car for a certain amount per race for about four races. We were never quite sure what their motivation was. We even took to trading in trucks at one point.

"We got through the season, but we were pretty broke at the end of it. James drove almost for nothing. In 1975 his earnings were about £75,000 – most of which he didn't get because we simply didn't have the money. In the end we settled for about £40–50,000. He was very good about it. He gave us lots of time to pay him and almost took a stake in the team. We agreed a deal. He got his money, I have to say."

But you enjoyed yourselves? "Oh, we did. When I think about it now I shudder. It wasn't unusual to finish a Grand Prix in Europe on a Sunday, get on the aeroplane, and be back in London by eight and then go partying until four in the morning and be back in the office or workshop at 8.30. But we were young. Sunday nights was usually the restaurant at the bottom of the Hilton – Trader Vic's – because of the cocktails. Absolutely lethal. You'd think you were drinking a fruit punch. We'd sit there and drown our sorrows or celebrate. A gang? Yes. There was a fairly regular bunch. Luke – Charles Lucas – drove the motorhome. He had quite a lot of money. We said we were the only team where the motorhome driver was the second richest member of the team [laughter]. The cooking was done by a chap called Tom Benson, who had a restaurant called Parkes in Beauchamp Place, and he did the bacon sarnies and the cocktails."

David Benson says: "You've got to put something about Hunt into proportion. At the end of 1975 Hesketh was running out of money and James had this wonderful opportunity because Fittipaldi got the money from Brazil to start his own team and left McLaren. During the 1975 season Fittipaldi set up the McLaren car perfectly and they had all the back-to-back information from one circuit to another, they knew exactly how to set the car up. Formula One started to get a bit more serious in 1973 and 1974, and James changing to McLaren for 1976 meant he had to be more professional. Suddenly you're working for a very big company, you are into a well-established and recognized team."

Teddy Mayer, running McLaren, said that when Fittipaldi made noises about reitrement he had only two names on his list – Niki Lauda and James Hunt. "You want someone who is physically fit and able, you want someone who is determined, you want someone who has proven that he is fast, and you want someone with the mental discipline to accept the frustrations that are involved in racing without having fits of rage."

In Brazil, the first race, Hunt put the McLaren on pole next to Lauda's Ferrari, something which established him within the team because he'd driven the car for the first time only the day before. In the race he ran a comfortable second behind Lauda when "one of the fuel injection trumpets fell off, which was an amazing thing, it hadn't happened for years. It then managed to dislodge itself and stick the throttle open." He cruised to a halt among the sweeping loops of Interlagos. Lauda won, Patrick Depailler (Tyrrell) second.

In South Africa he took pole, Lauda alongside him, made a moderate start – as he confessed himself – and "after 10 seconds Niki got the drop on me." Hunt was trapped behind Vittorio Brambilla (March), allowing Lauda to draw away. Once Hunt cleared Brambilla and a very determinded Jochen Mass (also McLaren) he squeezed and nibbled at Lauda's lead, but always felt, correctly, that Lauda remained in control. Lauda's winning margin, 1.3 seconds, was as misleading as such small fractions can be. To get to within 1.3. seconds of the car in front is hugely different from overtaking it.

The season of 1976 remains a tumult of a thing cast on stormy waters. Hunt's marriage to Suzy foundered, he confessing that he preferred to face the Grand Prix weekends alone and it was hard for her to stay at home. Into this stepped the unlikely figure of Richard Burton. "James attracted a lot of attention because Suzy going off with Burton, divorcing James and marrying Burton gave him an international status far beyond motor racing," Benson says.

"Suzy was marvellous, Suzy was a lovely girl, but very shortsighted (in the physical sense) and in fact that's how she met Burton. She and James had been in Gstaad and James had run out of money. He left Suzy and went back, I think, to Spain, maybe to try and raise more money or maybe he had prior commitments. Suzy was edging along a snowy footpath and she hadn't her contact lenses, couldn't see without them. Burton helped her across the road and it started from there.

"The whole of '76 was a very difficult year for James. He handled the pressure quite well. I think he actually enjoyed it. His relationship with me was very, very good, but one of the things that got in the way was how the *Express* highlighted his divorce. Suzy rang me once from the airport and said she wanted to talk about their break-up. We agreed to meet at Peter Hunt's office in London [Peter, Hunt's brother and business manager]. So I went there and we'd been talking for about half an hour. Peter arrived, was appalled I was with her, didn't know what she'd said. That soured some of the relationship. James later said to me: 'What were you doing there? You couldn't have bumped into her by accident.' I don't think he believed that she'd rung and wanted to speak to me. It was one of those difficult things because as a journalist you have to go, you have to do it."

Hunt accepted Ferrari had a stronger engine than his Ford in the McLaren, accepted Ferrari as firm favourites – they held "that intangible edge" – but judged the McLaren chassis better and, anyway, 16 races is a long way to go.

Regazzoni in a Ferrari took pole at Long Beach, Depailler alongside him, Lauda and Hunt on the second row. Regazzoni won easily enough, Lauda 42.414 seconds behind him, Hunt out on lap four, a crash with Depailler contesting the hairpin. Lauda 24 points, Depailler 10, Mass 7, Hunt 6.

Lauda went home to the Fuschl lake near Salzburg. He borrowed a tractor to work on his swimming pool, it turned over and trapped him underneath. "I had the luck to fall between the caterpillar wheels so I didn't get the whole weight on me and the earth was fairly soft, so that my head was buried in a cushion." He had broken ribs and extensive damage down one side of his body. The press, excited, lay seige to Lauda's house, a telephoto lense searching for him from a nearby montainside, journalists ringing up all the time, a Ferrari employee – dispatched to watch over him – emerging from the house to scatter reporters waiting there with a broom.

While Hunt prepared for the fourth race, Jarama, Ferrari politics reached out and gripped Lauda. In his book *For The Record* (William Kimber) Lauda produces the perfect chapter heading: *Suddenly, chaos.* Daniele Audetto, the team manager, credited with making Regazzoni win again – Regazzoni had been at Ferrari in 1970, '71 and '72, then '74, '75, but had won only three races – sent word that Lauda must rest, must not drive at Jarama. The talk was of replacing him there with a young Italian, Flammini, who'd won a European Formula Two race at Thruxton on April 19 a couple of weeks after Long Beach.

Lauda considered that putting a rookie in at this stage of a Championship was absurd and deliberately told a journalist that Italians were only good for "driving round the church tower". The anticipated rage from Italy suited Lauda perfectly: it announced that he was still in the ring and throwing punches. Lauda told Ferrari, with measured sarcasm no doubt, that at least he'd like to drive at Jarama in practice *if that didn't get in the way of their plans.* Doctors said he'd need two weeks to be fit and two weeks coincided exactly with the day of the Spanish Grand Prix. He lay in bed at Fuschl trying not to move, trying to breathe "decently."

At Jarama, new Formula One regulations came into force limiting the width and length of cars and banishing the large air-collector boxes which loomed behind the drivers' heads like some strange artefact.

Meanwhile, Tyrrell promptly startled everyone by unveiling a six-wheeled car. Depailler would say that "I will never forget the first session when we tested it at Silverstone. I believe I've never felt emotion like that. I was attracted to the car as if it has been my own child because in spite of its faults, in spite of its caprices, it was the expression of a big idea."

At Jarama Hunt took pole, Lauda alongside him...

Hunt tracked Lauda in the race, reasoning that at some point Lauda's ribs must start to hurt, and on lap 32 thrust inside at the end of the main straight. Lauda followed him home 30.97 seconds behind. (Depailler didn't finish, an accident on lap 26). A measure of euphoria gripped Hunt, who paid tribute to Lauda's bravery, shook a few hands, gave a brief interview to Stirling Moss, and went to the podium where he raised his arms and smiled, and smiled, and smiled.

The McLaren was wheeled into scrutineering to make sure it conformed to the new measurements and it failed by 1.8 centimetres, disqualifying Hunt, who heard at eight that evening. He reacted with almost fatalism, no point in getting upset, nothing I can do. He noted the astonishment of people around him that he didn't get excited – or worse.

Mayer, by training a lawyer, prepared to lodge an appeal with the Spanish Automobile Club the next day but, on the night of May 2 it stood: Lauda 33, Depailler 10, Regazzoni 9, Hunt 6. The appeal rejected, Mayer took it to the FIA's International Court of Appeal. Mayer's defence rested not on the fact that the

McLaren had been too wide – something beyond dispute – but that to disqualify Hunt negated natural justice because 1.8 centimetres was so small it could offer no advantage to the car. The appeal to the FIA would take time.

The Hunt media hype grew and grew, "hype of a kind not seen for a long time," Benson says. "In the postwar era Moss, Hawthorn and Collins got a lot of column inches. We weren't getting TV of that, of course, and curiously we didn't get TV of Hunt. The BBC banned racing because the advertising was at the point of the action. The BBC were trying to stave off sponsors coming into football, and stuff like that, and Billy Cotton Jr (then a senior executive at the BBC) took the decision not to cover motor racing, which made it a wonderful time to be writing about it."

Watson, driving a Penske, watched the hype. "I don't know who James Hunt was," he says. "It wasn't so much his behaviour in the car – he did a fantastic job as potential World Champion – but his behaviour out of it. On the social side he seemed to take a perverse pleasure in not conforming, understandable in somebody of 15 or 16, or even 18, but for a man in his late twenties misplaced.

"Perhaps I am more conformist than James, but if you are going to a function which is in your honour, or a black tie occasion, you dress accordingly or you don't go. He seemed to take pleasure in wearing jeans, like he was taking the mickey out of everyone. What lay behind it I simply don't know. The recognition in the press and as a celebrity was considerable. I thought that would be sufficient, but he seemed to need to make people squirm, make people feel uncomfortable in his company. He thought it terribly funny. He came from a very good family and a good education, he was extremely bright, so why he pursued this particular course I have no idea.

"At the fly-away races (intercontinental) he'd stay with other people rather than in the hotel. He had friends in certain countries. Maybe he intended to run less with the pack, to be more individual. In South America, a three-week trip, you'd go out to dinner in groups of four or five or six, you'd all be round the swimming pool, and James never seemed to be part of that. Maybe it came from the Hesketh thing because that was its own private world with its own esperanto, very yah, yah, *Heskethperanto*, all Public School, funny but very strange."

At Zolder, the fifth race, Lauda took pole from Regazzoni (1 minute 26.55 against 1 minute 26.60) and, according to Lauda, Audetto ordered him to run second to Regazzoni in the race if Regazzoni got a better start. Audetto added that he'd have pit signals hoisted to inform Lauda of this, to which Lauda replied that he could hoist signals of any colour. He wouldn't be looking.

Lauda led all the way, Regazzoni locked behind him while Hunt's gearbox failed on lap 36. Lauda 42, Regazzoni 15, Depailler 10. Hunt 6. Lauda led all the way at Monaco, winning it from Schecketer and Depailler, Hunt out – engine – on lap 25. Lauda 51...Hunt 6. In Sweden Lauda finished third, Hunt fifth. (McLaren had problems setting the car up.) Lauda 55...Hunt 8.

They set the McLaren up fine for Paul Ricard and Hunt took pole, Lauda alongside him. And luck broke for Hunt, broke completely and vastly. Lauda led, really attacking the circuit and drawing away from Hunt, but wisps of smoke siphoned from Lauda's exhaust, thickened and on lap nine he pulled off, engine gone. "I was driving along and it just blew," Lauda said, offering his own version of fatalism. "I'm upset, but what can I do?" He smiled and left.

Hunt won from Depailler by 12.70 seconds and, under heavy pleading from Mayer in Paris the following day, the Spanish disqualification was overturned –

"the first time," Benson says, "anyone had won two Grands Prix in that space of time." The decision cost Lauda three points, relegating him from first place at Jarama to second. Lauda 52, Hunt suddenly 26.

The British Grand Prix at Brands Hatch became a riven freak of an event.

Lauda had pole, Hunt alongside him, then Andretti and Regazzoni, Depailler and Amon. Lauda made a perfect start and from his position on the left of the grid moved towards Paddock Hill Bend, the right-hander. Hunt, slow away, could do nothing as Regazzoni ducked out into the middle of the track and moved into Paddock Hill Bend. Lauda turned in at the apex and Regazzoni went hard, hard, hard for the inside. Regazzoni clipped Lauda and the impetus turned Lauda's car. He grappled it more or less straight ahead. The impetus spun Regazzoni backwards.

Hunt savoured a millisecond of delight at seeing, as it seemed, the two Ferraris removing themselves. A millisecond later, with Regazzoni now spread broadside in front of him, he braked and turned the McLaren left, trying to get round Regazzoni by going over the low kerbing to the run-off area down Paddock Hill. As he braked he felt a thump as a car behind struck him. Hunt's right-rear wheel flicked against Regazzoni and launched him, toppling sideways. It happened so fast he had no time to move through emotions, even fear. The car landed the right way up. Hunt set off towards the track monitoring what damage might have been done. Plenty: the suspension affected, the steering affected, the McLaren scarcely drivable.

Behind him the shoal of cars darting here and there, searching for a path through, some even on the grass, had sorted itself out. Only Laffite (Ligier) remained. In the run-off area he'd found nowhere to go and struck the banking.

Hunt struggled up the incline to Druids where he saw *race stopped* flags being waved. He struggled down the incline to where a small roadway leads to the pits. He put the McLaren onto that, parked, left it and ran back to the pits. The race would have to be restarted, but who knew whether it would be declared a new race? Who knew if you could use your spare car? McLaren readied the spare, retrieved the race car and instantly began work on it.

In a few moments, Hunt, Regazzoni and Laffite's spare cars sat on the grid, waiting. Other teams protested this, creating chaos. The stewards met, weighed the situation and decreed that only cars which had completed the first lap could take part in the restart, no spare cars permitted. This echoed over the public address and the vast crowd, seeing Hunt excluded, made lowing noises of disgust and slow-handclapped.

Ferrari, McLaren and Ligier insisted they wouldn't withdraw their spare cars, deepening the chaos. In the midst of this Hunt's race car, the suspension repaired, was pushed to the grid, the spare pushed away. The stewards decided that to prevent chaos becoming farce the race should restart immediately.

Lauda led again, Hunt stalked him and on lap 45 slotted inside on the run up to Druids, the decisive gesture of the race. He beat Lauda by more than 50 seconds and sliced the Championship open, as it seemed, Lauda 58 but he 35. Ferrari, Tyrrell and Fittipaldi swiftly protested that Hunt should have been excluded – not running when the first 'race' had been stopped. Tyrrell and Fittipaldi were disuaded from pursuing it, but Ferrari kept on, thinking of the potential benefit to Lauda. The stewards rejected Ferrari, who now themselves went to the FIA's International Court of Appeal. That would move in the background for two months.

To demonstrate how well Hunt was coping with the hype, I give you this anecdote from Alan Brinton, at the Nurburgring for the German Grand Prix, the next race. "A Spanish journalist called Paco Costas wanted to do a piece with Hunt and asked if I could help. I said I'd see what I could do. We went along and saw Hunt and I said: 'Could you possibly take Paco round the Nurburgring, give him a lap?' Sure enough, James got into his hire car after practice and did it, no problem at all, me sat in the back."

Hunt took pole, Lauda alongside.

Once upon a time in his youth Niki Lauda liked the Nurburgring, enjoyed its endless challenges, enjoyed measuring himself against them, enjoyed improving his driving as he did so; but Lauda was 28 now, in his sixth season of Grand Prix racing and his 66th race. In his youth he'd rationalized the deaths of other drivers in various ways, but never dwelt upon them. He'd search back to try and pinpoint the moment he'd changed, when full awareness had come, and although he didn't find it he concluded it must have been after he reached Formula One.

He'd write a chilling paragraph in *For The Record* about the fire extinguishers when Roger Williamson died at Zandvoort in 1973 as being "about right for putting out a curtain that had caught fire," the barriers in South Africa which gave way when Peter Revson's car hit them in 1974, the beheading of Helmuth Koinigg at Watkins Glen, 1974.

The Nurburgring's dangers had been 'softened' under the weight of Stewart's safety campaign, but Lauda considered them unacceptable and said so publicly, speaking of the fear of mechanical failure and how long the rescue services might take to reach a driver. The Nurburgring still measured 14.189 miles. Some called Lauda a coward, which didn't trouble him. He knew he was right. He was also sure the German Grand Prix of August 1, 1976 would be the last at the Nurburgring. He accepted the majority decision of the drivers that they should race it. He judged some of those drivers couldn't take being called cowards, some were "too stupid" to see the consequences.

Rain fell on parts of the circuit, and when drizzle reached the pits the race was declared wet and everyone changed to wets except Mass (McLaren). Guy Edwards, on the last row of the grid in a Hesketh, thought "Mass must have had the balls of an elephant" to make a decision like that here. Hunt toyed with the idea of dries, dismissed it as a risk too far. Lauda didn't toy at all. Wets, please. Starting in second gear because of the track surface, Lauda gave the Ferrari too much throttle and felt his wheels rotating. Hunt had wheelspin, too, and Regazzoni stormed into the lead from the third row.

The order at the North Curve: Regazzoni, Hunt, Mass, Laffite, Pace, Peterson, Scheckter, Lauda. Regazzoni spun and rejoined, losing three places, but the order became irrelevant. The rain stopped, the track dried and completing lap one Peterson led, Mass catching him while most of the others pitted to change tyres. Lauda would remember his as being "a good quick change". Everything else he'd remember in strange, distorted fragments.

Mass grasped the lead towards the end of the second lap – Peterson still on wets – and constructed a vast lead. After his pit stop Hunt lay third. Edwards, who hadn't pitted, found Lauda "behind me for a while, then he overtook me and started to pull away. Then it got very damp again, very twitchy. He was having trouble with the car sliding all over the place." At *Bergwerk*, 11 kilometres from the start-finish line, Lauda moved into a slight left-hand kink, Edwards following. Edwards saw the Ferrari snap right, switch ends, snap left, thunder the catchfencing, batter a bank, explode into fire and ricochet back.

Edwards couldn't avoid clipping the Ferrari and neither, evidently, could Brett Lunger (Surtees). It may well be that a third car, the Hesketh of Harald Ertl, hit it too. All three drivers stopped and ran to Lauda, and so did a fourth, Arturo Merzario (Williams). Ertl saw two marshals with small fire extinguishers, but no protective clothing; he came back with a fire extinguisher and fired it into the cockpit for what Edwards estimates as between 6 and 10 seconds, long enough for them to undo Lauda's safety belts and, hauling and heaving, drag him out.

Hunt, far ahead and unaware of this, came all the way back round until a couple of miles from Bergwerk he saw *race stopped* flags and toured to the scene. Lauda had been taken away in an ambulance. Hunt stopped, talked to the other drivers and a concensus emerged: Lauda had been talking and, though burnt, it didn't seem that bad.

Hunt went to the restart assuming Lauda would be fit for the next race, Austria. The track now completely dry, he made a power play across the first lap and destroyed all opposition. He had the race won and he knew it. Scheckter finished 27.7 seconds behind.

Lauda was taken to Adenau Hospital, not far from Bergwerk, and that evening the word spread that it was bad, very bad. "Barrie Gill was doing the BBC," Brinton says, "and he came up to me in a great sweat, said he'd been held up and could I interview Hunt for him for the BBC? So I did. I can't remember what he said, but he made all the appropriate noises. I went back to my hotel and around eight had dinner with Brett Lunger. There was just one public phone, in a massive box in the hall. It rang, a call for me – the BBC. I don't know how they'd managed to track me down, perhaps Barrie had told them. A voice asked if I was still working on the story and I said I was having dinner with one of the blokes who'd helped pull Lauda out. The voice said 'I'll ring again in half an hour. Can you get Lunger to the phone?' I went back and Lunger said 'Sure'.

"When the phone rang again Lunger went into the box. It was an odd situation because this was the last day of the Montreal Olympic Games and Terry Wogan was over there hosting the programme. They'd linked him up from London to incorporate us. Lunger said his piece and handed the phone to me. I was asked what it meant for the Nurburgring. 'In my view this is the end of it as we have known it,' I said. 'This is a dangerous track, it's a terrific challenge, but I'm afraid it's become too dangerous for modern Grand Prix cars if anybody does make a mistake. A lot of people have been killed, a lot more will be in the future.' I'd left the door open and Lunger heard what I'd said. I went back to the table and he had a blazing row with me. He shouted: 'You can't say that about the Nurburgring.' It took me about 10 minutes to calm him down."

Lunger was of his time and bore the ethos of that, but his reaction is why Stewart began the safety campaign and why, now, it had become critical. Lunger had to be protected from himself, from his own courage, his own ethos. Every driver did.

It is true Formula One cars would return to the Nurburgring, but not until October 1984 and a new Nurburgring, only 2.822 miles, computer-planned for absolute safety and neutered to such a degree that some drivers wondered *is this really a race track?* The old Ring, brooding just over there, lay silent.

Hunt heard Lauda's condition the following morning – so serious he couldn't visit him. That morning, too, the British newspapers screamed the crash in heavy front page headlines. BATTLE FOR LAUDA'S LIFE said the *Daily Express*, NIKI FIGHTS FOR HIS LIFE said the *Daily Mail*.

This is no place to recount Lauda's recovery, how he was given the Last Rites, heard them and decided he would not permit himself to die. All this is well documented. Four days after the race he knew his lungs had recovered enough to enable him to live. Cosmetics would mitigate the savage burns to his face and ears and eyes, but never entirely restore them. For the rest of his days he would look seared; but he'd live, and live with that. He decided (typically) that whatever others thought when they saw his face was entirely their problem.

With a show of compassion which most mistook for petulance – because Hunt had been reinstated in Spain – Enzo Ferrari withdrew from the Austrian Grand Prix after making dogged attempts to have the race cancelled. It would have been patriotic, Ferrari pointed out, for Austria to do that with an Austrian in intensive care. Some thought this was buying time for Lauda to recover, but then some people are cynical...

Hunt took pole at the Osterreichring but, moving through the debris of Scheckter's Tyrrell (which had crashed when something on it broke), he damaged the McLaren and finished fourth. Lauda recovered staggeringly quickly and had lost none of his clarity of thought. "When he was in hospital," Benson says, "Marlene, his wife, rang me and said he wanted to talk to me. I rang him. He was concerned because he was having a Rolls-Royce refurbished, which I had arranged for him. Rolls had written to him about a problem restoring it – the Rolls was a Bentley." (Identical bodies, of course).

Distant dialogue...

Lauda: What shall I do, have a Rolls radiator put on or a Bentley radiator? What do the smart guys do?

Benson: The smart guys go for Bentleys. They're much rarer.

Lauda: OK, you tell them to make it back into a Bentley.

Benson: I'll do that, but I want to make a deal with you, not about what happened at the Nurburgring but the story of your comeback, how you got well.

"Niki liked that. He didn't want to talk about whether it was mechanical failure on the car, anyway. I found out what the *Express* would pay, he agreed, and I did the comeback." This story has a relevance which you'll see in a moment.

On August 21, the Saturday between Austria and the next race, Holland, Richard Burton married Suzy Hunt amidst laboured secrecy. A couple of weeks before, Burton contacted Judge Francis E Thomas Jr in Arlington, Virginia, and asked if he'd perform the ceremony. "They said they wanted it to be as quiet and simple as possible," Judge Thomas would say. He'd conducted the marriage of Henry Kissinger shortly before – no doubt how Burton heard of him.

Burton and Suzy left their New York hotel, flew to Washington, took a taxi and the deed was done in four minutes, Burton complimenting the Judge on having a Welsh name. "He was very friendly," Judge Thomas said. "Susan didn't say a heck of a lot, but she is very sweet and beautiful." They exchanged plain gold rings and returned to New York for a reception in the hotel. The owner had only three hours to prepare the wedding feast, but managed to have a commemorative menu printed in French in time. Hunt, golfing at Gleneagles, wished them well and Elizabeth Taylor, filming in Vienna, telephoned her congratulations.

On the Monday Burton returned to the film *he* was making, *The Heretic Exorcist part two*.

In Holland Hunt ran third, and when Watson went off line – his Penske quivered – took second. Peterson, leading, had oil pressure problems and towards the end Hunt and Watson grappled for the lead. Watson went out on lap 48 – gearbox – and now Regazzoni grappled, Mario Andretti (Lotus) pressing him. Hunt made it by 91/100ths of a second. Lauda 58, Hunt 56. Monza lay two weeks away.

Lauda felt fit enough to drive, or try to drive. Observers considered this something from the domain of miracles although (typically) he did not. Other observers considered this from the domain of madness, and he kept a cutting from the Vienna *Presse* newspaper which spoke of his burns, his blood-encrusted ear, the fact that he had no eyebrows and that he wanted to get back in his 'flying coffin.' The article concluded *Crazy!*

Lauda sensed Enzo Ferrari didn't want him to race at Monza because if Hunt went on to win the Championship Ferrari could claim a *moral* victory. Lauda could barely comprehend it nor (typically) did it particularly interest him. He journeyed to Ferrari's test track, protected his ear with foam because it hurt agonizingly against the side of his helmet, and drove 40 laps. It all felt quite normal except when he clambered into the car and people stood around not knowing what to do, but having to look as if they were witnessing a car crash.

Hunt had been speaking regularly to Lauda on the phone and knew he'd be back at *Monza*. It would have to be Monza for Lauda's return and the *Italian* Grand Prix, prey to many forms of hysteria about anything to do with *Ferrari*.

The Italian press, not noted for probity and themselves prey to many forms of hysteria, were writing: McLaren's fuel is illegal. (Wherever did they get that idea?) Texaco supplied McLaren and their transporter was halted at the *Italian* Customs for a while – surely only the Customs doing their job, although, cynics might say, doing it for the first time in their lives.

It rained so hard on the Friday that only three drivers ventured out in the untimed session, neither Hunt nor Lauda among them. In a macabre but inevitable way the world's media jostled the Ferrari pit for a glimpse of Lauda, a word with Lauda, anything Lauda. The people who got the closest look were in Milan, where the Grand Prix organizers insisted he went for a complete check-up to prove his fitness.

In the afternoon session, the track still wet, Hunt spun and damaged the front of the car to the derision of the *tifosi*. Lauda emerged to wild acclaim, but the Ferrari went into a slide. Lauda felt fear and reacted to it: he waited for the car to slide again, corrected it and knew he still had the nerve – and the skill.

A dry Saturday, but during qualifying the fuels were tested and officialdom declared McLaren's octane too high, the team's Saturday times cancelled. Hunt, however, could keep his Friday 'time' from the wet because the fuel hadn't been tested then and so, theoretically, it might have been legal. This left Hunt on the second last row of the grid (and only Watson on the row behind) and for a freak reason. After the Saturday session Otto Stuppacher became so sure he hadn't qualified his Tyrrell (1 minute 55.22 seconds) he departed, as did Arturo Merzario (Williams; 1 minute 47.31). On the Friday Hunt had done two minutes 8.76 seconds. Close to being out of it altogether if Stuppacher and Merzario had stayed...

Hunt reasoned that "I had to go for it, the only possible way I could score points," especially with Lauda on the third row. But...could Lauda stand the whole 52 laps and 187 miles?

Hunt did charge, and on lap 11 "missed a gear and made a bit of a mess-up. Tom Pryce (Shadow) came up alongside and I didn't try and block him, but I didn't think he'd try and repass me because it was pretty pointless. I tried to protect my position by still trying to get into the corner in front of him – a mistake because when we arrived together there wasn't room for me and off I went." Lauda finished fourth which, he said cryptically (and typically), some people thought quite good. Lauda 61, Hunt 56.

Three races remained, Canada at Mosport, the United States East at Watkins Glen and Japan at Mount Fuji. A driver could only count his 14 best finishes, no trouble to Lauda or Hunt who, even if they scored in all, would still have only 12 and 10 finishes respectively. A tranquil piece of simplicity, no permutations to worry so much about; and broken apart by the FIA, who now upheld Ferrari's protest over the British Grand Prix. Hunt lost 9 points and Lauda gained 3. Lauda 64, Hunt 47.

When the result was announced in Paris a journalist contacted Lauda and quoted him as expressing delight, expressing sentiments about how this was good for the sport. Hunt, already in Canada and playing squash, read the story and launched forth against Lauda. Lauda read that and had prickly views, to say the least. Hunt heard that and thought if Lauda thought he (Hunt) had "freaked out" it might be handy, might make Lauda stay away from him on the track.

Hunt took pole at Mosport, Lauda third row. "I have never enjoyed physically driving more than I did in Canada," Hunt would say, "because it was such a relief to get away from all the people, a real escape." On lap nine he took Peterson for the lead and won it handsomely 6.331 seconds in front of Depailler: Lauda eighth but running at the end, the suspension not feeling right. Lauda 64, Hunt 56 again.

Peter Dick, the young spectator who'd chatted to Graham Hill, remembers Mosport. "I was the world's greatest Niki Lauda fan and marvelled that he could be there at all only nine weeks after his crash. I had nothing against Hunt personally, but he was the man trying to come between Lauda and the title. I say this to explain how much I wanted Hunt to fail at Mosport, but that day, by his own estimation, he drove one of the best races of his career.

"Depailler hounded him for most of the 80 laps, literally snapping at his tail, and every time they came around I expected to see Depailler pass him. Under this relentless pressure Hunt never put a wheel wrong or even looked flustered, for that matter. I left the circuit shaking my head at the brilliance of the man."

A media-feeding frenzy sharpened its appetite (not necessarily a pretty sight or a matter of probity, either). Benson, to pre-empt it, approached Hunt at Watkins Glen, sat in his hotel room, and Hunt wondered what Benson wanted. An exclusive, naturally, *the story*. "I said: 'Well, that's what I did for Niki.' I showed him the piece, a whole page, and he read it and read it and put it aside. 'Now what are you going to do for me?'" Benson explained and thought he had a deal with the Hunt entourage for the rest of the season. He was wrong, the feeding frenzy too strong.

Hunt took pole at Watkins Glen, Lauda third row again. Hunt described the race as a "working thing." He had to win and drew profound professional pride from doing it, Lauda a distant third. Lauda 67, Hunt 65. Lauda judged the Ferrari team demoralized and puzzled. What could they do about Hunt?

The feeding frenzy grew, Lauda and cheating death, Hunt and memories of Lord Hesketh and Bubbles, Hunt a Wellington College *chap*, Susy married to

Burton. The angles didn't end, they expanded endlessly, and in the end they were whatever you wanted them to be, but everybody wanted them. Nothing like this had happened to Hawthorn or Hill or Clark or Surtees or Stewart; nor would it to Mansell: *everything* all at once.

Benson arrived in Japan to discover Hunt's entourage had done a deal with the *Daily Mail* – a direct rival – and their reporter was doing the story. "I think James felt very awkward about it," Benson says. (Benson rang his Sports Editor, who immediately set a reporter the task of creating Hunt's lifestory with whatever material was to hand, to feed the feeding frenzy and protect the *Express*. These were sharp Fleet Street days, dog eat dog.)

The writer Pete Lyons, remote from such internecine strife, penned this lovely paragraph in *Autosport*. "Hanging in the blue sky above the circuit was Fuji, the snowy white legend. The foothills round about were covered in curiously distorted familiar foliage. In the fields aged women stooped to tend the rice. Thronging the tiny roads towards the speedway were hordes of tiny Japanese cars, some familiar (but like the Asian plant life, oddly altered in detail), many others totally new to European eyes. Every signboard appeared to be covered not with messages but with cosmetic calligraphy, and the little food shops offered hot dishes of which the only recognizable feature was the steam curling off the top."

And, a lovely example of observation:

"Lauda was bouncing around the place on his toes, barking out technical commands to his team, hunching his shoulders away from hundreds of cameras and questions, responding to perhaps one in five entreaties with as few words as possible – except when he abruptly turned to address one particular remark with: 'What do you mean, I'm difficult to talk to?'"

Fuji: 2.709 miles, a long straight, a horseshoe right, a curving flow to a right shaped like a cat with an arched back, down a semi-dip to a sharp left-left, a long loop-sweep back to the straight; and a race of 73 laps. Andretti took pole, Hunt alongside, Lauda second row, but positioned behind Andretti. As with all qualifying, the dramas and the pressures resolved themselves into a geometry none could escape.

No such season could end in simplicity: race day misty, sombre and very wet, drenched, drowning and dangerous. In the warm-up four cars went off and Hunt pointed out that "approaching the first corner there's a huge puddle where you've got to brake for the braking area." The fear: aquaplaning, which no man can control. You skim over the spray to where the dynamics of the car take you.

Lauda sniffed the circuit briefly and headed back to the pits. Madness to drive in this, he thought, craziness, you can't see, and if you spin you might not even realize you're going backwards.

The drivers met and, according to Lauda, only three wanted to race. Hunt, vehement, said he didn't want to. While the argument moved to and fro, the officials floundering, the pace car did occasional laps to test the conditions and *it* aquaplaned. The argument moved through the starting time, 1.30. The weather improved marginally and the organizers announced another warm-up session, Lauda having none of that, thank you. He stayed in the pits and most others did, too. The organizers announced a 3.00 start, *nightfall* a mere 2½ hours away.

Watson, naturally present as the argument moved to and fro, has a philosophy about it all. When it comes right down to it (as they say), racers race. So – they'd race.

Lyons kept his eyes firmly open. "Hunt had to step across to his car on a sort of plank bridge constructed by his thoughtful mechanics to keep his feet out of the water on the ground. He had to settle down into a seat wet despite an umbrella that had been covering it. He had to pause while a mechanic with a drill pierced ventilation holes in his visor. He had to run his gloved hands over the wet steering wheel, ignore the dozens of camera lenses invading his cockpit, and try to be civil to the onlookers who wanted to have some sort of last contact with him. 'I'm not going to race,' he said in a very small, slow voice. 'I can't. I'm just going to drive around.' Then he leaned his head back as far as the crash structure behind it would allow and shut his eyes."

After the parade lap the start came with indecent haste in case further arguments developed. Andretti felt gingerly for the power and slithered far over to the right, leaving mid-track empty. Hunt went into it and in the horseshoe right at the end of the straight was throwing back a rolling ball of spray. Watson slithered outside Andretti and positioned himself behind Hunt, but virtually blinded by the spray. Lauda coasted, simply trying to make sure no other car hit him.

Hunt led as they completed lap one, Lauda 10th. An academic positioning and one which, like Enzo Ferrari's thrust at moral victory back there before Monza, did not interest him. He angled the Ferrari into the pits, and anxious mechanics in glistening Dayglo yellow anoraks dipped their heads into the cockpit. Lauda, arms folded across his lap, spoke quickly to them, unclipped his safety belt and rose. As he walked away someone wrapped a comforting arm round his shoulders, but he needed no comfort from others.

His life was more important than this. The team understandably suggested it might be explained as an engine problem, but no, Lauda said, he would tell anybody who cared to ask the truth. He'd live with the consequences of the truth because he'd be alive to do that. He stood in the pits and watched Hunt pass and pass in the lead, watched as the rain eased and stopped. It did not make him reconsider his decision in any essential way.

Niki and Marlene Lauda left the track in their hire car for Tokyo airport 60 miles away, Hunt still leading and needing only fourth. Brambilla moved past Andretti and attacked Hunt, but pitted on lap five for a front tyre change. Hunt led Andretti, but Brambilla charged again and by lap 16 was up into second again, eager and driving extremely fast. On lap 22 Brambilla tried to elbow through at the hairpin and spun. Mass moved past Andretti. Hunt had his team-mate behind him, an invaluable shield.

Mist hung like a shroud and the surface of the track dried, dried, dried – Mass unlucky to find a wet patch. He spun off, battering the front of his McLaren. *It's what can happen*, he would say, *when you drive artifically slowly*. The shield had gone. Lap 36: Hunt, Depailler, Pryce, Brambilla, Andretti, Regazzoni. On lap 40 Pryce sliced past Depailler and chased Hunt, but his engine let go. Depailler took up the chase.

Autosport reported: "The track was now dry enough for the rain tyres to become seriously overstressed. In fact all the wet air was gone, the clouds had blown away from the circuit, some blue sky had appeared overhead and the lowering evening sun had begun to slowly warm the scene. Incredible. Mount Fuji began to loom through the clouds, showing hints of snow-covered slopes. Cars began to sparkle. The still-wet tyre treads began to glisten."

The drying, drying, drying track surface clawed and plucked at the fabric of the tyres, stripping rubber from their deep grooves. Hunt's front left was already wearing and as he slowed to conserve it Depailler came up and went by, dragging Andretti through in his wake on lap 61. Andretti, prudent but with purpose, took Depailler who'd started to slither, left rear deflating. Depailler just missed the pit lane entrance and limped the 2.709 miles to get back to it. Lap 65: Andretti, Hunt, Depailler, Regazzoni, Jones, and all of them had lapped Gunnar Nilsson, sixth.

Hunt's left rear wore and wore, yard by yard, each rotation clawing and plucking. A season, a reputation, everlasting fame turned on a basic question: dare he risk a pit stop? As he drove a counter-question demanded an answer. Dare he not risk a pit stop? Teddy Mayer, neat and precise, watched from the pits as Hunt passed time after time, saw the car angling leftwards, gouging sparks from the suspension. The tyre was going down.

Hunt waited for the signal to come in, a monumental confusion of roles at the summit of a monumental season because Mayer judged Hunt sat in the best position to know when to come in: he could feel the tyre, feel the rate of deflation, would have to *feel* the moment to come in. How could Mayer feel that? "I couldn't get a communication going with the pits to know if I could come in. I didn't want to make the decision," Hunt said.

The question answered itself. With six laps of the Japanese Grand Prix to run Hunt's left *front* disintegrated on the long corner to the straight. Sparks sprayed ferociously now and what remained of the tyre lapped and flapped. But…Hunt had to cover only the distance to the pit lane. If the tyre had disintegrated 100 yards further on, 200 perhaps, 300 perhaps, he'd have had to limp the 2.709 miles, and who will say the tyre, flapping and lapping, would have lasted so far?

No chance.

He flowed into the mouth of the pit lane, pushing the McLaren quickly enough along it, and when he hit the brakes to stop it the car hung so low – the tyre totally deflated – they couldn't get the jack underneath. One mechanic bodily lifted a corner of the car while they did. Four new wet tyres took 27 seconds in the fitting, a long time and leading to another question. Where stood Hunt in the race? He had no clue, and McLaren, inscribing lap charts manually in the pre-Longines/Olivetti computer era, had little clue themselves. Hunt went back down that pit lane skimming with speed, blind in the thrust he would make, went back onto the circuit and stormed it, all guts and anger, because he could do nothing else. Truly he was fifth, but that he didn't know, and for a long while McLaren weren't sure either. Order: Andretti (who'd lapped everyone), Regazzoni, Jones, Depailler, Hunt.

Moving towards Tokyo airport Lauda heard on the radio of the hire car that Hunt had slipped back: a vague report, no proper details.

Andretti nursed his tyres. Regazzoni, sensing tyre trouble, nursed his Ferrari. Alan Jones (Surtees) had a slow deflation. Depailler made a strong surge towards Regazzoni and Jones. Moves in the race, jostling for positions in the race the way, as Watson says, it always goes, always will, racers racing the best way they can.

Hunt abandoned tactics and threw the McLaren at any speed it could reach. He'd lost the Championship, no doubt of that, but he'd ultimately be a Spitfire pilot: not finished until he'd fired the last of his bullets. Quite possibly in those moments he returned to a part of himself and what people thought he was: more Biggin Hill than Brands Hatch. "I'd overtake any car I could see."

On lap 70 Depailler's surge took him past Regazzoni and Jones, Hunt fifth, Hunt coming. Jones took Regazzoni. Hunt, the track moist enough for his new tyres to stroke whisps of wistful spray, saw and took Regazzoni and moved powerfully into the arched cat's back. Coming out of it he pitched the McLaren – an angry gesture – outside Jones and onto the racing line for the hard left-left. Jones didn't contest it, slotted in behind.

Last lap: Hunt pursued Depailler and Depailler chased Andretti nose-to-tail; and it finished like that, Andretti over the line and giving a little wave from the cockpit, Depailler easing alongside, Hunt roaring and pounding along about 100 yards away from both of them. Hunt covered his slowing down lap and eased into the pits this time. He began to shout at Mayer – "James could be hot you know" – although with the distorting effect of the helmet Mayer caught only the sense of the abuse. Mayer told Hunt he'd won the Championship by holding up three fingers, taut and vertical, to indicate where he'd finished in the race.

In the gaggle of people behind Mayer, others held up three fingers. Out of the car and with his helmet off people embraced Hunt and thumped his back. He jumped into the air a couple of times and fell backwards, rose and chattered: "Give me a drink, give me a drink. Did we really win?" The people who say they were the ones who answered this question (and the number who claim they did increases by the year) are irrelevant. He did not believe them. He wanted and needed official verification and would not be satisfied until he had seen the result *in writing*, no protests about anything looming.

Lauda neared the airport and as the result crackled on the car radio he moved into an underpass cutting it out. When he came out of the other side of the underpass the result, whatever it was, had gone into the ether, lost, just a temporal moment, a fleeting announcement on some radio channel which had already moved along.

At Fuji Hunt gripped a beer and gorged it.

Lauda heard the result inside the airport, rang Enzo Ferrari and had a conversation so cold he would never forget it. Lauda, back from the dead, did not seek understanding for his decision, only that a man has the right to govern whether he lives or dies and it should be respected. During the telephone call he found no respect.

Later in his career James Hunt experienced real fear contemplating getting into a Formula One car, a paradox among paradoxes. However, in 1976, Lord Hesketh judges that "he didn't force himself to the World Championship" – in the sense that he had to beat the fear. "He drove within what he considered his abilities. It's very difficult to become World Champion and be scaring yourself at the same time. A World Championship is a combination of all sorts of things, age and genetics and the competitiveness of the car, the will to win, and it had all been coming together for him from 1972 through 1973, 1974 and 1975."

A bizarre, bemusing aftermath.

"Did it change him?" Benson muses. "I think it changed him to some extent in that he went out of his way to try and prove *that he wasn't* changed. When I saw him in the hotel in Tokyo the next morning he was walking around barefoot in jeans and a tee-shirt, as he had always done, while he waited for the plane.

"He did a lot of that afterwards. The Hon Gerald Lascelles at the BRDC told him off for not dressing as befits a World Champion. It was difficult. There was a row at the BRDC with someone else, it was a dance, glasses were broken, stuff like that. I didn't know what the row was about. The *Express* News Desk got hold of me and I said: 'Look, I was at the dance, but I didn't see anything happen.' I gave them a few telephone numbers to get hold of people and left it at that.

James was always convinced I did the story under another name. It simmered down. I was annoyed at the time because the *Express* had been very, very supportive of James all the way from the very beginning, and when it came to the final deal with his entourage – we already had a verbal agreement, as I had with Niki Lauda – his entourage denied it to me in Japan."

Brinton remembers an award being presented, "I think by the Duke of Kent, and James turned up in sandals and no socks, jeans and open neck shirt. Everybody was embarrassed, highly embarrassed." It's where we began: deceptive deceptions and a man who had risked it, done it, and people who demanded of him what they wanted him to be, a conformist to them. He didn't demand they conform to him, an interesting juxtaposition and a very modern one.

Whatever, *they* judged it *bad form, Hunt, let the side down, poor show, 100 lines, I will not do this again, I will not do this again, I will not do this again*.

I've a question. Why should a World Champion not be what he wishes to be? Why should any human being? If Lascelles and other guardians (and custodians) of a safe life can slip into the berth of their very own parking places for their Jaguars at Silverstone – all the right badges, all the right pedigree, all the pomp of it, the imperial arrival – how have they escaped judgment? And who are they to judge?

It may be that in a century of two World Wars, perhaps 60 million dead and perhaps more, these things are not at all important either way.

Only a personal opinion.

THE ECHOES OF SPRING

In November 1978 John Surtees announced that Team Surtees were withdrawing from Formula One and he did so in forthright terms, entirely in character. "At the beginning of this year we set ourselves certain guidelines," he said. "We had a certain faith in ourselves. We knew we didn't have the best car but we were also sure that we didn't have the worst car, although it's been made out to be the worst car a lot of the time. And that affects everything: morale, sponsorship, everything. Sponsorship is now a vital factor because Formula One costs have got out of hand. I've always gone racing for pleasure and satisfaction, as well as my living, and there is no pleasure in hovering around the back of the grid."

Surtees had been running Vittorio Brambilla and Rupert Keegan. "Obviously we made some mistakes. I still had a certain amount of faith in Brambilla, at least in his ability to go quick, anyway. I thought to a certain extent he'd be an example to Keegan, give him advice about the car and so on. Now I'm not blaming Rupert at all for the fact that it was a disastrous season. I basically knew what I was taking on – someone who was (1) pretty brave, (2) blessed with fairly good car control, and (3) British. I was quite sure that with the right example and a good knowledge of the car Rupert could go quickly. At the same time I knew that if anything went wrong, if people told him enough times that he was wasting his time with the car, he would start to believe it, and it would affect him. He's very immature and very vulnerable.

"I'm a competitive person and, as such, it goes against the grain to be unsuccessful. I still enjoy the technical side of motor racing very much. I think the human side of the sport is deteriorating very badly compared to the morals and standards which people observed at one time – the whole spirit of the thing both on and off the track. It's become rather deplorable, but there's still a real hard core that doesn't change, the mechanics for example…"

This was a saddened, subdued end to a competitive career which had begun seriously on March 26, 1951 at Thruxton when he'd been riding a Vincent in a 1,000cc race. Before that, from 1948, he'd been in his father's sidecar, of course, and done some speed trials. Surtees' career represented a very real time-span – James Hunt was born in 1947, to select a pertinent example – and he left it exactly the same man he'd been when he joined it: trenchant, firm in his opinions and largely unrepentant. The final tally that season: 1 point from 16 races, Brambilla sixth in Austria.

Hunt had come fifth in the 1977 Championship, 13th in 1978, and was leaving, too, but leaving McLaren – a team visibly in decline, although reportedly not heartbroken to see him go – for what seemed a new challenge. Scheckter departed Wolf, the team bearing the name of Walter Wolf, a Canadian who had made millions in oil, and they signed Hunt.

Warr, formerly of Lotus, ran the team. "I'm split to a certain extent because my perspective of James is that he's the guy who shouldn't have won the Championship in 1976. Niki should have done. It was only because Niki is the character he is (withdrawing from Fuji, 1976) that he didn't win the Championship. That clouds it a bit because behind that overall impression James was actually a very good driver, intelligent and quick. If you look at the performances he was putting up in 1976 he wasn't sort of eighth on the grid or winning races by default, he was a pole-position-or-nothing man. He got the whole McLaren scene wound up and he must have had the motivational force to do that. He was always tough, physically he was tough, mentally he was tough, so it's unfortunate in a way: he was probably a much better driver than history might record for him.

"Of course England needed him at the time, and he was a bit of a product of the hype, you know, his rather casual ways, his irreverent attitude, the gorgeous girls. In all honesty I think he was a burning star, he wasn't ever going to be an enduring success, a once-only man. Having been fortunate enough to work with a lot of the very best drivers, there is more to it than ultimate speed, or ultimate grit, or ultimate intelligence, or ultimate whatever. They had to prove themselves by showing that what they had was an enduring characteristic, and I don't think James had that.

"I am sure his decision to drive at Wolf was partly because of pressure, that he wasn't going to get a good drive anywhere else. At Wolf we had established ourselves as a serious racing team. Take an equivalent today. Michele Alboreto, who's been at Tyrrell on the way up and a Ferrari works driver, is now with Dallara or something and James wanted to avoid that, and he wanted to cash in on his reputation and fame.

"He sensed, I think, several things. First, this was a serious team, so the world wouldn't say: 'Ah, he's over the hill.' It was a renewal of his relationahip with Harvey Postlethwaite, who he had a lot of time for. It was big money, and that satisfied whatever it was inside him that had to be able to say in the paddock: 'I'm earning more than you chaps.'

"To work with him was not easy at all. I came to the conclusion quite early in 1979 that he was just basically doing it for the wages, and his heart wasn't really in it any more. The team wasn't going that well, starting to struggle a bit with sponsorship, getting overtaken a bit in the race for aerodynamics in the ground effect era. Right from the word go we were pretty sure he wasn't going to be up to the mark.

"It was apparent in all sorts of things. For example, he had a bit of a nonchalant attitude. Most drivers who are keen stick in the garage and try and work through the problems with the engineers. His attitude was 'Well, do what you want and I'll see you tomorrow' and you thought 'Well, hang on a minute, this is supposed to be a guy helping us sort it out so that it's better tomorrow.' There was a level of interest which wasn't consistent with somebody who really had a burning desire to do well."

The facts of 1979, race by race, bear within them stark truth. Argentina, ninth row of the grid, out with electrics on lap 41; Brazil, fifth row, out with steering problems on lap eight; South Africa, seventh row, finished eighth a lap behind the winner, Villeneuve; Long Beach, fourth row, out with driveshaft failure on lap one; Spain, eighth row, out with brakes on lap 27.

"He sweated his racing," Hesketh says. "There are various things about James which I admire enormously. One of them was the day he turned up at Easton Neston when he was driving for Wolf. He'd been testing at Silverstone. He decided that he had scared himself, and of course there is scaring yourself and scaring yourself, and that was when he gave up. There are lots of people who don't make that decision, who go on and kill themselves. His decision had all sorts of contractual problems, too, because it's not like saying: 'We're at the end of a season, I am now driving beyond what I am capable of doing.' But because of that decision he was still able to bring his children and come and stay with me."

Warr remembers Hunt saying: "I don't want to go on with this any more." Warr said: "OK, if you want to quit, quit." Had he scared himself? "I think there could have been an element of that in it. Whether he had demotivated himself or frightened himself is something only he will ever know."

Hunt's retirement became a secretive (and amusing) saga, revolving round the considerable presence of Eoin Young, journalist, bon viveur and by temperament a man unlikely to be overawed by Formula One's comings and goings, or indeed anything else." My only previous contact with James had been in 1976 when I did the book with him [*Against All Odds*, Hamlyn]. We had a slight altercation at the end of doing the book and David Hodges finished it off. I'd literally never spoken to him after that." At Zolder, the race after Spain, Young lunched, as was his wont, at his haunt, the Elf motorhome. He espied "a character coming down from Wolf".

Distant dialogue...

The character: James wants to see you.

Young: I'm having my lunch.

The character: He wants to see you now.

Young: Well, tell him to come down.

The character: No, no, no, he wants you to come up.

"I'd never been in the Wolf motorhome before. Peter Warr was hovering around in the front of it. I said: 'Where James?' and he said: 'In the back with the door shut.' I went in and he was sat there looking at the table."

Distant dialogue...

Hunt: I've got something to tell you, but it's got to be in the strictest confidence. I'm going to retire at Monaco (the next Grand Prix and two weeks away). I want you to do the whole presentation of the thing.

Young: Can I pretend I didn't come in and you didn't tell me that? I don't want to know anything about it.

Hunt: Well, can we talk about it?

Young: I can't see what difference it's going to make. I think you are out of your mind. OK, you want to retire, retire, but you don't have to do it at Monaco.

Hunt: Come round to my hotel tonight, come round at 9 o'clock.

"The hotel was about two or three miles from where we were staying. I was having dinner with the usual bunch of journalists. I said: 'I've got to go now because I must see somebody.' They said: 'Who must you see, where are you going, what you doing?' It was unheard of for me to leave at that sort of time." Young, once settled near the bar of his own hotel and with dinner settling nicely inside him, normally wouldn't be enticed away into a fallout shelter with a thermonuclear strike en route.

"So I went to his hotel and he was with Jane Birbeck, called Hottie – Hot Loins (or as the foreign press called her, mispelling it, Hot Lions). She, James and I were up in the bedroom and they were going through the whys and wherefores of his retiring, whether he should retire. I got a tape running and he said: 'I don't want that.' I said: 'Listen, you asked me here to help you. At least I can tape what you say' – I don't think I've ever played it from that day to this – and the discussion went on and on, real soul-searching stuff. I said: 'You're crazy to do it at Monaco. If you intend to do it there so that everybody will know, well, it's the worst possible time. At Monaco it will be lost in the whole annual glamour-hype of the rest of the Grand Prix weekend. Do it before, do it after. If you're afraid you're going to kill yourself, stop now." Young returned to his hotel and no doubt the bar.

Hunt, on the fifth row of the grid at Zolder, ran fourth after half-distance, but spun off. He did not announce his retirement at Monaco and, like virtually everybody else, Nigel Roebuck of *Autosport* wasn't aware he intended to. Roebuck, in covering the qualifying, judged Hunt and Wolf – in the state they were in, eighth quickest on the first day, 10th on the second – worth no more than a paragraph.

Racing in his seventh Monaco Grand Prix, James Hunt was looking for his first finish. "I've got nothing much to report," he said after qualifying the Wolf for 10th spot. "It was a bit of a pain trying to get tyres of matched diameter, but otherwise everything's OK." And what of the brakes, the cause of so much trouble at Jarama? "No problem, they're working well. They weave quite a bit into Mirabeau and places like that, but they're stopping the car properly."

Another *Autosport* reporter, Marcus Pye, covered the traditional European Formula Three race supporting the Grand Prix. "The paddock was some tennis courts down past Casino Square and a long way away, off towards Italy! They had trucks and awnings and things like that, and they all pitched up early in the week. The practices were on Thursday and Friday and they took some covering with 55 entrants going for only 20 places."

The qualifying was commanded by a young, shaggy-haired Frenchman, Alain Prost, in a Martini-Renault. He fashioned a best lap of 1 minute 36.55. Other qualifiers included names which motorsport would come to know well, Michele Alboreto, Piercarlo Ghinzani, Chico Serra, Jean-Louis Schlesser, Stefan Johansson, Andrea de Cesaris, Mauro Baldi and, last of the 20:

Nigel Mansell (GB)   March-BL Dolomite 783/793   1:38.13

"I remember him as a guy who tried his heart out," Pye says. "That Dolomite engine was an absolute load of old rubbish, no torque whatsoever and the least suitable thing to drive on a twisty circuit. It was remarkable fortitude on the part of the man in the cockpit to get it into the race, quite extraordinary when you consider Brett Riley (his team-mate) couldn't, and everyone rated Riley at the time, he won a lot of races. I knew Mansell from Formula Ford, I'd met him a few times and he'd struck me as a shy, ordinary individual."

Tight it was, extremely tight, that Formula Three qualifying. Roberto Guerrero in an Argo-Toyota just missed the 'cut' with 1:38.16, a varied assortment of drivers marooned further back, Eddie Jordan, Jo Gartner, Mike Thackwell, Kenny Acheson, Philippe Alliot, Philippe Streiff, Thierry Boutsen. Riley could do no better than 1 minute 39.14, which put him 14 places below Mansell.

Pye wrote that *the Birmingham driver chiselled 1½ seconds from his Thursday time to scrape onto the grid. Interestingly, Mansell's Friday time would have given him joint fifth best time on the previous day. Suffice to say that he was delighted to put Britain into the race.*

"The race was fairly late in the afternoon. I watched the Formula One practice and then hung around in the pits while the Formula Three teams all dragged their kit up from the tennis courts. You couldn't bring support vehicles other than small vans and they had to drive the cars. It was a very pleasant afternoon by that stage, beginning to cool off, and even then the Dolomite overheated and probably popped its 27th head gasket of the season."

Of the race Pye wrote that *three laps from the finish the little Dallara of Guido Pardini finally picked off Luciano Pavesi's wide Ralt for fifth place. The Ralt eventually deposited its exhaust system and the red car led a train comprising Pavesi, Schlesser, Ghinzani and Michael Bleekemolen over the line before a long wait to Fernando Cazzaniga and Mansell, never far apart, and Roberto Capominosi who trailed round at the back throughout. Nigel was pleased to have reached the finish with his engine running very hot.*

Prost won by more than 5 seconds from Oscar Pedersoli, Mansell 11th. "Qualifying last and coming 11th seems very average in terms of bald facts," Pye says, "but in terms of the magnitude of the problems he faced at the start of the weekend it represented a genuine, almost incredible achievement."

In the Grand Prix Hunt retired on lap four, the driveshaft broken. "I was watching before Casino," Roebuck says. "There was a little kink in the Armco on the left which just about allowed a car to park with reasonable safety. The Wolf died coming up the hill and James pulled into it. He took his helmet off and he should have been immensely annoyed his race was over that soon, but he looked like a bloke who was relieved, glad it was all over. And of course he knew it was all over. We didn't."

Many were caught unawares. On the page adjoining the start of the Grand Prix report *Autosport* carried a Texaco advertisement showing Hunt in the cockpit, Warr crouched nearby talking to him, and beneath it the legend in very large type *James Hunt hasn't had an oil change in 3 years.* (Cynics might say that thus far in 1979 he hadn't gone far enough to need one.)

The following Wednesday Hunt rang Young and asked if he'd help with the announcement, scheduled for the morrow. Young declined: he didn't want to know anything about it. Instead, Hunt got Barrie Gill, PR expert as well as journalist, to do it. "The classic thing was," Young says, "that Hunt had said he didn't want anybody to know about it and I hadn't told anybody. I didn't even tell my wife. It must have been about 5 o'clock in the afternoon on the Thursday. She came into my office."

Distant dialogue...

Sandra Young: James Hunt's retired, it's just been on the radio.

Young: Oh gosh, what a surprise.

(Half an hour later the phone rang. It was James Hunt.)

Young: I hear you've retired...

Hunt: Oh Christ, I can't tell you how awful it is. I can hear Gill in the next office shouting down the line to a newspaper *I was the first journalist to know.*

Young mischeviously then telephoned *Autocar*, for whom he wrote, and said: 'Look, Gill's saying he was the first journalist to know. Can I tell the story?' So the next week's column was the sequence of events..."

In fact Hunt drove a Formula One car a last time at Donington on the Sunday at the Gunnar Nilsson Memorial Trophy – the Swede had died of cancer in October 1978. The cars didn't race, but took part in a time trial at racing speeds. Jones (Saudia-Williams) won, Hunt second, Andretti (Lotus) third.

"The primary reason that I retired was for self-preservation," Hunt would say, "but also because the sport had reached at this moment a situation where cars were completely dominating the drivers' efforts, and therefore I wasn't particularly interested in sitting in the car and being an irrelevant part of the result. I wanted to have more control over my own destiny."

Roebuck remembers: "That year James said many a time – because essentially he stopped because he was frightened – it was one thing to take a risk while you were in a car that could win, but he couldn't justify it to himself in a car that might be eighth with luck. The whole thing about him was, well, this thing about vomiting before a race is not a myth. He did. He really did. Once he got in the car he was all right…"

There's a tantalizing and enigmatic postscript to Hunt's active career. Patrick Depailler, number one driver at Ligier, a team going extremely well, had a hang-gliding accident. Depailler, who hadn't endeared himself to Tyrrell by breaking a leg just before he was due to drive for them in 1973, now broke both legs when the hang-glider crashed into rocks near his home at Clermont-Ferrand. Gerard Ducarouge of Ligier said pointedly that Depailler had now not endeared himself to *them*, and a decision on a replacement wouldn't be made until Ducarouge had spoken to Guy Ligier, although there were "a great many drivers to choose from." Ligier himself hinted that the team might have to go outside France for the replacement, and speculation mentioned Ickx, Keke Rosberg and Derek Daly.

Meanwhile… "the Ligier was *the* car in 1979," Warr says, "and all of a sudden James Hunt was coming out of retirement! In our contract with him there was something which said that if he did that he had to fulfill the remainder of the contract in a subsequent year, it didn't say anything about the current year. We were going to be made to look total fools: James retiring from us and then signing for the team which had the best car. It would really have rubbished us as a bunch of plonkers.

"I phoned Ducarouge and said: 'Listen, we're all mates in this together, the bloke's done the dirty on me, don't you sign him', and to Ducarouge's eternal credit he said: 'OK, I won't.' Ducarouge signed Ickx, who drove the rest of the season. In fact Ickx didn't cope too well because he hadn't been driving regularly in Grands Prix [one race for Ensign in 1977, three for them in 1978] and he faced the problems of the ground effect era."

Meanwhile…Warr caught Concorde to the States, where a driver called Keke Rosberg was doing CanAm racing, and signed him. Legend insists that Rosberg, hearing of Hunt's retirement, phoned Warr, who replied: "Hang on a minute, I'm on my way to the airport with a contract for you."

PORTRAIT:
NIGEL MANSELL

When everything has been raked over, dissected, analyzed, when all the evidence has been assembled – and by now there is a library of it – a strange question won't go away. Who is Nigel Mansell? Somehow you know the answer and somehow you don't. It gets pungent because you're sure you do.

At Christmas 1992 the impressionist Rory Bremner mercilessly parodied him in a sketch where the camera played alternately on Bremner aping Mansell and Bremner aping a naked Desmond Lynham of the BBC interviewing Mansell. 'Lynham,' who Bremner portrayed as so laid back he slumbered on air, rolled his eyes in monumental boredom as 'Mansell' explained how Frank Williams had agreed how many spoonfuls of sugar Alain Prost would get and how he, 'Mansell', would get fewer spoonfuls, and how could a man tolerate that?

In a most disconcerting way, satire sharpens reality, not by reflecting it but explaining it.

Bremner caught Mansell perfectly, the voice (an obvious target) and the slow, ponderous cadence of Mansell movements, Mansell gestures, the bleak aura of injustice which Mansell has borne down all these years. Bremner missed the warmth and the humour, perhaps because he didn't know they existed. They do.

There ought, I suppose, to have been a public outcry, as if Bremner had stormed a citadel and pulled its pillars down: *Our Nige*, hero and folkhero, myth and legend in his own race time, the plain man who took on the world and beat it, venerated, worshipped, the subject of endless uncritical adulation, a rock star of the track, a man made good on a massive scale, and so on. No outcry, though, just chuckling across the land.

The satire led to another question, not *Can you win the World Championship?* but *How do you handle it when you do?* The first part – winning – is tough enough, as a hundred drivers who have failed will tell you. The second part involves personality, presence, perception. Once upon a time the annual World Champion, as we have seen, carried the expectation that he would cast himself as Ambassador with the capital A to the whole sport during his term.

He certainly carried an expectation that he would defend the Championship, and though he didn't he had reasons, and they took him to IndyCars. So what? So there certainly ought to have been an outcry when Bremner suggested that, among others, Mansell had beaten a snooker table in the voting to become the BBC's Sports Personality of the Year. You could not have said that about Hawthorn, Hill, Clark, Surtees, Stewart or Hunt. Whatever they were, no satire would have sustained comparing a racing driver with an inert object. So: who is Nigel Mansell?

Plain? That's a hard judgment for someone who spent a decade mastering the intracies and delicacies of the world's most convoluted sport. In that decade – or more properly 12 years – he drove for Lotus, Williams, Ferrari and Williams again, experienced the bedrock of skirts which drew man and machine to the track in a savage suction, the turbo cars with their throttle-lags and astonishing speed, semi-automatic gearboxes which were a flick of a button on the steering wheel, active-ride suspensions which were initially very tricky indeed, car-to-pits radio, experienced every innovation and revolution which technology brought.

Much of Mansell's career, particularly the early years, is wreathed into folklore...that his father Eric, an aerospace engineer, took him to watch the British Grand Prix at Aintree in 1962; that Mansell spotted a kart in the forecourt of a Birmingham garage and persuaded Dad to buy it for a few pounds. It launched a career in karting, comparatively undistinguished. The magazine *Karting* exhaustively chronicles that branch of the sport, and while I was researching Mansell in karts I rang the editor, Mark Burgess (who has helped with my biographies of Ayrton Senna and Alain Prost). What cuttings had they on Mansell? Burgess murmured that he'd been fielding a lot of requests like this, people wondering if *Karting* had photographs, too, but he'd not been able to find anything. Some sources suggest Mansell drove for the England Junior team (and ended up a tree in Holland), some sources suggest he drove in the World Championships themselves. Burgess was surprised at the latter.

A press release, compiled by Tony Jardine in October 1984 for the John Player Racing Information Office – Mansell drove in 1984 for Lotus, whom John Player sponsored – made a solid attempt to place facts amongst the folklore.

Born: August 8, 1954, Upton-on-Severn.
First drove a car: Aged seven in an Austin Seven in a field.
First interest: Aged five, Jimmy Clark and Lotus while at school.
First race: 1968 at Shennington driving a 100cc Fastakart.
First win: 1969 at Turnhill, Salop, in a kart race.
Major kart successes: Seven times Midland Champion 1969–1971, 1973–1976; Welsh Champion 1970–71; Short circuit British Champion 1973; Northern Champion 1972.

When I used the word undistinguished about his karting career, you might think it an inapppropriate choice in the light of the paragraph above, but these were not major successes. Karting has all sorts of races, all sorts of meetings and all sorts of championships. Burgess places this into context. "The Midlands Championship was certainly the most important of the ones he won, but if you start talking in terms of the Welsh Championship people laugh. It's on a windy aerodrome and about five people turn up. Mansell drove in the 210cc class, which wasn't top notch – although it's one of those classes which has somehow survived, and there are still people in it who once beat Mansell!

"The top classes were the 100cc super or the 250cc. We do know Mansell was in the British Junior team, but if you're talking major success, that would be top 10 in the world, so you can't compare him with what Senna, Prost or Riccardo Patrese did. We have looked through our back issues and all we can find is the occasional mention of him in the results, nothing more than that."

We do know that Mansell was given the Last Rites in hospital after a crash at Heysham, Lancashire. In August 1992 a Blackpool news agency put out a report that "naughty Nigel Mansell's 24-year secret is out. He was just 15 when he entered the World Go-Kart Championships, but to do so he told the organizers of the RAC that he was 16-years-old."

It's this sort of item which confuses the historian and feeds the folklore. For example, the championships weren't called Go-Karts (it offends the karters deeply) and were never held at Heysham. Was Mansell really 15? The man who could tell us, Bert Hesketh, a senior official at the meeting, died early in 1993. In the report of August 1992 he was quoted as saying: "I remember visiting him after the race and joining in the prayers at the bedside." In fact, as he confirmed to me several months before his death, he journeyed to the hospital the following day, naturally concerned at a karter detained overnight.

He dismissed notions that he'd prayed at the bedside but, although not present when the Last Rites were administered, he'd been reliably informed they had been. He remembered Mansell as very quiet, just another karter. (Only one other driver to my knowledge has received the Last Rites, Lauda, after the Ring, 1976; and since both were helpless at the time they were administered it has to be coincidental.)

Hesketh didn't see the accident because he happened to be looking the other way. Mansell's steering broke, wooden staves separated one mini-straight from another and he battered into them. He was evidently unconscious or barely conscious when they took him to hospital.

Perhaps Mansell's ideal of himself as The Man Who Could Exercise Mind Over Matter was born in that hospital; subsequently there would be many more examples and they, too, are deep into the folklore; and we'll come to them. That he hammered and broke his body is beyond dispute at Heysham, and many other places in the years to come. The problem is to what degree the folklore seizes on that and, in the telling and re-telling, distorts it.

I don't suppose Mansell has spoken for a decade about his crash at Brands Hatch in 1977, for example, when evidently he broke his neck. The folklore carries it still, telling and retelling it, and that's where the distortion comes. In part this portrait, the last of the seven, is an attempt to cleave the man from this folklore. Not Easy. You notice I've had to use the word evidently twice in the space of 100 words...

Jardine's press release tells us: *Nigel worked at Lucas Aerospace, originally as Lab Technician on the development side of instruments. Production Manager, he worked on test beds and fuels. Projects included the multi-roll combat aircraft, RB211 engine and on the HS125. Moved to Girling where he was briefly a Senior Sales Engineer in the tractor division before going on to motor racing full time. Nigel has an HND in Engineering.*

It is a formidable background and argues both sympathy with and under-standing of things mechanical. It also argues a man of intelligence and ability. One assumes that simpletons weren't allowed near RB211 engines, never mind allowed to work on them.

He began single-seater racing in 1976. He found the money to buy a Hawke DL11-Ford – it was "elderly" – and contested five Formula Ford 1600 meetings, winning three and coming second in another. The car "was about three and a half inches out of alignment at the back," Mansell would say. "We could either have all the wheels in line and the chassis crabbing, or the chassis in line and one wheel out of alignment!"

His results carried no enormous significance because Formula Ford 1600 races at such places as Mallory Park, Castle Combe and Oulton Park – the three tracks he'd driven so far – were a melting pot of uncertain ingredients. Some drivers are kids just playing, some may have no talent and are simply enjoying themselves, some of the cars may be hand-me-downs a great deal more elderly than the Hawke. Some drivers may be good...

Mansell dug into his funds, found £3,000 and launched a complete assault on Formula Ford 1600 in 1977. Between March 6 at Silverstone and November 13 at Thruxton he drove in 51 heats and races in five cars, a Javelin JL5-Ford, a Crossle 25F-Ford, a Crossle 32F-Ford, a Puma 377-Toyota, and in the autumn a Lola T570-Toyota in Formula Three. The more experience you get the better, not least because it is so rationed by opportunities and expensive, and all experience is banked, stored, into your database. It will be useful if you are good...

Marcus Pye knew Mansell from Formula Ford days. "I'd met him a few times when he had the Hawke. He was a shy, ordinary individual. I only really got to speak to him later when he drove Mike Taylor's Crossle 32F, in which he was very successful. The 32F was really one of the classic Formula Ford cars of its time. I'd spoken to him a couple of times when he drove the dreaded Javelin, which shed wheels when you were going for a fast time."

At Brands Hatch in 1977 Mansell had the accident which – evidently – broke his neck. Mansell himself has said it happened in June and he was making his debut in the Crossle 32F. The records are quite clear: the crash happened on May 23. In the final of a round of the Townsend-Thoresen Championship the track dried, creating a "dry" line, and approaching a corner a slower car braked hard. Mansell faced a traditional choice: punt the car ahead or risk moving off the line onto the slippery stuff. He chose the latter, spun and crashed heavily.

Who occupied the slower car? A valid question because his version would surely be interesting (even if only so he could defend himself). Brands understandably don't keep incident sheets of every race, and in this era, the track in use the whole time, it would have needed – as John Webb points out – a warehouse to keep them in. *Autosport*, as far as I can ascertain, carried no mention of it – the race existed as one minor race among so many, the crash one crash among so many. Robin Bradford, who edited the Sportscard column which kept a watchful eye on the comings and goings at this minor level, has no recollection of the crash. That's understandable enough, too. The crash only became important in retrospect, when Mansell's career had become important. The career might well have ended at Brands. Beyond dispute Mansell hurt himself very badly.

Who was the other driver? Mansell claims the driver wrote to him years later announcing himself as the one who'd done it. Jardine remembers clearly that the driver arrived in the pit lane during a Grand Prix years later and wanted to meet Mansell. Jardine, fearing that Mansell may have been less than thrilled to make his acquaintance again, prudently shooed him back into anonymity.

Mansell was taken to hospital at Sidcup and told to lie still for several weeks. In deep depression he discharged himself, something which must have been extremely foolish. I remember exactly when we discussed it, an alcove of an hotel in Montreal in 1982, the first Formula One interview I'd ever done, and he recounted the tale and I had no reason to doubt it then or now. I only question whether he broke his neck because you're in a wheelchair if you do that, not a cockpit.

A specialist subsequently asked him: "Do you want to be alive or not?" He'd risked permanent damage. Maybe the Mind Over Matter found its birthplace here rather than Heysham, maybe not. Always – questions.

Towards the end of July he'd recovered enough to drive again, ironically at Brands Hatch, this time in the Crossle 32F in another Townsend-Thoresen round. He finished second in his heat, fourth in the final.

He won the other Formula Ford 1600 Championship – there were two – by taking pole, setting fastest lap and winning the final round at Silverstone in October. And, as we've seen, he tasted Formula Three, first in the Toyota at Donington in August, later in the Toyota at Silverstone and Thruxton.

Facing 1978, Mansell made a decision which is also in the folklore. To finance his assault on Formula Three he and Rosanne decided to sell their flat; the money bought five races in a March 783-Toyota, the first at Silverstone.

Peter Windsor, then an astute writer for *Autocar*, remembers that. "A good friend of mine, John Thornburn [who'd given Mansell what Mansell describes as moral support in the Formula Ford 1600 days] used to ring up quite a lot. He'd given Keke Rosberg his chance in Formula 5000 in England. One day he rang and said: 'I'm doing all I can to help this guy Nigel Mansell. He's racing Formula Ford, but he's an ace, I tell you he's the quickest thing since Keke.' I met Nigel at Silverstone at the start of 1978. He was on pole, Nelson Piquet second quickest, Derek Warwick third. I was so impressed with his confidence. He shook my hand – a firm handshake – and looked me straight in the eye." Windsor became a convert, something which would assume a clear importance.

With Rosanne working to pay the household bills, Mansell finished second at Silverstone, seventh at Thruxton, seventh at Brands Hatch, seventh at Oulton, fourth at Donington and then the money ran completely out. It was only April.

He did, however, receive a British Driver's Award shortly after and it gave him a drive in a Chevron B42-Hart at Donington in Formula Two, a genuine chance. Initially this would be a two-car effort, with Irishman Derek Daly in the other. During practice Mansell spun on oil and badly damaged the car. He ought to have been able to use the spare for the race, but by then a handsome young Italian, Elio de Angelis, arrived with a bagful of cash (his father owned a large cement business near Rome) and bought a ride, namely the spare. Overnight work to Mansell's car couldn't repair it enough to get into the race.

He needed luck and at last got some. Dave Price ran a Formula Three team, had March 783-Triumph Dolomites and a budget sufficent to pay two drivers. He already had a New Zealander, Brett Riley – whose childhood heroes were Clark, Graham Hill and Rindt, courtesy of the Tasman series – and was working his way through a short list. Mansell wasn't on it. Price hadn't considered him. Mansell journeyed to Twickenham, where the team were based, and by force of personality convinced Price.

"Mansell was not flattered by that car," Marcus Pye says. "He showed flashes of inspiration and he showed well from time to time. He truly had determination, absolutely. In those days my girlfriend lived at Goodwood and every Wednesday I'd go down there and sit on the banking at the racing circuit while she was at work and then we'd go out in the evening. At the circuit I'd watch the testing and there was always somebody of interest.

"Before one test session I drove round the circuit in my little Alfa. I got to St Mary's just after where Moss crashed and there was the lone figure of Mansell jogging round drinking in the atmosphere. It's a beautiful place to be in good weather. Remember Roy Salvadori's quote? 'Give me Goodwood on a sunny summer's day and you can keep the rest of the world.' That's about right.

"It was a 2.4-mile circuit, and because I was such a sloth I drove alongside him for half a mile talking out of the window to him. I did another lap and was quite amazed to find he was three-quarters of a mile further on when I saw him again. He jogged often, for the relaxation and to put him in the right frame of mind. He had a total, utter dedication to the whole thing. Most other blokes would have hopped into their hire cars and gone round in them. Whether he hadn't been to Goodwood before and was using this as a way to learn the circuit is completely irrelevant. You couldn't mistake the dedication, but otherwise he seemed a very, very ordinary bloke."

All are agreed that, putting the matter diplomatically, the Dolomite engine left a great deal to be desired. At Silverstone Mansell finished 11th, but came second a week later at Thruxton and won the third race, again at Silverstone, because Andre de Cesaris, leading, missed the chicane and received a one-minute penalty.

The March-Dolomite lacked genuine competitiveness and the results prove it, eighth, seventh, fourth, sixth, sixth, that sort of thing. At Monaco, Mansell came 11th in the Formula Three race on the weekend Hunt kept the secret of his retirement.

Over the weekend of July 12, 13 and 14 the Formula One world gathered at Silverstone for the British Grand Prix, and the Formula Three world gathered for their supporting race.

David Phipps "had had a good relationship with Colin Chapman – better than most people – since 1954 when I went to the factory at Hornsey one Saturday morning to look at the cars. I became involved in finding sponsors on a friendship-consultancy basis, if you like. I wasn't employed."

Now, in 1979, Phipps took Chapman to Silverstone, "although I can't think what the race was. The March with the Dolomite engine was hopeless in the dry, but in the rain Nigel was quick. I dragged Chapman out to the nearest corner – Woodcote, probably – to watch him in the rain and Chapman was quite impressed that this guy came through sideways and didn't spin off afterwards."

Whether this was before the British Grand Prix weekend is unclear. What is clear is that Nigel Mansell qualified 13th for the Formula Three race. Mike Thackwell, another New Zealander, took pole in a March-Toyota with 1 minute 27.07 seconds while Mansell did 1 minute 28.67. Prost (Martini-Renault) lined up immediately behind Mansell with 1 minute 28.74.

It is certain that as the race unfolded Peter Collins, then team manager at Lotus, and Windsor took Chapman to the chicane just before the start-finish straight.

Thackwell moved into the lead. Much further back *Autosport* reported: "The pretty red and blue Argo of Roberto Guerrero was being caught inch by inch by Eddie Jordan, who made a hash of the start. Once ahead of Michael Roe's Chevron, which had damaged skirts, the Marlboro March (of Stefan Johansson) tussled with Jorge Caton, and Mansell with Rob Wilson, Trevor Templeton and John Bright."

Chapman pointed out where Mansell lay in the race and Windsor and Collins pointed out how bad the car was. As Windsor describes it: "We said he'd got no power at all, but look how quick he is, look at the way he brakes."

Mansell finished sixth.

The situation was poignant because Carlos Reutemann intended to leave Lotus for Williams in 1980, creating a vacancy alongside Mario Andretti.

"We had a number of discussions," Phipps says, "and Chapman said: 'All right, you'd better organize a test session.' I was getting Peter Windsor telling me how fantastic Mansell was – I mean, I knew Mansell, I'd seen him several times – and I have to admit I was a bit wary because of his reputation. He'd had a lot of incidents. They might not necessarily have been his fault, but if you're not actually at all the races and you read about them afterwards you think a driver may be in over his head a little bit. In talks after the crash with de Cesaris, certainly, I learnt it was de Cesaris who caused it." (This happened at Oulton Park in September where de Cesaris tried an impossible overtaking move and Mansell somersaulted, the car landed the wrong way up and he suffered broken vertebrae.)

"You have to accept that men in positions like Chapman's get a lot of approaches. People use friends and confidants and consultants. Collins was pushing for Mansell, or at least Windsor was pushing Collins – anyway Collins was pushing for Mansell, but not too hard. You must be realistic. You can't go over the top for somebody who hasn't very much experience and say: 'Here is the guy to put in the Formula One car.' There were, however, reasons to have a British driver. The sponsors didn't ever say the team had to have one, but they'd be pleased if it did – rather than an Italian or an American or whatever. All of those things added up.

"I thought to myself: 'Well, this guy is quite good, and if he is treated properly he's potentially another good young British driver.' There were others about at that time, Stephen South, people like that, and we all had to lean on Chapman because he was keen to have an established driver. He didn't want somebody going round shunting the cars."

Watson, in his sixth season of Formula One and now with McLaren, remembers: "Windsor became a fan of Nigel's. I didn't know anybody other than him who was at that point, although I do know Chapman had faith in him. But Chapman was an opportunist, he would use people solely if he thought it would give Chapman some benefit. Nigel was keen and earnest, and nobody was desperately anxious to drive for Lotus at that time, anyway." By this Watson means the established, front rank drivers.

Chapman told Phipps: "You set up a test at Paul Ricard." The idea, Phipps says, was that "we'd have one or two people already in Formula One, Elio, Jan Lammers, Eddie Cheever. A test doesn't cost very much, the cars go testing anyway, and you can evaluate these guys. Chapman said: 'Round up some youngsters and we'll have a look at them.' I organized it to the extent of phoning the drivers, booking them into the hotel and telling them: 'You come on a Tuesday afternoon, you have a seat fitting, you drive on Wednesday and then you go away.'

"I was the one now doing the pushing, which was why Chapman didn't make the phone call himself to Nigel. I did. The point of it all was that he was still in considerable pain after his accident with de Cesaris, but nothing was going to stop him going there. I recall saying: 'I heard you'd broken your neck', and he said: 'Not really, it's all right, don't worry.' His attitude – I can't remember verbatim – was *I'll be there come hell or high water*."

This conversation is deep into the folklore, as is Mansell's flight to the south of France dosing himself with pain-killers.

Autosport reported: "Although it was actually deemed a Michelin tyre test, neither Renault nor Ferrari had any objections to Lotus sharing Paul Ricard's short 2.02-mile 'test' track. The Norfolk-based Grand Prix team took advantage to take along three cars, two type 79s and a type 80 for a selection of young drivers to try. There were many rumours before as to exactly who would be attending, but only Elio de Angelis, Eddie Cheever, Jan Lammers, Stephen South and surprisingly Nigel Mansell went. Apparently Marc Surer turned up but did not drive.

"It's fair to say that weather conditions weren't terribly favourable, strong winds and occasional showers sweeping the circuit. De Angelis was given the first run on Monday, putting in about 50 to 60 laps and eventually recording a best time of 1 minute 8.61 seconds. The following day Cheever had a drive over a similar number of laps, posting 1 minute 10.45. Lammers had his first experience of the 79 on Wednesday and lapped in 1 minute 10.08. Meanwhile, South had done many laps in both the other cars, eventually getting down to a very respectable 1 minute 7.74 in the 79T on Thursday.

"Mansell's first run in the other 79 was hampered by a broken gearbox, and when he did get out, late on Friday afternoon, the track was still quite wet after a shower. He did about 35 laps and got down to 1 minute 13.91. It was the talented young British driver's first run in a race car since his horrifying Oulton Park crash a few weeks ago."

David Phipps is instructive about this test. "Elio wouldn't go away! He said 'I pay my own bill', because obviously we paid for all the others. Cheever was very good and he'd had a lot of Formula Two experience, but I remember afterwards he seemed a self-defeated person. He came over and said: 'Well, I suppose you don't want my phone number, do you?' Very negative – whereas Elio, who had an entourage there, was desperate to get that drive. Lammers was quick, but both he and Elio were driving for Shadow in Formula One that year, so they had experience of that sort of car, that sort of engine power.

"Nigel made a pretty good impression on me...well, I mean, it's difficult to say. Put somebody from a Formula Three car into a Formula One car with nothing intermediate – and remember the experience of all the others – and he was pretty good. Being a cautious sort of person, I wasn't going to go overboard. I'm sure that somebody like Peter Windsor would have said 'fantastic' and suited that to whatever he wanted to get out of it. He'd have said: 'Well, he was 2 seconds slower than Elio but, of course, the wind was in a different direction' or whatever.

"Nigel was very straightforward about the test and I got on very well with him, but I'd have to say that I didn't see World Champion material there. I saw a lot of determination and the fact that he could actually drive the thing."

Chapman selected de Angelis to partner Andretti in 1980, but gave Mansell a testing contract and the promise of some Grand Prix races. While he waited for that he drove Marches in Formula Three and a Ron Tauranac Ralt-Honda in Formula Two. "He showed well in that," Marcus Pye says, "but at the time you really wondered why this guy was getting the breaks. From Formula Three to Formula Two is obviously a massive step in terms of financial commitment and he hadn't any money. You felt somehow it was all a lost cause."

Nigel Mansell made his Grand Prix debut at the Osterreichring in August, Chapman fielding a third car for him. Not surprisingly, Mansell qualified slowest, 1 minute 35.71 seconds against (and I know it's an unfair comparison) Rene Arnoux's pole time in the Renault of 1 minute 30.27.

Before the race Alan Brinton and another journalist, Patrick Stephenson, wandered over. "He was very approachable," Brinton says. "Pat was doing some work for the *Birmingham Post* so Mansell represented a local angle. He was sitting on a pile of tyres behind the pits, nobody else wanted to talk to him. I mean, who is he? Grand Prix debutant, you know. I always remember one phrase he used. *This is my first race, I'm determined to get to the top and when I do I can assure you I shall never change.* In retrospect you have to murmur oh dear, oh dear, in the light of what has happened, but it's the pressure, and to a certain extent I can understand that."

In *Autosport* Nigel Roebuck wrote: "Nigel Mansell failed to appear at the end of the 41st lap, having pulled off with engine failure after a very solid and courageous drive. On the grid, the Lotus mechanics had topped up his fuel tank, the excess from the churn blowing back and soaking his overalls. With time pressing, they had poured water over him in an attempt to minimize the damage, but the gasoline did its evil work and by the time Mansell stepped from the car his back was pretty well skinned. It was, of course, vital that he should create a good impression on his Grand Prix debut, and he stuck to his task with a lot of guts." He'd been 13th, itself of no particular meaning unless you're superstitious of course, when the engine did fail.

When he reached Heathrow the burns had tightened and he could barely walk.

The brakes failed in the Dutch Grand Prix and he spun off. At Imola, trying to qualify the spare Lotus for the Italian Grand Prix, he was hampered by brakes again and didn't make the race. He didn't go to Canada or the United States for the last two races.

In the background, hard rumours insisted that Andretti would sign for Alfa Romeo, which he duly did, and by late October softer rumours suggested Mansell would partner de Angelis in 1981. This dragged, and although Mansell insists Chapman assured him he had the drive, further rumours in mid-January suggested Jean-Pierre Jarier would get it. No matter. Lotus had nominated Mansell as their number two for the South African Grand Prix on February 7, a race in jeopardy because of the (then) vehement dispute between the governing body, FISA, and the Constructors' Association FOCA. The race took place, but was declared non-Championship.

Mansell would remember "passing Carlos Reutemann. I was following Elio, waiting for a good place to pass him, John Watson hot on my heels", but he went wide and damaged a skirt.

Mansell became a regular works Lotus driver and in the fourth race of 1981, Belgium at Zolder, finished third, although at the start a mechanic was run over on the grid – Mansell, not involved, was sure the mechanic had been killed. Mansell, shaken, went to the restart and spent a tract of it dicing with Villeneuve in the Ferrari.

He came sixth in Spain in June, and just before the British Grand Prix the *Daily Star* newspaper in London carried a telling feature headlined THE NEW JIM CLARK. The writer, Mervyn Edgecombe, coined this first paragraph: *Britain could soon be hailing Nigel Mansell as the motor racing champion of the world.* Edgecombe then went on to quote Chapman comparing Mansell with Clark.

"It's no use denying it – the similarities are there. Even at this early stage I instinctively know I've got a boy who is going to go all the way to the top.

"As well as being a very talented and exciting driver, Nigel's a tremendous attribute to the team. Even after such a relatively short period, I can already feel he and I are developing the kind of relationship Jimmy and I shared.

"I can envisage us building a successful relationship which I reckon will continue for the next five or six years, maybe 10. I think he is going to put us back on the pinnacle again."

Chapman died of a heart attack in December 1982. By then Lotus were struggling, de Angelis ninth in that season's Championship table, Mansell 14th.

Peter Warr took over the running of the team, an uneasy inheritance, and in conversation with him for an earlier chapter of this book I wondered about the relationship between Graham Hill and Clark, both of whom Warr had worked with. The question produced an unexpected answer.

"It's interesting, because there's a parallel with Nigel and Elio. Elio came from a very old patrician Roman family and he was almost a playboy, very wealthy, very laid-back, good looking, did everything with style. He smoked. I don't think he ever tried to keep fit in his life. In the evening in the hotel he'd have a couple of J & B whiskies.

"Nigel was in the Graham Hill mould, he'd come from a fairly ordinary English background, had this chip on his shoulder that he felt the whole world was against him. He worked really hard at trying to do this and trying to do that – in the Graham mould.

"Elio would turn up at the track. 'Ah damn,' he'd say, 'I haven't got my gloves, I've left them in the hotel' or 'the helmet, I cannot find it', so somebody would go and borrow him a helmet. He'd stub the cigarette out, get in the car, go out and be half a second a lap quicker than Nigel. And Nigel couldn't understand why it happened when he was working as hard as he was. Elio was a natural. He just did it and he liked it, and he was smooth, and he was quick, and all the rest. That's the same scenario that you had with Graham and Jimmy."

In April 1983 Mansell competed in the Race of Champions at Brands Hatch and retired after six laps. He thought something had broken on the rear suspension, "but the thing became even more dangerous. Every time I accelerated it was all over the place."

The Race of Champions proved to be a curious event, with only 13 starters and only one of them, Alan Jones, an actual Formula One Champion. Watson took part in a McLaren and he remembers Mansell. "There was this guy trying desperately hard in Formula One, but at that time he more or less appeared like anybody else among that generation of British drivers. He did have an ability and a talent, but I am sure no-one, even Peter Windsor, envisaged what we'd see later. Nigel was obviously competent. He was courageous in the car, he drove cars that were not particularly good and showed a remarkable level of courage to gain something from them.

"The first real glimpse was probably at Brands Hatch, that bloody awful Race of Champions in the middle of winter. To say the car looked lethal is an understatement, yet he was so committed, and this is the most notable feature of the man. I think everybody has to say they misjudged him. Something very powerful within Nigel motivates him and I don't know what it is. Of all the drivers I've been around he's quite unlike the majority. There is something within him which is so very strong, and I can't stick any particular label onto it. He had an ambition, a desire to fulfill what he expected to himself."

Mansell and Warr did not co-exist easily – Mansell has written hardened, sharpened words about Warr, and Warr has spoken hardened, sharpened words about Mansell. In 1984 Mansell led a very wet Monaco, thus leading a Grand Prix for the first time in his life, but spun off to general consternation. At Zandvoort Warr fired him to hire Ayrton Senna from Toleman. At this point in his career Mansell had finished no higher than third and, truth to tell, was perceived as a loser. Let me refine that brutal description: not a winner.

Nor was driving a Lotus easy. As Brinton attests: "Don't forget he had some pigs to drive, some real pigs, there's no doubt about it, but he would always be optimistic. I remember going up to Ketteringham Hall, where Lotus are based, one of those years when they'd announced their new car for the season, and he put on a show, patting it. 'This I know from the start looks good,' he said. 'It's going to be a world-beater.' All credit to him. In later years he resolved what must have been deep-seated doubts about active suspension because he had one or two rather nasty moments at Lotus, didn't he? He convinced himself, or was convinced, that it wasn't going to happen again." (Lotus pioneered active suspension.)

For 1985 Frank Williams took him to partner Keke Rosberg and described him in a celebrated phrase as "a good journeyman who will score points," a judgment reflecting the general opinion. There are many such, natural number twos who might possibly win a race or two if the cards fall right, but who rack up points and help in the Constructors' table, which is of no interest to the general public but of extreme interest to teams, sponsors and engine suppliers.

In 1985 Mansell picked up a couple of fifth places, then a sixth, another sixth, another sixth, so that after 12 races he had seven points. Contrast that with Rosberg: front row in Brazil, a race he led before the turbo failed; front row at Imola, fourth in Canada, front row and victory in Detroit, pole and second place at Paul Ricard, pole at Silverstone, leading Holland for 19 laps before the engine went, front row and leading Monza until the engine went again. Frank Williams had clearly been correct, just as those who insisted Mansell was not a winner had clearly been correct.

Across the following six weeks Mansell destroyed all these notions suddenly, absolutely and completely. In the Belgian Grand Prix at Spa on September 15, the race after Monza, Mansell moved confidently to second place behind Senna, the highest placing of his career. In the European Grand Prix at Brands Hatch on October 6 he hammered Senna by 21.396 seconds, the first win of his career. In the South African Grand Prix at Kyalami on October 19 he took pole and won a thunderous race from – Rosberg. In the Australian Grand Prix at Adelaide on November 3 he put the Williams on the front row, made a tremendous start, led and was punted by Senna.

How could a man who had achieved so little for some four seasons achieve so much so fast? There are strands to be followed, and the first is that frankly he seemed an unlikely superstar, which may have deceived many, including me. Tony Jardine's pen-portrait of him for the press, circa 1984, said:

Personal Details
Height: 5ft 10in
Weight: 11st 7lb (in off season) 11st 0lb (in race season)
Eyes: Brown
Favourite food: Roast lamb, cottage pie
Favourite drink: Brandy occasionally
Hobbies: Clay pigeon shooting, squash, flying, tennis
Favourite singer: Barbra Streisand
Favourite film stars: John Wayne, Clint Eastwood, Charles Bronson
Pets: 2 labradors – Abby and Kizzy. 2 cats – Purdy and Gemma.

Mansell made few compromises to what other people might have wanted him to be, although Brinton noticed one. "His accent was flat Midland – not

Brummie, he's not a Brummie boy, really. When he began to be noticed he got into a habit of talking differently, particularly when he knew there were foreigners around. He would articulate rather carefully. He wouldn't say: 'I don't know what to say,' he'd say: 'I do not know what to tell you.'"

None of this – staying loyal to cottage pie, refining the accent so it was easy to understand for non-native English speakers – goes any way to explaining the six weeks. We must look elsewhere.

Every race is a distillation of themes, but the focal point must inevitably be the winner of it unless there has been some momentous incident to overshadow that. Who remembers who ran seventh or came seventh, never mind why or how? Full across 1984 and 1985, something largely unrecognized had been gathering strength: Mansell. I propose to let this unfold by itself, race by race, so we can all see now what we all missed then:

1984
Brazil, Rio. Quickest in first qualifying, third row of the grid, highest placing in the race third, out – accident.

South Africa, Kyalami. Second row of the grid, highest fifth, out – turbo.

Belgium, Zolder. Fifth row of the grid, highest 13th, out – clutch.

San Marino, Imola. Ninth row, highest 16th, out – brakes on lap two.

France, Dijon. Quickest in second qualifying, third row, highest third, finished third.

Monaco, Monte Carlo. Second quickest in second qualifying, front row, led from laps 11 to 15, out – crash.

Canada, Montreal. Fourth row of the grid, highest fourth, finished sixth.

USA East, Detroit. Quickest in first qualifying, second row, ran second from laps 10 to 27 out – gearbox.

USA, Dallas. Quickest in first qualifying, pole, led from lap one to 35, skimmed wall, finished sixth.

Britain, Brands Hatch. Fourth row, highest ninth, out – gearbox.

Germany, Hockenheim. Eighth row, highest fourth, finished fourth.

Austria, Osterreichring. Fourth row, highest fifth, out – engine.

Holland, Zandvoort. Sixth row, highest third, finished third.

Italy, Monza. Fourth row, highest seventh, out – a spin.

Europe, Nurburgring. Fourth row, highest sixth, out – engine.

Portugal, Estoril. Third row, highest second from lap 12 to 51, out – brakes.

1985
Brazil, Rio. Third row, crash on first lap.

Portugal, Estoril. Fifth row, highest fifth after starting from the pit lane and lying 25th after the opening lap, finished fifth.

San Marino, Imola. Fourth row, finished fifth.

Monaco, Monte Carlo. Front row, highest second, finished seventh.

Canada, Montreal. Eighth row, highest sixth, finished sixth.

USA, Detroit. Front row, second from lap nine to 19, out – accident.

France, Ricard. Crashed at 180mph in Saturday morning untimed session, took no further part.

Britain, Silverstone. Third row, highest fourth, out – clutch.

Germany, Nurburgring. Fifth row, highest third, finished sixth.

Austria, Osterreichring. Front row, highest third, out – engine.

Holland, Zandvoort. Fourth row, highest fifth, finished sixth.

Italy, Monza. Second row, ran second for the opening three laps then pitted with a misfire, struggled on until lap 47 when the engine expired. Well, not really struggled. On lap 38 he set fastest lap, 1 minute 28.283 seconds, which translates to an average speed of 146.962mph (236.512 km/h) – only the second fastest lap of his career.

Monza had been September 8, the Belgian at Spa would be September 15...

The 28 races repay close scrutiny because, prisoner of an uncompetitive Lotus in 1984, he finished in the points every time the car ran to the end or he didn't crash. Up to Spa 1985 he finished every race seventh or higher if the car was running. Moreover he'd been on the front row three times and set that fastest lap at Monza. Together it suggests, in a mosaic of tantalizing prisms, something more than a journeymen going about his modest business. Journeymen do not start from the pit lane and gain 20 places by race's end; journeymen do not have a horrific crash at Ricard – striking a concrete post, being knocked unconscious – and after spending time in hospital come fourth in a Grand Prix a week later. Rosberg, himself a hard man, expressed open and sincere admiration of that, publicly, and no mistake.

Whatever the boy had or didn't have, he had balls.

There is another question to be faced. Honda, supplying the engines, were understandably covetous of their technology, which is not necessarily Oriental inscrutability – everyone is. Even when Honda occupied premises directly adjoining the Williams factory, the Williams staff, other than Frank himself and Patrick Head, were discouraged from going there by Frank, who decided he didn't want his people gossiping and distracting the work in hand. My hunch is he also made the decision so that Honda wouldn't have to say, politely but definitively, *please keep your people out because we'd prefer that they didn't see.*

Whatever, nobody at Williams knew what Honda were doing in the sense that Honda stayed inscrutable and the Williams mechanics didn't fire up the engines at meetings because Honda personnel did that. To put it starkly, the Williams team had to assume Rosberg and Mansell were being given equal treatment.

That Rosberg finished 1985 with 40 points, third in the Championship, might argue that he was a better driver than Mansell and Rosberg was the number one, anyway, as befits a former World Champion. Honda could have been forgiven for putting their main weight behind him. They were in it to win, after all, and until October 6 and Brands Hatch Mansell hadn't won a Formula One race in his life.

At Austria in August Rosberg said he was leaving to join McLaren. Subsequently, when the question of equal treatment raged over Mansell and Piquet the following season, Rosberg gazed back and said publicly that "Honda feel they can manipulate and control the game as they wish."

Did they now – 1985, Rosberg leaving, Mansell coming, coming, coming – put their weight behind Mansell? Does that explain why he was suddenly quicker? We do know that Mansell proved considerably quicker than Rosberg in both sessions at Spa, 1 minute 56.727 against 1 minute 57.582 in the first session, 1 minute 56.996 against 1 minute 57.465 in the second, but such finite judgments, unprovable and awkward, may depend on all manner of local circumstances. They exclude the possibility that Mansell was getting better and better.

At Spa Prost took pole, Senna alongside – and Senna's JPS Lotus-Renault covered the circuit 1½km/h quicker than Mansell in qualifying, a pace reflected in the race, Senna leading, Mansell chasing: of the 43 laps, in only 12 did Mansell go quicker than Senna, Rosberg – fourth – 1 minute 15 seconds away from Senna and 47 seconds behind Mansell. But Rosberg was able to harry Mansell early on and only fell away with brake problems.

Mansell constructed a mature drive, unhurried, accepting that he couldn't catch Senna and that he could not himself be caught. Prost, far behind him, tunnelled for points towards the Championship. In many superficial ways this ordinary Belgian Grand Prix was an ordinary Belgian Grand Prix, another race. Who saw that Mansell had moved an important step towards altering the power balance in Formula One? Did you? I didn't...

On the eve of the next race, the European Grand Prix at Brands Hatch, Mansell made a speech to some sponsors and their wives. Pye attended and pays his tribute to how charming – and amusing – Mansell can be on such occasions. "He stood up and gave his speech. He said: 'Well, you might ask me what it's like to drive a Formula One car. It's quick and all that, but the thing that really grabs your attention is the G force. We pull 4G. I'm trying, ladies, to put it in a way which won't embarrass you, but imagine you're lying in bed, your husband's on top of you and he suddenly weighs 32 stone.' It was really, really funny. They all fell about. He was brilliant at it, absolutely brilliant."

He was brilliant in the race, too. Senna (of course) took pole and took the lead, Rosberg surged past Mansell and Piquet and then attacked Senna. "I was a million miles an hour faster," Rosberg would say, "but I couldn't get by him. He was weaving and blocking me into Hawthorn's, and into Druids he took the inside line – and that's it for overtaking at Brands. There isn't anything else left. All I could try was at Surtees, which I did every lap."

On lap seven Rosberg lunged, spun and collected Piquet, who was right behind him – Piquet out, Rosberg crawling to the pits with a puncture. As he emerged from the pits Senna and Mansell rounded Clearways, Rosberg physically in front of them although a lap down. "I'd ruined my own race," Rosberg would say, "so I thought I'd give my team-mate a hand."

Rosberg blocked Senna. Mansell stole through and into the lead. He would not lose it, indeed would increase it remorselessly: at 10 laps, 3.6 seconds; at 20, 10.7; at 30, 12.8; at 40, 18.4; at 50, 25.4; at 60, 22.7; and then he eased down, the final margin being 21.396.

The emotion of the moment – and it was emotional, Rosanne in tears in the pit lane, Mansell himself extremely moved and not far from tears – obscured two aspects, that Prost – fourth – had become France's first World Champion, and Mansell had altered his career in the most fundamental way. Two weeks later he took pole in South Africa and stormed the race despite a heroic charge from Rosberg; put the Williams on the front row in Australia, led and then Senna punted him out.

Who was Mansell then? The Mansell you see now or the child of the Mansell you see now? He was essentially the same, dealing in malapropisms to make you wriggle in embarrassment but always a plain man coping in his own way with a multi-lingual, multi-cultural, multi-faceted global activity which excited many hundreds of millions. The boy from Brum (well, not exactly) would now knead Formula One, as it had so often kneaded him, and the dough would start coming in millions.

Goodyear have their own motorhome, a relaxed place. Brinton spent time there, as many other journalists did. Rosanne, he attests, was a regular inhabitant with the family – "Senna's first win at Estoril, l985, she sat in there with one of the kiddies who wasn't very well the whole time – and Mansell would come in and be a great joker."

He has an earthy, quasi-mischievous sense of humour and it expressed itself against one Anthony Marsh, then an on-track commentator, well-fed, famous for his lunch-time appetite and dubbed Bunter because he looked like that. Brinton remembers that Mansell "would come into the motorhome and Marsh suffered horribly. 'Bunter, on your third lunch today, mate?'" Marsh was an obvious, slow-moving target, but Mansell did it nicely, just a little gentle harpooning. Some of that was always with Mansell, the ease of being funny without hurting, the whimsical, ironical quip here and there.

For 1986 Piquet, twice World Champion, came to Williams as number one. That alone – the status of number one – would inevitably create friction, with Mansell emerging so strongly. The first three races established the tone – Piquet won Brazil, Mansell crashing with Senna; Senna won Spain from Mansell in a stunning finish by 0.014 of a second, Piquet out with engine problems; Prost won San Marino from Piquet, Mansell out on lap eight, engine: not much to choose between them.

Mansell won the fifth race, Spa, and won Canada two weeks later. Prost now had 29 points, Mansell and Senna 27, Piquet 19. Mansell took fifth place in Detroit and won France: Prost 39, Mansell 38, Senna 36, Piquet 23.

The British at Brands Hatch could be no ordinary race, Piquet pole, Mansell alongside him, while on the 10th row Jacques Laffite lined up his Ligier. Laffite has hammered out one of the most evocative descriptions of a man and his moments.

Red light. On the grid 26 cars howl enough to deafen you. The exhaust pipes are like cannons spitting thunder and fire. War? No, a Grand Prix. Twenty six drivers ready for the start, me among them. Green light. Accelerator pedal on the floor. Let the clutch out. A giant hand seizes me by the small of my back. Eight hundred and fifty horsepower thrust me forward.

Around me everything happens fast. The scenery has lost its contours: just a multi-coloured stream, but in front of me everything stays neat, precise. In a shower of sparks the other cars are doing the same speed as me. A flurry of gear changing. Second. Third. Suddenly a break in our flight. A yellow flash cuts across on the left: Boutsen. Brake. In front of me everything has stayed normal. The danger is not there. Accelerate again.

Unreal: there was nothing, and now a Ferrari. Johansson, just a profile, a red barrier. Miss him. Turn the wheel. Now a wall, straight in front of me. It's going to wipe me out. "No!" Useless to say that. Powerless. I've become an object, A Victim, I've become nothing any more. Beaten, dead. My greatest defeat.

A surge of arrogance: curse the wall, insult it. And the shock: implosion, compression, crushing. A sharp pain. Right flank pierced. Terrifying: in a few seconds everything has gone off balance. Stupor. Silence. Crumpled metal, torn plastic. The sound of voices: cries and calls. Where am I? Grand Prix, green light, wall…I'm in pain. And fear: am I crippled?

Within these moments we saw a motor racing crash, a sentence which is comfortable to write, as it would be, but the thing itself a surge-chaos-crash-surge and happening fast, cars flaying and floundering. Boutsen's Arrows snapped completely out of control – he had no idea why – and skimmed hard left, just missing the Lola of Jones, bounced the Armco towards Paddock Hill Bend and the impetus projected it back across the track. Johansson, faced with the Arrows broadside, dipped right on instinct, inadvertently forcing Laffite – on his outside – off onto the grass and in to the wall.

Almost unnoticed, Mansell, who'd made a superb start and led Piquet from the grid, felt something "explode" on the car – driveshaft, as it proved – and cruised round Paddock, cruised down the dip, his race already run. He had no way of knowing about the crash out of sight behind him. What Mansell did see were black flags stopping the whole thing.

The folklore again: how Mansell got into the spare car set up for Piquet, how he laid enormous pressure on Piquet at the restart and took him on lap 23, how Piquet laid enormous pressure on him and he resisted it, made no mistake as Piquet hounded, and hounded, and hounded. To put this into statistics, and there are times when mere numerals are very graphic, on only five of the 75 laps did more than a second separate them. Indeed, after 57 laps the gap stood at just 0.299 and even at the end, when Piquet accepted Mansell could not be overtaken, the gap moved out to no more than 5.574.

This race distilled everything about Mansell, bad luck leading to adversity, leading to a completely unexpected chance, then a drive of raw courage harnessing into sureness of touch and great power, and this is how close it was in the meat of the race. In what follows the + is what Mansell gained, the - what Piquet clawed back.

Lap 60	− 0.864
Lap 61	− 0.258
Lap 62	+ 0.075
Lap 63	+ 0.215
Lap 64	+ 0.236
Lap 65	+ 0.304
Lap 66	− 0.800
Lap 67	+ 0.405
Lap 68	+ 0.127
Lap 69	+ 0.244
Lap 70	− 0.136

Some time later I tackled Frank Williams on whether the team ought to have signalled Mansell to let Piquet go by as the number one, and Williams dismissed the notion in two telling phrases: that the team would have held the sport up to ridicule, and "you cannot stand on a man's career."

From this time on nobody would stand on Mansell's career, and only the Championship eluded him. He might have taken it in Mexico, although James Hunt set the scene for that in his very own trenchant way. On the Thursday before that meeting, as everyone arrived in Mexico City, *The Times* of London carried a long, perceptive and provocative feature by him headlined: An Outsider in the Pit Lane. The excerpts which follow are, I hope, representative.

Nigel Mansell seems perfectly suited to the mantle he has assumed among British sports enthusiasts and, indeed, the British public in general: That of Boy's Own hero. His disarming honesty, working-class charm and occasional naivety combine with his aura of determination to make him ideal material for those whose natural sympathy is with the underdog. Yet should he become the seventh Briton to win grand prix racing's World Championship in Mexico on Sunday, the cheering will be by no means universal.

Mansell's qualities are well appreciated by those who know him best...but there is another jury, hidden from the average sports fan, which give a running verdict on the worth of drivers and on their potential suitability for the role of World Champion. This is the collective voice of the insiders: the team personnel, the legislators, some of the senior sponsors and a veritable army of specialist media representatives.

There are perhaps 1,000 of them and they make up the grand prix circus. The sad and bewildering fact is that by and large they do not want Mansell to win.

Like any other high-earning sport, grand prix racing is a very ego-intensive business; after all, it is ego – controlled ego, that is – which makes winners and champions. Drivers are very protective of the World Championship: it is the pinnacle to which they all aspire, it can only be won by one man in each season, and a driver's ego is mightily strained when a chap he thinks he's better than, and possibly dislikes, takes the title.

When examining his suitability as a potential World Champion Mansell's personality raises many more questions than his new-found maturity as a driver. His naivety may appear quaintly attractive to the public at home, but in the business it is often seen as crossing the border into foolishness – unacceptable in sport's standard bearer.

The rough edges will be no problem as long as he shows the same capacity for rapid learning out of the car as in it. I speak from experience, because I was far more troublesome than he has been or is ever likely to be. I wish him all the best.

Mansell fluffed the start in Mexico and recovered to fifth, might have consummated the Championship in Adelaide but the tyre burst on the straight, giving a cascade of unforgettable and terrifying images.

He duelled Piquet all across 1987, but the consummation that season went when he ran onto a dirty part of the Suzuka circuit in qualifying, skittered at high speed into a tyre wall and badly damaged his back.

Williams lost Honda engines for 1988 and that season drifted away into frustration. The Judd engine didn't deliver enough power, and Mansell finished with 12 points. By then, anyway, he was going to Ferrari. There, he met the folklore of Ferrari and both fed on each other immediately – at Brazil, in the first race of 1989. The car, unreliable, wasn't expected to last beyond 15 minutes. It lasted the full 61 laps and Mansell beat Prost by 7.809 seconds, which provoked the ringing of church bells all round Maranello. No Briton had won in a Ferrari since John Surtees, Belgium, 1966.

But the unreliability threaded through the season so that all Mansell could do was fashion a few splendid moments, epitomized by Hungary where, rounding a right-hander, he thrust the car inside Senna; an extaordinary and genuinely thrilling example of creating everything from nothing. He ended 1989 fourth in the Championship on 38 points, no man's land. Prost had 81 (76 counting), Senna 60, Patrese 40.

Prost came to Ferrari for 1990 and Prost had all the luck, Mansell only a meagre share of it: fourth in Brazil, third in Canada, second in Mexico, set fastest lap at Silverstone, led the race twice but retired on lap 55, gearbox. He promptly announced his retirement, something which, he insisted, he had discussed fully with Rosanne and was not sudden. "There comes a time in everyone's life when they call it a day. I'm 37 this year and I'd rather quit when I'm at the top. I'm looking forward to spending some time with my family and hopefully at the end of the year turning into a little bit of a businessman."

He finished strongly, winning Portugal, second in Spain, second in Australia – but at Estoril hinted he might change his mind, and before Spain he did. Frank Williams had been to the Isle of Man with virtually a blank cheque and used his full powers of persuasion, which are formidable, to convince Mansell that the team had the car and the engine – Renault – to take him to the Championship.

Clearly Mansell would not have reconsidered such a public decision, and particularly one where he said he was putting his family first, if anything less than the Championship did not represent a real possibility. He cited, too, the sheer volume of people from a wide spectrum of motorsport and beyond who'd pleaded with him, and by a great quirk this extended beyond nationalism. Of course the Brits wanted their Brit, but many others did also, those who viewed the state of Formula One with a steady, wider eye, and sensed that any season which lacked the combative element of Mansell's driving would be seriously diminished. Hunt's feature of five years before might still be valid in many ways, but the great truth could not be avoided: you had three genuinely great drivers, Senna of sublime speed, Prost the pragmatic solver of problems, and Mansell of hurricane force. To lose any one removed a whole dimension.

Mansell pointed out reasonably enough that he'd considered trying sportscars, and Rosanne had said if he was going to do that her "anxiety factor" would be unaltered, so he might as well stay.

Mansell's critics saw this as weakness and malleability, a hard view when a man has dedicated virtually all of his adult years to becoming World Champion, has twice been within grasping distance of it – Adelaide 1986, Suzuka 1987 – and has an offer on the table giving him a ripe chance at it.

Renault held the key because no matter how expert Patrick Head and the design team, no matter how sophisticated the chassis and aerodynamics, Williams could not win without sufficient power. That is not the trite statement it might seem. To take the Championship, you could not avoid the power Honda fed into the Marlboro McLarens and would have to match or beat it. Williams proved that to themselves in 1988 when they had Judd engines. Only once over the whole 16 races did Mansell set fastest lap – Silverstone, a wet race which allowed him to compensate – and the true difference can be illustrated by what happened two weeks later at Hockenheim, a speed circuit, which Senna won:

	Senna	Mansell
Lap 1	2:12.533	2:28.597
Lap 2	2:06.702	2:12.529
Lap 3	2:05.949	2:08.883
Lap 4	2:06.089	2:07.770
Lap 5	2:05.426	2:07.905

To be fair to Judd, Williams were experimenting with active suspension, which didn't help – the car would become, in Patrick Head's own phrase, "a bit of a pig's ear", and Frank himself has confessed that they didn't see the move to Judd as "potentially a major disaster", but added that that was what 1988 became.

Renault, of course, were well versed in Formula One, having run their own team between 1977 and 1985, supplied Lotus and Tyrrell in 1986, departed and returned with Williams in 1989. Patrese and Boutsen made solid progress, Patrese finishing one place above Mansell in the Championship, Boutsen one place behind. In 1990 Boutsen again finished one place behind Mansell, but Patrese fell back to seventh. Neither Boutsen nor Patrese, both highly competent drivers, could stir a hurricane; neither had that elusive combination of factors and facets which made them regular winners likely to grip the Championship round the throat and not let go.

Moving into 1991, their third season, Renault were preparing to measure themselves directly against Honda. Renault had taken a corporate decision to apply whatever resources they deemed necessary, the only way to do it. Renault even saw this in a wider context, as a way of proving to European manufacturers that the Japanese could be beaten. Frank Williams was impressed and said so. Whenever he'd visited the Renault factory near Paris he sensed that, having risked their reputation, Renault were putting muscle into the programme, plenty of it, real muscle.

What would Mansell do with it? In a sense 1991 became a rehearsal, albeit a strange one. Senna set off at a gallop, winning the first four races, which led many to speculate about another Marlboro McLaren slaughter, the rest chugging along always off the pace. The reality proved different. Senna himself recounts that in one of these races Patrese caught him, Senna cut past a backmarker and assumed be wouldn't be seeing Patrese again for a while, glanced in his mirrors and – Patrese back on him already. Senna saw a great deal in that moment: that his car would be vulnerable across the remaining 12 races.

Mansell ought to have won the fifth race, Canada, but the car broke down in unexplained circumstances within sight of the line. After that Mansell galloped all the way to Portugal in September, where a mix-up during his pit stop sent him off down the pit lane with a rear wheel not secured, the wheel bounding away into the Tyrrell pit, Mansell marooned, beating his fists in frustration. He won Spain, challenging Senna wheel-to-wheel along the straight in a macho moment which Frank Williams savoured to the full; but it was too late, and any mathematical chances of the Championship went when Mansell, tracking Senna, plunged off at Suzuka with brake problems.

Prost took a sabbatical in 1992 after harsh words between himself and Ferrari, but it cleared the theatre of Formula One for Senna and Mansell to meet head-to-head, McLaren's technology against that of Williams, Renault against Honda, Elf against Shell. The head-to-head never happened. Mansell overwhelmed the season, the hurricane blowing everywhere, blowing on everyone, blowing them aside.

It's somehow fitting that CHAMPIONS! should climax with the 1992 season because, all else aside, it enables us to reflect and compare, a difficult and potentially misleading exercise, but surely worth the attempt.

In 1958 there were 10 races. Hawthorn won once, took pole four times, was also on the front row four times, set fastest lap five times and led 125 laps out of 592.

In 1962 there were nine races. Graham Hill won four times, took pole once, was also on the front row three times, set fastest lap three times and led 316 laps out of 624.

In 1963 there were 10 races. Clark won seven times, took pole seven times, was also on the front row once, set fastest lap six times and led 506 laps out of 598.

In 1964 there were 10 races. Surtees won twice, took pole twice, was also on the front row three times, set fastest lap twice and led 89 laps out of 722.

In 1965 there were 10 races. Clark missed Monaco for Indianapolis and from the remaining nine won six, took pole six times, was also on the front row three times, set fastest lap six times and led 354 laps out of 583.

In 1968 there were 12 races. Graham Hill won three times, took pole twice, was also on the front row twice, set no fastest laps and led 175 laps out of 853.

In 1969 there were 11 races. Stewart won six times, took pole twice, was also on the front row three times, set fastest lap five times and led 416 laps out of 807.

In 1971 there were 11 races. Stewart won six times, took pole six times, was also on the front row three times, set fastest lap three times and led 347 laps out of 671.

In 1973 there were 15 races. Stewart withdrew from the last after the death of Cevert but from the remaining 14 won five times, took pole three times, was also on the front row once, set fastest lap once and led 215 laps out of 914.

In 1976 there were 16 races. Hunt won six times, took pole eight times, was also on the front row three times, set fastest lap twice and led 319 laps out of 1,030.

Repeating the proviso of how precarious such direct comparisons are, era vaulting to era, there's one aspect you can't miss. The driver does not need to dominate every qualifying session, every lap of every race, to win the Championship. He can get there tactically, seizing enough chances along the way, simply keeping on. That is revealed by looking at Hill's record against Clark's.

It's a reasonable assumption, however, that every driver would have dominated every qualifying session and led every lap if he could – adding only another proviso, that when the Championship tightened and tactics did come into play, they drove for percentages if that was what was required: Hawthorn needing only second place at Casablanca, and so on.

Nor does any of this cover what makes motor racing virtually unique, the equipment. Nowhere else is equipment vital: nobody suggests that Liverpool only won so many football matches because they had the best boots, that McEnroe could never have won Wimbledon without one make of racket rather than another, that Botham only made runs because he had one make of bat rather than another. Only horse racing resembles motor racing, in that if one horse – the jockey's equipment – is hugely better than the others it will be difficult, if not impossible, to beat, particularly if such as Piggott are on it. The horse will cover the ground faster.

Clark's Lotus in 1963 and 1965 was hugely the best car, and it covered the ground faster, but how good or bad was the opposition? What comparisons do you use? Hunt made significant progress towards the 1976 Championship while Lauda recovered from the Nurburgring crash, which begs a subsequent question: was Hunt's McLaren a better car than Lauda's Ferrari? How do you separate the performance of the driver from the potential of the car?

After a certain point, if one driver has a hugely better car he will cover the ground faster and will be difficult, if not impossible, to beat. If you've a mind for this sort of thing you can wander endlessly in the maze of it, balancing one perspective against another, wringing your own comparisons, playing your own mind games, Hawthorn versus Stewart, Hunt versus Graham Hill.

From whichever direction you approach 1992, what Nigel Mansell achieved looms so colossal, so all-embracing that you need a context to press it into.

There is no dispute that the Canon Williams-Renault was hugely better than the rest. Mansell exploited it more than any man had exploited any car since Clark in 1965. We shall see.

In 1992 there were 16 races. Mansell won nine times, took pole 14 times, was also on the front row once, set fastest lap eight times and led 692 laps out of 1,036.

The full extent of this cannot be escaped, whatever basis you care to use for comparisons. It was more wins, poles and fastest laps than Hawthorn had in his entire career *spanning seven years and 45 races*; more poles than Hill had from *176 races*; more poles and wins than Surtees had from *111 races*; the same number of poles and one win less than Hunt had *in his entire career spanning seven years and 92 races*.

Moreover, Mansell might have constructed an even more massive monument, being content to let others set fastest laps (because he didn't need to), and at least twice allowing Patrese by as a gesture to a team-mate. Otherwise he'd have led more laps and equally would have won Monaco, too, if a wheel weight hadn't come off, making him pit for what he thought must be a puncture and thus lose a very, very safe win. Even then he finished second.

Mansell destroyed all significant records for a single season. The poles, 14, beat Senna's 13 in 1988 and 1989. The wins, nine, beat Senna's eight in 1988. The points total, 108, was also a summit, although with the caveat that only because a win had been worth 10 points since 1991. In 1988 Prost scored 105 – translating to 112 if he'd been getting the 10, not nine.

Patrese, who had the same equipment, couldn't compete with Mansell. The hurricane blew him away. Senna had a package which couldn't compete, and for which Senna's racecraft, thinking and intelligence couldn't compensate.

No man had won the first five races of a season, and if Senna's four in 1991 were deceptive, this manifestly wasn't. McLaren weren't catching Williams. Nobody was. The fabled five-in-a-row represented only opening shots; Silverstone brought a climactic, Mansell destroying the qualifying record with a lap to stand against any, anywhere, anytime, and within half a lap of the start of the race destroying the whole field, too. This is Mansell moving away from Patrese, Senna's times thrown in for interest.

	Mansell	Patrese	Senna
Lap 1	1:33.601	1:36.868	1:39.127
Lap 2	1:26.914	1:29.628	1:30.433
Lap 3	1:26.679	1:28.645	1:28.909
Lap 4	1:26.327	1:28.537	1:28.484
Lap 5	1:26.578	1:28.249	1:28.560

Eleven times Mansell set fastest lap, climaxing on lap 57 (1:22.539), Patrese's quickest 1:25.519, Senna's quickest 1:25.825. Maybe we should dwell on that. Berger had a best of 1:24.875, Schumacher 1:24.344. Putting it stark as a knife thrust, only Schumacher reached inside *2 seconds* of Mansell's best. Mansell began lapping backmarkers after a mere 13 laps.

Silverstone was typical of the broad acres of 1992, Mansell able to race by himself, pace himself, run alone, a lonely discipline demanding different qualities than the racer. He'd mastered that, too.

An awesome thing. Mansell found virtually every circuit responsive, hospitable, didn't matter if the corners flowing at him were the 'new' Kyalami, or Spain in the rain, or Monaco, the sweeps and straights of Silverstone, the autobahn of Hockenheim, the nip-and-tuck of the Hungaroring; although that was different, very different, the Championship now in play and Mansell not in pole.

During the race he contrived to overtake Berger three times, sharp and hard, contrived to come back from a crippling pit stop (another putative puncture frightener) and forced a mighty, majestic path past any who stood in his way. He couldn't reach Senna and circled second, comfy and easy, the ultimate percentage for the Championship. Hawthorn would have understood, except that Hawthorn played the percentage in the last race of 1958, Mansell with five races left. Within days it became messy, a verbal deal done with Williams at Hungary sealing down 1993 rescinded by Williams, a tawdry saga of whether Prost had already signed for 1993, of whether Senna – who with an extremely provocative, almost cataclysmic gesture, announced to James Hunt he'd drive free for Williams – would drive a wedge into it.

This climaxed at Monza when Mansell announced his retirement again, and during the press conference a Williams employee tried to persuade him out of it. Mansell chugged on through his carefully prepared statement, a most peculiar conjunction.

The predictable public outcry, breasted by an abortive demo from *The Sun* newspaper at the factory decorated by not-so-seductive Page Three girls, reverberated here and there. The reverberation centred on a concensus of gut feelings among The Great British Public. Why when we get a World Champion do we drive him out? (No pun intended). Conversely, in a recession, with unemployment mounting and people counting their pennies, why did Mansell not settle for less money since it would be still in the millions, and he already had many millions?

Was the presence of Prost the problem? Mansell had enjoyed undisputed number one status with Patrese – what Mansell calls his "comfort zone" – and would he get that with Prost? (Innuendo: Prost French, Renault French, Elf French, Mansell from Upton-on-Severn.)

Enter Hunt and, inadvertently, Murray Walker, commentating on the BBC during the Japanese Grand Prix, Mansell's second last Formula One race, when the saga still limped onwards. The race had moved into a fallow period (nothing much happening) and Hunt said sharp words about Mansell not defending the Championship in 1993, so sharp that Mansell threatened legal action.

You can blame the Williams team for the way they handled the saga (badly, and without sensitivity), but you cannot fault their logic: we have a chance of Prost and Mansell, so why not? If Mansell goes we still have Prost. We can have Senna. If Prost won't tolerate Senna, bearing in mind their particular histories, we still have Prost. When any Formula One team has the car every driver wants – and needs – that team is in an immensely strong position, but also a potentially delicate one. The team is deep into the jostle of egos and conditions and demands and 50-page legal contracts. It brings us back to Rory Bremner's parody of the spoons and the sugar.

Moreover, the whole of Formula One now had to address the question of costs; were finding, as Frank Williams would say, that technology swallowed more and more resources, while simultaneously a large percentage of the budget went simply to pay the drivers. In this climate Williams offered Mansell a pay cut and he declined.

So he went to IndyCars, where Clark and Hill and Stewart had been so long ago, and a vast slough of publicity followed him there, mostly analyzing the dangers and how difficult he'd find oval racing. Other commentators examined the complicated IndyCar system of flags and pace cars, probed the tactics of when you pit and when you don't, and how you play the flags to your advantage: sophisticated stuff and demanding knowledge, judgment and finesse. How would he cope with all this, remote from everything he'd known before?

Immediately he was quick. What else would he have been? What else could he be?

The IndyCar people, and particularly Paul Newman and Carl Haas of his own team, loved it. The team started to pump out statements that at Mansell's first test "some 80 members of the working news media – about half representing organizations outside the United States – were at Phoenix International Raceway as Mansell was scheduled to take his initial laps on an oval track. It certainly was the most extensively reported test session in the 81-year history of IndyCar racing." Mansell had transported Mansell Mania across the Atlantic, just like that.

He promptly transported it across the Pacific to Surfers' Paradise, Queensland, a road circuit, and thus familiar in character. He beat Emerson Fittipaldi by some 5 seconds and became the first rookie to win his first IndyCar race since Graham Hill took the Indy 500 in 1966. Mansell professes surprise at how "physically demanding" it had been and "if you overdrive these cars you can go slower, so I still have a lot to learn."

At Phoenix he faced an oval and broke the track record in the first practice session, went hard in the second, went too hard. In Turn One, and at a speed estimated at 170mph he lost his Lola-Ford and struck the wall backwards with such force he broke the concrete. He woke up in the medical helicopter as it landed at the hospital. The story of a life, the bravery, the injury, the fight-back he'd make to be fit for the race after, Long Beach. But…had he been too brave?

Raul Boesel, once of Formula One and now with the Simon/Duracell team, would say "Mansell tested a lot at Phoenix and he was extra-confident, but the problem with oval circuits is that it is very difficult to judge the limit. That's the most critical point. He also drives, I'd say, on the edge of oversteer and I repeat, it's very difficult to judge when you need to readjust the car or the point where you can catch it if something goes wrong. He was on that edge. You always think if you've caught the car once, twice, you can go further, but that's when the oval catches you. It was definitely better for him to find out at Phoenix than Indianapolis, because at Indianapolis if you have something like that the consequences can be a lot worse."

Mansell arrived at Long Beach "sore and stiff," broke the track record, took pole and finished third. He led the Championship with 36 points, his team-mate Mario Andretti on 32, Teo Fabi on 26.

And he came to Indianapolis, where they still speak of Clark and Hill and Stewart, but particularly Clark. Minutes before qualifying began, A J Foyt announced his retirement, and his impromptu little speech dissolved into tears and long silences while he composed himself. He'd first raced the 500 in 1958, the year Hawthorn founded the CHAMPIONS! dynasty, had won it four times, and although reluctant to praise any other driver as a matter of principle, always spoke with admiration and affection about Clark.

Mansell qualified eighth and drove a very great race in the authentic sense, confirming – if any confirmation were still needed – his global stature. He led, but deep into the race Emerson Fittipaldi (Penske-Chevrolet) and Arie Luyendyk

(Lola-Ford) outfoxed him when a green flag was hoisted and Mansell finished third.

Subsequently, Derek Daly, another former Formula One emigre, expressed the firm opinion that Mansell might have gone to Indianapolis "scared" by all the people who'd told him scare stories, but Mansell dismissed such notions by what he did in a couple of hours of qualifying, opening the way for his great race. This was made more poignant by the exploits of Michael Andretti, partnering Senna in the Marlboro McLaren in Formula One, who scarcely looked a leading Formula One driver, and whose limitations were being mercilessly exposed by Senna's exploits.

Mansell then stormed Milwaukee, an oval...

To find perspective about Mansell became more and more difficult. To help in that, here is John Watson, wise in the ways of motor racing. "Nigel is almost like a caricature. If you see him out of the car he does not look like a racing driver, and he doesn't live the sort of life the public associates with a racing driver. He knows what he is comfortable with, and therefore he is sophisticated in that sense, but he is not into the image of being a racing driver. That is, living in Monte Carlo.

"What was more important to him in living on the Isle of Man was that it is part of Great Britain, and everything about it is British, the food, the way of life. The people in the street speak English, so in that sense he is not sophisticated. The twist, then, is that he recognized what he was comfortable with as opposed to Monte Carlo. Miami? Again they speak English, Florida offers a very pleasant lifestyle, lovely weather, a practical place to live, and if you are wealthy enough you can choose the areas that are nice.

"What Nigel does – which I think is unique – is gain tremendous strength from Rosanne. She should be given half the awards for Nigel's achievements. That woman has lived with a guy who can be difficult. He is maybe misunderstood, but he doesn't help that by his way of expressing himself. She deserves enormous credit because she is as much a part of the process of success as he is.

"What I find admirable is that when he goes to, say, the Monaco Grand Prix he brings his wife and children with him and he eats with his family. He is a family man, he doesn't run round, he's not a playboy, he's very straight-forward, fundamentally uncomplicated. Through tremendous belief and persistence he has grown – and he is still growing – and he has not yet fulfilled his potential. He may not get any faster, but he may become even better.

"Personally I am delighted because it says a lot for mature men. For example, Michael Schumacher is very young, exceedingly quick and has tremendous long-term potential, but there is Mansell at 39, soon he'll be 40, and I don't think there is anybody around who's quicker.

"You can argue that if you put Senna or Schumacher into that Williams they would do exceptional things, too, but Mansell was blinding. At Silverstone in qualifying in 1992 he did 1 minute 18.9. I cannot put into words what that must have been like, because the degree of personal commitment, the degree he dug into his boots, the sheer courage that was required, together with the skill and everything else ... well, that time is unbelievable, stunning, truly magnificent. You are talking about him taking a second off his quickest lap. To find a tenth of a second at that level is impossible in most cases, you're scratching to do it and goggle-eyed if you do.

"He needs deperately to be loved, and that is a weakness in his total character, but the need enables him to do what he did at Silverstone. He is pumped up like hell, but if there wasn't a crowd, he wasn't getting the sort of support from them that he does get, it might have been different.

"This is why I think his racing in America is going to prove very interesting. [My interview with Watson was before the IndyCar season began, and I'm not being unfair including his observations because they are instructive in a wider context.] He will not have the kind of jingoistic support he has become accustomed to, he'll have a different type of audience, a difference sort of media. Undoubtedly he will be bloody quick, but it is totally different.

"He may win them over very quickly, in which case he will do outstandingly well. On the other hand, if it does not come together and you're racing in a car anybody can go out and buy, nothing different about it technically, no advantage, it will be a true indication of his greatness, or it may open up questions about his character.

"The problem is that he himself compounds his downsides. It is now almost a standing joke that as soon as he opens his mouth you are going to get: 'Oh, I had a problem with this and that.' Actually, in his own way, maybe he has got to the stage of parodying himself. I don't know. The other evening I went to a presentation in London. He turned up on crutches having had an operation on a bone in his foot. He said: 'I had to have a second operation because the epidural began to leak.' It could only happen to him, just...just him.

"Senna can get out of the car and say things and be critical. Did the Honda people ever jump to attention when they had a new engine and Senna was critical. Yet when Nigel is being critical he is a whinger. 'My car is not good, my car is not good', and he has a credibility gap. That gap has closed, but it still exists. I don't mean with the media, I mean with the team.

"If you offered any team either Senna or Mansell I'd think Nigel would be second choice, and it is a great shame because Nigel has done something truly remarkable. He did not have the dream style like, say, Stirling Moss; he has gone down the path of bump and grind, pillar to post, and I am happy to say he is capitalizing on that. I'd say he's very astute generally. The deals he makes are pretty good deals. The downside of that was the situation with Williams and Prost..."

There was talk, late in '92, that perhaps Mansell might 'guest' in Formula One, his IndyCar commitments permitting, and some enterprizing soul even consulted airline guides, worked out how many trans-Atlantic flights it would involve, which races he could do here, with races there. It was a good story on its day, but betrayed an undercurrent. Formula One, which initially had seen Mansell as the journeyman all those years before, now needed him.

He was asked if he could perhaps drive in 12 of the 16 Formula One races. "I think maybe Superman could, but I'm not Superman. It's just not possible. I think there are only seven races that don't conflict, anyway." He spoke, also, of the Silverstone invasion of 1992. His supporters got a lot of criticism for that, "but if you remember I stood by them, hard and fast, and I still do now, today."

Question: "They love you?"

"I love them."

The need to love, and the need to be loved. Perhaps, as John Watson implies, that's really it. That time in *The Times*, Hunt called him the outsider of the pit lane, and outsiders are either happy to be on the outside, working out their own destinies, or urgently need to be inside.

In the matter of coping with publicity, of coping with becoming a public persona – a profound alteration in the life of any person – Mansell was obliged to face mounting demands on a scale difficult to imagine unless you're the recipient. Some, like Lauda, were indifferent to adulation and distrusted nationalism. Some, like Prost, accepted it as it came, accepted it as it went away again. Some, like Clark, found it cloying and obtrusive and extremely unwelcome. Some, like Hunt himself, wandered through it and kept on wandering, whatever fears wracked him on the circuits when he drove. Some, like Hawthorn, resented every intrusion and, particularly after Le Mans in 1955, regarded reporters with subdued hostility – and Hawthorn had not known the full intrusive appetite of the media, circa 1993, nor known the full intrusive effect of the television camera constantly poked into your face every place you went.

When Clark received a mild version of adverse publicity after the Von Trips accident – journalists waiting outside the farm at Duns – he became extremely indignant. Graham Hill coped beautifully, naturally, and created publicity. Of them all he was born out of his time. He would have understood the medium circa the Nineties intuitively, and worked it to maximum effect. Mansell learnt at least to be at ease with it, no mean feat when the world had become 15-second sound bites and the way you spoke, every mannerism, each shift of an eyeball, laid bare.

It remains touching that so many drivers were content to give their addresses and telephone numbers for publication in *The Motor Racing Register* in 1965. It also remains eloquent of an era gone, and no doubt gone forever. As I write these words, Monica Seles has just been stabbed between the shoulder-blades by a spectator at a tennis tournament. Yes, 1965 is very long gone in every aspect.

It's very curious to see Nigel Mansell as the love-child of Formula One, and very curious to see Formula One lovelorn when he released his embrace from it, but that is what happened, no less. After another saga (nothing to do with Mansell) Williams named Damon Hill as Mansell's replacement for 1993. Hill handled it well. He was after all 30, or perhaps 31, but more probably 32; not only film actresses guard their vital statistics. (Gilles Villeneuve did, too.) Under the media appetite Hill would be obliged to speak endlessly about his father, and I'm as culpable as any. It's what you got in the chapter on Graham.

Damon provided the last conjunction or the latest continuation, whichever you prefer. His father raced Hawthorn and had been at Casablanca, Morocco, in 1958, the day it began, and it's endured all the way to here.

Reflecting, Mansell says: "The world moves on", and if this is not the most profound philosophical insight you've ever read it remains true. The world moved on the instant Williams told Damon Hill he'd partner Prost, moved on as Mansell moved to IndyCars and captivated another continent.

He made the occasional acerbic remark about Formula One, but we were ready for that because he was vindicating his own decision to go from it. He had reached an immensity, and it was more immense because of the loveless years: this year he had Paul Newman enthralled, *the* Paul Newman, half a million at Indianapolis in tumult, American kids being christened after him, hardened chat show hosts on national television charmed, commentators gabbling about what he could make a motor car do in those clipped, pointed phrases Americans wield.

In 1991 you'd have judged him as a man who nearly did, but somehow never did.

In 1992 you'd have judged him as the man who finally did, but just once after this long wait.

In 1993 you'd have to judge that his place among the CHAMPIONS! requires reassessment. Given the same cars, which of the other six – Hawthorn, Hill, Clark, Surtees, Stewart and Hunt – would you have wagered your life to beat him? Only he truly took on Senna elbow-to-elbow, will-to-will, wheel-to-wheel and emerged unbroken, unbowed and undeterred; and many feel the only comparison with Senna is Fangio and...Clark.

Mansell takes his place among the CHAMPIONS! for the reason that no man can deny: he earned it, then he did it, exactly like the others.

THE BRIDGE OF SIGHS

Autumn 1992 through spring 1993, and in such a book as this you gather shards of memory scattered so long ago, but which still refract light. They don't easily fit into the flow of the narrative, for one reason or another, but they acquire a separate strength because they are random, unexpected, and fashion a prism. Here they are.

DEREK BELL is at the Motor Show, Birmingham, where he's just announced his scheme to teach people how to handle fast road cars properly. His first pupil will be decathlete Daley Thompson, who sits just over there smiling broadly and chatting to anyone who comes by. "In the last three weeks," Bell says, "I went to the *Club des Ancient Pilotes*, all the old racing drivers, Carroll Shelby and Dan Gurney and Stirling Moss, Clay Regazzoni bless him, people going back as far as time began. One of them was a chap called Tony Gaze, an Australian, and a tall, elegant, very nice-looking man who'd raced in the early Fifties. He said he'd been a pilot in the war. He asked where I lived and I said: 'Chichester', and he said: 'Oh, I was based there. I couldn't fight back home so I came to fight in the RAF. We'd go on four sorties a day and the adrenalin we got was just like racing.'

"These guys who were racing drivers, they were not stupid, they were very brilliant, calculating men, the same kind who would fly a Mosquito and a Spitfire. They weren't content sitting back, so don't give me crap that they were just playboys. They were brave, bloody clever guys and, like the Mosquitos and the Spitfires, it was something you had to do, very definitely. It's changed, and I'm glad its changed, but that doesn't alter the fact that it was like that. Jimmy Clark, for example, was annoyingly modest to those around him, but in those days drivers weren't promoted and presented the way they are today, there was no sponsorship. They didn't make much money out of it, and they weren't in it for the money anyway. They did it because they loved it."

By coincidence **DICKIE ATTWOOD** comes along, a trim, neat, precise man, shakes hands with Bell and settles in front of my tape recorder. He nurses firm views, although he tempers them before they become trenchant. "People always ask what the makeup of a racing driver is, and there are so many combinations of things starting with eyesight and moving into everything else. You could probably make a computer do what the best guy in the world can do, and the best guy in the world would probably still beat the computer. I don't really know what it is. An extra sense perhaps.

"Jim Clark was a smooth driver, he did make several mistakes but they didn't cost him very much. The classic mistake was at Brands Hatch when he just seemed to drive off the circuit coming out of what used to be called Bottom Bend and he destroyed the car, but Jimmy never cut himself, he never had any injuries at all. Mind you, I saw him at Monte Carlo coming out of the Gasometer hairpin, he bashed both wheels and the rear of the car on the left-hand kerb and missed the hydrant on the side of the road. He had the elements of luck, but he was so far and away the best that maybe the luck followed him until that day at Hockenheim.

"There have been a lot of drivers in the world who never got into the right car, or never got into a racing car at all – a lot of undiscovered blokes out there who have natural balance, the combination of eyesight, touch, feel, all of it, but it's never put to the test. There could be other Jimmys, but there was only one Jimmy in his era, like Stirling Moss before him. Jimmy was just quicker than anybody else. Why? I don't know.

"I never asked him how he could do it, and I don't think it is a question you pose. That would be like one professional asking another, and you just don't. He wouldn't have known, anyway. I don't believe he was aware of it, he was number one all the time and it became part of his make-up. I can't explain it, I'm sure he couldn't explain it, and nor could anybody else. They may have tried, but at the end of the day they never got to the bottom of it."

Tell me about the atmosphere. "That's the whole thing, isn't it? You go back nearly 30 years and the world was a different place. All the drivers got together after a race and had a bloody good bash. There wasn't the publicity, there wasn't the television – I think television has been an enormous influence. The pressure of the world has become so intense that I cannot contemplate what it's going to be like in another 20 or 30 years.

"The Sporthotel at the Nurburgring was the only place to go, it was convenient, right on the circuit, but everywhere we went we all stayed in the same place. Of course the back-up people didn't exist, you didn't have the number of crew men. You simply couldn't get everybody in the Sporthotel now because the entourages are too big. Unless you were there then it's difficult to imagine. It was like club racing is today, I think, that sort of atmosphere, relaxed, good fun, great times. I feel sorry for the people now because they missed all that.

"There was a morality about racing, but along with that you have to consider the safety of the cars of the day. You did not bang wheels, you didn't really get near enough to a guy to start an incident because it was too dangerous. That is what is wrong with a lot of racing today: they crash into each other knowing they are in a safety cell. It's not as clean and fair as it used to be. Michael Schumacher charging into Ayrton Senna a couple of times in 1992, that's the exuberance of youth over the older, more experienced guy, but it would not have happened years ago, you just didn't take those sort of risks. You'd have got killed, yes, that's right. There wasn't much grass alongside the old circuits, just telegraph poles and people standing behind them. It's like trying to compare the old Spa with the one now. These people talk about the glorious new Spa. To me it's totally boring. A lot of the circuits built in the last 20 years have constant-radius corners, geometrically correct but not interesting at all. You simply cannot compare the two Spas."

Clark hated Spa, didn't he? "Yes, but he won there four times. He drove it and everybody else drove it. We never thought of having drivers' strikes or anything like that. You got on with it whatever the conditions were."

JOHN SURTEES sits in his office in Edenbridge, a pleasant drive through woodland from the M25. He deals in property, has just written a couple of books, and is heavily into restoring old bikes – a hobby, he describes it, and no doubt the echo of a whole life. He's also raising money for the nearby St Piers Lingfield centre for children with epilepsy.

"Jimmy Clark I had a great affection for. He was a genuine character and an honourable person, unlike a few others. He truly got something out of his motorsport, he was good at it, but at the same time it was very important to him and he created a relationship with a car.

"He was still able to switch off and become another person, and that gave him an advantage. He could recharge his batteries to a degree many of us totally involved couldn't. We treated it as a seven-day week, a way of life. Jimmy could not work that way. That's partly why he built up such a relationship with Chapman. Chapman said: 'Jimmy, go away, I'll sort the car', and Chapman would get on with it."

Surtees remains active, if not hyperactive. "If somebody approaches me and says they want a particular machine I'll do some research, find it and fix them up with it; if necessary I'll put it back into its original condition – totally original, so that it not only looks right but is right. What worries me these days is that I see so many period bikes tucked in museums which are so-called restored. All they have is a slap of paint on them. There's so much material out there without innards! They're not really running examples."

VIC ELFORD is living in Reno, Nevada, after a tortuous but interesting career centred around motorsport. "The first time I met Jim Clark was in 1964 or 1965. Because of the success of the Cortina, Ford got about 30 or 40 of us who had starred in them from Britain, from Germany, from the States, from Australia, all over. They took us to Cortina d'Ampezzo in the Italian Dolomites for the weekend. A load of journalists were there – I've an idea John Blunsden was among them [he was! – JB] – and Ford told us we'd be driving Cortinas down the toboggan run! We'd also be taking the journalists down and they sat there crapping themselves when they heard.

"The night before, we had a fairly well-lubricated party and after it was over Colin Chapman, Jimmy, myself and someone else got in a Cortina which Ford had lent us and we went to the top of the run to have a try-out, see what it would be like. Jimmy drove. It was night, of course, and we came thundering down this thing with the car going left and right, bouncing off the walls. They had gaps in the walls which were normally packed with snow and ice when the sledges were coming down. The Cortina bounced a little bit wrong, Jim got a little bit out of sequence and bashed the left front into one of the gaps. That destroyed the car. How did Clark cope with a sheet-ice toboggan run in the dark? OK [chuckle]. He just sort of let the thing steer itself between the walls.

"I met him at other places," Elford says, "and I knew him reasonably well, but by no means intimately. He was a marvellous chap and I would like to have known him a lot, lot better. He was unpretentious, didn't throw his weight around. I can't imagine a greater difference than between Jim Clark and one or two of the prima donnas today in Formula One."

JOHN WEBB lives in Spain and, he says, he's a pretty good suntan. "Clark was an absolute, complete gentleman. I knew him to the extent that he used to come home to dinner. He'd be totally relaxed there, a gentleman in every way. I'm sure he understood what he had, although not in the sense that people do today because money didn't come into it very much. As a hobby I ran a little outfit called Webbair, which took all the Grand Prix drivers, mechanics and press to the races. Clark was always a bundle of fun on the aeroplane. I think I remember him as a person more than as a driver because he was a delightful man."

JACKIE STEWART who, never let us forget, won more Grand Prix races than Clark and waited 19 years for another Briton to move past his total, has a touching refraction of light, or two. "My memories of Jim will always be of his incredible inability to make decisions. I tell a story which epitomizes that. We were to race at Sebring, we were in a hire car crossing Florida, the countryside flat as a pancake. Here was a single-track railway line and a level crossing. We looked left and it's clear for 10 miles, we looked right and it's clear for 10 miles, we looked back up again to the left – still clear for 10 miles. Jim's driving. He turns to me and says: 'What do you think?'

"He didn't want to be faced with any form of decision-making. His nails were bitten almost to the core, there was hardly any nail on any of his fingers. Here was the coolest, calmest, most calculating racing driver in the world, and he continually bit his nails and chewed his fingers with nervousness; and if there was anybody who was going to have an ulcer it would have been Jim Clark. In a way he was a terribly highly-tensed man and yet…the moment he slipped into a racing car he changed."

PETER WARR was both an official with FISA and Secretary of the BRDC, based at Silverstone, when we went to a very British pub in Silverstone village for a ploughman's lunch. Somehow it's the right place and the right thing to order if you're to talk about the seven British winners.

"If you think about it, you loved or hated Stewart, Hunt you loved or hated, Mansell you love him or hate him, but Clark…there wasn't anybody I know who didn't adore the guy, didn't worship him, not a single person. I have never met anybody who said: 'Oh, he's a bastard', or even: 'Oh, he can't take a joke.'

"Senna is the one I compare with Jimmy because he is the most complete racing driver of today, and by that I mean all the physical attributes, reaction times, the skill, but he's also got the mind, the intelligence, he works at his race. I accept that you can't compare the two because the era now is very different. Jimmy'd come to Silverstone and you'd see him in the sportscar race in the morning, Formula One after lunch and finish with a saloon car race. Well, they're not allowed to do that now, but Senna, I am convinced, is the only one who could have done the programme Jimmy did and been as good in everything.

"When Jimmy drove Patrick Lindsay's ERA at Rouen during the French Grand Prix weekend he'd never driven anything before with the accelerator between the brake and clutch pedals, yet in three laps he was quicker than Lindsay, who'd been driving it for several seasons.

"Ayrton showed us just how good he was when, if you remember, in a Mercedes celebrity race at the new Nurburgring in 1984 – all the hot shoes were there in identical cars – he blew them away. That was the only real time we've had a clue that Senna would have been the same if the era had been the same as Jimmy's – that he could have stepped into anything and been bloody quick. That is the measure I make: that he is a complete race driver. Jimmy told me once that whenever he could he left 18 inches between himself and the edge of the road on the exit from a corner to give himself a small margin.

Distant dialogue...

Warr: Listen, you know you've got this fantastic reputation for going through practice and then, when there's a minute and a half of the session left, you pop it on pole with a time nobody can get near. How do you do that? Do you use more revs, do you change gear in a different place? How do you actually go about doing a lap that is substantially quicker than one you have done before?

Clark: I don't really know. (Clark sat and pondered.) If I stop and think my way round one of those laps, I do everything exactly the same.

Warr: But that can't be quicker.

Clark: Well, except I brake a little less hard.

Warr: But that means you are committing the car to a corner at a speed at which you haven't previously entered it. How do you know it's going to do what you want it to?

Clark: Well, it's just a feeling. You *know* it's going to do it.

"If you go on from there, I remember one year at Jerez and in qualifying Senna had done a 1 minute 17.6 seconds, a 17.7 – anyway it was half a second faster than everybody else."

Distant dialogue...

Warr: That's it Ayrton, you don't have to go out again.

Senna: No, no, no, I just sit here in the car.

Warr: But it's pointless.

Senna: No, no, no, I just sit in the car for a bit. (Senna sat and pondered for about 15 minutes, quiet, with his eyes nearly shut, and called Warr over). I can do a 1 minute 16.9. I've been thinking my way round the lap and I can do it.

Warr: But it's not necessary.

Senna: Yes, but I'd like to see if I can do it.

"We put the other set of qualifying tyres on, out he goes, 1 minute 16.9 absolutely on the button. He'd replayed the lap 10 times in his mind and worked out where he could pick up the difference. That's the most astonishing thing about these guys, what sets them apart. I'll give you another example. When we got to the Alan Jones-Carlos Reutemann era with the Williams FW7, which was the definitive ground effect car, Jones didn't have a problem at all, but Reutemann did. Take a corner like Copse at Silverstone, he'd say, the difficulty is getting your mind to accept that the car will turn in at that speed, you can't get through the mental barrier of a voice inside you saying *it's too quick, it won't do it, I'm going to finish in the wall*. So the guys who have what Jimmy called instinctive *feel*, who just know the car will if you do it right, are very few and far between. I think Prost has some of that, too.

"James Hunt? One has to be careful. Of course he did a lot of commentating, and many people who didn't know him when he was racing formed an opinion of him as a result of his public image. You've got to divorce that from when he was a good race driver. He continued to enjoy the same thing that used to make him turn up at the BRDC annual dinner-dance in jeans and sneakers instead of a dinner jacket. He still had the same element in him – hadn't he? – where he felt he had to say something controversial, it was expected of him, and that's how he got brainstorms – because his public expected it of him."

The Hunt enigma continued to make **ALAN BRINTON** wonder. "I've seen him at the BBC. I was coming out, there he was, no socks, he looked awful. I said: 'Where's your car?' He got onto his rusty old mountain bike and flew off. Did you see him at Silverstone last year (1992)? He pulled into the press car park in an Austin A35 Countryman, rusting all over, with his wife and two kids. 'Great little car,' he said, 'great little car. Never given me any trouble, great fun to drive.' Is that affectation or what? At the BBC I've seen when he's due to be on air and people are saying: 'My Christ, 10 minutes to go, where's Hunt?' At the last minute he'd stroll in eating fish and chips or he's got a pie from somewhere. 'What are you worrying about? I'm here, aren't I?' But I wonder if he'd waited round the corner to make his entry with one minute to go." Hunt himself gave a variation of this, part confirmation, and we'll come to it in just a moment.

ANDREW COWAN is still in rallying, working for Mitsubishi on one of those modern industrial estates which seem to be constructed of pre-packed plastic blocks, clean, functional and all the same inside. It's near Rugby and a long way from Duns, in time as well as distance.

Was it difficult for Clark to live in Paris away from all the things he knew and loved? "No, because that wasn't going to be the way of life for him in the future. I don't think he dreamed of doing a Jackie Stewart, going to settle in Geneva or anywhere like that. Even the money drivers were earning when Jimmy was World Champion wouldn't be enough to let him say to himself *what am I going to do with all this?*

"He was advised to become a non-resident of Britain and thereby qualify not to pay so much tax on his earnings. Those earnings were peanuts compared to what they would have been even three or four years later.

"He was a farmer at Edington Mains and he was going to stay a farmer at Edington Mains. He had a lovely farm and he loved it. I don't think he would ever have given that up. His heart was at home in Scotland, at Edington Mains. He could have gone anywhere and spent any amount of time to race a car – he was unmarried, he didn't have any ties – but he was coming home to Edington Mains, no question about that.

"It was astonishing the people that made friends with his parents, people from all over the world. They wanted to go and walk where Jim Clark walked even when he was racing, and a lot of people – like Bette Hill – stayed in contact with them up until the time of their deaths. Jimmy's own death was impossible, it was impossible. I've often heard it said that that Formula Two race didn't mean anything on a safe and boring circuit, but that didn't matter to Jimmy. The race – every race – was important to Jimmy irrespective of what car or where.

"He once told me that when he had a place in Bermuda and was on holiday there he received a call from the States asking him if he'd like to drive one of those saloon cars they race, the big slipstreaming jobs where they weld the doors. Somebody was staying with him – I think it may have been Graham Hill – and Jimmy said: 'Yeah' and then to Graham: 'Come on, it's a two-car thing, we'll both go over', but Graham said: 'No, I'm going home.' Jimmy went and drove, and although he broke down he said: 'The slipstreaming and stuff like that was right up my street.' It wasn't *how much are you going to pay me*, or *is it dangerous?*, but this is something *I haven't done before, I'd love to do that*. And that was Jim."

What would you like to say about him that you haven't already said? Cowan pauses so long before he finds himself ready to answer that when I'm transcribing the tape of the interview I count the length of the pause: 14 seconds. "The sad thing for me is that I don't think he ever realized how good he was and where this could have led him. In his wildest dreams he'd never have believed that 25 years on every time you pick up *Autosport* – like last week again – there's a photograph of Jim Clark, and that's happening the world over. That makes me sad because he's not here to enjoy it. I feel it because I was travelling all those years in my rallying, spending a lot of time in the southern hemisphere, and Jimmy loved New Zealand, Australia, South Africa. Everywhere you went, and you go, people hear your Scottish accent and ask: 'Did you know Jim Clark?' It still happens. It's like it's just there, it's alive."

OSWALD BREWIS has a warm Borders accent, almost a lilt, and there is warmth and a quiet maturity in his voice, a resonance. "I've seen Jimmy become very rude with people, but I don't think I ever saw him lose his temper. He could give people the brush-off, let's put it that way, especially prior to racing. If someone came up and shoved a microphone in his face he could be *extremely* rude. A lot of people hadn't the sense to do otherwise. He could be brusque, there would be no hesitation, that would be it. He could also get very angry, and he *looked* angry. None of us went near him on those occasions, we left him alone.

"I don't remember him ever speaking of danger, well, I suppose he did in the sense that they all did – about dangerous corners, dangerous bits which at that time there wasn't a hell of a lot done about. Spa particularly was one which bothered him, he was certainly well aware of danger, but no, he didn't talk about it."

What would you like to say about him that you haven't already said? "It's such a shame that we didn't have him with us a lot longer. He was almost still learning the business, he was so good, but I don't think he was at his peak. He had so much more potential. No, I don't think he would have gone back farming. He might have continued to *operate* his farm…"

JIM ENDRUWEIT lives in Norwich these days. "Jim Clark was the last of the gentlemen drivers, one of nature's gentlemen. He had great determination, but he never threw his weight about, he was always polite and he inspired a tremendous loyalty from his crew. The blokes would do anything for him, work all night standing on their heads if they had to. Jim didn't deal in excuses. If he made a cock-up, he made a cock-up.

"He'd sit in the pits, go out and do a few laps, come back in and sit on the pit counter apparently not doing anything. I guess he was psyching himself up, working it all out. Suddenly he'd get off the pit counter and say: 'OK, I'll go and do three.' He'd do a warm up lap, a sizzler, a slowing down lap, he'd come in and say to me: 'That's it', and he had pole. He'd get out of the car and go and sit on the pit counter again…

"He'd have tremendous discussions with Chapman about the car. In engineering terms Jimmy was inarticulate, he could tell you what the car was doing but he'd be using his hands. 'You go into this corner and it does this.' Chapman could and would interpret what Jimmy was saying and would tell us: 'OK, give this a tweak, give that a tweak,' and that is how it used to be."

MATTIE, ISABEL AND BETTY are sitting in Mattie's house in the countryside not far from Edington Mains. They speak clearly and crisply and have a simple worldliness which is both touching and extremely impressive. On some shelving in a corner stand the books about Jim, and the one by him, and the videos about him. These are in no sense flaunted, just there; and other books are there, too, *All Arms and Elbows* by Innes Ireland, with a private hand-written dedication to Mattie which I won't repeat, but which absolves the whole Clark family from any responsibility for his leaving Lotus.

Since, during the course of my interview, the sisters often prompted each other, added cameos and memories in another's mid-sentence, and since they all think the same way I quote them collectively. Perhaps it's more accurate like that, anyway.

"He always arrived at the British Grand Prix as late as possible to avoid the fuss. He didn't get home much because there were races every weekend. He didn't discuss his driving when he did home home, he came to relax. He was keen on jazz. Chris Barber played at a theatre in Berwick not long ago, and Jim had known him through his keenness on jazz. Chris Barber said he felt he wasn't very far away from a friend. Jim was a bit homesick in Paris, although he could get by in French. Jabby Crombac was very good to him – Jabby's son is called Colin James and his dog was called Lotus! We used to worry because our parents had knocks on the door from strangers all the time, and our parents always took them in. The trophies were there all around the house, but they never lost anything, nobody ever took one."

One of the sisters said: "Someone in a retirement home in Kelso told me they'd been thinking about me the other day. 'I've just been writing to my brother who lives in Clark Street, Johannesburg.' The street was called after Jim and I didn't know.'"

The last word must go to Mattie, the eldest. "I would say the level of interest – in the sense of letters from strangers, visits and so on – is beginning to tail off now, but when I go down to the graveyard in Chirnside I still find flowers there with no name on."

My interview with the sisters took place in December 1992, before the pace began to gather towards April 7, 1993. The level of interest would increase in huge proportions and a full month before, *Startline*, the magazine of the British Automobile Racing Club, wrote this: "The Jim Clark Room in Duns, Berwickshire, which opened in 1969 to house the majority of the World Champion's trophy and award collection, is being totally refurbished to commemorate the 25th anniversary of his death. The Room looks set to be the focus of many an enthusiast's pilgrimage in 1993 and, since space is restricted, the organizer, Jeff Taylor, would be grateful to hear from any members who may be considering a group visit.

"The Room will be open from April 2 to late October, with normal opening times being Monday to Saturday 10am – 1pm and 2pm – 5pm, and Sunday 2pm – 5pm. Group visits outside these hours may be available. There will be a modest charge, with concessions."

JEFF TAYLOR, Berwickshire District Council's museums officer, adds to this. "The Clark family gave the old town council about 120 of Jimmy's trophies and awards in late 1968. They became the Jim Clark Memorial Room, although essentially just the trophies and awards without explaining anything much about them. We've now tried to make The Room the story of his career from the beginning, using photographs to fill in the gaps.

"We have visitor's books which run to 20 tomes and last year we recorded the 200,000th visitor. We're averaging about 5,000 a year and anticipating that will go up. People come in and they know all about what happened in the races for which Jimmy got the trophies. You should see their eyes if you open a case and let them touch one. We're also producing a Jim Clark Trail leaflet so people can go to Chirnside, where he's buried, and see the memorial clock there, can go to Charterhall and Winfield, where he raced in the early days and then back to Duns."

A curious thing happened long before the reopening of The Room. Taylor received a phone call from Professor Sid Watkins, who has a house at Coldstream where he relaxes and fishes. Watkins said he had a very important guest coming who wished to remain incognito, but would like to have a look. Taylor, intrigued, gently coaxed the name out of Watkins.

Ayrton Senna.

Senna had been invited to Loretto to make a speech; one of the boys was a friend of Senna's family and Brazilians take this sort of thing seriously (perhaps we do, too) and spent the weekend staying with Watkins. He journeyed to Duns and Taylor let him in.

"Without being disrespectful to Senna," Taylor says, "he didn't seem in any way overawed by all the trophies because he's plenty of his own and trophies are trophies. He was much more interested in what Clark was like. I imagine they were the same type of people, quiet, reflective. I looked at him and I thought: this is a very controlled man."

BETTE HILL is sitting in the lounge of her house near Clapham Common. It is decorated by the sort of mementoes you'd expect, a photograph on a wall of Graham with Prince Charles, many photographs of children and grandchildren arranged in frames across a table; some David Wynne statues. Not the Jackie Stewart mural montage, but the same idea on a more modest scale.

What did you think of Jim Clark? "He was a difficult character. I couldn't really sum him up in a few words because he was spoilt – which is natural in a boy with four older sisters. He was talented so he expected the best, and in many cases he got it. He would never make up his mind; very, very aggravating and irritating to the people he socialized with. We had occasions where we'd be flying from A to B and he'd want to go to A, B, C and D before we got there. He'd say: 'Oh, no, we can do it this way', but invariably he ended up doing it the way everyone else said.

"He didn't make up his mind whether he was going to marry Sally Stokes or not. That was on and off, which must have been absolutely traumatic for her. When she did finally marry someone else he said: 'I didn't tell you to go and get married!' He didn't want to commit himself, he would never commit himself to anything, really and truly. He was a great nail-biter, he was strung up."

In December 1992 Nigel Mansell won the BBC Sports Personality of the Year, although the occasion had to be intrinsically different from when Hawthorn sat at the same ceremony 34 years earlier and chatted to John Surtees about taking up cars. Dinner jackets were no longer *de rigeur* and, surveying the ranks of guests – each of whom had known that pressure Dickie Attwood describes so graphically – there was very little innocence left, if any. Collectively these people had made fortunes, but arguably none more than Mansell. As it happened **DAMON HILL** sat next to Mansell, Martin Brundle next to Hill: a pleasant conjunction, Damon son of Graham who'd raced Hawthorn and all the threads between connected.

The next day at the Williams factory Hill was confirmed to partner Alain Prost in 1993. Frank Williams opened the press conference by saying: "Patrick Head, who is my partner and the technical director of the team, and myself decided that Damon was the ideal candidate for the vacancy which has existed for rather a long time. Primarily Damon's attraction to the team is that he is actually very, very fast. He has demonstrated that, I think, to the surprise of a few people in recent testing, but additional to his speed, Damon was also selected because he understands Grand Prix cars. This year, whether he knows it or not, he's clocked just over 9,000 kilometres in testing our active ride car and approximately the same number the year before, again in our active ride car. Primarily our requirements from him are not to crash the car and to get on the podium as often as he can."

Hill, quietly-spoken, polite, the kind of person you like straight away – although already 32, no kid this – made precisely the right noises. He had, after all, only taken part in two Grands Prix, getting a very uncompetitive Brabham into the British and Hungarian races and goading and cajoling it to the finishing line.

"I think that motor racing has changed quite a lot in the last 10 years. It's become generally far more competitive – more people competing in it with the advent of Formula 3000. All the winners of Formula 3000 have gone on to be successful Formula One drivers, and the competition is such that a lot of the drivers now coming from there are ready to compete in Formula One. I've done three years of Formula 3000 and two years of testing with Williams. My racing experience is quite extensive and I'm not overawed in any way. I'm very familiar with the car and I relish the opportunity."

You must have answered this before, but do you think you got into the sport in the first place because of your dad, or do you think if your dad had been something else you'd still have been here today?

"I love doing dangerous things, unfortunately. [Soft smile] I just…you know, I can't help that. I started off with bikes, that was me trying to do my own thing, and I wasn't too easy into car racing, so it's difficult to say. Obviously it's an influence and I haven't been able to avoid it. What else might have happened I'm not sure, but the point is that it's tremendously exciting driving a racing car, and it's even more exciting when you're racing one. I find it attractive and I might well have done it if my father had been a bank clerk or something. After all his father was a stockbroker."

It's a topic I pursue after the press conference. "I'll tell you something. I think of him after every race I finish, but I don't think about him all the time because I've got to live. But after every race I've finished I think to myself I've done the best I could have done. I feel like he's there – you know what I mean? – saying *well done*. In some way I don't feel it quite as much now as I used to. I went through a phase of…well after he died I was in a sort of daze for about five years, and then when I started racing I think, in a way, I was getting closer to him, to understanding how he was or how he might have been. Having my own family now, I can relate to how it must have been for him having us and racing at the same time. He enjoyed the fame and being a personality and all the rest of it. Unfortunately the price is that you can't be everywhere at the same time so he wasn't at home much. I feel as if I'd like to have seen more of him, probably because he died prematurely just when I was getting to know him."

While the Mansell Mania was being played out during the 1992 British Grand Prix you got that Brabham to the finish, albeit 16th. Dad would surely had been proud of that?

"It doesn't do to think about it too much because the fact is he's not here. I don't feel like he's not here, though. There's enough material and film and books of him. We've got albums. We can cast ourselves back a bit. Also he was such a character that he made a massive impression in my mind about what is right and what is wrong, the way to proceed in life. I'm not saying I'm a clone of his at all, I don't think I am, I think I've got many differences, but ..."

... but you're a battler and so was he.

"That was obvious from his career. He wouldn't allow himself to give up and I don't think he'd expect it of his children ever to give up. That's one unforgettable lesson. If you give up you'll never make it."

KEN TYRRELL, known to many as Uncle Ken, has modest premises by big-team Formula One standards, but the better for that. The factory, like the team and the man himself, are on a human scale. Of Surtees he will say: "Amazing to be able to do it on bikes and in cars. I mean, the number of people who will ever be able to do that is...well, you'll be lucky to see it in a whole lifetime. OK, I saw Surtees do it in my lifetime and perhaps – I say perhaps – my grandson will see it again. That's how difficult it is to do both."

ALAN BRINTON has a mischievous sense of humour, a shrewd eye and a large array of mellow, chewed, mahogony-tinted pipes. He doesn't wave them about for emphasis as many do, just puffs them along in gentle, repetitive chugs, drawing comfort from them. "I don't think anybody was more determined to win than John Surtees, nobody was more determined. Oh dear, oh dear. A difficult man? Yes. A man who had difficulties, with Ferrari, for instance? Yes. But a highly intelligent person. He didn't just ride for MV, he learnt Italian. I remember going to see him seven or eight years ago with somebody from *Auto Motor und Sport* from Stuttgart, and he started a very deep discussion on the German political situation.

"He was living in an Elizabethan house which he'd restored. The interesting thing was that he'd spent a lot of money and a lot of time in the restoration, but it was in perfect taste. It didn't look as if he'd spent all that money or time, the house appeared just the way it should. Now you wouldn't expect that from his background – his father a rough-and-ready motorcycle dealer and rider and a real toughie. Really, deep down, John is highly intellectual. I think he's still showing that in his love of old bikes and what they mean to a certain generation."

TED PAPSCH sits in his back garden in Farnham, Surrey – Farnham, a place heavy with association. Hawthorn's garage was not far away, the house his mother lived in just over the way, the house Derek Bell lived in nearby. Hunt used to come and visit Bell and Papsch's daughter, a professional hairdresser, would cut his locks. By a paradox Papsch never spoke so much as one word to Hunt, "though I admired him tremendously." Papsch, small and lively and with an accent which chews words gloriously ("I only remember the good times, not the bad") holds firm opinions.

"The tyres they raced on, the understeer, the oversteer…if modern drivers drove modern cars without any modifications on the same circuits – no resurfacing – that those boys like Mike, Stirling Moss, Fangio, Ascari drove, they wouldn't even break the lap record. They wouldn't even last. Those boys were supermen. The modern cars steer themselves: and you look at the speeds those boys did with steering which was just impossible, drivers sitting high up, the pressure from the wind nearly blowing them flat, the petrol flopping around from one side to another, small tyres. The smell of the exhaust fumes hit you – it was motor racing and I don't think it's motor racing any more."

Late February 1993 and Lotus launch their new car at Claridge's. There are drinks before and 100 people, maybe more, congeal and talk in a long, broad reception room. The car, held on an angled ramp in the next room, is covered by a sheet which is definitely not a shroud. The ceremonial unveiling will be later, a striptease as these things always are, but the car, if you get my meaning, always keeps its G-string on. A bit like the definition of the bikini: what it reveals is important but what it conceals is vital.

Walter Hayes, small and neat, moves urgently among the crowd. He seems to have hurried down the years constructing empires which endure, like the Cosworth which Clark drove that day at Zandvoort in 1967 and Lotus will use in 1993. **PETER COLLINS**, now running the team and always conscious of its history, has a ready handshake, a genuine smile, and the knack of remembering people's names so that socially he glides. Hazel Chapman, impeccably groomed as ever, stands and people pay homage to her, as they should, as they should. James Hunt, wearing a *dark suit, collar and tie*, looms, a stooping semi-benevolent-looking figure content to chat to whoever comes along. Johnny Herbert's Dad, an electrician, has a merry twinkle in his eye. So that's where Johnny got it from. Under severe questioning Dad says he never kicks Johnny's bottom because he never needs to. Much laughter. It's that kind of occasion so far.

A stentorian, hired voice summons the gathering to move next door. A broad conference room. Collins speaks from a platform, the car remaining at that angle on the ramp behind him, a feline shape under the sheet. "We [he and Peter Wright, the technical director] were appointed consultants to the team on the day that Saddam Hussein invaded Kuwait. We then compounded that situation by committing to the 1990–91 World Championship as the war broke out in the Gulf and the world entered an economic recession. The last two years have been very difficult for the team as we embarked on a five-year programme to return to the front of Grand Prix racing and to win the World Championship.

"Team Lotus, under Colin Chapman, created an enviable record of success. It is our objective as caretakers of Colin Chapman's legacy to add further to that success. Grand Prix racing is without doubt one of the greatest global sporting spectacles. It has seen the passing of great Champions such as Jim Clark, Rindt, Villeneuve and the retirements of Jackie Stewart and Niki Lauda, and never has its popularity waned."

Collins wasn't being unkind, and we won't explore sentimentality again. It's too late in the book for that. Collins spoke the truth, the ones who are gone are gone, and yet...somehow you couldn't have a Lotus occasion without the mention of Clark.

Herbert and the new driver, Alessandro Zanardi, are openly enthusiastic about the car (what else would they be?) and at the instant of unveiling it does look feline, caressed by wind-tunnels, soothed by whatever the computer says is the shape to be, but sharply-smooth, in evolution a creature poised to stretch itself across the savannah devouring the earth beneath it as it reaches for its prey in a primitive quest based on superior speed. Anthropologists suggest that the cheetah may achieve 70 miles an hour across the savannah at full stretch, impelled by hunger and the urgency of the kill. Maybe, maybe not. From a standing start Johnny Herbert would overtake this cheetah in something under 3 seconds and continue towards thrice its speed – which may not be quick enough in Formula One in '93. The finite judgment comes only on the track when it's being pumped hard against all the opposition, stretching, stretching, stretching, just as they are.

After the striptease we're back in the broad drinks room, Brinton engages in some banter with Hunt about bringing food into the BBC when he's commentating. "Quite right," Hunt says, "I've found a place which does Big Macs," and grins the Public Schoolboy grin which says *if I want to, why can't I?*.

Hunt, voraciously hungry, takes tidbits from every passing tray the waiters ferry and chats to a pretty girl who's evidently in marketing or organizing something for him. He retains that presence you can't mistake: not just achievement, but the ease of an athletic body, slack but which could become taut at any instant. Otherwise you can't play the big game and never could, the Nurburgring, say, and its 187 corners. Reactions may slow, dulled by the years, softened by inactivity at such a level of absolute intensity, but the shards and the refractions never really go away and neither does the prism. Who truly could have guessed that Hunt had less than six months to live?

I sit in an alcove with Hazel and we discuss doing an interview, though she's unhappy to speak into a tape recorder, prefers I take notes. That's curious if only because, as I point out, my notes might not be accurate, but her voice on the tape will be. She's insistent, it's a bit late to work into a couple of thousand words of what remains of my shorthand and so the interview ebbs away, never really happens at all. We do, however, discuss April 7, 1968. She remembers being in the hotel room at St Moritz, remembers Jim Endruweit coming through to it on the phone from Hockenheim, remembers Colin repeating out loud everything Endruweit was saying twice. She turns to face me and her eyes are brimming with tears. She composes herself, says how good Clark was and adds that he did have the best car to drive...

The following night **GRAHAM GAULD** rings because I've dropped him a note thanking him for a copy of the *Ecurie Ecosse* book and stressing the value of the background it contains. Gauld is deep into the final preparations for the Jim Clark memorial dinner he's arranged (and far from being undersubscribed he's caught in a rush). He is determined to make it a celebration not a wake. Among others he's spoken at length to Chris Barber, who points out that his ex-wife is living in Scotland these days and someone wrote a tribute to Clark which she could sing, although the tribute – never performed – is intended to be accompanied by bagpipes. How about doing it on the night? Gauld declined politely. He knows how hauntingly sad bagpipes can sound, that's not the mood. One of these days, Gauld says, he intends to write a book on the psychology of the racing driver and he applies that specifically to Hockenheim, April 7, 1968. He's been doing some research into reaction times and how low in fractions of one second a leading driver can get them. He has an assortment of precise figures and he's built them onto Clark's speed when the accident began, how wide the track was (26 feet), how far away the tree across the grass. He's balanced that against the reaction times of ordinary human beings and concluded that Clark, at 150 miles an hour, had had time to correct and recorrect the Lotus whereas the ordinary human being would already have been off the circuit and onto the grass *before he knew the accident was happening...*

I wondered how Gauld would react himself to the 25th commemoration. He was there at the beginning of the career, in the passenger seat a time or two or three, taped the interviews and wrote the books from the tapes (some of the material, unused, candid as you like and, as we've heard, laced with the f-word), was as close as any to the man and much, much closer than most.

Gauld responded candidly: he anticipated he'd react like the professional journalist he's been down all these years, but unconsciously he contradicted that immediately with a most curious and entirely authentic handful of words. "The people who get emotional about Jimmy are the ones who didn't know him well. The people who did know him well don't react like that *because they haven't accepted it, they still think he's out there somewhere and they'll meet him again one day.*"

Does Hazel Chapman? It's not the sort of question you ask, and I didn't as the guests dispersed from Claridge's into the darkness of London, and all of them, even Johnny Herbert, waiting until the car had been pumped hard at Kyalami, South Africa, first Grand Prix of 1993, to find out.

DAVE SIMS certainly wonders what the anniversary dinner will be like. He works for Tom's, the Toyota sportscar team, at the factory in deepest Norfolk. It's a culture-shock to drive into the little village of Hingham, a slumbering place, and discover not only a glistening factory, but a very hot-looking car in the foyer with the names of John Watson and Johnny Dumfries on the side.

What was Clark like? "If you didn't know him for what he was you'd never guess. If he wore his suit maybe you'd take him for a banker, when he wore his country clothes he became a farmer. Above all he was an absolute gentleman, an absolute gentleman, very, very, very clever, very switched on. He could read people's thoughts, yes, a good reader of a person. He sussed out who worked on what and if they were performing up to scratch.

"Once he got into a car he had this phenomenal ability to sink into it, do a few laps, come in and say: 'This is OK', or 'This is what I need', and he'd put his finger right on it. He was able to feel the cars as if they were part of him. He was easy to work with – he didn't have the engineers scratching their heads, he could tell them. He didn't ever make a fuss. You could blow two engines, he'd miss a practice session, then put it on pole. [Chuckle.]

"Italians know their motorsport, and every time I visit Italy people still come up and say to me: 'Ah, Jim Clark's mechanic.' Last year we were testing in Group C at Monza, a bloke came up to me – must have been aged 45, 50 – and asked me for my autograph. I said: 'What do you mean, I'm not a driver,' and he said: 'No, no, no – Sims,' and I said: 'Yes, Jim Clark's mechanic.' I thought: Blimey…"

BOB DANCE, known as The Vicar because of his thirst for tea, retains a warm Norfolk accent and a sense of perspective, no matter how many pit lanes he's worked in down the years, how much of the sport's great and sad moments he's witnessed. "I had great respect for the drivers of the Sixties," he says. "You never knew if you'd see them again at the end of the afternoon: no seat belts, roll-over bars which didn't support the cars, fuel tanks which leaked. Motor racing was dangerous and sex was safe…"

TONY BROOKS sits in the lounge of his large and delightful house on one of those estates, if you can call it that, where all the houses are large and delightful and to be found down narrow, tree-shaded roads. His wife Pina, who's Italian, has harmonized all the colours in the lounge so that they are both simple and restful and at the same time extremely striking, something harder to achieve than you might think. The quietude reflects Brooks. Like Clark he is a gentleman in the authentic sense of that word, and he telephoned the morning after our interview to say he hoped he hadn't been controversial, hadn't been hard on anyone. He hadn't.

"There are an awful lot of average mountaineers who would be able to match the great mountaineers, who would put together great climbs if they had a safety net and knew they could get away with making mistakes, but mountaineering would not be the same sport. Motor racing is not the same sport as it was in the Fifties because of the risk element and you must recognize that.

"You needed to know that one mistake could be your last. Now a driver can say to himself that if he makes a mistake he might lose a few seconds and, if worst comes to worst, he'll be out of the race. That is a totally different attitude of mind. In our day you would not get the bumper-to-bumper syndrome because we would have killed each other. It is relative, of course, but most of today's top drivers would be dead if they had had their accidents in the cars we drove.

"You lose friends because they die of cancer, they are killed on the road, you lose friends from natural causes and to adjust to the loss of a friend is really the same whether he happened to be a motor racing driver or not. Having to cope with bereavement is not unique to motor racing. Obviously we lost a lot of friends, which you were very, very sad about, but we all took part in motor racing realizing that these were the risks. Therefore, one took the attitude *well, he died doing what he really enjoyed, it gave him a kick*. That's how you'd explain it to yourself. *He died that way, better than in bed after a long illness.*

"What is different is that you had positive evidence of the risk you were taking. I had total confidence in what I was doing and the way I was driving, I was not going to make a mistake. I recognized that others could have accidents, or I could come round a corner, find oil on the track and have a fatal accident because I could do absolutely nothing about it, but the fact that I never made a serious driving error – as opposed to a stupid mistake like the Aston Martin accident at Le Mans – which resulted in a serious accident supports my theory. My confidence that what I was doing was not going to lead to my death enabled me to keep on.

"You'd have races on aerodrome circuits where the barriers were probably barrels but lots of open spaces so you could make mistakes and know nothing very serious was likely to happen. Drivers would become very tough competitors on them. As soon as you got those same drivers on the road circuits like the Nurburgring or Spa or Portugal, they would become much less serious opposition because, I believe, a small mistake could result in a monumental shunt. That's what has changed. I come back to the analogy of the average mountaineer…"

DAVID BENSON sits in the new *Daily Express* office and it glistens, Fleet Street so near and yet far away over Blackfriars Bridge. He tells a story, circa 1960, when he'd had a rotten day, been to Heathrow to collect a parcel which wasn't there and so on. Worse, it was his birthday. He gravitated to the Steering Wheel Club in London, fell into the company of Reg Parnell and said he'd buy him dinner – you ate well at the club and didn't need a bank loan to do it. Parnell said he had a young driver, who'd just driven Formula Junior at Oulton Park, coming along to meet him and Benson said: "No problem, he can join us." As it happened, they were four at table before the driver arrived, so he sat at an adjoining table, eating and listening quietly. Benson called for the bill and a soft Borders voice said he'd prefer to pay for his own. "No," Benson insisted, "it's my birthday, it's my treat." "No," the soft Borders voice insisted, "I'd prefer to pay for my own." Jim Clark did.

JIMMY STEWART is an enervated, cascading voice down the telephone and a man at peace in his retirement. Just the day before, the day Gauld rang me, Jackie had been up to Dumbarton with his son Paul, and Paul's engagement had just been announced – she's quite a girl, Jimmy says, good family, good job with the Mark McCormack organization, drives an expensive BMW. Ah, elderly irony among so many ironies.

Jimmy drives nothing now. His apartment overlooks the river, he's comfortably within reach of the shops, the buses, the railway station, and he asked himself what he wants a car for and finds no reason. He walks four or five miles a day and plays golf, handicap slipping to his dismay away from 3, but amongst it he has come upon contentment. Not many ex-racing drivers have. Life's good, he repeats, life's good. What else would you ask of a man? And then we fall to laughing over how he might be a bandit about the golfing handicap. He doesn't exactly confirm or deny it, but laughs again, another reverberation down the telephone, clean and pure as Highland spring water. One thought: as we spoke he showed no envy of Jackie, no trace, nothing like that, nor any suggestion of what he might have done himself if circumstances had been different. Yes, there were offers from Connaught to dip himself into Formula One, Connaught were on his back, but…

Another old story among so many, but this time a happy ending and you don't get many of those. Nor laughter down the telephone.

JABBY CROMBAC, close friend of Clark, went to cover the South African Grand Prix, first race of the 1993 season, and at Kyalami "a complete stranger came up to me and wanted to talk about Jimmy. This stranger must have recognized me from a photograph in one of the old books."

PETER COLLINS sits at Ketteringham Hall, a genuine country house rather than a Grand Prix team headquarters (although it doubles as that nicely enough), and we've just finished a long interview about Benetton and Gerhard Berger (for a different book). The talk moves, to Senna and to Clark.

"I saw Jimmy five or six times when I was young and the smoothness was extraordinary. *He* was extraordinary. If they couldn't give him the rev range he wanted he'd deliberately put two wheels onto the dirt in corners to spin the wheels quicker to get the revs *he* wanted…"

Collins voice trails away into a silence of awe, a quarter of a century after he witnessed it.

At **DONINGTON PARK** for the European Grand Prix in April 1993 Hunt seemed entirely himself, entirely the man he'd become, tall and stooping, a shambolling gait, a keen eye. I mentioned that there were specific questions I needed to raise with him on his chapter in this book and he said: "Sure, love to," and we tentatively arranged to have lunch sometime. Early in June I needed another specific question answered – nothing to do with this book, but important in the Berger one – and we chatted on the phone, his rounded voice polite as ever. "Ring again if there's anything else I can do."

He'd remained approachable, easy to talk to, entirely natural and unaffected. He was what he was. Two weeks later he died in his sleep at his London home. The answers to the questions in his chapter of this book will remain unanswered now.

He'd had financial difficulties – one newspaper made its main story on the front page that he died penniless – but he'd had those before. Perhaps – who knew? – the abuses he'd heaped upon himself years before when he drove Formula One took some final subterranean toll, surfaced all at once and took him away.

He spanned two distinct generations, as a Grand Prix driver from 1973 to 1979 and a BBC commentator from 1980 to Canada, June 1993. At the BBC he balanced the natural excitement of Murray Walker with becalmed, sharpened, sometimes barbed insights. He regularly enraged viewers because he said what he thought and devil take the hindmost. His verbal assaults on Riccardo Patrese and Andrea de Cesaris became talking points in themselves.

Walker once confessed that both he and Hunt felt such an urgent need to communicate that the BBC allowed them only a single, communal microphone so they couldn't talk together.

The day Hunt died Nigel Mansell flew to England to go to Madame Taussaud's to shake hands with his own wax image. Someone asked him about Hunt and Mansell expressed the incomprehension. "At 45, you just don't think about things like that." He shook his head.

The written obituaries to Hunt struggled to put his life into focus, but most agreed that he'd been a pain in the neck when a driver and progessively matured into good company, humorous, self-deprecating, neither concealing nor embellishing his financial plight. One obituary, in *The Independent*, written by a man half a decade off the pace, suggested Hunt hadn't matured at all and that drew a heap of abuse on the writer in a readers' letters page.

Richard Williams of *The Independent on Sunday* (the sister paper) got much closer to the real Hunt in a long tribute. Williams quoted Bubbles Horsley at length, and with Williams' permission I quote a tract of what Horsley said, which complements what he said in the chapter on Hunt.

"He kept his mates. That was one of the things. All his mates were from when he was racing his Mini, or playing squash or golf, or school-mates. He moved in and out of the glamorous world, completely at ease with it, and yet it never got inside him. They didn't convert him, if you like. The marketing men convert people – like Mansell, a Brummie lad struggling for years, now a superstar with his own jet, moving around like royalty. They've converted him. They've got him. They never got James. James never had those desires. No matter how much money he had, he never would have wanted a jet."

Williams suggested Lauda's crash hung over Hunt's Championship. "Because of that I think he felt his Championship wasn't taken as seriously as it should have been, that there were people who said that if Lauda hadn't had the crash James wouldn't have won it that year. And I think that was a regret. I think that hurt him, because if you actually looked at the facts and the figures it was not true. It was a fair win. You can't take that away from him."

Williams suggested Hunt departed Formula One because of fear. "Yes, he got frightened. It was demoralizing for him. In the end he said: 'I don't want to kill myself struggling for seventh place.' That's what got to him. How it manifested itself, whether as fear or frustration, whether he sought to escape from that in drink, girls, whatever…possibly. He must have known that his career was in decline, that he wasn't in the right team, that it wasn't working for him, and yet his talent hadn't declined. It's rather like a film star who's suddenly getting bum scripts but he needs to do it because that's what he does, he needs the money and therefore he does it. But in the end the scripts got so bad…"

Entirely in keeping with the wonderful, improbable days of and at Hesketh, Horsley recounted that money became so tight "we didn't have enough to go to the French Grand Prix and I saw his [Hesketh's] Rolls-Royce parked in front of the house, so it went." *Went*, as in Horsley sold it. "He came back and said: 'Where's my Rolls-Royce?' I said: 'It's gone.' He wasn't very pleased. He forgave me when we came second, though." By this time, too, Horsley was buying engines with the proceeds from selling the team's tee-shirts.

Williams posed the question, or rather assertion, that Suzy, Jane, Sarah and Helen all looked like the same girl. "Well, they always do, don't they? You've got chaps who like Jags, and chaps who drive Mercs, and chaps who drive Ferraris. I think with James they were good foils for his character. He had a way in all his relationships which was…I don't know how to say this…I won't say his wives were one of the boys at all, but it was apart from love and sex. They were pals as well. That was very important. Suzy was wonderful and we used to call her gannet. She was very tall and flopped about like a young bird, as though she was going to fall over. She was always breaking things – her wings would flap out and crash, another lamp off the table. Jane was great company and so was Sarah. Helen, too, although she was much younger than him, and I think he was moving into a quieter phase of life. A lot less partying in the last two, three, four years. And she's quite quiet, so she was perhaps the only one who was slightly out of the mould." Did the relationships end in the same way? "No, with Suzy and Jane it was amicable, with Sarah it wasn't, unfortunately."

A final reflection from Horsley… "When you're driving in Formula One your days are completely organized for you. You don't have to think. When that stopped he was lost for a bit and it led him to have some problems with his relationships. But he'd turned the corner. He was much, much happier in the last year or so. He wasn't drinking, he was getting much fitter, he was beginning to see a bit of light at the end of the tunnel. And also, of course, discovering that life doesn't really change if you're driving around in an A35 van and bicycling everywhere. It's not actually that different from driving around in a £70,000 Mercedes.

"James was a very good father, he understood people and situations. He could take a small child who was very unhappy about something and walk off with him and talk it through and really communicate – he was a marvellous communicator, which was why he was so good on TV. The child would come back grinning and everything would have been solved, just with a few words. That was one of his great strengths but people who're brilliant at solving other people's problems often struggle with some of their own, don't they?"

Maurice Hamilton in *The Observer* caught much of Hunt in a single paragraph. "Last March, Hunt attended the memorial service in London for the other World Champion to have died of a heart attack, Denny Hulme. When it was over, Hunt changed into cycling gear on the pavement, stuffed his suit in a rucksack, bade a cheery farewell and pedalled off. We never dreamed his funeral would be the next one – probably because he did not wish us to know about the troubles he was packing in his old kit bag. The fact that we cared said much about the true warmth of his character, which had only emerged in the afterglow of stardom."

THE FUNERAL on the Monday of the following week was confined to close friends and relatives. His girlfriend Helen Dyson, who'd been flown back from a holiday in Greece by the private jet of McLaren's Ron Dennis, attended, and so did Lord Hesketh.

A quiet, dignified resting.

There would be a memorial service later, a chance for a larger circle of acquaintances and admirers to pay their homage, and it would be an enormous circle. One way and another James Hunt had touched a deep chord in Britain and far beyond.

(I sent a copy of each part of this book which involved them to Jean Howarth and Innes Ireland so that they might be happy with the content and correct anything about which they were not completely happy. At this point in the manuscript Innes added in neat handwriting: "A few months earlier, James turned up at the memorial service for my son Jamie. Strangely, Denny's service was held in this same church. James was similarly attired as for that and chained his bicycle to the drainpipe at the entrance to the church. It never occurred to me that James would be there, but I valued his presence greatly. I only write this to strengthen the sympathy James had for children. Use it if you wish.")

ROY SALVADORI, who raced Fangio and Clark and Hill and Surtees and savoured Stewart, savoured Hunt, mourns (June 1993) the absence of Mansell, but says "I can't imagine a book about British drivers which does not include a very, very big paragraph about Stirling Moss. If you talk to any of the drivers who want to be honest in their old age I defy you to find somebody who will say that anybody was better than Moss. We all know that he was the best."

But now, Salvadori mourns that the combative factor of Mansell has gone, although he still enjoys the races hugely, probing for what's going on, seeing a whole race and all the drivers in their various contexts.

Salvadori is a resident of Monte Carlo and has an apartment which overlooks the grid, the painted bays which remain all year charting the theatre of a sudden great moment when hell unleashes and the day after a quietude returns, tourist traffic chugging and grunting as if the race had never been.

Could Hawthorn have passed this way – the ordinary streets of the Principality – in a metal car virtually unprotected, could Hill have lapped it at 76 miles an hour and enslaved the Principality? Could Stewart have lapped it at 85, prudent as you like, Roman Polanski filming him and he – Stewart – a shaggy-haired icon of the late-Sixties, early-Seventies, easy and tense and public on the film? Could Surtees have fought and battled and struggled here, willpower over temporal difficulties? Could Mansell have gone round – Ste Devote, Casino, the judder towards the tunnel, the tunnel, the downhill rush to the chicane, the delicacy of slipping around the swimming pool – at 91? And all of them leaving only faint, dimmed echoes? Yes. It happened and it's gone away, and will come back again next year then go away again. The Bay of Sighs, if you will.

Salvadori can watch from his balcony at his leisure, and reason. By a final irony he vindicates Hunt's posthumous doubt about the Championship, 1976, although Salvadori doesn't specify that and, as it happens, he doesn't have to. "There is no World Champion who got there by accident. If you go through the whole history of World Champions they've all stood up on their own merit."

JEAN HOWARTH, who won't ever lose the presence of a lady, shares a homely cottage nestled into the Berkshire countryside with her husband, Innes Ireland. She is far more than a former model. She ruminates gently about Mike Hawthorn.

Sports people traditionally find it difficult to cope with retiring immediately after an active career. How would Hawthorn have coped?

"He was an extremely good after-dinner speaker, he would have been much wanted. He was charismatic, and I don't think he would have faded from the public view. He'd have carried it off, the right presence. Goodness knows what Mike would have made of Mansell."

That's both ends of The Bridge of Sighs, a broad span.

The sleepers on that second bridge at Silverstone still tremble.

Mike Hawthorn competing in the Riley Ulster Imp, his first racing car and the one which brought him his first win. His subsequent successes in this car and a Riley Sprite set him off on a meteoric career.

His first serious racer. Hawthorn returns to the Silverstone paddock after practising for the 1952 *Daily Express* International Trophy in the Formula Two Cooper-Bristol.

By 1953 Mike was driving for Ferrari. Here he is one year on at Silverstone and obviously enjoying himself. The grin was even wider after he recorded his first win for the Italian team.

Back at Silverstone again for the British Grand Prix in July, but this time he blotted his copybook with a monumental spin opposite the pits. Miraculously he recovered, but he had to settle for fifth place.

The boyish good looks
which ensured Hawthorn
such a hectic social life.

At the end of 1954
Hawthorn drove the new
Vanwall Special at a non-
Championship race at
Aintree, where he
finished second behind
arch rival Stirling Moss'
Maserati, the two sharing
a new lap record.

Hawthorn was at the top of his form at the Nurburgring in 1957 when his Ferrari
finished less than 3 seconds behind Juan-Manuel Fangio's Maserati after what is
widely considered to be the Argentinian's greatest race.

A characteristic Hawthorn pose – wearing his well-worn sports jacket and puffing on a pipe while taking a look at Tony Brooks' Vanwall at the Nurburgring. Tony would win the 1958 German Grand Prix with Hawthorn second, but it was to be a sombre day, Mike's Ferrari team-mate and 'Mon Ami Mate' Peter Collins being fatally injured.

In happier times, Hawthorn and Collins in earnest discussion with Ferrari engineer Carlo Chiti. One of the two pals' happiest days was when they finished first and second in the 1958 British Grand Prix, Collins scoring his third and final GP victory.

The forecourt of The Tourist Trophy Garage at Farnham, Surrey, with Mike Hawthorn's name adorning the facia above the showroom. He would leave from here on his last journey in January 1959.

Mike leaning on the front wing of VDU 881, the considerably modified Jaguar Mark 2 in which he would die shortly after this faded photograph was taken.

The two faces of Graham Hill. The image most often seen was of the verbal entertainer, always ready with the perfect wisecrack to fit the occasion. The darker side, which usually had a more restricted audience, offered an invitation to tread carefully.

Hill's first Grand Prix victory came at Zandvoort, in Holland, the first of his four successes in 1962 with BRM which would lead him towards the first of his two World Championships.

Graham Hill and his Lola-Ford pose for the mandatory winner's picture at Indianapolis in 1966. There was some doubt as to whether he or Jim Clark – the 1965 winner – had actually won the confusing race, but not by Graham, who remarked: "I've drunk the milk!" (the traditional drink given to the winner).

Hill and Clark confer before the Lotus-Ford 49's debut at Zandvoort in 1967. Hill was somewhat miffed that so much praise should be directed at Clark for his victory whereas Hill, who had led until his timing gears broke, had done all the testing due to Clark's absence as a tax exile.

Graham Hill almost made the Monaco Grand Prix his private property. Here in 1969 he leads Jean-Pierre Beltoise's Matra on his way to his fifth victory through the streets and his second for Lotus following his hat-trick there for BRM.

Here we are again! Hill stands to attention with Princess Grace and Prince Rainier for the fifth time as the victor's national anthem is played. There was no champagne-spraying at this royal occasion!

The way Hill rebuilt the morale of the Lotus team in 1968 after Jim Clark's death was magnificent, as was his personal achievement of racing again in South Africa in 1970, only five months after his terrible accident at Watkins Glen. Here he helps his still painful left leg into the cockpit of Rob Walker's Lotus in which he would finish sixth.

A melancholy occasion. In 1975 Graham Hill was entered for the Monaco Grand Prix for the 18th and final time, on this occasion in his own Embassy Hill, but the past master failed to qualify. A few weeks later he announced his retirement.

Hill the entertainer. Here is Graham in full flow at Ford's celebratory dinner to honour Jack Brabham on his retirement.

What might have been. Hill was convinced that Tony Brise was a future World Champion, but sadly they would both perish when Graham's plane crashed near Elstree on November 29, 1975.

265

They appeared to have something on their minds on this occasion, but the Jim Clark-Colin Chapman special relationship was central to their mutual success during their eight years together in Formula One.

On a winning roll. Clark crosses the line to win the 1963 British Grand Prix at Silverstone, the fourth of the seven Grand Prix successes that season which would lead to his first World Championship.

A year on and the scene changes to Brands Hatch, where he won his third British Grand Prix in succession, his Lotus being chased here by Graham Hill's BRM, which was just 2.8 seconds behind at the flag.

Jim Clark had witnessed a lot of tragedy at Spa and he loathed the place, especially in the wet, but this did not deter him from scoring his fourth Belgian Grand Prix win in a row there in 1965.

In Jim Clark's day, the victor's champagne was for pouring and supping, not spraying. Team Lotus mechanic Bob Dance clearly expects Clark and Chapman to save him a drop at Brands Hatch, where Clark had just secured the 1964 British Saloon Car Championship in a Lotus Cortina.

Clark's victory at Indianapolis in 1965 was as decisive as it was inevitable, the Establishment being duly humbled by the combination of driving and technological brilliance. Jimmy enjoyed his success, but he was less comfortable with all the ballyhoo which would follow it.

After his second World Championship in 1965 Clark had a lean 1966 season under the new 3-litre rules, his only victory coming here in the United States Grand Prix at Watkins Glen, where his Lotus-BRM recorded the only success for BRM's H16 engine.

Back home in 1967 for his fifth and final victory in the British Grand Prix, Clark typically led all the way from pole position in his undeniably quick but so often tricky to handle Lotus-Ford 49.

Jim Clark in a moment of relaxation. His brilliance was matched only by his modesty, even after he had mastered the self-doubt which haunted him during his earlier years. He simply couldn't believe he was that good.

John Surtees burst onto the motor racing scene in 1960 thanks to a Formula Junior Cooper supplied by Ken Tyrrell, which he drove with impressive speed and precision honed from his World Championship motorcycling career.

Surtees made his Formula One debut with Lotus and was runner-up to Jack Brabham in the 1960 British Grand Prix, only his second race for the team. He would move on to Cooper and then Lola before winning the 1964 World Championship with Ferrari.

Surtees had to work hard for his third place behind Jim Clark's Lotus and Jackie Stewart's BRM in the 1965 French Grand Prix at Clermont-Ferrand, an electrical fault causing his Ferrari's engine persistently to misfire and throw his car off line through the circuit's many corners.

Blotting out all the activity surrounding him, Surtees has a few moments of deep concentration as he prepares for the 1966 *Daily Express* International Trophy race at Silverstone in his 3-litre Ferrari. He would finish second behind Jack Brabham.

After leaving Ferrari abruptly in mid-season, Surtees joined an expanded Cooper team and scored a morale-boosting victory with his Maserati-engined car in the 1966 Mexican Grand Prix, this time leaving Brabham to do the chasing to the finishing line.

Following a three-year period of mixed fortunes with Honda, BRM and then his own McLaren, John built and ran Ford-powered Surtees cars from mid-way through the 1970 season. Although he found the going tough he seemed to get a lot of pleasure from being complete master of his own show.

Surtees combined the roles of team owner and driver until 1972, then concentrated on management, his best season thereafter proving to be 1976, when Alan Jones scored points in three races. He would finish fifth here at Zolder, in Belgium.

John Surtees today at his lovely home in Surrey, where he is a happy family man and surrounded by the machinery which remain at the heart of his continuing fascination with sport on two wheels and four.

John Surtees is today the elder statesman of Britain's surviving World Champions and a master restorer of machinery and buildings.

Jackie Stewart's introduction to Formula One came on the Friday evening before the 1964 British Grand Prix, when Jim Clark and Colin Chapman – seen here watching him intently – lent him Clark's spare Lotus for a few laps of the Brands Hatch circuit.

The following year
Stewart was driving for
BRM and took his first
victory in the *Daily
Express* International
Trophy race at
Silverstone.

BRM team-mates Stewart
and Hill, and already the
seasoned team leader is
having to endure the
ribaldry of the brash
newcomer. The
symbolism of the broom
between their helmets is
not immediately clear.

Stewart struggling in vain with the fast but fragile H16 BRM in the 1966 Italian Grand Prix at Monza, where a year earlier he had scored his first GP victory.

The combination of Stewart, a Matra chassis and a Ford V8 engine launched Ken Tyrrell on his career as a Formula One entrant in 1968. Here Stewart is on his way to a lucky victory in the Spanish Grand Prix, after the fragility of the high wings had launched Hill and Rindt into major accidents with their Lotus-Fords.

Wings were severely restricted after the Barcelona fiasco and this is the neat solution provided on Stewart's Matra, which is heading for another victory, this time in the Dutch Grand Prix.

Once he was established as a Grand Prix star, Jackie Stewart made sure that his appearance reflected the cult image of the time, which meant growing his hair long, if not quite as long as Helen's.

Tyrrell and Stewart became as formidable a pairing as Chapman and Clark had been. They admit that at times they drove each other to distraction in their pursuit of excellence, but the end results made it worthwhile.

Stewart won his three World Championships in alternate years, his third coming in 1973, aided by this drive to victory in the British Grand Prix at Silverstone.

Stewart the corporate man. Since his retirement from racing at the end of 1973 Jackie has enjoyed an equally successful and financially lucrative career as a consultant to major industrial and commercial companies, which means he covers far more air miles than the busiest Grand Prix driver.

A Grovewood Award, which he is receiving here in 1969 from Bruce McLaren, established James Hunt as a young driver of great promise.

Hunt's association with Lord Alexander Hesketh was cemented in the cockpit of a Formula Two Surtees, but when good results proved elusive they turned to what they considered would be the easier world of Formula One.

James proved he was much more than a public school playboy when he made his Grand Prix debut in a Hesketh March at Monaco in 1973 and was classified sixth despite suffering engine failure two laps from the end of the exhausting race.

On Stewart's retirement, Hunt slipped easily into the role of Britain's premier Grand Prix idol, helped by the off-circuit activities of his deliberately flamboyant team, which made at least as many headlines as his own prowess on the track.

Lord Hesketh had to wait until the 1975 Dutch Grand Prix for his greatest wish to be fulfilled – to win a World Championship race and still make it all look like fun. Here he greets Hunt at the end of his slowing-down lap.

When the Hesketh team's finances ran dry Hunt's Formula One career seemed in jeopardy, but suddenly there was an unexpected vacancy at McLaren following Emerson Fittipaldi's decision to form his own team. Hunt was invited to replace him and promptly celebrated his good fortune by winning the Race of Champions at Brands Hatch.

At McLaren there was a house rule that everybody should be properly dressed, and James complied. It was when attending social functions away from the track that his scruffy and often totally inappropriate appearance tended to give offence.

James never drove better than during his 1976 World Championship season. Here he is leading John Watson's Penske and heading for another victory in the Dutch Grand Prix.

The contested victory in the confusing 1976 British Grand Prix. Hunt, first across the line, thought he had won and received Niki Lauda's congratulations, but officialdom later upturned the result and awarded Lauda the race.

A Champion's drive in Japan. Lauda's early retirement had eased the pressure, but James had to overcome a puncture and a pit stop before collecting those vital 4 points to claim the title.

Hunt's move to the Wolf team seemed like a good idea at the time, but it proved otherwise and led to a mid-season decision to retire in 1979. One career was over, but an equally successful one as a TV commentator would win him many more admirers.

Nigel Mansell, the Formula One new boy for whom a testing contract soon turned into a regular Grand Prix drive from 1981.

Full of promise, but plagued by bad results, Mansell was finding things tough going with the JPS Lotus 91 in 1982, when he only twice finished in the points.

Another year on and the hair had grown a little longer and the frown a little deeper. Following Colin Chapman's death things were never quite the same.

The switch to the Williams team in 1985 transformed Mansell's prospects and at the end of his first season there he scored his maiden victory in the European Grand Prix at Brands Hatch ahead of Senna, Rosberg and Prost.

Mansell was usually out of luck at Monaco, and in 1986 he could only finish fourth after starting from the front row for the third year in succession.

Mansell and Frank Williams found little to smile about while watching the timing monitors during 1988 after their loss of Honda engines to McLaren.

Mansell's move to Ferrari had got off to a surprising start with a debut victory in
Brazil, then the team's difficult 1989 season was brightened by his brilliant drive to
win the Hungarian Grand Prix.

Nigel's decision to retire at the end of 1990 was reversed when he was offered No 1
status back at Williams, and the attraction of Renault power to chase that elusive
World Championship.

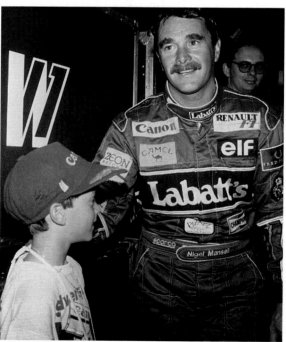

Mansell's near miss of the title in 1991 was followed by a runaway in 1992 beginning with five consecutive victories, the sixth of his nine coming here in France, where he finished in front of team-mate Riccardo Patrese and Martin Brundle.

After clinching the World Championship in Hungary things turned sour for Mansell, and he looked relieved when his Formula One career ended in Adelaide and a new one in IndyCar racing beckoned.

PART TWO

by John Blunsden

MEMORIES OF THE CHAMPIONS

I count myself extremely fortunate that my years as a motor racing writer have coincided with the peaks of the careers of all seven of the great drivers featured in this book (or eight if I may be permitted to include Stirling Moss, who was a World Champion of his time in all but title).

Inevitably, I was present when they achieved some of their greatest successes, and I was also witness to some of their darker moments. It is always satisfying to be present in a professional capacity at moments of historical significance, but one of the greatest satisfactions of sports journalism is that it also allows one to get to know the subjects of whom one is writing as people, not just as performers.

Some of the 'Super Seven' I came to know better than others, but all of them for one reason or another have left an indelible mark on my memory, and rightly so because to a man they have been exceptional people, each one different, but in his own way exceptional – each one highly motivated and brim-full of determination in the pursuit of excellence.

What follows is just a taste of their impact on someone who so often admired their deeds; who sometimes but not always shared their opinions; who from time to time had fun with them in a verbal sparring match; who did his best never consciously to waste their time; who hopes that he always treated them fairly in print; and who, above all, is grateful for the opportunity from time to time to have shared their company.

MIKE HAWTHORN and Stirling Moss

I have always been aware that whilst journalists are entitled to voice opinions, they should never indulge in personal bias. However, I recall that back in the Fifties it was extremely difficult to be both a 'Stirling Moss' and a 'Mike Hawthorn' fan. Though united by their exceptional talent and in their burning ambition to knock "all those bloody foreigners" off the motor racing perch, they went about their business in such sharply contrasting styles that it was easy to identify with one or other of them, but very difficult to do so with both.

The fact that I found myself more comfortable in the Moss camp probably dates back to one evening in 1951 – long before I was earning a living by putting words on paper, and at a time when I knew little of Mike Hawthorn other than that he had been driving a pair of prewar Riley sportscars very quickly indeed – when I first spoke to Stirling on the telephone (a mutual friend had given me his number). The details of the conversation, which must have gone on for more than an hour, are irrelevant, although they revolved around the possible purchase of a 500cc Formula Three car. What matters, and what impressed me so much at the time, was that a very busy and already highly successful racing driver was freely prepared to give so much of his time to a complete stranger, painstakingly and patiently offering the benefit of his knowledge and experience. His enthusiasm for the sport came pouring down the telephone, but equally impressive was the care with which he explained in great detail the various pitfalls and how to avoid them.

Through that rewarding and wide-ranging conversation I was immediately convinced that Stirling's spectacular success so early in his career had been achieved not just through his exceptional virtuosity as a racing driver, but also because of his attention to all the extraneous factors which can impinge on the level of a driver's success in motor racing, things which so often were either unidentified or ignored by other drivers.

He had set out as a teenager determined to prove to his parents that it was possible to make the grade as a professional driver at a time when racing was still essentially an amateur activity, and in pursuing this it became clear to me that he was applying a level of professionalism which extended far beyond its purely monetary connotation.

At that time, remember, Britain was woefully short of competitive racing cars at the upper level, so it was essential that the performance disadvantage of 'racing British' should be reduced by whatever legal means were available. Stirling voiced the opinion that a racing driver owed it to himself – and to the people he worked with and the public – to maximize the potential which his driving ability offered him, and this meant achieving the ultimate standards of personal as well as technical preparedness.

Whatever he was driving, he would seek to be that much better prepared than anyone else when he lined up on the starting grid. It was a level of dedication which caused a certain amount of amusement in those days – motor racing still had much of the 'Tally-ho' atmosphere left over from the fighter pilots of the Second World War – and what has long since become standard practice in professional motor racing was even regarded in some quarters as being slightly unsporting. Yet when the prospects of success at the highest level seemed so remote, Stirling's self-imposed standards of pre-race preparedness seemed to me to make a great deal of sense, and they tended to become the yardstick by which I began to judge the performance of others, including, in due course, Mike Hawthorn....

Like many people, I first heard of Hawthorn when I read of his exploits at the wheel of the two Riley sportscars, and then, of course, he hit the headlines early in 1952 with his first drives at Goodwood in Bob Chase's Formula Two Cooper-Bristol. He had already been christened 'The Farnham Flyer' by the media by the time I first came into contact with him at Silverstone a few weeks later, and I remember clearly the minutes prior to his heat in the *Daily Express* International Trophy race. Inevitably, he and his car had become a centre of interest in the paddock, but I sensed he was finding it a distraction and couldn't wait to drive away from the crowd on to the track, where he could concentrate on the task ahead.

I watched his race from the inside of Woodcote Corner, and within two or three laps it was clear what all the fuss had been about. It was not just that

Hawthorn was quick, very quick, it was that he looked even quicker. With the skinny tyres of the day, a long, fast, right-hander like Woodcote called for a lot of work on the steering wheel if you were really trying, and Hawthorn was certainly trying. His tall frame seemed to overflow out of the low-sided cockpit of the Cooper and his arms were pumping like an express train each time he swept through the corner, holding his car on the limit of adhesion. It was wonderful stuff to watch. I recall that he won that heat, but then had some sort of trouble in the final, a long pit stop putting him out of the running, but though he went home empty-handed, no-one had matched him for entertainment value that day.

While Moss' determination to 'drive British' whatever the odds was putting a brake on his own career, Hawthorn's leapt ahead when he responded to Enzo Ferrari's offer for the 1953 season, recognizing that it was the best possible passport to success in Formula One, as he was to prove in the French Grand Prix at Reims in that nail-biting photo-finish victory over Juan Manuel Fangio's Maserati.

Over the next year or two, Moss had to work harder than Hawthorn for his success, not because of any deficiency of driving skill – on the contrary – but because of some of his decisions off the track, which all too often left him to fight his battles in inferior machinery. Then the tables were turned when Moss was invited to join Fangio in the Mercedes-Benz team, and Hawthorn began to struggle with the early Vanwall.

It was at this point that I thought Hawthorn's inconsistency compared with Moss began to become more noticeable. On occasions his driving would have a magical quality, but then would come a lack-lustre performance which the more cynical would put down to a manifestation of his pre-race partying and nocturnal activities. However, it has to be said that this was not always a fair accusation because what was not widely known at the time was that Hawthorn – who had been condemned by some sections of the media for avoiding his National Service – was not even eligible to serve because he was medically unfit, a fact which he chose not to reveal.

Nevertheless, I long felt that Mike, in enjoying life in the broadest sense, did his racing career no favours, and I think it was not entirely down to the cars they were driving that from 1956 to 1958, the year when Hawthorn narrowly beat Moss to the World Championship, he was able to score just one Grand Prix victory to Moss' nine, four of which came in Hawthorn's Championship season.

From the start, Hawthorn had been a fun-loving extrovert, but not everyone responded to his sometimes outrageous pranks, not that this seemed to worry him because I never thought he was over-endowed with diplomacy. Also, towards the end of his all-too-short career I felt that even the humour and the pranks were sometimes a little contrived, that deep down he was not enjoying life quite as much as first impressions might have suggested.

It is widely known that he was emotionally crushed by the 1955 Le Mans accident and by the inevitable probing afterwards into the whys and wherefores of motor racing's biggest ever tragedy, in which he had been one of the drivers closest to the centre of the catastrophe. Thankfully, I was not there, but it has always struck me as cruelly ironic that the disaster should have occurred at the end of one of the finest demonstrations of sportscar racing between two artists at the wheel – Hawthorn in his Jaguar and Fangio in his Mercedes – ever seen at the circuit.

I believe that even after he had come to accept, as so many had insisted, that he should not shoulder the blame for what had been a classic motor racing accident, he turned ever more closely to those who were part of his 'set' and raised the barriers that little bit higher to those who were not. His great pal Peter Collins ("Mon Ami Mate") was, I found, much more approachable, and though no wallflower himself was, I think, a little exasperated at times by Mike's more extreme behaviour.

Certainly, Collins' death at the Nurburgring in 1958 upset Hawthorn greatly, and it removed much of the enjoyment which his forthcoming World Championship might otherwise have yielded him. Given all the circumstances, it was not, perhaps, so surprising that he should decide to retire from racing rather than go on to defend his title in 1959. All the pleasure had gone out of it.

A few weeks later I was in Monaco covering the Monte Carlo Rally for *Motoring News* when the news filtered through that Mike had died in a road accident near Guildford. I can remember it as if it were yesterday. The first reaction was disbelief, then something bordering on annoyance that he would do something so foolhardy; without even knowing the facts, there was already the potentially dangerous assumption that he had done something wrong because it seemed to fit the image. (Years later – by a coincidence this was also in Monte Carlo – I related this feeling to Jean Howarth, Mike's fiance and now Mrs Innes Ireland, and she rebuked me, saying that in all the time she had known him Mike had never scared her on the road. She was so convincing that I had to believed her.)

That day in 1959 I was thankful I was not working for a daily newspaper. Less fortunate was my future business partner Alan Brinton, who at that time was motoring correspondent of the *News Chronicle*. He knew the paper would have been trying to contact him so we rushed back to his hotel hoping to pool our combined memory bank (covering a rally, neither of us had any racing reference material with us). Sure enough, the paper had been on, and I think we had about 20 minutes for Alan to compile some material and phone it across.

Working for a weekly, of course, I had more time, and in any case the editorial team back in London would tackle the main story while I concentrated on the rally. But afterwards, I tapped out a piece for our 'Culpeper' column, which I repeat here because I think it accurately portrays what Mike meant to so many of us at the time of his death:

'For those of us who were in Monte Carlo last week, the first thing we heard was the question, passed by word of mouth, "Have you heard about Mike?" The horrible news that followed shocked us, at first into disbelief. It just couldn't be true. It must be some garbled rumour – perhaps he has had a bit of a prang and is injured.

All too soon we were to know that it was no rumour – that Mike was dead. Even then it took a long time before the full impact of the tragedy went home. Never again to see and enjoy the Hawthorn bonhomie around the circuits and in the club rooms was something not easy to grasp. For although he had vacated the cockpit, he was to remain a familiar figure wherever there was the sport of driving or talking about motor cars.

In a way, we were proud when we saw the headlines in the eagerly awaited British papers the following morning. No event, even the end of the war, had carried such heavy print, and invariably he was identified not as "Hawthorn" or "World Champion", but simply as "Mike". To the whole country, it was like losing one of the family, and the papers paid the appropriate tribute.

Without doubt, Hawthorn was THE personality of the race tracks, and his *joie de vivre* had a magnetic quality that instinctively drew people to him. He was the sort of character on which people tried – but never really succeeded – to model themselves. For Mike was always the individualist – he conformed to no set pattern, indeed he disliked convention for its own sake, just as he abhored fakes in any guise.

He was the chap who loved to "have a real bash", even when the odds were stacked heavily against him, and some of his best drives during the past eight years are not even featured in the record books. He invariably gave of his best when fighting at close quarters, for "pressing on" was the natural way for him to go motor racing.

Both on and off the track, he had to endure great tragedy during his all-too-short career, and many people did not realize that his overflowing sense of fun hid a far from happy young man, whose emotions had been severely strained.

Those of us who knew a little (few knew all) of the "story behind the story" learnt to forgive his occasional outbursts of abuse, bad temper and non-co-operation. For even then, his steadfast insistence on doing and saying what he liked, regardless of the consequences, was most refreshing. Whatever Mike said, you knew he meant it, unless, of course, you were the victim of his tremendous wit and sense of fun.

As a driver, he was already lost to us, and who knows, time may prove that in that respect he was just about replaceable. But as a man, as a character, as a tremendous personality, there could never be another Mike Hawthorn. Long shall we mourn and remember you, "Mon Ami Mate!"'

Yes, he was quite a character, was Britain's first World Champion.

GRAHAM HILL

Most people who rubbed shoulders with Graham Hill during his racing career will testify to the fact that he was something of a 'Dr Jekyll and Mr Hyde' character. At times we loved and applauded him, not only for his racing deeds, but also for his deep concern for the underprivileged away from the circuits, yet on other occasions we were infuriated by his black moods and by the abuse he would then dispense so liberally.

To the public at large he was a consummate ambassador for the sport – a natural performer with a microphone, a born entertainer who could invariably lift and amuse an audience, exuding a talent which was supported by impressively good looks, a sharp sense of humour and impeccable timing.

He could also drive a racing car impressively well, but one always sensed that he had to work harder at this than he did when he was holding the stage. On the race track and in the pit garage he was a grafter, and one developed tremendous respect for the way he persevered to match the accomplishments of others, such as Jim Clark, who were more naturally gifted and for whom things always seemed to come so much more easily.

Perhaps borrowing a page from the Moss book of how to maximize your opportunities, Graham was forever striving for that fractional improvement from his car, testing with an almost obsessive commitment every possible option of spring, damper and rollbar setting, tyre pressure and brake balance (setting up a racing car chassis was a relatively rudimentary procedure in those days) until he had convinced himself – if not always his mechanics – that he had found what he considered to be the optimum set-up.

It was most often when he was engaged in this work, and especially when the solution to his problem of the moment was proving elusive, that 'Graham Jekyll' was inclined to depart the scene and 'Graham Hyde' took over. Woe betide anyone who approached him during these occasions with a question – even a seriously considered and seemingly relevant one – which broke his concentration. On a good day, the response might be nothing worse than a short, sharp and sarcastic rebuke; on a bad one it was best not even to wait for the reply.

Yet despite – or perhaps because of – the minefield one had to tip-toe through in order to approach him, it was perhaps as well for motor racing journalists that Graham was around. At least he was never afraid to let you know, loud and clear, when you were being a pain, whereas some of his contemporaries – and I think in particular of those delightful people Bruce McLaren and Dan Gurney – had such friendly dispositions that they rarely if ever reacted strongly when cornered by a journalist in a moment of high tension, even though beneath their armour of self-control I am sure they must have been extremely irritated by the intrusion.

Graham taught most of us – I say most, because some never *did* seem to learn! – that in a motor racing environment there are two golden rules for journalists. The first is that before the mouth is opened the brain should be put into gear (Question: "Are you going to win the race today?" Answer: "No, I shall be too busy strangling journalists who ask me bloody asinine questions!"), and the second is that there are times when the mouth should not be opened at all.

It was the national and other non-specialist press who tended to 'misread' Hill most frequently, but in those days, through journals like *Motoring News*, *Motor Racing* and *Sports Car Graphic*, I was still at the heart of the specialist press and consequently my conversations with Graham tended to take on a more specific purpose and invariably were most rewarding. Away from the pressures of the pit road, a one-to-one chat could be a most enjoyable occasion, with questions flowing in both directions. For Graham's genuine enthusiasm for the sport was of a rare depth, and whilst one heard that in financial matters he was a very tough negotiator, one knew that if the chips were down he would have even done it for nothing, as he had early in his career – it might have made his black moods even blacker, but that would merely have served to make him drive himself and his car even harder.

Graham made the grade through sheer grit and determination and – perhaps as importantly – by his willingness to drive anything, anywhere, whenever the opportunity arose as he was developing his career. The versatility which he developed and refined during those often difficult years was later to serve him well, and it was pleasing to those of us who respected him so much that his major successes stretched far beyond Formula One. Indeed, in sheer entertainment value, perhaps he was at his best in less sophisticated cars, which he could hurl around the tracks in spectacular style. Yet this was the man whose sustained control and judgment of the Monte Carlo street circuit was to net him those five victories in the Monaco Grand Prix – a wonderful achievement that would not be surpassed until 1993.

Unfortunately, it took a severe and painful accident to reveal to the world at large the full depth of Graham's guts and determination. I was at Watkins Glen when he suffered his bad accident in the 1969 United States Grand Prix, and the following morning I called to see him at the local hospital before flying home. His legs were obviously in a very serious mess, but even prior to the extensive surgery they would obviously require he had begun his own rehabilitation. I asked him if there were any messages for anybody back home, and he said: "Yes, tell everybody I'll be on the grid in South Africa" (the first race of the 1970 season). I made the usual encouraging noises, as one does on those occasions, never really believing that he would drive a Formula One car again. Five months later in Kyalami he had to be lifted gently out of the cockpit of Rob Walker's Lotus-Ford in which he had just collected a World Championship point for finishing sixth at the end of probably the most courageous drive of his distinguished career. I was not there, but I am told by those who were that it was all extremely emotional, with several hardened onlookers in the paddock area reduced to tears.

I have always thought that that was the moment when Graham should have retired from the cockpit and begun his new career as an entrant and constructor. But his sheer joy of being able to drive a racing car again was not something he was about to deny himself after having endured so much pain and exhaustion in his efforts to speed his rehabilitation. Unfortunately, it would be another five years before he would finally relinquish the cockpit, having been able to secure, in the brilliant Tony Brise, who was destined to die with him, a young driver whom he recognized as having the capability of bringing his team major success.

In the intervening period, those of us who watched Graham's own efforts at close quarters became increasingly worried that as his speed inevitably declined so his determination – which at times became sheer stubbornness – to carry on driving as well as carrying the burden of team control would lead to another bad accident. Little did we know that what we all feared would eventually come not on a race track but from the air in that terrible crash so soon after we had cheered Graham around Silverstone on his 'goodbye' lap in 1975.

That cold and foggy November evening I was relaxing in the lounge at home, listening to the BBC news, when the newsreader announced that reports were coming in that a light plane with several people on board had crashed near Elstree, adding that it was believed that the plane had been travelling from the South of France.

There was no indication as to whose plane it was, but I immediately feared the worst because I knew that the Hill team had been testing at Paul Ricard, and I also knew that Elstree was Graham's 'home' airfield.

I immediately went out to my study and began opening my files, convinced I was about to begin a difficult and sad task, and that I would have to work quickly. Then I rang the sports department of *The Times* to warn them of my fears that it could well be Graham's plane that had crashed. They told me that there had just been a flash on the wire confirming that sadly this was so. At moments like this the adrenalin flows freely and personal feelings are pushed into the background as the mind is concentrated on the unpleasant task at hand. It is only after all the facts have been gathered, and the copy has been written and passed to the paper that it is possible to indulge in one's own feelings.

I recall thinking later on that night that the Graham Hill I would want to remember was the man from the Sixties and all his efforts and achievements associated with that decade, not so much the Graham Hill of the Seventies, which for him had ended so prematurely and tragically and with so much unfulfilled. All these years later, I still feel the same way and the majority of my most vivid recollections of him tend to stem from that earlier period.

There are so many of them. Like his antics on the playing field during the cricket matches between the Formula One teams and the Lord's Taverners which often used to enliven British Grand Prix weekends in those relaxed times. Or holding court well into the evening at the 'Tip Top' bar at Monaco, just up the road from the Mirabeau, rubbing shoulders, not with his team's corporate guests, but with his adoring fans who no doubt for months afterwards would proudly announce that they had had a drink with Graham Hill. Then there were the many times when we waited in anticipation for his first words when he grabbed hold of a microphone and gave us one of his wicked winks, because we knew for sure that they would be hilarious, possibly even a touch risque, but never obscene.

On a more serious note, I still recall vividly that weekend of the Spanish Grand Prix at Jarama in 1968 when he used an effective cocktail of badgering and compassion to galvanize the grief-stricken Lotus team back into action so soon after the death of Jim Clark, and of course his victory that weekend, laced with a spot of good fortune though it may have been, was the perfect tonic to help restore team morale.

I think Graham was one of a minority of top-class drivers who could use controlled anger to lift his game without imperilling either himself or his rivals, and to my mind this was never demonstrated more clearly than at Silverstone in 1960 when he stalled his BRM on the front row of the grid and then took his car right through the field into the lead. I watched the later stages of the race from the inside of Club Corner, where his pursuit of Jack Brabham's oversteering Cooper had us all on tip-toe, and there was a huge cheer when he first came round in the lead. Then, about six laps from the end, there was an agonizing groan from the spectator enclosure as we heard that he had slid off at Copse Corner. It seemed a cruel way to have to end such a magnificent demonstration of sustained aggression, especially when we heard afterwards that Graham had been suffering from deteriorating brakes for several laps, was constantly having to pump the pedal, and had simply arrived too quickly into Copse when lapping a backmarker.

That was another of Graham Hill's unfulfilled ambitions – to win his 'home' Grand Prix – but never mind, because in my view he achieved so much more in the pursuit of his career than went into the record books. He really was a worthy ambassador for his sport; OK, he could be a stroppy so-and-so at times, but he was also a man of many fine qualities with which, I am sure, he would have continued to benefit motor racing for many more years but for his ill-advised attempt to beat the fog over Elstree on that grim November evening.

JIM CLARK

Some memories stick in the mind so vividly that they will never go away. For example, like many people I can remember exactly where I was on the afternoon of November 22, 1963 when I heard over the car radio that President Kennedy had been shot. I had just left the *Motor Racing* office at Brands Hatch and was driving towards the main grandstand and the front gate.

By an extraordinary coincidence, on the afternoon of April 7, 1968 I was at precisely the same spot, although this time on foot, when I heard some more shattering news. I was on my way back from the paddock to the press box having checked up on some retirements during the BOAC 500 endurance race when I saw Walter Hayes, at that time Ford's public affairs and motorsport director, heading towards me, and seemingly in a state of agitation.

"I have the most terrible news, which I think you should know," he began. "Jimmy has been killed in Germany." The christian name was all that was necessary – in motor racing there was only one Jimmy, and this made what Hayes was saying all the more unbelievable. It couldn't happen to Jim Clark, it just couldn't because he was always so much in command. But of course, it had.

"I've told them in the commentary box, but I've asked them not to put out anything about him being dead, certainly not until after the race," Hayes went on. "I think that over the next hour or so the fewer people who know about this the better." Even in that stressful and emotional situation, Hayes, renowned for always being in command of things, was making a cool judgment having recognized the broader implications of the news; it was important that people's focus should not be diverted from the race taking place in front of them, especially those with a job to do in cars and in the pit and paddock areas.

Inevitably, the telephone lines were already humming by the time I had returned to the press box, and the next few hours were filled with that unpleasant cocktail of sadness and high-intensity activity known so well by motor racing journalists.

That evening I know I was not alone amongst the pressmen at the circuit in caring little that Jacky Ickx and Brian Redman had scored a close-fought victory over the works Porsche 907s with their Ford GT40. It just didn't seem to matter any more. Despite the precautions, by the end of the race the news of Clark's death had spread through the grapevine and the post-race celebrations were muted. Our minds were preoccupied by the realization that we would never again be able to share Jimmy's company or be entertained by his supreme skill behind the wheel. And, of course, the inevitable unanswered question: "What went wrong?", because we knew it couldn't have been driver error. I cannot remember which driver said it, but it doesn't matter because he was probably speaking for nearly all of them when he said: "Hell, if it can happen to Jimmy, what chance have we got?" For weeks afterwards I sensed that Clark's death severely weakened many other drivers' protection of self-confidence.

Jim Clark came into motor racing carrying so much inbuilt talent that I am sure he never had to train himself in the accepted sense; everything seemed to come so naturally to him. In those days of narrow-treaded tyres, relatively unsophisticated suspensions and minimal knowledge of aerodynamics, racing cars – whether saloons, sportscars or single-seaters – tended to slide their way round race tracks and it was easy to see who were the really quick drivers. But Jimmy invariably seemed to be in a class of his own, making even the 'quick' drivers look pedestrian. At times it was almost uncanny, yet I think he was genuinely surprised at the level of his own performance compared with that of others. Unlike them, he didn't need a 'forgiving' car in order to perform to his personal best, he just adapted his technique to compensate for his car's inadequacies, and as his team-mates would testify on many occasions, there were often plenty of those.

Watching him streak away from the grid – usually from pole position – into an immediate lead was a mixed blessing. At one level, the demonstration of car control which followed was invariably a joy to watch, but of course all too often Jimmy's presence meant there was little prospect of a close race. Usually, he thoroughly enjoyed setting the pace and the standard, but sometimes after a particularly dominant performance he would seem almost apologetic about it, inferring that it was simply that he had had the best car.

At times this was true, the trouble was no-one else could drive it quite like he could. Such were his speed of reactions and sense of balance that his cars could be tailored for ultimate pace rather than driver comfort, although towards the end of his career, when cars were becoming more 'technical', I am sure he became more interested in the engineering side and its influence on chassis performance, and his growing self-assurance in that area, under the guidance of his friend and father-figure Colin Chapman, became more visible.

Inevitably, his mechanics worshipped him, and as his technical knowledge increased he became ever more comfortable in their company. Yet I sensed that Jim Clark was only truly at ease in two environments – either sitting behind the steering wheel of a racing car or working on his sheep farm in Scotland. Indeed, I always thought it remarkable that someone who was so utterly in command in the cockpit of a racing car and in the highly stressed conditions of a demanding and dangerous motor race could be so nervous and ill at ease away from them. Although many of Jim Clark's accomplishments on the race track were of nail-biting intensity, it was his own nails which took the punishment when he was away from the circuits.

We used to see quite a lot of him in hotels because it was Colin Chapman's policy to stage a press function whenever a new racing car was unveiled or when there was something special to celebrate, as was frequently the case when Jimmy was around. Colin was an articulate speaker, with an easy flow of words to meet any occasion, and it was always a painful experience for us to watch Jimmy becoming increasingly nervous while Colin was in full flow as the time came ever closer when he would have to move up to the microphone himself. How he loathed those things!

Only towards the end of his tragically short life did he begin to master the torture of speaking in public, but his hatred of doing so never really diminished. The problem was that fundamentally he was a very shy man in the company of more than a handful of people at any one time. He also had a certain distrust of the press, partly I think because he didn't fully appreciate the job we were required to do, but perhaps more tellingly because he felt he was not always treated fairly by journalists.

I had no commitment to a national newspaper on that afternoon in Monza in 1961 when Clark's Lotus and Wolfgang von Trips' Ferrari collided on the back straight during the second lap of the Italian Grand Prix, so I was spared from having to intrude on his all-too-apparent grief after the accident. In those days, Monza, especially when the banking was in use, was a notorious slipstreaming circuit, and I decided to watch the opening laps of the anticipated wheel-to-wheel battle from the earth bank at the rear of the press car park overlooking that back straight.

The leading group of cars were still closely bunched as they rushed by for the second time, but they were just beyond the limit of my vision when 'Taffy' von Trips (with whom I had been chatting in the paddock only minutes earlier because he seemed likely to be crowned World Champion by the end of the afternoon) apparently moved slightly to the right and collided with Clark's car; Jimmy managed to keep some sort of control of his Lotus, but the Ferrari was launched at horrendous speed towards the public viewing area above the track on the left, where von Trips and a dozen spectators were killed on the spot.

It was another example of the classic racing accident, and as had been the case in the even more appalling Le Mans disaster six years earlier it was no fault of the drivers involved that in those days circuit safety standards left so much to be desired and that any high-speed collision in the proximity of spectators was likely to have disastrous consequences.

But Jimmy, who was always deeply affected whenever anyone was badly hurt or worse at a race meeting, suffered considerable mental agony in the aftermath of the accident, and during the days that followed he came increasingly to resent the inevitable intrusion by the press into his mental anguish and grief. Thereafter, his relationship with some sections of the media was to remain cool and guarded.

Fortunately, for those of us involved with the specialist magazines the relationship was more relaxed and Jimmy could be good company with people he felt he could trust. As the years went by this mutual regard became deeper, but right to the end I sensed that he only felt truly relaxed in the company of a journalist or reporter if they had been known to him for a long time and therefore warranted his trust.

My longest conversation with him took place towards the end of 1965 when we were far from home. We spent a couple of hours sitting alone on a pile of tyres stacked in the corner of the Firestone warehouse at Riverside Raceway, in California, during a long break between practice sessions. I was over there on my annual visit to the Los Angeles offices of *Sports Car Graphic*, and Jimmy had come across for the Group 7 sportscar race for which Team Lotus had sent out two of the notorious Lotus 40s for him and Richie Ginther.

It was Richie who had described the '40' as "rather like a Lotus 30" (itself a fairly diabolical-to-drive car) "with 10 more mistakes", and Jimmy was inclined to agree with him; that he managed to bring his car home in second place that weekend was yet another demonstration of ability over physics.

Despite his car problems, Jimmy was in a reasonably relaxed mood, though conscious that he was probably wasting his time being over there and looking forward to returning to Europe, even though he knew that having just won the World Championship for the second time he would inevitably be drawn into another round of social events and public appearances, which he would have preferred to do without. Did he enjoy the West Coast American way of life? Not really, and certainly he didn't like all the ballyhoo over there since he had won the Indianapolis 500 earlier in the year.

Yet for all his reticence, I sensed that he was beginning to enjoy the trappings of his success. The Border sheep farmer was coming to terms with living first class and rather liking it, provided he could do so on his own terms, which meant out of the public gaze. He was beginning to have more fun amongst racing people, and I reminded him that a few weeks earlier he had been one of the ringleaders of the traditional end-of-season Team Lotus versus the press bunfight at Monza. This invariably started as an orderly dinner at a long table until someone would surreptitiously hurl a bread roll from the 'Team' end of the table in the direction of the press. Retaliation then became inevitable, and things would degenerate until the ammunition became upgraded into wine-filled rolls spiked with toothpicks, whereupon order would eventually be restored in the interests of life and limb. But while the battle raged, Jim Clark would prove himself as adept a bombardier as he was a racing driver.

When he moved abroad to avoid the penal UK taxation regime of the time there were fewer opportunities to meet him in relaxed circumstances, but early in 1968 came the suggestion that he might well be returning home quite soon. I was looking forward to the possibility of another of those long Riverside-type chats. But of course it was not to be; sadly, the memories have had to suffice.

JOHN SURTEES

It must always be difficult for someone who has reached the pinnacle of one sport to arrive in another as a beginner. It must have been even more difficult when the two sports were motorcycle and motor racing in the days when certain elements of the car fraternity seemed to consider anyone associated with two wheels to be an interloper and something of a second-class citizen.

Geoff Duke, with two motorcycle World Championships already on his scoresheet, switched from two wheels to four at the end of 1951, but he didn't really enjoy the experience and returned to his first love during the following year, adding four more world titles between 1952 and 1955.

John Surtees made a similar transition in 1960, and although like Duke he retained his connection with motorcycle racing (he won two of his seven motorcycle world titles after he had started to race cars) and was less than enamoured by the reception he received from some of the 'car people', he stuck at it. John has always been a very determined character, and I have always felt that it was his knowledge of Duke's experience as much as his natural desire to succeed in any task he undertook that made him even more determined, not just to make the grade in motor racing, but to prove that he was better than anyone else at it.

I am sure that Surtees' deep-rooted determination stemmed from his father, Jack, who was a noted sidecar racer in his day (I believe John had his competition baptism sitting in Dad's 'chair') and for whom life had been far from an easy ride. Jack's racing career was drawing to a close and John's was just starting when I first set eyes on them in the early Fifties. This was at Brands Hatch, where I used to be a regular visitor on Wednesday or Saturday afternoons in order to watch the open practice sessions.

The two Surtees were regulars there, and time after time I noticed that John would invariably be first out onto the track whenever a motorcycle session began, and would then pound around lap after lap, seemingly glued to his machine in the immaculate style which became his hallmark, while Jack watched eagle-eyed from the paddock entrance and then laid down the law whenever John stopped for a briefing.

Even this early in his career, it seemed to me inevitable that here was someone who would be going on to great things, if only because his dedication to perfection was all too apparent. It didn't matter what the track conditions were like, there was always something to be learnt by getting out there and coping with them, and I'm sure it was this single-mindedness which enabled John to rise so quickly in the sport and to take on the very best – people like Duke – at such an early age.

In a sense, history was to repeat itself with John's move into motor racing because once again he found himself racing against, and therefore being compared with, the very best almost from the start. I was not a witness to his initial test drives in an Aston Martin sports-racer and a Formula One Vanwall at Goodwood, where I believe he was soon lapping on or very close to Stirling Moss' pace, but I was at the circuit a few weeks later to watch him make his racing debut in a Formula Junior Cooper-Austin which Ken Tyrrell had loaned to him for the opening meeting of the 1960 season.

After seeing Surtees steer the car into pole position on the grid (for his first race!), a group of us walked back towards the banking overlooking the chicane to watch what, regardless of the outcome, would be a small piece of motor racing history. Notwithstanding his practice time, few of us expected John to be able to match the pace of Jim Clark's Lotus-Ford once the flag dropped, but we were in for a considerable surprise.

On that opening lap the Cooper held a clear lead into Woodcote and through the chicane, and although Clark went by during the second lap, Surtees later retook the lead. Then his inexperience showed when he became blocked in by backmarkers, which dropped him to third place, but he fought back again and we saw him take second place from Trevor Taylor in the other works Lotus by out-braking him into Woodcote in a brilliantly judged manoeuvre on the last lap. Even before the race Surtees had been able to demonstrate that his exceptional speed of reactions had given him impressive car control; now we had seen that far from being inhibited in his new environment, he was prepared and able to mix it wheel-to-wheel with anyone, with no favours asked or given, and was likely to become as formidable a competitor on four wheels as he had been – and indeed still was – on two.

Of the seven World Champions under discussion in this book, I think that John Surtees has probably been the least well understood of them all by the press. Some writers who quite rightly still applaud his very considerable and versatile achievements on the track are still inclined to recall his racing days – first as driver, then as constructor/entrant – with mixed feelings, remembering him as a somewhat prickly character who was often self-opinionated, sometimes cantankerous and overly argumentative.

On occasions, perhaps, he *was* so inclined when things were going really badly – and all too often in his racing days they seemed to be – but I believe the real John Surtees was always a considerably different person from the image he sometimes portrayed, and in making this assessment I give thanks for the opportunity which came my way in the early Sixties to get to know him well when we attempted to get a book off the ground together. Although we had to abandon the project because we both found ourselves unable to devote sufficient time to it – 16 years later the book was resurrected and brought into print most ably with the help of Alan Henry (*John Surtees: World Champion* – Hazleton) – I found the hours which we did manage to spend together to be most revealing. This was not simply because of the interesting tales John was able to recall for me – these were invariably fascinating, though frequently frustrating to a collaborator because time after time they would lead John off at a tangent from the matter under discussion! – but because in working with him away from the pressures of the race track, though not always those of his ever-ringing telephone, he emerged as someone so very different from my own preconception of him.

He was at that time an intensely private person, and it had not always been easy to interpret what was going on in his mind. Consequently, I have to confess I had formed the opinion that he carried a considerable chip on his shoulder, that he seemed to feel that he was surrounded by incompetents, that he was probably regretting having come into motor racing in the first place, and that he was only remaining in it because he still felt he had a message to deliver to certain other people.

In fact, as I quickly discovered, he was actually revelling in the challenge which racing on four wheels had offered him, he was getting genuine pleasure (as distinct from cold self-satisfaction) out of what he had been able to achieve, he had already developed a deep appreciation of the history of the sport, and he was being driven by a burning ambition to contribute to its enhancement.

Rightly, in my opinion, he felt he had quite a lot to offer in that direction. Not as a high-profile ambassador in the accepted sense, because he was not an extrovert like Graham Hill, who revelled in an audience and could handle a microphone with devastating timing and wit, but as a performer in the true sense because the perfectionist in him was forever searching for and identifying ways and means by which things could be done better.

More often than not, any prickly behaviour on his part was, I believe, born of frustration that he was being thwarted in his efforts by others, all too often for politically motivated reasons. Nowhere was this seen more vividly than during his years with Ferrari, with whom he had that extraordinary love-hate relationship. He had genuine affection both for the man and for his team, and for what they stood for in historical terms, but his relationships with certain individuals involved were always brittle; John has always put great store on integrity, and therefore has tended to react strongly against behaviour which he sees as falling short of acceptable standards.

I quickly discerned that 'Big John', as he was sometimes known, was – and still is – an acutely perceptive person, who can smell trouble at a thousand paces. Yet beneath that sometimes tough outer skin I discovered a highly sensitive and, I suspected, in some respects a slightly vulnerable disposition. This, I believe, helped to explain the suddenness of his break-up with Ferrari at the very time when he was poised to reinforce his ties with the team; in the highly charged environment of Formula One, he could cope with all the on-track pressures that were thrown at him, but of the counter-productive pressures in the pit road he could only stand so much.

Of Britain's seven World Champions, John Surtees to my mind has emerged as being by far the most genuine example of a true motorsports enthusiast. Why else should he in recent years have gained so much sheer joy in restoring and then riding or driving so many machines from the past? Why, indeed, should he have collected such an impressive array of them in the first place? Not, I am sure, for financial gain – though I am certain that a man who has had so many business interests both within and beyond the sport has a highly developed sense of what is and what is not a good buy – but because he is acutely aware of the role they played in the past, and through owning and/or using them, he has been able to touch their sense of history.

John Surtees, I believe, gets at least as much enjoyment today out of his association with motorsport as he did at the height of his riding and driving achievements, and rather like Stirling Moss, the role of elder statesman and occasional competitor sits very comfortably on his shoulders. During his professional racing career he was usually so preoccupied with the task or the problem of the moment that his face rarely projected enjoyment and would only occasionally break into the broad grin which characterized his more relaxed moments, such as when he became the generous and felicitous host at the season's end parties he used to hold at his home – and how enjoyable those occasions were.

Towards the end of his involvement in Formula One, his efforts to sustain his own team proved to be a bruising experience, and when eventually he had to leave the scene due to inadequate resources – he had been let down once too often – many of us felt a deep sense of sympathy towards him, even though the news was by no means unexpected – the writing had been on the wall for some time.

But at least he had the satisfaction of knowing that he had tried honourably, even though he had been denied the contentment of seeing one of his cars win a Grand Prix. He had deserved at least that much, and if today that little piece of unfinished business still rankles, he doesn't let it show. Indeed, these days John Surtees' contentment and pleasure with life is written all over his face, usually accompanied by that broad grin, and I believe he is now held in higher esteem than ever before by those who perhaps are only now beginning to assess the true value of his contribution to the sport.

JACKIE STEWART

Racing drivers are notoriously shy when talking about how much they earn (and why not?), but one day, not long after his retirement from racing, I found myself in conversation with Jackie Stewart, discussing the matter of a fee. It was not one he would be charging, but one that I was proposing to charge a third party.

He said: "Let me offer you a piece of advice. Never, *ever*, under-price yourself. If you do, people will think you are mediocre, someone who can do the job the same way as anybody else. Charge more, and people will expect you to do the job better. Charge them a lot more and they will expect the very best. Then you have to make sure that you *give* them the very best that money can buy, ensuring that whatever they are having to pay you they will be getting outstanding value for money, better than they can find anywhere else."

That, I thought, summed up perfectly Jackie's philosophy, not only throughout his racing career, but also during the years since his retirement, when he has earned far more than he ever did as a driver by working as a consultant to commercial and industrial clients – and giving them outstanding value for money.

From quite early in his racing career it was clear that Jackie was very conscious of his financial worth, and it was all part of a considered plan that he should ensure that he was paid it. It was in June 1966, while he was recuperating in a London hospital following his accident in the Belgian Grand Prix, which had left him trapped in his badly crumpled BRM until rescued by Graham Hill and others, that he first talked to me at length about money.

He told me that the financial ravages of the motor trade in which his father had been involved had given him a deep sense of insecurity when he was a youngster. Consequently, from quite an early age he had determined that whatever he did in life he would make sure that he earned enough from it so that his own children, should he have any, would be protected from a similar burden of financial uncertainty.

"At the time, I assumed that in due course I would join my brother in running the family garage business, so I was intent that when that day arrived the whole operation would be run as skilfully and efficiently as was possible so that it could be developed into a prosperous and expanding business. But then along came motor racing, and when I discovered I was quite good at it, suddenly my potential earning power was extended far beyond my wildest dreams."

Clearly, Stewart had not been slow to adapt to his changed situation, and already he had rewritten his script for life. Despite his temporary discomfort he said: "Today I count myself very fortunate indeed that I am paid what many people would term a lot of money to do something that I enjoy so much and for which I seem to have a certain talent. But my aim in life now extends far beyond just achieving financial security; I plan to use my time in racing to create a platform for whatever direction my career takes me afterwards."

Already – and remember, Jackie still had only two Grand Prix wins to his name at the time – he was taking the long-term view, conscious that any racing driver had only a limited period of high earning power. Clearly, his mind was already focused on what would follow. He also told me of his intention to embark on what was to prove to be a highly controversial campaign – to improve the safety standards in motor racing. In this, his BRM team patron Louis Stanley had already taken a head start on him through his creation of a mobile Grand Prix Medical Unit, and sitting up in bed that afternoon and flushed by relief at having escaped so lightly from his potentially fatal accident, he was most fulsome in his praise for Stanley and for the way he had masterminded Stewart's emergency treatment immediately after the accident and his subsequent speedy return to London from Spa-Francorchamps.

Warming to his theme, he said: "Louis has the right idea. There is a real need for skilled on-the-spot medical facilities, as we saw in Belgium, but safety extends far beyond responding to accidents. We need to reduce their likelihood and severity by making circuits safer places to race on, and that's what I intend to fight for, even if it makes me unpopular in some quarters." Just how unpopular he would be with certain people even he probably hadn't anticipated, not that this would have deterred him; Jackie Stewart was born with a stubborn streak in him, for which nearly everyone in motor racing should be grateful because it caused him to stand his ground so resolutely on this important issue. Much of the safety consciousness from which motor racing subsequently has benefited has stemmed from the pioneering work led by Stewart and a few others all those years ago.

I recall that in the late Sixties some of the arguments he had with his detractors on this thorny subject were at least as heated as his battles on the track, and quite frequently they took place in front of an inquisitive audience because quite unashamedly he used the media whenever he could in order to promote his cause, usually with good effect. For a man whose public image was important to him, it was a brave strategy because at one stage his stand on safety issues was in danger of receiving more publicity than his accomplishments on the track, his World Championships notwithstanding.

Yet some of his performances – particularly those for the Tyrrell team – which I witnessed provided the most telling evidence that Jackie Stewart was a driver of rare distinction. Apart from his latent ability, I think his two most formidable weapons were the quality of his preparedness and his smoothness. As part of the former, he became something of a testing addict, and he used to give Ken Tyrrell a hard time with his incessant requests for ever more test sessions in order to try the latest tyres that Dunlop and in later years Goodyear could offer him. But it was all in a good cause. He once said to me: "I feel content when we have done enough testing between races to ensure that when we come to the next Grand Prix we are able to achieve a level of performance in the first practice session on the Friday that the others only attain by the first session on the Saturday. If you can start off with that sort of advantage, you can keep building on it into the second day and be that much more in control of the situation all weekend." That, I thought, was a typical Stewart remark – being in control of the situation.

Never, of course, was this seen to more dramatic effect than during the 1968 German Grand Prix, that remarkable race on a wet and foggy Nurburgring where we saw Jackie and his Tyrrell Matra emerge through the murk to receive the chequered flag more than 4 minutes ahead of the Lotus of Graham Hill, the runner-up. Here was the evidence, if anyone had needed it, that Jackie was the Formula One 'smoothie' of his time, demonstrating a driving style dedicated to sustaining his car constantly in a state of balance in ever-changing conditions. It is a quality which he has continued to promote very successfully in recent years through the medium of his race circuit-based high-performance driving courses.

I always thought that his car control was seen at its best through a long, fast bend, of which there was none better than Silverstone's Woodcote Corner in pre-chicane days. I remember in particular the final qualifying session before the 1969 British Grand Prix, when the battle for pole position became a private contest between Stewart and his Matra and the Lotus of Jackie's friend and close neighbour Jochen Rindt. Stewart looked to have won it, but then a dislodged stone punctured a tyre and caused him to crash on the outside of the corner. It looked a nasty accident, but he climbed out, sprinted to his team-mate Beltoise's car and then lapped even faster in it, but in the meantime Rindt had put in a 'flier' to claim the fastest time. It was a fitting overture to a memorable wheel-to-wheel battle between Stewart and Rindt at the front of the Grand Prix, which I watched from the inside of Copse Corner, where we were all kept on tip-toe until the see-sawing contest was ended prematurely by Rindt being forced to make a pit stop when a wing end-plate began to rub into one of his rear tyres.

Because he has maintained a close connection with the sport over the past 20 years, many of us have seen more of Jackie in various of his current roles than when he was driving, and in particular we have been able to watch and study him performing at close quarters. It can be an impressive sight. For a start, he is a fluent and articulate public speaker who prepares his lectures and speeches with infinite care. During his driving course days he emerges as a most effective tutor, and I for one have benefited greatly from the opportunities which have come my way to share a car with him on a race track and allow my inadequacies to be revealed. I defy anyone who has sampled one of his courses not to have come away from them a faster, smoother and safer driver.

Whatever the project in which he is involved, he pursues it with an almost breathtaking energy, commitment and attention to detail which has nothing whatever to do with monetary reward, as I discovered on an occasion during the Seventies. At the time I was asked to assemble a group of people who, on a completely voluntary basis, would be prepared to research and identify developments in the safety field which were of either actual or potential benefit to motor racing. It proved to be a more time-consuming task than any of us had anticipated, but despite his already hectic business schedule Jackie willingly took up the challenge, and his input, I recall, exceeded that of the rest of us put together.

Much of his work these days, of course, takes place beyond our view, notably his test driving and product evaluation for car and tyre manufacturers, but I'm sure that indirectly we derive considerable benefit from it. I am told that he pushes, pushes, pushes his clients all the time in his pursuit of even the most subtle of improvements, and I can imagine that on occasions he becomes a considerable thorn in the side of the 'bean counters'.

In my experience, second-best in anything is anathema to him, which is why on at least two occasions I have derived great joy and satisfaction in beating him. The first was in the Seventies on one of his Formula Finesse exercises with Ford, when somehow I contrived to keep the ball in the bowl on the car's bonnet while shaving a few tenths off his time through the driving slalom; he took his defeat graciously and handed me a Rolex watch which I still treasure as a reminder of a brief moment of glory.

During the Eighties we had a longer-running battle which continued through a period when at Grands Prix we each enjoyed the hospitality of the Goodyear motorhome during our periods of relaxation. At lunchtime our minds would always become focused on the same target – a particularly succulent line in cheese-and-chutney sandwiches. He would always do his best (has he ever done less than that?) but invariably I would beat him by a whisker to that all-important last one! As I would explain to him between mouthfuls, it was a case of horses for courses.

JAMES HUNT

The harbour area of Monte Carlo on Grand Prix weekend has always been a magnet for journalists hungry for a few extra scraps of gossip, and in 1973 the boys from the tabloids had a field day. A newcomer was in town, who over the next few days would generate nearly as much ink as all the established teams put together.

Even for those of us accustomed to the extravagances of Grand Prix racing's once-a-year yachtsmen, the arrival on the scene of Lord Alexander Hesketh and his entourage was something special. You couldn't miss them because not only did they have one of the largest floating entertainment centres in the whole place, it was sitting on pole position, bang in the middle of the harbour area opposite the new swimming pool around which for the first time the race track would be required to deviate.

The hospitality on board was lavish and we were all made most welcome, yet there was something unreal about it all. How could a group of extroverts, so dedicated to the task of having a ball, possibly have any serious intentions about Formula One?

The centre of attraction – especially of course amongst the females – and seemingly enjoying every minute of it was the tall, fair-haired graduate from Formula Ford and Formula Three, whose demonstrations thus far of his impressive speed on the race track had been punctuated by a number of heavily publicized shunts and the odd punch-up – unlikely credentials for success in the increasingly hard-nosed environment of Grand Prix racing.

That first evening in Monaco, looking beyond the champagne glasses at the assembled company, it occurred to me that James Hunt was being cast in the role of Clown Prince of the production, but that Alexander and his almost equally rotund team manager, Bubbles Horsley, were really the two biggest Jokers in the Pack. Clearly, all three knew a great deal about how to enjoy themselves, and their partying that weekend almost certainly out-performed the opposition on the champagne and socializing barometer. But there was little evidence to suggest to me during those few days of frenzied activity that the driver at the centre of it all could possibly become Britain's next World Champion after Stewart (who was destined to retire later that year having secured the title for the third time).

But by the end of the weekend, Hunt, who was destined to spend so much of his sadly brief life surprising people, had already raised quite a few eyebrows in the pressroom. Defying all predictions, he had qualified his March comfortably, and on the Sunday we watched with increasing admiration as he kept it clear of the barriers throughout what was physically the most exhausting race in the calendar, only for his engine to expire a few laps from the end. Happily, despite his late retirement, he was still officially classified ninth of the 10 finishers, which needless to say was deemed justification for the popping of a few more champagne corks.

In fact, as we were soon to discover, behind all the extravagance and jocularity there had lurked a considerable measure of serious intent, and James quickly came across to us as a driver who was setting his sights high. In his favour he was immensely fit, as indeed he would need to be during the years ahead in order to shrug off the after-effects of his sometimes lurid lifestyle, while his first visit to Monaco had already demonstrated to us his impressive stamina, even though – like anyone in his first Formula One race there – by the end of it he was completely spent.

During that first season, Dr Harvey Postlethwaite and his race engineers helped to turn the team's 'off the peg' March into a far from uncompetitive car, and this, coupled with James' hard-charging style, soon transformed the Hesketh team into serious contenders, a fact which seemed to make some of their more extrovert off-circuit behaviour all the more incongruous. In fact, I believe that on many occasions their earnest pursuit of the outrageous was nothing more than a well-orchestrated game of playing to their image, as a means of emphasizing their defiance of convention for its own sake. Behind the facade, they were as dedicated to success as anyone; the difference was they went out of their way to prove that you didn't need to be po-faced in order to achieve it.

In this, Hunt played his part well, and I remember clearly the flood of goodwill which flowed his way from the press tribune on the afternoon when he beat Niki Lauda and his Ferrari to the finishing line at Zandvoort in 1975. Little did we realize that it would be the only Grand Prix victory which he and his noble patron would enjoy together before the money ran out the following winter. That their shortage of finance should coincide with an unexpected vacancy at McLaren, following Emerson Fittipaldi's surprise decision to leave and form his own team, was undoubtedly James' luckiest break since entering Formula One, and he was quick to acknowledge this when we talked at length at Jarama one morning when practice for the 1976 Spanish Grand Prix was delayed by the lack of a medical helicopter.

It was only after spending this time with him that I came to realize just how deep-thinking a person James was, and how broadly based were his interests. He was very conscious of the higher level of expectation from his new team, who were the current World Champions, and his own determination to deliver had become even sharper as a result. Although his personal life had continued to fill the pages of the newspaper gossip columns, there was, I thought, a new seriousness about the way he went about his business on and around the race track.

He also talked to me enthusiastically about his other business interests, notably his wine bar and club in Spain (which sadly, like so many of his investments, would not endure) and of the serious consideration he was giving to buying a farm. Much as he craved for the World Championship (which was destined to come his way by the narrowest of margins at the end of that year), I gained the distinct impression that morning that James did not foresee a long career for himself in motor racing.

His mind was already on other things, other challenges, which perhaps helps to explain why later, when at the height of his fame as the current World Champion, he seemed to go out of his way to amaze and at times offend people by his unconventional behaviour and appearance, as though he had to remind everyone, however exalted, that he was, and always would be, his own man. At that time I was far from alone amongst journalists in roundly condemning him for appearing (sometimes late) for formal public appearances in jeans, a provocative tee-shirt and sandals. In this I thought he did himself little credit, and the image of his sport considerable harm.

That said, I believe the quality of his driving during 1976 made him a worthy World Champion, notwithstanding Niki Lauda's terrible accident which served to swing the points battle in Hunt's favour. James drove like a true Champion that year, though never quite as well, I thought, afterwards. In fact, having put so much personal effort into winning the title, I think some of the fire went out, along with much of the enjoyment. Increasingly, he became very wound-up before a race, yet he had tremendous guts, and it was a typically brave act, I thought, that he announced his retirement so suddenly, in mid-season, because he had decided that the risks (in an admittedly uncompetitive car) were no longer acceptable or endurable.

Ironically, in some respects I think his retirement from the cockpit was the making of James Hunt, for the man who emerged was so much more relaxed simply because there was no longer that conflict between his natural inclination to do his own thing and the personal discipline of being a professional racing driver. He remained close to the scene, of course, and increasingly we used to enjoy his company and appreciate the outspokenness and at times the perception and wisdom of his views, which he was always pleased to air most eloquently.

Perhaps this is why someone had the inspired idea of sitting him in a BBC Television commentary box alongside Murray Walker, not that his new career with a microphone was without its pitfalls, especially in the early days when his laid-back approach sometimes tended to blur his vision of what was going on in front of him. I remember on one occasion in particular becoming quite insensed because of his vehement condemnation of Jacques Laffite for an accident in Spain in which the Frenchman had clearly been the innocent victim. We argued at length about it afterwards, but without any animosity whatsoever.

Indeed, it was extremely difficult to fall out with someone whose warmth, charm and sheer good company far outweighed his aberrations. The many thousands of words in tribute to him which were written after his untimely death said it all, because many of us in the media had had the privilege of sharing his company and getting to know him so much better than most 'superstars'.

It is a matter of record that he suffered severe financial distress during his final years – the legacy of costly divorce proceedings and failed business enterprises – but he rode his problems with great stoicism, never burdened others with them, and indeed did his best to laugh them off. I first caught sight of the ancient and battered Austin A35 which had become his long-distance transport when he parked it close to my car in the press car park before the 1992 British Grand Prix and with tongue in cheek I ribbed him for letting down the tone of the place.

He rose to the bait. "You don't know what you're missing", he claimed. "Oh yes I do", I countered, "I used to run one about five centuries ago". "Magnificent car", he went on. "You can pack a house in it, and it goes for ever on a gallon of petrol", and then added, with a wry laugh, "besides, it's all I can afford after a couple of expensive divorces!"

In and around London he would use his upright pedal cycle with the carrier basket on the handlebars, and occasionally we would arrive together at the BBC Television Centre. "It's just super for keeping fit", he would enthuse, "and of course it's much quicker than a car in all those traffic jams. In fact, I love traffic jams; then I can gloat over all those frustrated drivers breathing in exhaust fumes!" James certainly knew how to face adversity with a smile on his face.

It was at the 'Beeb' that I met him for the last time, only hours before he died. He seemed to be on top form, and I'm sure he felt that way, too, though clearly he could not have been. We had only a short chat, mainly about race prospects, then he rushed off in search of a bar of chocolate before settling down to his final race commentary on the Canadian Grand Prix, which on this occasion he and Murray were to do at long-distance.

Minutes earlier James had taken a phone call from the Montreal circuit from Gerald Donaldson, the esteemed journalist and author with whom he collaborated on his syndicated newspaper columns. They had got to know each other very well as a result of this work and had become close friends. James had read Gerry's biography of Gilles Villeneuve and had been so moved by it that he had asked him if he would help him with his own life story, which he planned to write, not immediately, but perhaps in a couple of years' time. He promised him that it would be something very special in motor racing autobiographies, and I am sure it would have been.

Sadly, we are much the poorer for having been denied the opportunity to read it, at least in the form in which it had been conceived, although Gerry's planned tribute to a remarkable life will doubtless prove a worthy substitute. In the meantime, some of us can count ourselves very much the richer for having been able to share the company and friendship of one of motor racing's most remarkable characters.

NIGEL MANSELL

When covering a Grand Prix for a newspaper or magazine in the days when there was greater freedom of movement, we tended to follow certain routines during the weekend, the details of which would vary according to the circuit. For example, when the Belgian Grand Prix was held a Zolder, it was almost inevitable that at least once a day during practice a few of us would head away from the pit and paddock area towards the first corner, a fast but relatively sharp and testing left-hander.

It was a good place to watch drivers at work, to compare their techniques, and to study the relative handling characteristics of different cars. Sometimes we would be joined there by one or two drivers whose own cars were temporarily out of action. In those days, long before everything was either televised or recorded on computers, it gave them a good opportunity, without having to walk too far from base, to watch the opposition – and perhaps most importantly their own team-mate – in action.

In 1981, towards the end of one of the practice periods, I was joined there by Nigel Mansell, who earlier in the session I had noticed was giving it all he knew through the revealing left-hander. Now Elio de Angelis was out on the track in the other Essex Lotus, and if anything he was smoother through the corner than Mansell had been, but he was also consistently just that fraction slower on the stopwatch. "You're gaining at least a tenth on him through here", I remarked, which brought a smile of satisfaction to Nigel's face and the brief reply, "Good".

This was to be Mansell's sixth Grand Prix (he had taken part in just two the previous year and the first three in 1981, but then Colin Chapman had withdrawn his team from the San Marino Grand Prix in protest over the banning of his revolutionary twin-chassis Lotus 88). But although it was still relatively early days for a Formula One newcomer, Mansell's score sheet to date was beginning to look less than impressive. He had completed just one race, in 11th place, which was also the highest he had ever run in a Grand Prix; in the other four he had twice been stopped by engine failure, once by brake failure and once by an accident.

I could sense the feeling of frustration which was grinding away inside him, and already there were ominous signs of the Lotus team becoming polarized into two camps, one behind each driver, with Mansell's looking the weaker of the two despite his personal endorsement by Chapman. But at least that day the major frustration for the drivers – the loss of the Lotus 88 on which so many of the team's hopes had been based – was being shared equally, and faced with having to go back to using what, by Formula 1 standards, were outdated and increasingly uncompetitive cars, Mansell seemed to be coping with the situation more effectively than his senior driving partner. By the time practice ended Mansell was 10th on the grid, four places ahead of de Angelis.

In those days there seemed to be far more people around who were prepared to 'rubbish' Mansell (perhaps because he was never slow to complain of injustices or to speak his mind whenever things were not as he thought they should be – which seemed to be quite frequently) than there were those anxious to praise him, and I found myself very much in the minority at that time in believing that behind all the moaning there was a rare talent bursting to be revealed.

Walking back to the pits with him that day, I sensed that he was far from happy with life and he seemed genuinely surprised when I said to him: "You may not believe it right now, but one day it will all come good, and before you realize it you'll have achieved so much in Formula One you'll want to write a book about it!" Then he turned, smiled wryly and said: "It's nice to know *someone* has some faith in me."

I failed to raise the book subject with him again until 1986, during his second season with Williams, which was probably a mistake because by then he had a retinue of managers to handle commercial matters and contracts, and I soon discovered that their idea of a fair reward for his time far outstripped mine or my ability to pay it.

By that time, of course, virtually everything else had changed for Mansell, too, for his talent had been exposed for all to see. He had always been a charger, but now, backed by a highly competitive car operated by a very efficiently managed team, he was also a consistent winner and obviously a World Champion in waiting. He had become the new British motor racing hero to thousands of race fans who, having been starved of a home-grown Champion to cheer since James Hunt had won his title way back in 1976, had gratefully seized on *Our Nige* as their best hope of seeing their dreams fulfilled.

Some of his driving by this time had developed an awesome intensity, but back in the pit area we often witnessed tension of a different sort. His main problem during that first period with Williams, of course, was that he had gone there as number two to Nelson Piquet, and by demonstrating fairly convincingly his ability to out-drive him he had sewn the seeds of the discontent which would haunt him until he left the team for Ferrari. Also, it didn't exactly smooth the atmosphere within the team that Mansell clearly disliked Piquet intensely as a person.

Never one to hide his feelings, Nigel became the subject of almost guaranteed copy for the media, especially the tabloids, who could be relied upon to grab and where necessary embroider every morsel of his outpourings. Even those of us who wrote for what we considered to be the serious newspapers found that our Sports Editors all too often wanted a 'Mansell angle' to what could and perhaps should have been a more evenly weighted story.

Up to a point they were probably right, because whether it was practice, qualifying or the race itself, it was virtually certain that Mansell would be taking himself and his car closer to their respective limits than anyone else. For the editors back at base he became the dream ticket to headline-making copy, a driver who would risk bursting a blood vessel in his determination to extract the last ounce of commitment from himself and the last drop of speed out of his car. But I often wondered what must have been going through the minds of the other drivers when they saw the British press week after week heading *en masse* for the back of Mansell's pit garage after every session and then dutifully waiting there, sometimes for 20 minutes or more, for him to emerge and report 'what it was like out there'.

In the earlier years we were usually told about some sort of Hell on Earth, but gradually the histrionics were brought under control, whereupon his post-track interviews took on a much more positive and informative flavour. Also, the more he became used to us, the more comfortable he seemed to be in our presence, and in his more relaxed moods, especially when he was exercising his considerable sense of humour, he became at times the most enjoyable and amusing company.

Yet to me he has always been something of a paradox. For example, how is it that a man can hold himself on a knife-edge of balance at the very limit of adhesion in a racing car and then be so inordinately accident-prone out of it? If there is a hole in the ground or a loose pavement stone you can bet your boots he'll find it and do himself some grisly injury, usually on the eve of a race. How is it that someone who is so emotionally moved by the devotion of his race fans can on occasions infuriate those with whom he is required to work most closely because of a seeming lack of sensitivity towards their feelings? I believe there were times when he would have generated much more goodwill within his team if he had been as free and fulsome with his praise for others' efforts as he was with his dutiful mention of his sponsors.

But for all that, no driver, surely, has ever spared himself less in pursuit of that so often elusive goal of a World Championship. He has hurt himself on far more occasions than most bodies would tolerate, and although he might be inclined from time to time to exaggerate the effects of minor mishaps, on many other occasions the pain has been far more serious than he would ever let be known.

In financial terms, he could not have come to the top of his sport at a more opportune time, even though the sort of income figures (invariably based on guesswork) that have been quoted for him from time to time in various quarters are probably well wide of the mark. "Contrary to certain people's opinion, money is not a problem for me," he told me one day in Canada when he was in the middle of negotiations for a new contract. "Most people don't realize, because normally I never talk about financial matters, that I became a millionaire when I signed that contract with Colin Chapman all those years ago, and I can tell you I've had a pay rise every year since!"

But although the timing of his racing career has made Mansell a very wealthy man, in at least one other respect it could scarcely, I suggest, have been less fortunate. Today, all the classic ingredients of a top Formula 1 driver – exceptional skill, stamina, bravery and fitness – are it seems insufficient in themselves to guarantee the success they warrant. Alongside them it would appear to be necessary to demonstrate some equally uncompromising but less savoury qualities. It helps, for example, to be self-centred, cunning, manipulative, opportunistic and devoid of any sentimentality whatsoever, in other words, to be blessed with devastating political skills.

This is where I believe Mansell has fallen short throughout his racing career. He is simply not a political animal, which in itself is, I suggest, highly commendable, but it does help to explain how over the years he has found himself on so many occasions floundering in a jungle of confusion and disappointment in his negotiations with people whom he has assumed always meant what they said and whose straightforward honesty and sense of fair play he took for granted.

I think perhaps his happiest months in Formula One were during the early part of his two-season stay with Ferrari when his gutsy performances in an all-too-often fragile car earned him the title *Il Leone* (the lion) not only by the *tifosi*, but also by the people in his pit and back at the factory, who have always generated tremendous goodwill to a driver prepared to stick his neck out. But later, the political skills of Alain Prost completely destroyed his morale there.

His relationship with Frank Williams was, I thought, always a brittle one, being based on mutual respect for each other's abilities rather than personal qualities. In 1987 a few of us were invited over to the Isle of Man to talk to him while he recuperated from the back injuries sustained in his practice accident in

Japan. He was obviously in considerable pain and could only walk slowly and with great difficulty, but his real hurt, he said, was that Williams had seemed more concerned by the loss of a car for the race than for his own welfare and that he had been obliged to defy team orders in order to fly home for treatment.

His final fall-out with the team in 1992, having just secured that richly deserved World Championship, was a drama which Formula One could ill afford and for which it has since been paying a heavy price, even though the drop in race attendances following his departure were probably caused more by unacceptably high admission prices in the middle of a deep European recession than by Mansell's absence. After all, spectators used to flock to Grands Prix long before Nigel started to win them.

Nevertheless, Formula One's loss has been CART and IndyCar's gain, and although after crossing the Atlantic he probably burnt too many bridges behind him to make his return to Formula One a realistic prospect (short of a fundamental restructuring of the sport) the possibility of him racing again in Britain within an expanded IndyCar series is one to which I am sure countless thousands of his admirers would respond with barely controlled enthusiasm. Should that day arrive, the biggest traffic jam the country has ever witnessed because of a sporting event is almost a foregone conclusion, but many thousands would doubtless deem it an acceptable inconvenience in order that they should see once again motor racing's leading entertainer performing before them at the height of his powers.

Like the six who went before him, and the seventh who deserved to be numbered amongst them, Britain's latest World Champion has done it 'his way', and we can be thankful to all of them for that. And thanks, too, for the memories...

WORLD CHAMPION STATISTICS

R = retired, DIS = disqualified, W = withdrew before race. Note: figures in brackets in season's totals indicate the number of points before dropping under the only-so-many-finishes-count rules.

MIKE HAWTHORN

Born Mexborough, Yorkshire, April 10, 1929. Died in a road crash, January 22, 1959. First race, Brighton Speed Trials 1950 (Riley Ulster Imp). First Grand Prix, Belgium 1952 (Cooper). Grand Prix career: 1952 Cooper, 1953–54 Ferrari, 1955 Vanwall, Ferrari, 1956 Maserati, BRM, Vanwall, 1957–58 Ferrari. 45 races, four poles, three wins.

The 1958 Championship

Jan 19	Argentina	Buenos Aires	3
May 18	Monaco	Monte Carlo	R
May 26	Holland	Zandvoort	5
June 15	Belgium	Spa	2
July 6	France	Reims	1
July 19	Britain	Silverstone	2
Aug 3	Germany	Nurburgring	R
Aug 24	Portugal	Oporto	2
Sept 7	Italy	Monza	2
Oct 19	Morocco	Casablanca	2

Points: Hawthorn 42 (49), Moss 41, Brooks 24, Salvadori 15, Schell and Collins 14.

GRAHAM HILL

Born Hampstead, London, February 15, 1929. Died in a plane crash, November 29, 1975. First race, Up-to-1,200cc Sportscars, Brands Hatch, 1956 (Lotus 11-Climax). First Grand Prix, Monaco 1958. Grand Prix career: 1958–59 Lotus, 1960–66 BRM, 1967–70 Lotus, 1971–72 Brabham, 1973 Shadow, 1974–75 Lola. 176 races, 13 poles, 14 wins.

The 1962 Championship

May 20	Holland	Zandvoort	1
June 3	Monaco	Monte Carlo	6
June 17	Belgium	Spa	2
July 8	France	Rouen	9
July 21	Britain	Aintree	4
Aug 5	Germany	Nurburgring	1
Sept 16	Italy	Monza	1
Oct 7	USA	Watkins Glen	2
Dec 29	S Africa	East London	1

Points: Hill 42 (52), Clark 30, McLaren 27 (32), Surtees 19, Gurney 15, P Hill 14.

JIM CLARK
Born Fife, March 4, 1936. Died in a Formula Two race at Hockenheim, April 7, 1968. First race, Sprint for cars over 2,000cc, Stobs Camp, Hawick, 1956 (Sunbeam-Talbot). First Grand Prix, Holland 1960. Grand Prix career: 1960–68 Lotus. 72 races, 33 poles, 25 wins.

The 1963 Championship

May 26	Monaco	Monte Carlo	8
June 9	Belgium	Spa	1
June 23	Holland	Zandvoort	1
June 30	France	Reims	1
July 20	Britain	Silverstone	1
Aug 4	Germany	Nurburgring	2
Sept 8	Italy	Monza	1
Oct 6	USA	Watkins Glen	3
Oct 27	Mexico	Mexico City	1
Dec 28	S Africa	East London	1

Points: Clark 54 (73), G Hill 29, Ginther 29 (34), Surtees 22, Gurney 19, McLaren 17.

JOHN SURTEES
Born Tatsfield, Surrey, February 11, 1934. First race, Formula Junior, Goodwood 1960 (Cooper-Austin). First Grand Prix, Monaco 1960. Grand Prix career: 1960 Lotus, 1961 Cooper, 1962 Lola, 1963–66 Ferrari, 1966 Cooper, 1967–68 Honda, 1969 BRM, 1970 McLaren, 1970–72 Surtees. 111 races, eight poles, six wins.

The 1964 Championship

May 10	Monaco	Monte Carlo	R
May 24	Holland	Zandvoort	2
June 14	Belgium	Spa	R
June 28	France	Rouen	R
July 11	Britain	Brands Hatch	3
Aug 2	Germany	Nurburgring	1
Aug 23	Austria	Zeltweg	R
Sept 6	Italy	Monza	1
Oct 4	USA	Watkins Glen	2
Oct 25	Mexico	Mexico City	2

Points: Surtees 40, G Hill 39 (41), Clark 32, Bandini and Ginther 23, Gurney 19.

1965, Clark's second Championship

Jan 1	S Africa	East London	1
May 30	Monaco	Did not compete	
June 13	Belgium	Spa	1
June 27	France	Clermont-Ferrand	1
July 10	Britain	Silverstone	1
July 18	Holland	Zandvoort	1
Aug 1	Germany	Nurburgring	1
Sept 12	Italy	Monza	10

| Oct 3 | USA | Watkins Glen | R |
| Oct 24 | Mexico | Mexico City | R |

Points: Clark 54, G Hill 40 (47), Stewart 33 (34), Gurney 25, Surtees 17, Bandini 13.

1968, Hill's second Championship

Jan 1	S Africa	Kyalami	2
May 12	Spain	Jarama	1
May 26	Monaco	Monte Carlo	1
June 9	Belgium	Spa	R
June 23	Holland	Zandvoort	9
July 7	France	Rouen	R
July 20	Britain	Brands Hatch	R
Aug 4	Germany	Nurburgring	2
Sept 8	Italy	Monza	R
Sept 22	Canada	Ste Jovite	4
Oct 6	USA	Watkins Glen	2
Nov 3	Mexico	Mexico City	1

Points: Hill 48, Stewart 36, Hulme 33, Ickx 27, McLaren 22, Rodriguez 18.

JACKIE STEWART

Born Milton, Dumbarton, June 11, 1939. First race, Charterhall, 1961 (Marcos GT). First Grand Prix, South Africa 1965. Grand Prix career: 1965–67 BRM, 1968–69 Matra, 1970 March, 1970–73 Tyrrell. 99 races, 17 poles, 27 wins.

The 1969 Championship

March 1	S Africa	Kyalami	1
May 4	Spain	Montjuich Park	1
May 18	Monaco	Monte Carlo	R
June 21	Holland	Zandvoort	1
July 6	France	Clermont-Ferrand	1
July 19	Britain	Silverstone	1
Aug 3	Germany	Nurburgring	2
Sept 7	Italy	Monza	1
Sept 20	Canada	Mosport	R
Oct 5	USA	Watkins Glen	R
Oct 19	Mexico	Mexico City	4

Points: Stewart 63, Ickx 37, McLaren 26, Rindt 22, Beltoise 21, Hulme 20.

1971, Stewart's second Championship

March 6	S Africa	Kyalami	2
Apr 18	Spain	Montjuich Park	1
May 23	Monaco	Monte Carlo	1
June 20	Holland	Zandvoort	11
July 4	France	Paul Ricard	1
July 17	Britain	Silverstone	1
Aug 1	Germany	Nurburgring	1
Aug 15	Austria	Zeltweg	R
Sept 5	Italy	Monza	R

| Sept 19 | Canada | Mosport | 1 |
| Oct 3 | USA | Watkins Glen | 5 |

Points: Stewart 62, Peterson 33, Cevert 26, Ickx and Siffert 19, Fittipaldi 16.

1973, Stewart's third Championship

Jan 28	Argentina	Buenos Aires	3
Feb 11	Brazil	Interlagos	2
Mar 3	S Africa	Kyalami	1
Apr 29	Spain	Montjuich Park	R
May 20	Belgium	Zolder	1
June 3	Monaco	Monte Carlo	1
June 17	Sweden	Anderstorp	5
July 1	France	Paul Ricard	4
July 14	Britain	Silverstone	10
July 29	Holland	Zandvoort	1
Aug 5	Germany	Nurburgring	1
Aug 19	Austria	Zeltweg	2
Sept 9	Italy	Monza	4
Sept 23	Canada	Mosport	5
Oct 7	USA	Watkins Glen	W

Points: Stewart 71, Fittipaldi 55, Peterson 52, Cevert 47, Revson 38, Hulme 26.

JAMES HUNT

Born Sutton, Surrey, August 29, 1947. Died London, June 15, 1993. First race, Snetterton, Formula Ford 1968 (Alexis). First Grand Prix, Monaco 1973. Grand Prix career: 1973–74 March, 1974–75 Hesketh, 1976–78 McLaren, 1979 Wolf. 92 races, 14 poles, 10 wins.

The 1976 Championship

Jan 25	Brazil	Interlagos	R
Mar 6	S Africa	Kyalami	2
Mar 28	USA West	Long Beach	R
May 2	Spain	Jarama	1
May 16	Belgium	Zolder	R
May 30	Monaco	Monte Carlo	R
June 13	Sweden	Anderstorp	5
July 4	France	Paul Ricard	1
July 18	Britain	Brands Hatch	DIS
Aug 1	Germany	Nurburgring	1
Aug 15	Austria	Zeltweg	4
Aug 29	Holland	Zandvoort	1
Sept 12	Italy	Monza	R
Oct 3	Canada	Mosport	1
Oct 10	USA East	Watkins Glen	1
Oct 24	Japan	Fuji	3

Points: Hunt 69, Lauda 68, Scheckter 49, Depailler 39, Regazzoni 31, Andretti 22.

NIGEL MANSELL
Born Upton-on-Severn, August 8, 1953. First race, karting, Shennington, Banbury, 1963. First Grand Prix, Austria 1980. Grand Prix career: 1980–84 Lotus, 1985–88 Williams, 1989–90 Ferrari, 1991–92 Williams. 181 races, 31 poles, 30 wins.

The 1992 Championship			
Mar 1	S Africa	Kyalami	1
Mar 22	Mexico	Mexico City	1
Apr 5	Brazil	Interlagos	1
May 3	Spain	Barcelona	1
May 17	San Marino	Imola	1
May 31	Monaco	Monte Carlo	2
June 14	Canada	Montreal	R
July 5	France	Magny-Cours	1
July 12	Britain	Silverstone	1
July 26	Germany	Hockenheim	1
Aug 16	Hungary	Hungaroring	2
Aug 30	Belgium	Spa	2
Sept 13	Italy	Monza	R
Sept 27	Portugal	Estoril	1
Oct 25	Japan	Suzuka	R
Nov 8	Australia	Adelaide	R

Points: Mansell 108, Patrese 56, Schumacher 53, Senna 50, Berger 49, Brundle 38.